A Journey Round the World: A Cycling Memoir

David Sore

Matador
9 De Montfort Mews
Leicester LE1 7FW, UK
Tel: (+44) 116 255 9311 / 9312
Email: books@troubador.co.uk
Web: www.troubador.co.uk/matador

ISBN 978-1848760-561

A Cataloguing-in-Publication (CIP) catalogue record for this book is available from the British Library.

Printed by the MPG Books Group
in the UK

Matador is an imprint of Troubador Publishing

"There comes a time that one must decide, of one's dreams, either to risk everything to achieve them, or to sit for the rest of one's life in the backyard."

Robert Manry, a copy editor
from Cleveland, Ohio,
who spent 78 days
crossing the Atlantic Ocean
in a 13½ foot sailing boat.

Contents

Appendices

Maps Facing Page

Introduction

A world tour represents the ultimate challenge for many cyclists. Since the majority of tours are circular by nature, beginning and ending at the same point, which is usually the cyclist's home location, a circular tour round the world is generally seen as the biggest tour that can be made. It is possible, of course, to make longer tours without encircling the world. Many such tours have been made, but a world tour involves an element of simplicity which these tours cannot have.

Many people whom I met on my journey thought I must be the first cyclist to attempt such a feat, as relatively few of us have achieved it, and the activity attracts little publicity. Those of us who have delved into the history of the subject will know that the first world cycle tour was completed a long time ago, by an English-born American - Thomas Stevens. He made his historic journey between 1884 and 1887 on an 'ordinary', alternatively known as a high wheeler or a penny-farthing, starting and finishing in San Francisco. There are no archives recording the names and details of all those who followed Thomas Stevens, though attempts have been made to compile such a list, which continues to get longer. Before the end of the Nineteenth Century, the list could include the names of the first married couple and the first trio of men. What is beyond doubt is that a world tour has been completed since by many people, both male and female, from various countries, and starting from different positions. There is no defined route which must be followed, but it is generally considered that the minimum qualifying requirements are that most of Europe and Asia be crossed, and North America at the widest section.

The route followed will depend on a number of factors, not least the prevailing political situation in the countries travelled through. It will be obvious that a country on the route should not be at war, either as the result of invasion or internal strife. A stable situation must be a prerequisite for travelling safely through any country. Writing about my journey many years after the event, I am grimly aware of this simple truth. I never expected to encounter problems in

North America, Japan, Australasia or Europe, but there were already problems in parts of Asia before I left England in 1966. The war in Vietnam was relatively recent, while problems in Burma went back many years. What I could never imagine when I travelled through Asia and Europe in 1969 was that so many of the countries concerned would be affected in future years by the most horrendous convulsions, on a scale and of a nature which defied belief.

1969 was not a halcyon year for overland travel through Europe and Asia, but it was part of a reasonably settled period which prevailed for many years after the end of the Second World War. The late 1940's and the next decade were very much a period of reconstruction. Few people had the resources to spend on extensive travel for a number of years. With recovery from devastation, I could not conceive how circumstances would change in so many countries during the 1970's and thereafter, while I attempted to rebuild depleted financial resources. By the time I had made a partial recovery, I was on the way to settling down. The demands of this next stage of life meant that it would be a long time before I would be able to sit down and write the story of my journey.

I looked eastwards during this period with growing disbelief as apparently stable conditions unravelled in one country after another. When I travelled through Yugoslavia, I did not realise that the federal republic was being held together by the powerful Communist machine and the leadership of President Tito. My maps and guidebooks might tell me that I was moving through the states of Serbia, Croatia and Slovenia, but the borders were simply lines on maps. I sensed no bitter hatreds waiting to break out following President Tito's death in 1980, and the collapse of Communism at the end of the decade. In Iran, the overthrow of the Shah in 1979 was the first of a number of major events which closed overland travel through that huge country in its pivotal position on the route through Asia. War between Iran and Iraq, starting in 1980 and dragging on until 1988, meant that Iran remained closed for many years. If you couldn't travel through Iran, there was no sense in thinking about travelling through Afghanistan. Events there rendered pointless any such plans, of course, where various internal coups during the 1970's were followed by Soviet invasion in 1979. Withdrawal during 1988 and 1989 did not bring peace, but ushered in a long period of civil war during which different factions competed for power. The events in New York and Washington on 11 September 2001 focused world attention on Afghanistan once more, foreshadowing further turmoil. In Cambodia, the horrors of the Khmer Rouge regime between 1975 and 1979 set back travel in that unfortunate country for more than two decades.

The briefest outline of such chilling events is reminder enough that I did not travel through a static world. Looking back, I had to consider myself incredibly fortunate to have been able to make the overland journey when I did. It was part of a period which included momentous events, with England winning the soccer World Cup in 1966 and America sending the first man to the moon in 1969.

As you travel with me through this exciting period, a golden era for much of the world, it is impossible not to recall such major events. For me, it was very much a journey of self-discovery in exceptional circumstances as I immersed myself in the life of so many countries. I must record my thanks to very many people for their kindness and consideration on the long journey. I mention by name only a few, conscious that, even after the passage of considerable time, many might wish to remain anonymous. They will recognise where they are referred to: I can only apologise if these considerations on privacy are misplaced.

The passage of time inevitably presents problems concerning maps of the journey. I have generally referred to countries under their current names, but with some exceptions. I don't think anyone will be confused. As you share some of my experiences on what was a unique journey, taking me to countless famous locations which I never dreamed of seeing, plus to thousands of others not so famous, I hope I have conveyed some of the excitement felt as I travelled the world; it was a world from which I drew continuous inspiration as I observed it with a sense of wonder. Not the least consideration was a personal view that the journey was made using one of the finest forms of transport ever invented, bringing me so close to everything I was fortunate to experience.

David Sore
Cambridge

A Journey Round the World: A Cycling Memoir

David Sore

Chapter 1

The Beginning

Wednesday, 23 March 1966

The hours ticked by as I waited at my parents' home in Bury St. Edmunds for my ticket and final sailing instructions. Preparations were almost complete. I had been informed a few days before that my ship, the *s.s. Bristol City*, would be departing from Swansea on Friday, 25 March. I had hoped that the port of embarkation would be closer to Bury, but that would not matter as long as I had plenty of notice of the final instructions. When no letter had arrived by first post on Tuesday that week, I phoned the offices of the shipping company in London to express my concern. I was advised that the final instructions were being posted that morning.

The instructions arrived, informing me that I was to be at King's Dock at Swansea no later than 3pm on Friday. As I packed my belongings, my mother came up to my room to tell me that it was very windy outside. I said I hoped it was blowing in the right direction. Just before ten o'clock, after final farewells, I was on my way, with the immediate prospect of covering 240 miles in two and a half days. I had set my mind on travelling to the port of embarkation in the manner in which I expected to spend a large part of the next few years. But how long would I be away for? I had never had a holiday longer than two weeks.

As I left the shelter of the town and headed west, I found that the wind was not only blowing in the wrong direction but it was strong as well. After about two hours, as I approached Newmarket, I began to realise that I was not going to cover the target of 100 miles before the day ended. As the wind became progressively stronger, I was getting more and more tired. If there had been a tail wind, or no wind at all, I might have stood some chance of realising the day's objective, but I was not yet in any physical condition to battle against a strong head wind for many miles.

I contemplated staying the evening in Cambridge, and taking the train to Swansea the next day. Cycling the journey was now out of the question. I checked to see that the youth hostel was open for staying overnight. It was closed for six days! The decision was made to take the train to London and spend the evening there. I had not expected to see London again for a few years, and the idea of seeing it one more time had some appeal.

As I cycled along the Thames Embankment in the early evening towards the youth hostel in Holland Park, I was startled to see two heavily laden cyclists clearly on a similar mission to myself. I felt the bond which unites all long distance cycle tourists and stopped to have a word. They were from Syria, on a world cycle tour, and had been on the road for two years. After extensive travelling in Europe, they had arrived recently in England. Since they wished to cross to America in the future, they were interested to hear about my imminent journey.

Leaving them I continued to Holland Park, and in the evening went into the centre of London with a couple of fellow youth hostellers for, what was for me, a nostalgic last evening in the capital for some time, admiring the bright lights on the Houses of Parliament, on St. Paul's Cathedral and on other public buildings as seen from the River Thames.

The train left Paddington at noon the next day. I settled back in my seat as we sped to Bristol and on into Wales, arriving in Swansea at 3.40pm. I wondered to myself what the arrival time might have been if I had been presented with a favourable wind on leaving Bury and been able to cycle the journey.

I headed for the docks some time after 2 o'clock on the Friday, eager to get under way. My ship was taking on cargo at this, its last port of call, and thus the port to which the passengers had been directed. There was ample room for the bicycle. I was astonished to find that the ship could accommodate a maximum of five passengers. It was one of a relatively small number of cargo-passenger boats plying the Atlantic. It allowed the traveller with time to make a leisurely crossing of the ocean and adjust gradually to the different lifestyles on each side, not to mention the adjustment required by passing through five time zones on the way to New York. It seemed an appropriate way for me to prepare myself for the forthcoming journey into the unknown.

My fellow passengers had similar reasons for choosing a slower passage across the Atlantic, and we introduced ourselves to each other as we came on board. We were going to get to know each other quite well during the next ten days of the crossing, as we had little to do but eat and sleep, talk, read, exercise ourselves by walking round the deck, and think.

There was time to think back over various formative influences which had resulted in the course of action in which I now found myself. Starting an engineering apprenticeship with the English Electric Company at Stafford in the summer of 1958, I was thrown together with sixty or so others at the apprentices' hostel at Dunston Hall. We were all new to each other. Exchanging experiences at dinner, one of the group, Simon from the west country, informed us that he had recently returned from Germany, having cycled across Belgium to Germany to visit an uncle stationed with the army there. I marvelled at this feat. Simon was on the same course as myself and the following summer introduced me to the Youth Hostels Association. As we attempted to hitchhike through France to the Riviera, many fruitless hours were spent at road junctions trying to obtain lifts. We encountered one or two cyclists, whose freedom to control their own movements got me thinking. If they could come out here and cover considerable distances, so could I. I would be completely independent, and there would be no more long frustrating waits by the roadside.

The following summer I undertook my first cycle tour, in North Wales, a sympathetic fellow student lending me his large saddle bag in which I carried everything needed for a two week journey. It was a revelation. The immense feeling of satisfaction which the tour gave me is difficult to describe. The bicycle was taken to the continent for the first time in the summer of 1963, for a memorable journey through Belgium to the Rhine, returning via Luxembourg. When I renewed my membership of the YHA in October, I became a life member. I had discovered a way of travelling that appealed to me greatly. The next two summers were also spent in Germany, taking the train into Germany each time for tours of the Black Forest and Western Bavaria in 1964, then Eastern Bavaria and the Bavarian Forest in 1965.

Up to and including 1964, all the tours were undertaken with the modest gear range provided by the three speed hub gear on my semi-sports bicycle. I had to walk up every long hill. My cycle dealer, Henry Burton, told me about some conversion equipment he had fitted to a doctor's bicycle which allowed him to have a wider gear range, in particular some very low gears for climbing in the mountains. If I calculated the gears I wanted, Henry would fit the necessary equipment to my bicycle. The engineering training now came in useful, and the tour of 1965 was carried out with the new equipment. I did not have to walk up a single hill. The world literally lay at my feet, or rather at my pedals.

Of my fellow passengers on the *Bristol City*, three were returning to North America, a middle aged Canadian couple from Montreal and a young American from La Crosse, Wisconsin. A young Englishman from Bristol completed the list of five passengers. Our backgrounds were quite different. The couple, Douglas and his wife, were on their way home after a long vacation in Europe. By the time they returned, they would have been away nine months, including four in Spain and then four in England. Douglas had been operating a chain of restaurants in and around Montreal prior to leaving for Europe; it had clearly been a successful venture. The American had been away from home for about four years, travelling in Britain, Germany and Spain. The Bristolian, Malcolm, was studying for a Ph.D. on some aspect of chemistry and was on his way to the University of California in Los Angeles to take up a research post.

The light faded as we awaited departure. At 9pm the boat moved away from King's Dock into the Bristol Channel. We were on our way. The next morning land was sighted to the north as we travelled a few miles from the south coast of Ireland. By the evening we were in the open sea, and the wind seemed to be getting up. I had not yet found my sea legs and retired to my bunk. The wind increased further and sleep was impossible. There was ample time to ponder whether a fast jet crossing of the Atlantic might have been a better option after all.

At breakfast next morning, a Sunday, each of us wanted to know how much sleep everyone else had managed. The passengers took all their meals with the ship's officers, and it was some consolation to learn that the seasoned sailors had enjoyed little more sleep than the rest of us. The conversation then centred on an exchange of ideas on how best to prevent oneself being thrown from one side of the bunk to the other as the ship rolled and pitched continuously. The strength of the wind did not diminish until late in the evening, and I spent most of the day in a reclining position on my bunk.

Conditions improved, allowing us to settle into a routine. The regular excellent meals provided by the crew, plus the tea and coffee breaks, divided up each day into neat periods. We were all tempted to eat far too much for the energy we were using, and invariably spent periods walking round the deck, keeping out of the way of the crew as they repainted the crane booms during the long days at sea. Long periods were spent leaning over the rail at the stern, looking at the foam wake created by the propellers as we cut through the water at about 15 knots.

Thursday was a significant day as we sailed below Newfoundland. It was General Election Day in Great Britain. Just before we went for dinner at 6pm, then 11pm in London, we heard the first results on the BBC World Service. By the late evening when I retired to bed and the first 400 results were in, Harold Wilson was apparently heading for victory with a considerable majority. He was being given a mandate for his current policies, and would be freer to operate now that he no longer had just a majority of four.

The weather deteriorated, setting back the scheduled arrival time to late Monday afternoon. We would then have been sailing for ten days. On the Sunday morning we came down to breakfast to be informed that there was an unofficial dock strike in New York. Just how long was it now going to take to obtain a berth as a queue of ships waited to load or unload their cargoes? We made good progress throughout the day in a calm sea.

The following morning I spent an instructive hour after breakfast on a tour of the ship's engine room with the 4th Engineer and the other passengers. As a former engineering apprentice, I was particularly interested in this treat of the voyage. Built by John Redhead & Sons Ltd at South Shields for Bristol City Line of Steamships Ltd, the ship was launched in 1959, with a life expectancy of approximately 15 years. It was thus already half way through its life. The ship was driven by a steam turbine built by C. A. Parsons Ltd. With a length of 435 ft and width of 59 ft, the ship weighed 5500 tons and could carry 700 tons of cargo. There were 45 officers and crew, and 5 passengers. In the afternoon we were invited up to the bridge to look at the navigating equipment, followed by drinks in the captain's cabin.

At 8pm we arrived off New York. The ship passed below the graceful Verrazano-Narrows Suspension Bridge linking Staten Island and Brooklyn and dropped anchor. It was now dark and hundreds of lights on the bridge road and the main suspension wires made for a most attractive sight. We were just inside the harbour, and about seven miles to the north, thousands of glittering lights gave form to the familiar Manhattan skyline.

Before we could proceed further we had to be cleared by Immigration, who would not be coming out to the ship till the next morning. They came out early at 4.30am and we were soon eager to proceed to dry land. There was a further problem, however. The longshoremen were still on strike and our berthing position was presently occupied by another ship. During the days prior to arriving off New York, my fellow passengers and I listened anxiously to the news broadcasts for hope of a report that the strike was over. The possibility had been aired that the ship might divert from its course and berth at some other port, rather than run the risk of standing idle off New York for an indeterminate period. Halifax, Nova Scotia, was mentioned; a piece of information I did not receive too gladly. It did not fit in with my planned itinerary.

After the early awakening for Immigration, a full morning was spent gazing with wonder into the distance at the Manhattan skyline seven miles away, now clearly defined in the light of day. Two miles off the tip of Manhattan Island we could see the Statue of Liberty. I was optimistic about our prospects for moving, and was informed after lunch that the ship would probably start moving to its berthing position near the town of Elizabeth about 3pm. We were on our way at 4pm and berthed an hour later near Elizabeth. It was about 10 miles direct from Manhattan, but several miles further by road. Although cleared by Customs in the early evening, it was too late to start on the long trek into New York. The captain informed us that all passengers could spend the night on board ship.

We were keen, however, to put our feet on dry land. I accompanied the Canadian couple into the centre of Elizabeth by bus. They wanted to find a chemists' shop. An enquiry for directions told them to take the main drag for a number of blocks where they would find a drugstore near the corner of the intersection. I was learning fast about my new country.

NORTH AMERICA

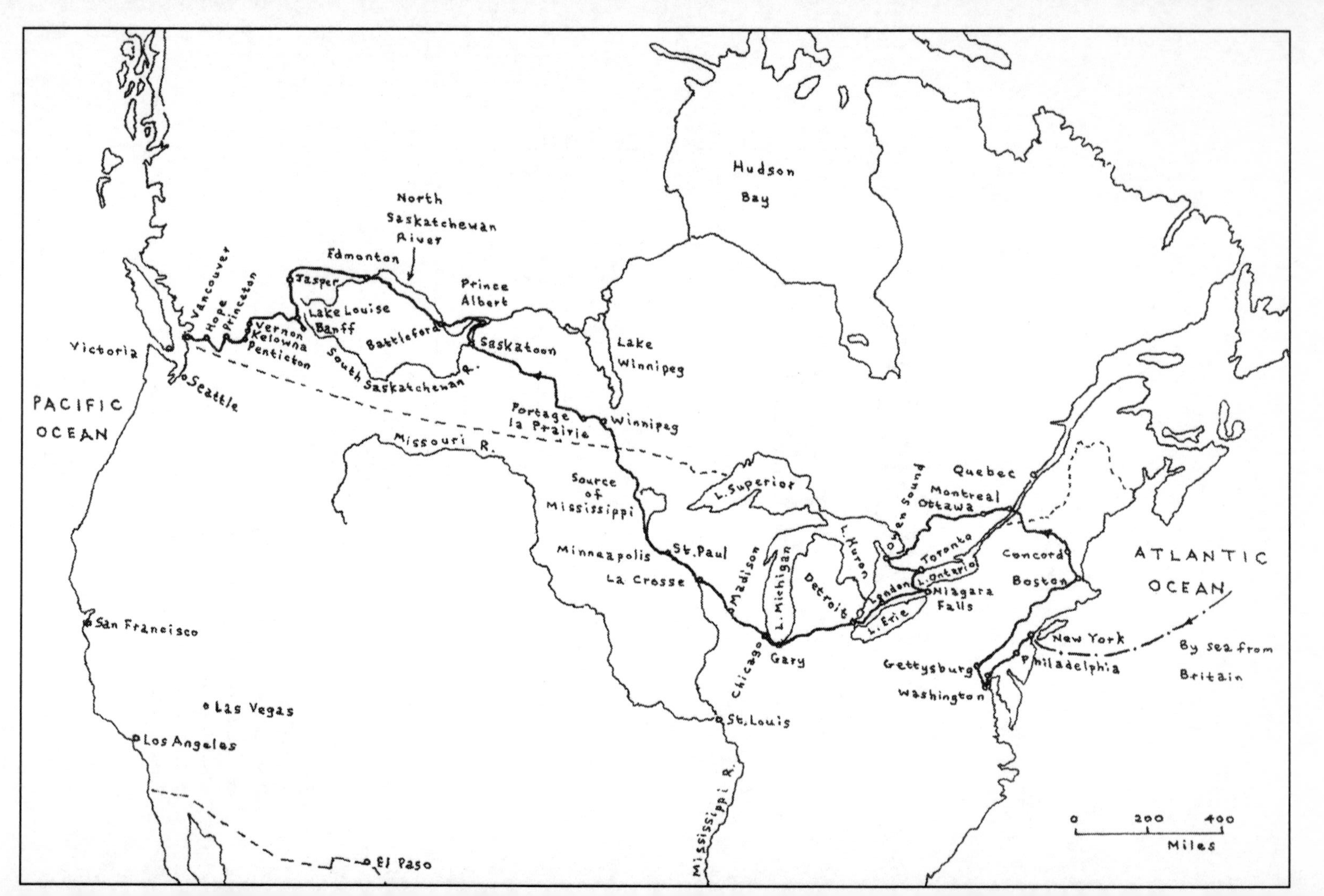
Hudson Bay
North Saskatchewan River
Edmonton
Jasper
Lake Louise
Banff
Battleford
Prince Albert
Saskatoon
South Saskatchewan R.
Vancouver
Hope
Princeton
Vernon
Kelowna
Penticton
Victoria
Seattle
PACIFIC OCEAN
Lake Winnipeg
Portage la Prairie
Winnipeg
Missouri R.
Source of Mississippi
Minneapolis
St. Paul
La Crosse
Madison
Chicago
Gary
L. Superior
L. Michigan
L. Huron
Detroit
Owen Sound
London
L. Erie
Toronto
L. Ontario
Niagara Falls
Ottawa
Montreal
Quebec
Concord
Boston
New York
Philadelphia
Gettysburg
Washington
ATLANTIC OCEAN
By sea from Britain
San Francisco
Las Vegas
Los Angeles
El Paso
St. Louis
Mississippi R.
0 200 400
Miles

Chapter 2

A History Lesson

Wednesday, 6 April 1966

I left the ship at 9.30am to start on the long trek into New York. A dock official had provided me with a map of the New York area after I had convinced him that I really was intending to cycle into the centre of Manhattan. I decided to go over the Goethals Bridge nearby to Staten Island, cross the island to the north-east corner and take the ferry to Manhattan. After a few minutes I was at the approach to the bridge and saw an ominous sign: "No Bicycles - No Pedestrians". I explained to the police officer controlling traffic onto the bridge that it would be most convenient for me to be able to cycle over the bridge. However, roadwork was proceeding on the bridge, and a sidewalk which once existed had been removed owing to the virtual extinction of pedestrians in this area. He could not therefore allow me to proceed, but invited me to seek confirmation from his superior who was just along the road. I explained my position with great reasonableness, but the whole matter was viewed with disdain.

I decided not to wait for a truck to give me a lift over the bridge, turned around and made for New York via Newark, Jersey City and a ferry across the Hudson River. All went smoothly for five miles, when suddenly from nowhere appeared two dogs, one on either side of me. They looked ferocious and bounded along beside me, yapping the whole time and making the occasional jump for my ankles. I pressed down on the pedals to increase my speed. After what seemed an eternity my adversaries gave up the chase, leaving me free once more to adjusting to riding on the right-hand side of the road and avoiding the big American cars. The experience was a little worrying. It drove home the rarity of cyclists in this part of the world, and several other dogs barked at me as I continued towards New York. I was clearly regarded as a source of danger. In the days following I thought often about what I might do to protect myself in the event of a sudden attack.

I arrived on Manhattan Island at about 2pm and made my way gingerly to the William Sloane House YMCA in the heart of the city. The Empire State Building was just half a mile away. The dock official who had furnished me with my first map of the area had advised me to head there, and I was pleased to be able to obtain a room. As darkness fell I looked out of the window spellbound at the sight of thousands of little rectangles of light from the windows of the skyscrapers all around.

The next four days were spent in the big city, lapping up the sights. The first morning was spent walking round the central area, feeling my way as I took in Fifth Avenue, Broadway, Times Square and the Rockefeller Centre, followed by a tour of the United Nations buildings in the afternoon. One of the best ways of getting a feel for New York is to take the 35 mile boat cruise round Manhattan Island, and this was done the next morning. In the afternoon I could not wait any longer. I had craned my neck upwards a number of times as I passed the Empire State Building. It was time to ascend the building for some memorable views.

I was fortunate to be in New York over the Easter weekend and thus able to witness the Easter Parade on Fifth Avenue on the Sunday morning, an occasion for the ladies to display their Easter bonnets. The parade centred on the area around the Rockefeller Centre and St. Patrick's Cathedral. Close to where I was standing one young lady in particular received a great deal of attention from the photographers. Her hat was not exceptional, but she exuded glamour. That was all that mattered.

*****

I was now keen to get under way. Since arriving in the city I had done no cycling. The roads were so dangerous, but that had to be accepted. With all my baggage once more on the bicycle, the image of a cycle tourist which I now presented to everyone else somehow always reassured me concerning my safety. The baggage had the effect, in my mind, of surrounding me with a protective shield. With the large Union Jack on the saddlebag I was also advertising myself as a visitor from Britain, and hoped it would result in some consideration.

This didn't seem to be happening as I made a detour northwards for a ride through Central Park and then headed south along Fifth Avenue. It required some concentration to keep out of the way of what seemed scores of buses. I took the ferry to Staten Island, leaving the Manhattan skyline retreating slowly into the distance, and crossed the island to the south-west corner. At the approach to a long bridge linking the island with the mainland was a familiar sign which I had seen at the Goethals Bridge eight miles north a few days before: "No Bicycles - No Pedestrians". I had no alternative but to unstrap my bags and hope a suitable truck would come along with a sympathetic driver who could provide me with a lift. After half an hour a small empty pick-up truck came along and I was on my way. I offered profound thanks to the driver as he deposited me at the other end of the bridge, on the mainland in New Jersey.

This first part of the journey was taking me through a densely populated and heavily travelled area. Much of the high speed traffic was on the growing interstate highway system. My maps showed a network of expressways, thruways, turnpikes, parkways, skyways, tollways and beltways, from all of which I was, of course, barred. But it required some careful map study to seek out a reasonable route which kept me away from this highway system.

Midway through the afternoon found me passing through the town of New Brunswick. I decided to go about 15 miles further to Princeton, home of the famous University, where I would settle down for the evening. My plans were changed suddenly half an hour later when, cycling past a café, a middle aged lady stopped me and introduced herself as a former enthusiastic cyclist. Before marrying she had been a schoolteacher and had taken parties of schoolchildren on cycling holidays, including one tour in Alaska. I was very impressed. I gladly accepted her invitation to stay with her and her family five miles south-west of Princeton. I followed her car as she led me through the city. We spent the evening exchanging experiences on where we had cycled, and I collected a few tips on cycling in my new territory. I was overwhelmed by this display of hospitality, on what was my first day out of New York

The next morning I decided not to go back into Princeton, but to continue onwards to the historic city of Philadelphia. Entry to the city from the north-east involved an interminable journey through a huge commercial area, past an astonishing mass of advertising signs and overhead cables. I made for the youth hostel in Fairmount Park.

By the time I reached it in the late afternoon, drizzle had turned to rain, which continued throughout the evening.

Further rain the next morning could not spoil my visit to Independence Hall where, on 4 July 1776, the Second Continental Congress adopted the Declaration of Independence, formerly announcing America's separation from Britain. The Revolutionary War had been going on for more than a year, and was to continue for a further five years till 19 October 1781 when the leader of the British forces, Lord Cornwallis, surrendered at Yorktown, Virginia. America had won her independence and, in the summer of 1787, in the same chamber in Independence Hall in which the Declaration of Independence was adopted, the Federal Convention sat to draft the Constitution.

I listened with great interest as this chain of events was unfolded by a guide. Three parties of young schoolchildren visited the Hall, originally the Pennsylvania State House, while I was there, and no effort was spared to drive home to them how the British ransacked the building, tearing its timbers down for firewood, when they occupied Philadelphia during the winter of 1777-8. During this long, bitter winter, George Washington was encamped with his army at Valley Forge, some 18 miles north-west of Independence Hall, and all were suffering terrible hardships and privations.

As I eavesdropped on one of these talks, the eyes of the guide and myself met and I raised an eyebrow in response to this virulent attack on the British. The female guide guessed that I might be from the other side, and I sensed a slight embarrassment. But the younger listeners would have plenty of time in the future to put these historical events in a wider perspective.

Leaving Philadelphia I had my first ride in the countryside proper, off main roads and away from heavy traffic. It was very pleasant. The countryside was not at its most attractive yet, however, and it would be a few weeks before this occurred. Spring was just arriving, the trees were still almost bare and I would be present to watch the buds come out and the leaves slowly fill the empty branches.

As I passed through a number of villages, I had to keep a close lookout for dogs. If one saw me at the approach to a village and started barking, it was certain that I would receive the attention of a dozen others before reaching the other end of the village. And why did everyone keep such big dogs? My hair bristled often at the sight of so many Alsatians. I discussed the matter with several people and suggested that it might possibly help if I bought a few dog biscuits to offer as a substitute for my ankles. "I shouldn't bother" was a consistent reply. "They're fed much better things than that, and won't touch them." I resigned myself to Fate.

Ambling along the country roads on my way to Baltimore I was startled by an unusual sight. Coming down the road towards me was a horse and buggy. As we drew closer I observed that the couple occupying it were dressed entirely in black. I saw many more people like this as I travelled further. I was in the area of the Amish community, a farming people who came originally from Northern Germany in the 1720's. Their way of life had changed little since they first came to America, rejecting many worldly things, including TV and radio. They could ride in cars but not own them. I was told more than once that they disapproved strongly of having their photograph taken, and one could not be sure that they did not carry a shotgun beside them to deter the would-be photographer. A combination of diffidence, respect for religious beliefs and thoughts of self-preservation meant that I did not manage to take a single photograph of them.

The scenery changed as I approached Baltimore, the chief commercial city of Maryland, and found myself passing through a large commercial area, past a concentration of neon signs and overhead cables as on the approach to Philadelphia. I toured a fascinating ship, the *s.s. Constellation*. This wooden frigate was the U.S. Navy's first ship and was launched in Baltimore in 1797. She saw action on many occasions and had a formidable list of distinctions. In the Second World War the famous ship served as the flagship of the U.S. Atlantic fleet.

From Baltimore it was just a short ride to the federal capital, Washington, D.C. There was so much to see in this attractive city, including the White House and the Capitol. The tour through the White House was all too quick, with so many people to accommodate, that I was in and out of the famous residence before my mind had hardly accepted the fact that I had managed to get in. The tour of the Capitol, housing the legislative branch of the Federal Government, was much fuller. Following the guided tour, I returned the following day to attend a meeting of the Senate. I sat for some time listening to the "distinguished Senators" - so they referred to one another - discussing the position of the Indian in the Great Society. The position was not a happy one, and I was able to see something of this firsthand during the ensuing months.

I had arrived in Washington at the end of the Cherry Blossom Festival, an event which had its origin on 27 March 1912 when the wife of President Taft planted the first Japanese cherry tree. The wife of the Japanese Ambassador planted a second tree as a token of friendship between the two countries. The ceremony officially accepted a gift of 2,000 Japanese cherry trees, which were planted in Potomac Park. The little trees grew, and every springtime the park is a beautiful sight, the blossom of some 2,000 trees making unforgettable sights. I soaked in as much as I could, and visited monuments in the park to three famous presidents - Washington, Jefferson and Lincoln. I was deeply impressed by the marble statue of the seated Lincoln by Daniel Chester French behind the columned facade of the Lincoln Memorial. I could not leave Washington without crossing the Potomac River to the Arlington National Cemetery to see the grave and temporary memorial for the most recent President, John Kennedy, his life cut short by an assassin's bullet less than four years before.

*****

I had wanted to see something of the early history of America before starting the real journey across the continent. The next stage consisted of a wide sweep round through the countryside to Boston, taking me through the states of Maryland, Pennsylvania, New Jersey, New York, Connecticut and Massachusetts. The immediate goal was Gettysburg, just across the state border in Pennsylvania and 80 miles to the north of Washington.

A National Museum informed the visitor of events concerning the biggest battle of the American Civil War. Here from 1-3 July 1863 the Confederacy made their last great offensive. The three days of the battle involved 85,000 Union and 71,000 Confederate soldiers, and at the end of the third day 44,000 soldiers had lost their lives. An electric map described the progress of the battle, and it was interesting to see photographs in the Museum of former President Eisenhower, poring over the map with his former Second World War colleague Viscount Montgomery. The former President, who lived just three miles from Gettysburg, had taken Montgomery there on one of his visits in retirement.

The following morning I left the tourist home where I was staying for a cycle ride round some of the 16,000 acres of the battlefield. The rolling terrain now included 2,400 monuments and markers. Some four months after the battle, on 19 November 1863, and with the Civil War still to continue for another 17 months, President Lincoln journeyed to Gettysburg to take part in a ceremony of dedication of part of the battlefield ground as a National Cemetery for Union soldiers. I found myself reading a marker recording Lincoln's short address during the ceremony:

> "Four score and seven years ago our fathers brought forth on this continent a new nation, conceived in liberty and dedicated to the proposition that all men are created equal. Now we are engaged in a great civil war, testing whether that nation or any nation so conceived and so dedicated can long endure. We are met on a great battlefield of that war. We have come to dedicate a portion of that field as a final resting-place for those who here gave their lives that that nation might live. It is altogether fitting and proper that we should do this. But in a larger sense, we cannot dedicate, we cannot consecrate, we cannot hallow this ground. The brave men, living and dead who struggled here have consecrated it far above our poor power to add or detract. The world will little note nor long remember what we say here, but it can never forget what they did here. It is for us the living rather to be dedicated here to the unfinished work which they who fought here have thus far so nobly advanced. It is rather for us to be here dedicated to the great task remaining before us - that from these honored dead we take increased devotion to that cause for which they gave the last full measure of devotion - that we here highly resolve that these dead shall not have died in vain, that this nation under God shall have a new birth of freedom, and that government of the people, by the people, for the people shall not perish from the earth."

The Gettysburg Address has been described as "the greatest expression of English literature ever expressed by man." I had never encountered the full Address before and was tremendously impressed. I read the immortal words a number of times before leaving the location. I was glad indeed not to have travelled direct from New York to Boston. Seeing the historic sites in Philadelphia,

Washington and now Gettysburg was giving me a first class background on which to develop an understanding of America.

From Gettysburg I turned north-eastwards to York, just 34 miles away, arriving there just after midday. It was a glorious sunny day. Walking round the town during the afternoon my attention was captured by the posters outside the cinema. I simply had to stay in the town, and in the evening went to see *The Sound of Music*. I was enthralled, becoming a lifelong fan of Julie Andrews.

The next morning I passed through Lancaster, a centre of the Amish community encountered earlier on the run towards Baltimore. In the late afternoon I arrived at Hopewell Village, a National Historic Site, in French Creek State Park. From 1770-1883 the village was the centre of a typical colonial iron-making community. The furnace and the houses had been restored to their original condition when the village thrived.

As I travelled the few miles towards Pottsdown to look for accommodation for the evening, a motorist stopped and invited me to his home for dinner. I was glad to accept this invitation from Pat, meeting his wife, Gloria, originally from Australia, shortly afterwards, and their two teenage children. I remembered this warm hospitality for some time. I remembered especially being left in the house by myself the next morning to continue breakfast while the mother drove the children just a short distance to school. They were conscious that I would have cycled, but it was not the American way.

Gently rolling farmland gave way to hillier, wooded country as I approached New Jersey. Crossing the state near its north-west boundary with Pennsylvania, I was generally travelling with the lines of the hills. As I entered New York state and turned east towards the Hudson valley, the hills were suddenly across my path and I was climbing for the longest periods so far in America. Travelling through Palisades State Park, I was rewarded by the sight of a group of small deer, which scuttled off into the forest as they saw me.

Thick mist reduced visibility at the summit of the hill ranges. Rain started to fall as I approached West Point, but I was able to walk round the grounds of the U.S. Military Academy for an hour or so. The rain came on heavily as I continued up the valley to Newburgh for the evening. I delayed my departure the next morning, Sunday 1 May, to see what the weather was going to do. As the sky brightened I set off for just a few miles further up the Hudson valley, and had a memorable afternoon visiting the home of former President Franklin D. Roosevelt and then, two miles north, the Vanderbilt Mansion. The home of the former President at Hyde Park, now maintained as a National Historic Site, is a truly fascinating place to visit. It made me want to read more about the life of the great man, and of his wife Eleanor who had a distinguished career herself and had died just recently in 1962.

The Vanderbilt Mansion was a magnificent example of the great estates developed by financial and industrial leaders in the era following the Civil War. Built in 1896-8, it was the country home of Frederick W. Vanderbilt, a grandson of Cornelius Vanderbilt who founded the family fortune in steamboating and railroading. Touring the Mansion, it was easy to imagine myself in one of the stately homes of England.

I turned east to travel across the north-west corner of Connecticut into Massachusetts. The terrain was quite undulating, taking me through a number of forested areas, mainly of silver birch. The immediate destination was Westfield, home one of America's largest bicycle manufacturers, the Columbia Manufacturing Company. Arriving there late one afternoon, they were interested to see me and accommodated me in a motel for the evening, my first time in this American institution. The following morning I was conducted on a most interesting tour of the factory by the Advertising Manager.

On arrival in Boston the next day I made initially for the offices of Raleigh Industries of America. A few days before leaving England I had been given a tour of the Raleigh factory in Nottingham. I was going to be travelling on a Raleigh bicycle. The company had been unable to provide me with any kind of technical support or financial sponsorship, but the marketing staff whom I met expressed genuine interest in my plans. I was given the names and addresses of the company's agents in all the countries I might possibly be visiting, and invited to contact them. One of the staff in the Boston office knew of me as he had recently been in England. At this particular time the company was thriving and exporting considerable numbers of bicycles to America.

Registering at the large YMCA later, I inquired about a safe place to store the bicycle. "Take it up to your room in the lift" was the astonishing reply. I thus had the bicycle in the room with me. When I opened the door for the first time, there was the sight of a TV: I felt I was being well looked after.

Boston was the scene of so much of America's early history. I followed the Freedom Trail, a one and a half mile route taking me past many places associated with Boston's and America's early struggle for freedom. Walking along the dockside I came across a plaque describing the events of the Boston Tea Party. In addition to all the historical wealth of Boston, there were two famous institutions of higher learning to visit. I could then add to my C.V. that I had studied at the Massachusetts Institute of Technology and Harvard University, the latter founded in 1636 and America's oldest University. Following the Heritage Trail, it took me round much of the University and also to the home for more than 40 years of the poet Henry Wadsworth Longfellow.

One of the delights of my few days in Boston was to attend a Promenade Concert by the Boston Symphony Orchestra. I had arrived in Boston during the second week of a nine week season of Promenade Concerts which took place each spring. First established to provide a longer season for members of the Boston Symphony Orchestra, the concerts were an institution, as was their venerable conductor, Arthur Fiedler. In England I must have heard the orchestra on the radio scores of times. I still recall vividly that wonderful evening as the 72 year old maestro led the orchestra through a mixed programme of classical and light music. The performance of Ravel's Bolero, a work I must have heard on "Two Way Family Favourites" by this very orchestra countless times, was a thrilling experience. Near the end of the concert was a very topical item, a selection from *The Sound of Music*.

*****

I had so far covered almost 1,000 miles on the bicycle, only to be further east than when I had arrived in New York. Now I started to move westward. A north-westerly route out of Boston brought me to Lexington where, on the Common, was a statue of Capt. John Parker, commander of the Minutemen, who were engaged on this Common in the first fighting of the American Revolution. The terrain was flat as I followed the Merrimack River into New Hampshire, but hills were visible in the distance. The terrain became undulating as I left the river and headed north to Alto at the southern tip of Lake Winnipesaukee, a huge lake some 15 miles long and 5 miles wide to the south of the White Mountains, surrounded by pine forest. The setting was outstanding with the result that it was a major holiday area.

I rented a cabin beside the lake and decided not to travel the next day. Rain had come on, and it was far too attractive an area to rush through in poor weather. After spending the morning reading I walked down the road to the restaurant, expecting to return to my cabin shortly afterwards. I could not have imagined how the rest of the day was going to change as I became the beneficiary of some generous hospitality which I would never forget.

I had no sooner entered the restaurant when I found myself in conversation with an older man there. Everett knew much of England and France as he worked for sometime in the travel industry. We knew many places in common. He was retired from normal work but still had a lot of energy, and kept himself occupied by involvement with a number of organisations and by running errands. An errand had brought him to the restaurant, and he invited me to accompany him to Farmington, 10 miles to the south-east, to fetch some spirits for the restaurant. I found myself being driven round the local countryside, being shown many points of interest, including a Fishery Hatching Station. We stopped for a drink at his home, which was empty as his wife was away caring for her ailing mother. I then found myself going to dinner with friends of his, a retired bank official and his wife. Returning to Alton Bay, we stopped for a short time at Everett's daughter's home, having stopped there briefly earlier in the afternoon. Arriving back at the cabin at 10.45pm, I could not believe how the day had developed.

The following day was a glorious one from the start, and how glad I was to have bided my time before cycling along beside the western shore of Lake Winnipesaukee and then the smaller Lake Squam, and particularly after yesterday's adventures. The scenery changed as I approached the White Mountains. At Plymouth I was hailed by a former English woman from Bristol, and stopped to talk to her. The large Union Jack on my saddlebag was useful in identifying my origins to other people travelling on the road.

Moving slowly through the White Mountains, I stopped often to admire the view. I stopped to see the Flume, an 800 ft natural chasm extending along the flank of Mount Liberty. Ignoring the sign telling me the pathway along the chasm was officially closed, I soon found I was not able to proceed far. Large patches of snow were everywhere in the narrow chasm which the rays of the sun could not reach, and sheets of ice hung down the chasm walls, evidence to the wintry weather this area was still getting.

As I left the White Mountains to turn west into Vermont the vista opened up again to rolling green hills, with much of the terrain covered in forest. I was now close to the Canadian border, and it was time to forget about America, at least for a short period, and concentrate on the beauties, the history and the people of an even younger country.

Chapter 3

A New Country

Wednesday, 18 May 1966

As I left St. Albans in Vermont for the Canadian border 13 miles north, the terrain levelled out, and I became optimistic about reaching Montreal in one day. I was eager to get there even though it meant cycling 80 miles. This was going to be a new record for me for a day's run, and considerably more than my daily average of closer to 60 miles in open terrain with nothing to delay me.

The entry to Montreal was via the ungainly structure of the Jacques-Cartier Bridge, taking me across the St. Lawrence River at high elevation. The heart of the city had a fine mountain backdrop, on the slope of which was located Parc Mont-Royal. I walked up the hillside to the park a number of times, to gaze down on the major buildings in this most attractive location. Back down in the city centre I was conscious of a different atmosphere among the people. The French influence was very strong, and there was a grace and style about many of the ladies.

For my first three nights in Montreal I stayed in a small youth hostel about two miles west of the city. I then had to leave due to prior bookings and sought a room at a tourist home close to the heart of the city. This was much more convenient, but it was an interesting experience arranging the booking. The young couple at the home spoke hardly a word of English, and my French was quite rusty due to lack of use.

The Jacques-Cartier Bridge which had brought me into the city crossed the St. Lawrence via St. Helen's Island. On my last full day in Montreal I went back to the island to see the developing structures for Expo 67. (Update: St. Helen's Island has been the venue for the Canadian motor racing Grand Prix since 1978.) At 9pm I left the tourist home to climb the hillside to Parc Mont-Royal for the fourth time, this time to look down on the city at night. Only a small number of the major office buildings had lights on - today was a Canadian National Holiday, Victoria Day - but literally thousands of spots of light registered the presence of the private houses ringing the central part of the city. From the high vantage point, moving spots of light indicated traffic crossing the three bridges spanning the St. Lawrence near the central area. It was an enchanting sight.

When I had booked in at the tourist home, my brain had worked overtime as I showed the young couple there my bicycle and explained where I was intending to go. Now it was time to set off on the next stage, a journey of approximately 120 miles along the north bank of the Ottawa River to the federal capital. During the few days in Montreal, the countryside seemed to have undergone a transformation. The trees were now full of leaves, and everywhere was a rich green as I travelled through pleasant farming country.

I encountered the hottest day so far as the temperature rose to the middle 80's. I had to make use of my water bottle for the first time, filling it at a café when I stopped for a drink. I arrived in the capital with two very red arms.

It was time to renew acquaintance with the Canadian couple who had been on the boat with me to New York. They were moving to Ottawa and had left me with an address of friends in the city in order to make contact again. From the friends' address I spoke to Douglas on the phone and was soon on my way. It was good to see the couple again and to enjoy their hospitality for a couple of days before they had to leave for Toronto on a business trip. I then transferred to the YMCA in the heart of the city.

I had arrived in Ottawa in the last week of May. It was perhaps the city's most colourful time, the time of the Annual Tulip Festival. I headed for Dow's Lake to see, on the eastern bank, the largest bed of tulips in the city, 130,000 bulbs of many colours. They made a glorious picture, and were just a fraction of the total number of bulbs planted in the city for the festival. The original bulbs had been a gift from Queen Wilhelmina of The Netherlands in gratitude to Canada for offering her refuge during the Second World War.

I toured the Parliament Buildings and attended a meeting in the House of Commons for about an hour. I listened to several members lamenting the labour troubles in the country at the time. A dock strike in Montreal was having a serious effect on the economy, prices were rising, and threats of strikes loomed from the lumber industry in British Columbia, Air Canada and on the railways. Britain was not the only country with pressing economic problems. As I listened intently to the debate, it was easy to pick out the heavy-jowled John Diefenbaker, former Prime Minister and now Leader of the Opposition. He was the first Prime Minister I had seen in the flesh.

It rained for most of the day on my last full day in Ottawa, a Sunday, but it enabled me to get down to some letter writing without feeling I should be outside. I was getting excited at the prospect ahead, the opportunity to see the first of a number of family relations. My maternal grandmother had been one of ten children, including five brothers. Four of them had emigrated to North America in the 1900's, one eventually returning. As I pored over maps while planning my journey, I realised it was going to be possible to visit all the descendants of my great-uncles without having to make a major diversion from the route which I would otherwise have chosen to take across the continent. The first letters were written to advise cousins near Owen Sound and in London that one of their English cousins was on his way.

The direct route from Ottawa would have taken me south-westwards through Ontario to Toronto, but I now headed in a more northerly direction towards Algonquin Provincial Park. The heavy rain of the day before had ended, though I did have to contend with a number of showers during the next few days. The rain seemed to make the rich farming country through which I was travelling greener than ever. As I approached the Park the terrain became more undulating and increased areas were covered in forest. I became aware of a change on the roads. The amount of traffic was much reduced as I left the larger centres of habitation behind me.

I was disappointed not to see any wildlife as I journeyed through Algonquin Park, but the noise from construction work on the road had probably caused all the animals to move further into the forest. I emerged from the Park into an area of lakes, rivers and forest, a popular recreational area, especially for canoeing. At Birkendale I saw the Lake of Bays for the first time. As I travelled round the lake on the east side, the road passed through forest of mainly yellow birch, with considerable numbers of maple trees. All along the road the banks were covered with trillium, the provincial flower of

Ontario. Whenever the road ran close to the shore, breaks in the trees allowed views over this most attractive lake, providing me with one of my most enjoyable rides so far.

I was making for Baysville at the south end of the lake. There were a number of youth hostels in the area, and I organised my route to stay in the hostels at Baysville, Coldwater and Collingwood the next three nights. Youth hostels had been an integral part of all my earlier cycle touring in Britain and Europe. They enabled like-minded travellers to meet, converse and stay together in sympathetic surroundings. It was too early in the season here to get many visitors during the week, so that I had the undivided attention of the houseparents during memorable stays. I arrived at Baysville to find the houseparents, Mr. Fred Mills and his wife, an elderly and very kindly couple, totally absorbed watching preparations on the TV for the latest spaceflight. The Gemini 9A flight, with Thomas P. Stafford and Eugene A. Cernan as crew, was about to get under way. I looked forward to these flights myself, and had got used to hearing the sonorous tones of the NBC commentator as he announced at short intervals "We have ignition", "We have lift-off", "The rocket has cleared the tower, all systems are go." I put my bags down and joined the couple in front of the TV.

Mrs. Mills was a retired teacher and decided to help the youth hostels as she enjoyed having young people around her. As I started to write my diary during the evening, the couple invited me into their quarters for a cup of tea and a chat. We were still talking at one o'clock the next morning when I decided I ought to retire for the night. I delayed my departure the next morning before starting for Coldwater. The houseparent at this hostel was equally welcoming, a widow with a grown-up family, and I spent a second long evening in conversation. The following morning at breakfast I had my first maple syrup.

A different kind of welcome awaited me when I arrived at Desboro near Owen Sound to meet the first of my Canadian relations. It was a unique experience to be meeting them in this way. There I met a daughter, Teena, of my late Uncle Fred, and her husband Eldon. They were middle-aged with a married daughter living just a few miles away. I had arrived on a Sunday and was taken out to meet the rest of the family. On my last evening in Desboro I gave a slide show to all the relations, showing them the photographs accumulated so far.

Two days before, I had accompanied Eldon as he collected cattle from adjacent farms and took them to market in Toronto, a round trip for the day of 220 miles. Now it was time for me to start my own journey to the provincial capital, which would take me two days. The road was straight for mile after mile, with the terrain flat for much of the time. Heavy rain was encountered on the first day, and early in the afternoon a motorist stopped to offer me a lift to Toronto. I hoped he understood why I had to decline, but I was cycling by choice and was not getting wet underneath my waterproof clothing.

A fine sunny day followed and I sailed along into Toronto with a breeze from the north-west right behind me. As I wended my way through vast suburbs and stopped to look at my map, a young man stopped ahead of me and came back to talk. He had done some youth hostelling in England. "If no one else does this, welcome to Toronto," he said, hearing that I was going into the city for the first time. I proceeded to the University lodging house, which acted as a youth hostel during vacations. It was now the middle of June, and just a few students remained on the campus.

I was sent along to a double room occupied by an exceptional student from Kenya, who had won several scholarships. After getting to know him we spoke for a long time during my second evening there. Martin had come to America on a scholarship and taken a first degree in social studies at the University of California, obtaining the highest marks on the course. As a result he had been offered two further scholarships, by the Rockefeller Foundation and the International Exchange. He was using the former to study international relations for a higher degree and said quite firmly he was determined to come out top again. We discussed human relations for a long time, principally relations between blacks and whites. I was relieved when he said that he considered that the British had done a tremendous amount for the Kenyan people. However, when he returned to Kenya at the end of his studies, he had plans which this generous expression did not reflect. All the time he had been in America he was conscious of a perception that the white man generally felt that the black man was inferior to him. He had travelled in the Deep South, and was determined to show through his studies that he was not personally inferior to any white man. He professed to being a fervent nationalist, and his experience had been such that, on his return, he would join a nationalist group and see that the white residents suffered as he had seen the black people suffer in America. His achievements had not been limited to the academic field. He had boxed as a middleweight in the Commonwealth Games in Australia, winning a silver medal. He was someone to watch.

One building in Toronto dominated the memories of my stay, the New City Hall. Designed by Viljo Revell of Finland, it had been completed only the year before. To me it was a work of genius, and the most inspiring building I would see on my entire tour. It comprised a circular domed council chamber with two curving office towers behind it, 260 and 326 ft high. I gazed in wonder at the building and returned in the evening when it was floodlit. I spent some time taking photographs, recognising that my time there was limited. But the photographs would enable me to recapture those moments at any time in the future.

I was attracted in a different way to an older building, the fairy tale castle Casa Loma, situated on a hilltop just north of the central area and built by the soldier, industrialist and financier, Sir Henry Pellatt, between 1911 and 1914. It followed several years studying Old World castles. I was reminded of the castle of Neuschwanstein in Bavaria, visited on my second cycle tour in Germany in 1964. On a tour of Casa Loma, Regina, an attractive University student, was the guide. I was left with a reminder of this as she offered an official postcard to everyone who gave her a tip at the end of the tour. On the front was a fine photograph of her standing in front of the castle with her signature below. I still treasure my card. What an inspired way to raise additional funds to assist her through her next year at college!

One day in the city I came back to my bicycle after visiting offices to see paper sticking up between the saddle and saddlebag. There were in fact two pieces. On one was written "Best of British luck!" The second piece of paper was the corner of an envelope bearing the printing "N.V. Philips' Gloeilampenfabrieken Eindhoven Nederland" and the message "Lots of luck with your trip, from the Netherlands". I looked around for signs of the persons responsible, but they must have long gone. It is difficult to overestimate the positive effects of gestures like this. They made my day and I kept the pieces of paper as souvenirs. The large reservoir of goodwill which I had towards everyone as I enjoyed the time of my life now overflowed.

One female student still at the University showed interest in my bicycle. Dianne was cute with her blonde hair in pigtails and no more than five feet tall. I took her for a ride on the front carrier of my bicycle one afternoon. We had gone about a mile when a police car drew up. "I think one of you had better get off," the officer said quite simply. Dianne got off and we watched as the car went off into the distance. She then remounted and we returned to the University. The unusual sight had attracted a number of looks on both the outward and return journeys.

I left Toronto to follow the Lake Ontario shore to Hamilton at the west end, then turning east to travel through fruit-growing country to visit one of North America's major attractions, the Niagara Falls. I crossed back into America at Queenston, a few miles north of the Falls, as a brochure informed me that was the best side to be on for the famous views. An elderly official at the start of the Lewiston-Queenston Toll Bridge looked quizzically at my transport. "Is that a motorcycle?" Assuring him it was not, I paid a nominal charge and was on my way, following the east bank of the Niagara gorge which was some 200 ft deep and 300 ft wide. I spent two hours at the Falls, watching as the water thundered over the American Falls and the Horseshoe Falls. After organising accommodation at a tourist home nearby, I returned in the evening to gaze once more at this magical attraction, now floodlit.

I was keen to get six miles west to Thorold early the following morning to see three of the massive locks of the Welland Ship Canal. Until this impressive feat of civil engineering was completed in 1932, there was no way for freighters to pass between Lake Erie and Lake Ontario. Now a series of seven locks along the 25 mile canal, each 859 ft long and 80 ft wide, allowed freighters up to 750 ft long and 75 ft wide to deal with the 326 ft higher elevation of Lake Erie. By comparison the *s.s. Bristol City* on which I had crossed to New York was a modest 435 ft long and 59 ft wide. I spent over an hour watching huge freighters entering the locks, then rising or falling some 46 ft before proceeding to the next lock.

I continued west through flat farming country. As I neared Wellandport a car stopped ahead of me and I was asked what part of England I came from. The driver had emigrated to Canada from London several years before. I was offered a lift for several miles, but he seemed almost prepared for my reply. In parting I gladly accepted some strawberries offered. A turn to the north-west at

Cayuga allowed me to follow the east bank of the Grand River, giving me my most pleasant travelling of the day.

At Brandfort the next morning I stopped to visit His Majesty's Chapel of the Mohawks, built in 1785 and the first Protestant Church in Ontario. The name reminded me that I had encountered my first Indians in Canada the previous evening at a hotel in Caledonia. I then needed to push onwards as my destination for the day was London, Ontario. Following the River Thames from Woodstock I covered 79 miles on what was a glorious sunny day.

I was keen to meet my relations in London, including my cousin Will whom I had met several years before on a trip to England. During a stay of several days he showed me slides of a trip made out west many years before, helping me considerably in planning a route across the Rockies to Vancouver. Many people had said to me in recent weeks: "You have not seen Canada until you have seen British Columbia."

The temperature rose into the mid-eighties while I was in London, and I made generous use of the shade provided by the many trees in the "Forest City", with its wide tree-lined streets. The humidity was also increasing, making for tiring riding as the journey continued through a tobacco farming area towards the south-eastern corner of the province. Staying overnight in a small hotel in Chatham, my room was like an oven after the heat and humidity of the day. It was difficult to sleep, and I could only wonder how many more nights would be spent like this. The following day the temperature rose to 92°F as I approached Windsor. In the early evening I rode over the Ambassador Bridge spanning the Detroit River. The next stage of the journey would be in America.

Chapter 4

To the Mississippi

Saturday, 25 June 1966

On my first morning in Detroit I was eager to get to the main Post Office to collect the latest box of slides at the General Delivery section. I walked about two miles to be there about 9.15. Why wasn't it open? As I returned towards the city centre I learned that I had entered a new time zone. Michigan was an hour behind Ontario. This episode emphasized to me in a very positive way that I was moving west. I turned my watch back to continue with a longer day than expected.

I walked around the central area to get a feel for the city, seeing the major buildings. After lunch I sat on the grass by the Cobo Hall and Convention Centre, studying the travel literature collected. The area thronged with people as Seventh Day Adventists gathered for their 50th World Conference. As I looked round I saw people from Africa, Asia, India, Pakistan and Japan. There was quite an atmosphere.

One leaflet resulted in me cycling eight miles north in the evening to the Michigan State Fair Grounds to hear my first open air concert. It was performed at the Music Shell by the Detroit Symphony Orchestra. I shall never forget that magical evening as I sat in the open air under the stars and, in a varied programme, listened to a performance of Chopin's Piano Concerto No.2. The soloist was a young artist, Sheila Stephenson. As the delicate melodies wafted across from the Music Shell, a slight breeze caused the leaves of aspen trees nearby to quake gently, and the high temperature of the day slowly dropped. I had never enjoyed a piece of music so much.

As I cycled the eight miles back to the YMCA late in the evening along Woodward Avenue, which was absolutely straight, I felt unsafe for the first time. Would the motorists roaring past me see my small dynamo lights, and, more importantly, me? For I was now in the motor car capital of the world. Ford, General Motors and Chrysler all had huge plants here. I went on a tour of the Ford Rouge Plant at Dearborn, a vast complex where not only were a large number of car components manufactured and cars assembled, but the raw materials themselves were processed. The giant complex had its own blast furnaces and rolling mills and produced its own steel. It was the first time I had seen a car assembly plant.

The tour round the assembly plant one morning was interesting, but a visit on the afternoon of the same day was more memorable. Three miles from the Rouge Plant was the Henry Ford Museum, housing the world's largest collection of vintage cars. The museum in fact covered the whole field of transportation. Especially interesting for me as a cyclist was a superb collection of veteran bicycles, the first I had seen. I was particularly attracted to one machine which was a special rather than a veteran bicycle, the "Oriten" 10-man bicycle.

It was built by the Waltham Manufacturing Company in 1896 in Waltham, Massachusetts, as a promotional venture to advertise the alleged superior qualities of the company's single and tandem machines. The Oriten had to be pedalled at a minimum speed of about 20 mph to stand by itself, and the normal speed on a run was 45 mph. It was exhibited at bicycle meetings throughout the country, and local dealers would charter it for a few days to stimulate sales. I wrote to the Museum later to see if I could obtain a colour slide of the Oriten, receiving the following intriguing reply:

> "A check of our slide files reveals that the only view we have of this bicycle shows it being supported by ten high school girls. While the girls are quite lovely, there is, unfortunately, relatively little of the bicycle showing in the slide. However, we could supply you with a copy of this slide for $1.00."

I sent off for a copy, and was delighted with the result.

*****

My route out of Detroit through mile after mile of suburbs required some planning, as I made for Saline to the south of Ann Arbor to stay at the youth hostel there. It had a fascinating history, being on premises which originally formed part of a canning factory. This had been part of a big co-operative endeavour which unfortunately did not survive the big slump of the 1920's. The owner decided to use part of the buildings for a youth hostel after being impressed with what he saw of the organisation in Britain and Europe. Saline was the first hostel where I had the company of a fellow hosteller, a young man from Toledo just across the border in Ohio who had cycled the 35 miles north for a day's run.

The journey across Michigan took me through gently undulating farming country. I was glad there were no steep hills to negotiate as the heat was now intense. It started to come on when I was around London, Ontario, and was to last for several weeks till I reached Manitoba. For days on end the temperature soared into the middle 90's, and the humidity was high as well. I stopped often for drinks and ice-cream.

During one of these breaks I had my first encounter with the press, and in somewhat unusual circumstances. I was making no attempts to contact the media but, as I spoke to a man in Coldwater, the vicar of his church came along. The vicar, Fr. Man of the Episcopal Church, invited me to have a drink with him in a local café. He had been in England for three months during the war. I didn't ask him, but I guessed he might have been a padre with the American forces. Meanwhile, his parishioner had called the local press and a reporter suddenly arrived to obtain a story and take some photographs.

I was taken aback by all this attention. I then had to push down on the pedals to keep up with a planned schedule. I had written to my great-uncle in Gary, Indiana, to advise him that I hoped to arrive in Gary on what was now the next day. After a night at the Friedenswald youth hostel, a distance of 85 miles lay ahead of me. Conditions were easy, however, and I reached Lake Michigan at Grand Beach in the late afternoon. The name conjured up visions of exciting terrain, which did not materialize as I hurried through the industrial town of Michigan City, and along a wide road through forest to the industrial city of Gary. Smoke from steel mills rose into the air.

When I arrived at the home of my uncle he was outside talking to a neighbour. "What can I do for you, young man?" he asked. He didn't recognise me. For some reason he collected his mail from the Post Office. He hadn't been there for several days, and my letter was waiting to be picked up. I had therefore arrived unexpected. After introducing myself properly, my Uncle Joe realised who I was, and we had a laugh over the incident. We had met a few years before when he had come over to England to see his sisters, including my grandmother. He took me to a local restaurant for a meal. I was ravenous after the longest day's run so far.

The following day he gave me a guided tour of Gary, showing me the main public buildings. On a visit to the museum I learned that Gary was not founded until 1906, when the whole area was covered with sand dunes and scrub. Its population now approached 200,000 and new steel mills were being constructed. As we walked round Gary we stopped for drinks a number of times. It was so hot. The country's Major League baseball tournament was in progress, and the frequent stops for refreshment allowed us to keep up to date with the latest games via the TV's in the bars.

My uncle was a big strong man who had spent his working life on the railways. The next day was a Sunday and he took me 25 miles north by train to Chicago to introduce me to the sights there. A quieter day followed. It was the 4th of July, Independence Day, and we sat outside the house, with the Stars and Stripes flying as at so many other houses in the neighbourhood.

I left for Chicago the next morning for a grim ride through industrial areas and decaying housing districts. I was glad to get to the YMCA in the heart of the city, to be allocated to the smallest room I had ever stayed in. But the room was just a base from which to explore the city. I walked along State Street - "That Great Street" - as it was named on the street signs and immortalised by Frank Sinatra. Grant Park by the shore of Lake Michigan afforded fine views of the Chicago skyline. At the Band Shell in the park an orchestra was rehearsing a Mozart concerto for an evening concert. A few hours later I attended my second open air concert, hearing various concertos by Mozart and his "Eine Kleine Nachtmusik".

Conscious of an imminent stage of my journey, I went to the Board of Trade building to see the world's largest grain exchange in operation. After seeing a film, I watched the business on the trading floor from the Visitors' Gallery. Below was a vast milling throng of men, engaged in the buying and selling of wheat, maize, oats, rye, soybeans, soybean oil and meal, cotton and cottonseed oil, and other commodities. The scene reminded me of a trip several years before to the London Stock Exchange. There was the same first reaction of total chaos, and the trading floor was just as littered with pieces of paper.

Chicago was the home of America's largest bicycle manufacturer, the Schwinn Bicycle Company. I left the YMCA early one morning full of anticipation at the prospect of seeing something of their manufacturing operations. I was disappointed on reaching the premises to find the company closed down for the annual summer holiday, and decided to visit the conservatory in nearby Garfield Park. Leaving after a couple of hours, I turned to where I had left the bicycle locked against the fence. It was gone. I walked around the area for several minutes, hoping to catch sight of it. Touring the area later in a police car, the officer advised me that I stood little chance of seeing the bicycle again. Three months later when I was in Vancouver, I wrote to the police to confirm the latest situation. A police captain wrote to me: "I am sorry that you had trouble in our town."

I headed back to the YMCA to get the address of the Raleigh agent for Chicago from my diary. The agent directed me to a cycle shop north of the city, where I was able to purchase a second-hand bicycle of a similar type to the one stolen. During the next two days I overhauled it and fitted it with lower gears. At a hardware store I enquired about an adjustable spanner to replace the one which was in the stolen saddlebag. "You mean a wrench, buddy".

Suitably chastened I couldn't get out of Chicago fast enough. It was Sunday, 10 July. It would have been interesting remaining in the city for the day as there was to be a big civil rights rally at Soldier Field in Burnham Park. The chief speaker was to be Dr. Martin Luther King.

*****

As I headed north out of Chicago, I became aware of a change in attitude towards me by motorists and truck drivers. I had no flag on the new saddlebag, and motorists blared their horns loudly, while others shouted remarks which could not be commended to print! I was clearly being taken for an American. It was apparently all right for an Englishman to travel in the U.S.A. on his bicycle, but for one of their own kind to think of travelling in this way was unforgivable. Horns were blared loudly with the hope that I would go off the road to allow the motorists to pass with the minimum of inconvenience. There was no co-operation.

I was going to have to buy a new Union Jack at the earliest opportunity. Thankfully the situation eased off as I left the last suburbs of Chicago and passed through farming country. The corn was now yellow in most of the fields. Arriving at a recreational area around Fox Lake in the late afternoon I sought a room in a small hotel with some apprehension. My concern was justified. The temperature had climbed to 98°F during the day, and entering the hotel room was like entering a blast furnace. I had no plans to camp on this part of the journey as it was taking me through so many towns and cities, but I was beginning to regret it.

Entering Wisconsin I travelled through more fine farming country, now by field after field of maize, the area having an air of considerable prosperity. The large barns characteristic of the area were brightly painted and well maintained. When I sought water for my drinking bottle from a farmer sitting outside his farmhouse, he confirmed that the area was first class farming country. The sizes of farms in the area varied from 80 to 160 acres. He said one man should be able to look after 80 acres, and he had done so himself.

As I approached Janesville I decided that, if I could find a good cycle shop in the town, I would stay there and do one or two things to make my new machine more reliable for the long distances ahead. I was lucky and was given space in the workshop to fit new tyres and tubes, inspect the hub gear and front wheel bearings, and fit a new cyclometer so that I could once again record accurately the daily milage. I didn't know it at the time, but I had just passed the half-way stage of the journey across the continent, having completed 3,000 miles. There still seemed a long way to go. In the state capital Madison to the north, a knowledgeable cycle dealer recommended a more suitable derailleur gear than the one I left Chicago with. It was duly fitted. All this work increased my confidence in the ability of the new bicycle to serve me in the months ahead.

The hot weather continued. As I stopped for drinks I was the recipient of hospitality numerous times as local residents insisted on treating me. I was able to read in the newspapers that the whole of the eastern United States and much of the mid-west was basking in a heat wave. In Chicago the police turned on fire hydrants in the heat of the afternoon to allow children to cool themselves. When the hydrants were switched off in a Negro area to the south-west of the city, possibly the one I had travelled through on my entry to the city, rioting started. The Negroes complained that they were being treated unfairly: hydrants were still on in a nearby Italian district. Sunday's civil rights rally had left the Negroes very conscious of what they perceived as their rights. Then a massacre occurred of eight student nurses by an armed man. I felt I had left Chicago just in time.

Heavy rainfall while I was in Madison cooled the air for a short time as I headed north-west to La Crosse. The traffic was now much lighter as the terrain became increasingly hilly. I was travelling through an area of craggy peaks and deep winding valleys, the only considerable area in the northern United States which did not get flattened by glaciers during the Ice Age. I hoped the road would not take me into too many of the valleys as the temperature rose again and climbing out of the valleys was arduous work. The summits afforded sweeping views over the surrounding country.

I descended to La Crosse and to the valley of the Mississippi River. La Crosse started as a trading post in Indian territory. The French traders named it Prairie La Crosse after a game they saw the Indians playing which reminded them of their own game. North of La Crosse steep hills rose from both sides of the river, reminding me of a journey up the Rhine valley three years previously. Many people of German origin were settled in the area, probably drawn by the same association. Stopping overnight at a tourist home in Alma, I had hardly unpacked my bags when the daughter and son-in-law of the couple who lived there invited me to take a drive with them to the top of a local hill. They wanted to show me the glorious view over the Mississippi into Minnesota on the west side from a vantage point 500 ft above the valley. Back down in the valley I walked up to a lock and dam on the river, the 600 ft long lock allowing large barges to pass through.

Although I was following the river as it flowed between tree-clad hills, the hills often fell steeply straight down into the water. The road then climbed into the hills, offering memorable views over the valley. I passed through the small town of Stockholm, witness to the fact that many people of Scandinavian origin had settled in the area. My next major destination, St. Paul, apparently had one of the largest Swedish communities in the country.

St. Paul also had one of the most attractive State Capitols I had encountered so far, and I thoroughly enjoyed my visit there. The guide was an elderly woman who was immensely knowledgeable about everything connected with the building, and so enthusiastic. Her manner towards several children in the group I was with suggested that she had been a schoolteacher.

Just eight miles separated the centres of St. Pauls and Minneapolis, its twin city, but the visitor was advised to take a slightly longer run and pause for a while by a small waterfall in Minnehaha Park, the falls which inspired Longfellow when he wrote his famous poem "Song of Hiawatha" in 1855. Above the falls was a statue of Hiawatha and Minnehaha, erected in 1911.

Minneapolis was described as the city of lakes. Lakes covered the whole city area, and areas adjacent to the main lakes were set aside as parkland. Additional parks provided throughout the city area resulted in the Minneapolis park system being judged one of the finest in the country. From Minnehaha Park I followed a number of the lakes on my approach to the city centre. There was Lake Nokomis, which I almost encircled before following Minnehaha Creek to Lake Harriet, then Lake Calhoun and Lake of the Isles from which it was just a short distance to the centre via what was undoubtedly a residential area of very high quality. In the city centre I was attracted to one building more than any other, the Headquarters Building of the Northwestern National Life Insurance Company. Designed by Mioru Yamasaki and built only a year and a half before, it still looked absolutely new. So many people thought it must be a major public building that the insurance company had to lay on organised tours to satisfy the public interest in it. I joined one of these tours and was most impressed. I had earlier seen equally striking buildings by Yamasaki at Harvard University in Boston and at Wayne University in Detroit.

Longfellow's poem about Hiawatha described vividly the Indian legend that the great Hiawatha could lead his people out of any danger that might come to them in the Minnesota wilderness. Reading about this by the falls, I wondered exactly where this wilderness was. I found out a few days later when I rode into it, after following the Mississippi northwards through farming country. A few miles north of St. Cloud near the small community of North Prairie I had to leave the river. For the last 200 miles or so from La Crosse there had been a road on each side of the great river, one being quieter than the other and therefore more suitable for cyclists. Now there was only one road, on the east bank. I followed minor roads northwards as farmland gave way to an increasing amount of forest and lakes. Approaching Motley late one afternoon, the sky looked very stormy to the north. As I looked round quickly for accommodation I came up to a truckdrivers' motel. I was pleased to obtain a room, at a bargain price of $2.50. Rain lashed down for an hour shortly after I had got under cover, with the bicycle beside me in the motel room.

After a further day's travelling I left a hotel in Park Rapids in keen anticipation. The road climbed gradually as I cycled through pine forest and followed the eastern shore of Lake Itasca for four miles to a shallow stream flowing northwards from the top end. I had arrived at the source of the Mississippi. A sign nearby informed visitors:

> "Here 1475 ft above the ocean the mighty Mississippi begins
> to flow on its winding way 2552 miles to the Gulf of Mexico"

A supreme challenge awaited the visitor to this unique location. By means of stepping stones, one could walk across the mighty river without getting one's feet wet. Visitors came and went away while I was there. The majority did not fancy their chances of a dry crossing and removed their footwear before starting. For many it was a wise decision as some of the stones were just submerged and were very slippery.

Some 40 miles north of this memorable spot I crossed into the Red Lake Indian Reservation, a vast area of tribally owned land centred around the Upper and Lower Red Lakes. On the 637,000 acres (just under 1,000 square miles) of the reservation, a third of which was made up of the two connected lakes, lived some 3,000 Chippewa Indians. Unlike almost every other Indian reservation in North America, this one had a considerable measure of self-government. The economy was based largely on fishing and on the utilization of their large timber holdings.

I saw the school, church, hospital and main administration buildings in the village of Red Lake, the largest of three villages on the reservation. I was told that I might see the Chief in one building and looked forward to the possibility with eager anticipation. I found him in his office in conventional western clothes, wearing a trilby hat, talking on the telephone and with a cigar in his other hand. The image I had expected was shattered. There were just one or two good houses in the centre of the village, but most of the Indians lived in shacks which were, in the main, a depressing sight. Was this the sort of thing President Johnson had been advised of when I heard him talk three months earlier in Washington about the position of the Indian in "The Great Society"? This ambitious anti-poverty programme was intended, of course, to improve the lot of the deprived and disadvantaged everywhere.

It was not easy to see how conditions at the reservation could be improved rapidly as it was 'closed'. Private industry could not therefore come directly to the area and exploit its advantages. It was easy to feel angry about the legacy of the policies followed less than a century before as the western frontier advanced and the Indians found themselves on reservations with their natural way of life wiped out.

On my entry to Red Lake village two Indian boys had come along beside me on bicycles and spoken to me about the area. Now as I left the reservation they sped out onto the road on their bicycles, accompanied by a third boy, as I passed a house two miles west of the village. They accompanied me for about six miles, bombarding me with questions about England and my trip over here. We passed a shack about every half mile, with fishing nets to be seen by the lakeside. After 10 miles the houses stopped and I entered a wilderness area. As the road left the lakeside I entered forest, mainly birch, which lasted for miles. Just before I left the reservation a car carrying two adult Indians stopped by me, curious to find out where I was going. They offered me a refreshing can of beer as I stopped to talk to them.

It had been a most interesting day, which wasn't over yet. Four miles off the reservation at Thorhult I reached the first white community. There was no store there to get food for the evening, so I continued for five miles to the next community at Fourtowns. It was a glorious evening for travelling, and this time I was in luck. While at the store I found myself talking to a group of men at the bar there. First one invited me to stay at his home for the night, then another. They were all going to the home of the father of one of them for a game of cards and a meal and invited me along. A hectic evening followed, the like of which I had never encountered before. Two of the men at the bar were local farmers, a third one a chiropractor at Thief River Falls about 40 miles to the west, and another an optometrist in the same town. They apparently gathered like this most Wednesday evenings, an opportunity for this outgoing group to let their hair down once a week. Before we left one of the men said he would like me to meet one of the first Americans. As he beckoned me towards the doorway of another room, I had visions of meeting a descendant of the Pilgrim Fathers. I was taken aback to suddenly see an Indian woman smiling at me. I completely fell for that one, and we all had a laugh.

My bicycle and baggage were put on the back of a small truck, and we were off to the home of the father of the optometrist. Otto lived in a simple small cabin on the edge of the forest near Grygla, a few miles to the west. Several other people joined the group later in the evening. There was plenty to drink and we all had a meal. Otto seemed to like having all this company descend on him once a week. As the night advanced it was arranged that I stay at the cabin. I got to bed at one o'clock, occupying one of two bunk-type beds.

Otto provided me with an excellent breakfast the next morning and I left the rustic setting at 10.30am after a final bottle of beer with him. I would never forget the hospitality of that evening. I left the forest behind as I journeyed through farming country. The farms were widely scattered and were almost the only population in the area. A new dimension came into my route planning. I could not be sure if small places marked on my map represented communities where there might be a small store. It was essential not to allow my supplies of food and drink to get too low.

The country was now almost flat and the road was long and straight. The line of the road could usually be seen disappearing over the distant horizon, with the road visible for a much shorter distance due to a mirage created by the heat. Another day's travelling brought me to the small town of Roseau. As I took the baggage off the bicycle outside the hotel, the manager of the local store invited me to visit his home later in the evening. After a cup of coffee he showed me his snowmobile, which he used during the harsh winters in this area. I started to feel that I was in the far north. But another huge country only started 10 miles north of Roseau, and the following morning I crossed the 49th parallel into Canada.

Chapter 5

Across the Prairies

Friday, 29 July 1966

A sign at the border carried the words "Welcome to Manitoba - the Keystone Province". In 1877, in an address at Winnipeg's City Hall, the Earl of Dufferin, Governor-General of Canada from 1872-1878, referred to Manitoba as "the keystone of that mighty arch of sister provinces which spans Canada from the Atlantic to the Pacific." He was the first vice-regal representative to visit Manitoba.

The provincial capital of Winnipeg was just 100 miles away by road from the border crossing. Sparsely populated country continued on the Canadian side of the border, with widely dispersed farms. I travelled for much of the day through almost unbroken forest, reaching Steinbach, principally a Ukrainian settlement, at the end of the day. The hotel receptionist mentioned that, a few days before, she had seen a cyclist like myself in Whiteshell Provincial Park to the north-east: I would have to keep a lookout for him. Before leaving the next morning, I heard a short news item on the radio about the soccer World Cup. England had just beaten West Germany 4-2 in the final after extra time. I had completely forgotten about the competition, which had gripped the nation's attention as England advanced to her finest hour.

Winnipeg proved to be a most attractive city to visit, with its clean buildings and wide tree-lined avenues. At the first opportunity I toured the Legislative Building to gain a better insight into the history of Winnipeg, and of Manitoba. I heard of Winnipeg's beginning as the fur trading post of Fort Garry, and of the arrival at this site in August 1812 of colonists to establish the first permanent agricultural settlement in Manitoba. Crossing the Red River I walked around St. Boniface, the largest French-speaking city outside the province of Quebec, and part of Greater Winnipeg. A memorable evening was spent at the Rainbow Theatre in Kildonan Park, reputed to be Canada's only outdoor theatre. There, under the stars, I watched a performance of *My Fair Lady*.

On my last full day in the city I wrote out 18 cards. I had promised so many people I would send them a card now and again, and Winnipeg was a milestone on my journey. Earlier, I visited the Winnipeg Grain Exchange to learn what I could about the marketing of grain produced on the Canadian Prairies. I was as prepared as I could be for the journey ahead, a ride across the vast expanse of the prairies. Was it really one big wheat field? And ought I to take a train for the next thousand miles as so many people had advised me so as not to die of boredom?

I left Winnipeg with a feeling of adventure. I was also looking forward to meeting a whole group of relations who lived just a day's travel away near Portage la Prairie. They were descendants of my late great-uncle Fred, one of four uncles who had emigrated to North America during the early years of the Twentieth century. They had responded to advertising campaigns to go out and help to settle the wide open spaces of the prairies. Five of the six children of my uncle lived in the small communities of High Bluff, St. Ambroise and St. Marks to the north-east, and one to the south of Portage. They were all involved in farming. It was mainly cattle raising country, and I had arrived at haymaking time. Large amounts of hay were needed to feed the cattle during the long, severe winters when the cattle were confined to the barns. I spent several days in the area, being taken from one family to another and getting to know everyone. Alex showed me his fishing nets and snowmobile, and drove me the few miles north to Lake Manitoba; he often went fishing there during the winter, taking the catch to Winnipeg to sell. Alice borrowed a projector, enabling me to give a slide show at her church in Portage la Prairie to relatives and friends. She also contacted the local paper in the town, arranging for me to give an interview as I left the area. All my baggage was back on the bicycle once more for an accompanying photograph.

As I departed, I was conscious of a meeting at a café a few days earlier on the approach to Portage. A young man said to me: "If you head straight west to Regina and Calgary, you will travel through the heart of the wheat land. When you get right in this area, you can turn and see nothing but wheat in every direction. You may not see a single tree or a house." I told him I was intending to take a more northerly route via Saskatoon and Edmonton. It was going to fit in with a planned ride through the Rockies: in addition, there were more addresses to visit close to the route.

I turned northwards just a few miles west of Portage. The weather was now pleasantly cooler, and I put my sweater on for the first time for weeks. When the sun broke through the clouds it suddenly warmed up again, and I had the sweater on and off a number of times. Stopping at a store at Woodside in the afternoon for a drink and ice-cream, the owner would not accept payment. His young son and a friend had a lot of questions to ask me about the bicycle. As I demonstrated the gears to them, the store owner's wife invited me into the house to have a cup of coffee. There I met two RCMP's, one the father of one of the boys. All the parents were as interested in my trip as the younger members, and I ended up giving a further demonstration of the bicycle gears. A few weeks earlier one of the boys had seen two cyclists like myself as they passed through on their way from Vancouver to Montreal. At Gladstone at the end of the day, other people mentioned seeing the two cyclists on their way across the country.

A cloudy day followed as I made for Erickson. Near Neepawa the road sloped upwards affording views over a patchwork of fields. A longer gradual climb began as I turned directly north to Erickson and approached Riding Mountain National Park, a vast rolling plateau some 1000 ft higher than the surrounding prairie. The 30 mile journey through the park involved a ride through evergreen and spruce forest, following the shore of two attractive lakes, Clear Lake and Moon Lake, and with many wildflowers by the roadsides. I emerged from the north end of the park to more wide views over the prairie below. I savoured the view, as a number of weeks were going to pass before I gained any similar elevation. I swept down to Dauphin, losing 1000 ft in little more than two miles. An older man there looked me up and down. "Is the Government paying you anything to do this?" It got me thinking about the undoubted goodwill aspects of the tour. Maybe I should write to the Prime Minister on my return?

I seemed to gather an increasing number of people around me whenever I stopped, whether at a hotel in the evening or during the day for a break. My saddlebag sported a new Union Jack purchased in Winnipeg, but apart from this arousing curiosity about my identity, a cycle tourist was a very rare specimen on the route which I was following. Younger boys invariably asked:

"How many gears have you got?"
"Twelve."
"How fast can you go in twelfth gear?"

Time and again this question followed the first one. I tried to explain that the purpose of having a large number of gears was not to go fast but to enable me to climb steep hills. As I elaborated I wondered sometimes if the message was getting across to my young prairie listeners, most of whom probably had bicycles but who could have no conception of what is involved in climbing up a long steep hill. I said that I normally travelled at about 10 mph.

"How far do you travel each day?"
"About 60 miles."
"Where are you going to?"
"Vancouver."
"Where did you start?"
"New York."
"You mean......?" The question was often not completed as they looked once more at my transportation.
"Don't you get very tired?"

This question invariably prompted one of my monologues. I tried to explain that, after a few days cycle touring, your general fitness and stamina levels improve considerably. These must be built up on a foundation of a reasonable level of health and fitness. You get tired, but it is a tiredness which ordinary rest allows you to recover from completely. Provided you then stay within your own individual energy capacity, you can go on indefinitely. This is a difficult concept to get across, but it lies at the heart of cycle touring. Cycle tourists are not born with innately higher energy levels than anyone else, but they learn how to harness their resources more effectively. The human body can be likened in many ways to an internal combustion engine. A body without exercise is like a badly tuned engine. With exercise, it is astonishing how much energy can be tapped into, how much more efficient the body can become. Everyone I met could see that I was of just average build. I would generally leave them with looks of disbelief, possibly feeling that there must be some additional indefinable factor.

After I had entered Saskatchewan and passed through Yorkton, the terrain began to have a new interesting feature as a railway line began to follow the road. Every eight miles or so was a community, and every community had two, three or four grain elevators standing beside the railway line. The tall elevators were about the only landmark on the horizon and left a vivid impression on the memory. As you approached a community from the distance, rectangular blocks on the horizon denoting the elevators did not seem to get any larger until you were almost on top of them. Their true shape then took form, you passed them and almost immediately looked towards the new western horizon for the blocks defining the position of the next community. Some of the communities through which I passed had intriguing names - Theodore, Mozart, Kandahar, Dafoe, Jansen, Guernsey, Viscount - and I wondered what story might lie behind each name. At almost every community a large, low building indicated a curling rink. The prairie dwellers were fanatical players of the sport. It was a major winter recreation; an activity which the harsh winters gave plenty of time to follow when work on the farms was limited.

The relative quiet of the journey was broken at intervals as a giant freight train rumbled past, transporting grain from the elevators to the main shipping terminals, west to Vancouver or east to the lake head - the twin cities of Port Arthur and Fort William on the north shore of Lake Superior. The diesel locomotives could pull about 160 - or more than a mile - of freight cars. When a long train came past, you thought it was never going to end.

There was considerable diversity in the scene. Wheat and other grain crops covered much of the land, but on this northern route there was also dairy farming and cattle rearing. There were also considerable areas of scrub and poplar forest. Everywhere one was conscious of the immense space.

Trees were often very scattered, a feature I became especially aware of around lunch time, or when I wished to stop for a rest. After the first few weeks of the journey I started having picnic lunches to reduce spending. The meals in the restaurants and cafés were good value, but I could never resist following up with apple pie and ice cream. Just before lunch time I would endeavour to buy a bottle of soft drink, then continue, looking for a tree under which I might shelter from the hot sun while I had a leisurely lunch. It was often far from easy. There were usually trees to be seen, but they were often well away from the road or inaccessible with the bicycle. After finding a likely spot I would approach it with trepidation, expecting to be driven back every second by a swarm of mosquitoes, suddenly active at the presence of food - human food! Wearing shorts I exposed far too much battle area to the hungry beasts. The first time I was bitten in northern Ontario my arms swelled up considerably.

In the immensity of the prairies, one thing decided whether a cyclist was going to have an easy ride - the wind. When it started to blow there was little to mitigate its strength. I also learned with dismay one other fact of prairie life - the prevailing wind blew from the west. I listened with fortitude to a remark made to me many times. “It would be better if you were going the other way.” When the wind blew directly against me, I had a gruelling day’s run. But when it was behind me it was glorious. I could coast along almost without effort, gazing at will at the scene around me, all thoughts of a previous day’s struggle evaporating in an instant.

The country was seldom completely flat for very long, but rolled very gently. I tried many times to capture the vastness of the scene in a photograph, but it was very difficult. One needed to be there, to turn a full circle slowly, and to see in every direction the enormous fields of corn, broken now and then by patches of scrub and trees, with just the occasional farm-house standing well back from the road. If a railway line was near, grain elevators would almost certainly be seen somewhere on the horizon, maintaining eternal vigilance over the scene.

I found the whole experience absolutely fascinating. After following the railway line for three days and for 200 miles from Yorkton, I arrived in Saskatoon, the second city of Saskatchewan, and a milestone on the journey across the prairies. It had been twelve days since I left Winnipeg, and I was looking forward to a few days in a city again. Before exploring, I wrote a short letter to relations in Battleford of my brother-in-law to advise them I was on my way. On my entry into Saskatoon I had admired the setting of the city on the steep banks of the South Saskatchewan River. I went back across the river to the east bank to see the setting again from different vantage points, to look at the group of bridges crossing the river near the centre, and to take photographs.

Many hours were spent at the Western Development Museum, totally absorbed in what must be the finest collection of early farm machinery in North America. The Museum also had a fine collection of early household furnishings and utensils, and one could begin to savour some of the spirit of the pioneers who opened up the Great Plains not very long ago.

The direct route from Saskatoon would have taken me north-west to North Battleford, but I decided to make a detour. A lady at the company I had left in Stafford had given me the name and address of a cousin in Prince Albert to the north-east. It was 100 miles away by road, but represented just a blip on a thick line on a large map recording my advance across the continent. The detour to Prince Albert took me past wheat fields and cattle rearing country, and through significant areas of pine and poplar forest. At a small hotel at Duck Lake at the end of the first day out of Saskatoon, the manager told me that Duck Lake was the oldest town in Saskatchewan. Many years ago the population had been 1300, but it was currently down to 700. An important historical event had taken place nearby at Batoche, during the winter of 1884-5, known as the Northwest Rebellion. The manager treated me to a delicious steak meal, and the following morning returned the money I had paid for my room. Such gestures of hospitality remained in my memory for long afterwards.

Arriving at Prince Albert the following afternoon, I made my way to the fire station to introduce myself to the person I had come to see. Mr. Slater was the Chief Fire Officer and was able to talk to me for some time before I departed to see more of the town. A leaflet informed me that Prince Albert and its surrounding district was the oldest settlement in the province, and the town was celebrating its Centennial Year in 1966. A fur trading post had been built a few miles away in 1776, and I felt the detour had taken me into the far north. The map showed me that the close road network across the prairies started to peter out only 25 miles north of Prince Albert.

Two further days travel brought me back to the main route at North Battleford late one Sunday afternoon, 21 August. Crossing the North Saskatchewan River I began to wonder where the farm of my brother-in-law's relations was. It had a box number for its mail address related to the smaller community of Battleford 10 miles to the west. I noticed a phone booth and gave them a call. The parents were out but Leslie, the son, tried to give me instructions for the farm 22 miles to the south-west. Having just completed 66 miles I did not relish another 22. While I waited at the phone booth to see if

Leslie had been able to contact his parents, a car suddenly pulled up and I was soon on my way, with the bicycle in the back of the car. The parents had been at a meeting only a few miles away. The journey to the farm took me through some very hilly farming country, and almost entirely on gravel roads. I was glad of the lift.

I spent two memorable days on the 1000 acre farm where cattle were raised. On the first morning I accompanied Leslie, who was 11, and his father to round up 40 cows into a corral in readiness for the visit of two vets. All the cows were to be vaccinated for a particular disease and checked for tuberculosis. Earlier in the spring every cow had produced a calf, and all had survived. I spent a busy morning operating a squeeze gate along a passage leading from the corral to confine each cow while the vets did their work. Failing to hold 2 of the 40 cows properly, I wasn't sure if I was going to qualify as a farmer.

After the morning's work an entirely different kind of afternoon followed as Mr. Scotton took Leslie, his younger sister Kathy and myself into Battleford. While he attended to some business matters I took the children to another branch of the Western Development Museum which proved to be as interesting as the one in Saskatoon. Fort Battleford National Historic Park was nearby. The fort was established by the North West Mounted Police in 1876 to assist in the settlement and development of the surrounding area. It was an area inhabited by more than 25,000 Indians, whose way of life came into inevitable conflict with the advancing settlers.

A quieter day followed during which I assisted with gathering in bales of hay. The farmers were working flat out to make the most of the glorious weather. There had been considerable rainfall lately in the area, though I had encountered much less on my route. The average temperature was dropping slightly, and extra clothing was starting to be taken out of my bags.

I was brought into Battleford by truck to save me a long ride on gravel roads, refreshed by these new experiences. They had included a horseback ride with Leslie. There was no saddle for my horse and, as I bounced up and down, I knew that I preferred the iron horse with which I was now reacquainted. Progress was slow as a number of people stopped to talk to me, and the temperature rose once more to 90°.

Approaching the border with Alberta, a new feature appeared on the scene. Near Lloydminster I saw an oil derrick in a field. Looking beyond to surrounding fields, six further pumps or "nodding oil-cows" were visible, with a large storage tank some 30 yards from each pump. The pumps were in the middle of good wheat fields, but one doubted if the farmers considered them a nuisance. I read later that there were 10,500 oil wells in Alberta, and expected to see a few more as I continued.

The provincial capital of Edmonton lay some 140 miles from the border. As I advanced through this new province, wild roses were often to be seen by the roadside. The choice of the wild rose as the Provincial flower of Alberta seemed appropriate. At Mundare I made a slight detour off the main road to visit the Ukrainian Museum, seeing several national costumes, a large number of valuable early Ukrainian bibles and other publications, Ukrainian paper money and, among many handicrafts, a number of beautifully painted eggs. I was drawn to the museum by a number of experiences during recent weeks. I found myself travelling through or staying in a number of places with an almost exclusively Ukrainian population. In other places the population was almost entirely another ethnic group, highlighting a significant difference between Canada and America. Emigrants to America were encouraged to assimilate into the local population quickly and think of themselves as Americans after relatively little time in the country. Emigrants to Canada were not subject to a similar pressure and many communities apparently identified as closely with their ethnic origin as with considering themselves Canadian.

Twenty miles west of Mundare I detoured to travel through Elk Island National Park, being rewarded by the sight of a herd of buffalo in a paddock. They were the first buffalo I had seen, one of few remaining herds in North America. A youth hostel in the park provided me with overnight accommodation, and welcome shelter during the night when heavy rain fell. Emerging from the park on the north side I found myself on a gravel road for three miles before joining the main road near Lamont. The wet gravel made for heavy going, the first time I had encountered the problem. I was going to have to clean the bicycle while in Edmonton, which was now only 35 miles away.

The provincial capital was the last important milestone on my journey across the prairie provinces. Like the previous milestone of

Saskatoon, Edmonton also stood on the banks of a river, this time the North Saskatchewan. During a number of walks round this attractive city, I crossed the river to the south bank to admire the skyline of the main public buildings to the north. An interesting morning was spent touring the Northern Alberta Jubilee Auditorium, given to the province in 1955 to mark its 50th year. It was apparently one of the finest auditoriums in North America. On the afternoon of the same day I went to the Queen Elizabeth Planetarium to spend an absorbing hour learning about the night sky and the current space programme. This building was also very new, commemorating the visit to Edmonton in 1959 of the Queen and Prince Philip.

Being in another provincial capital, I was keen to visit an older building, the Legislative Building. I was amused to find that one girl in the reception office was a recent emigrant from Manchester, and the guide of the party I joined was a Scot who emigrated in 1955. In the party was a man visiting from Canterbury in Kent and an American lady who had emigrated from England a few years before. I began to wonder which country I was in. But I was at the northern gateway to the Rockies, which now beckoned strongly.

Chapter 6

Through the Rockies

Sunday, 4 September 1966

Two days travel from Edmonton brought me to Edson, 125 miles to the west. A short climb followed, and from the crest of the road I had my first view of the Rockies. They were still 60 miles away, but a long range of peaks was clearly visible, so clear was the air. The peaks remained visible for much of the day as I travelled through almost unbroken pine forest.

Near the entrance to Jasper National Park a small black bear, about three feet high, came out of the trees 30 yards ahead of me. It saw me before I could stop, and turned back into the trees. It was the first bear I had seen in the open. A large sign nearby provided some information on the Athabasca River, which I was going to be following on the journey into the park:

> "There in the valley lies the mighty Athabasca River - a part of Canada's first transcontinental route. After the discovery of the Athabasca Pass in 1810-11, famous explorers, untiring voyageurs and resolute fur traders followed the river to its source in the Rockies, then made the gruelling trek over wind-swept mountain passes to the Pacific. The River remained as part of the great Trans-Canada route until the completion of the railway in 1885."

The following day I passed through the entrance to the park to begin what must be one of the most beautiful journeys in the world, the journey through the Rocky Mountains down the Banff-Jasper highway. For the next week I cut my daily milage down drastically as I ambled down the highway, trying to take in as much of the magnificent scenery as I could. A chain of mountains stretched on either side of the highway for 150 miles, almost unbroken but ever-changing. I had this paradise to myself for long periods as the main holiday period was over and traffic was very light. And for almost the entire run for me, the weather was glorious. I was especially conscious of this as my stay in Edmonton just a few days before had been accompanied by several periods of heavy rain.

With a chain of youth hostels along the highway, the extent of each day's travelling was guided by the hostel locations. This should have solved accommodation matters, but a problem arose which I had not anticipated. With the main holiday period ended, the hostels were unmanned from Labour Day, the very day I entered the park. Keys were available in Edmonton for the later traveller, information which I learned too late when I met a couple from the hostel organisation near Edson. I therefore generally improvised shelter around the hostel buildings, grateful for the exceptionally fine weather. I was in luck, however, on my first night, at Maligne Canyon hostel, finding the girls' dormitory unlocked. I settled down, not expecting anyone else to arrive to cause complications! At Jasper nearby I stocked up with food supplies for a number of days.

In addition to the mountain scenery, there were so many things to see, so many detours to make; there were the world-famous resorts of Jasper, Lake Louise and Banff; there were the lakes with their fantastic colours and in superb settings - Peyto, Bow, Louise, Moraine and many others; there were the mountain passes on the highway itself, Sunwapta Pass at 6,675 ft and Bow Pass at 6,785 ft; and there was the Columbia Icefield, centre of the greatest known accumulation of ice in the Rocky Mountains.

The ice-field was situated almost halfway between Jasper and Banff, and the highway took me beside a huge tongue of the ice-field, the Athabasca Glacier. It was a sight such as I had never seen before. I turned off the highway for a steep climb of one and a half miles up the hillside beside the glacier to an elevation of 7,150 ft, the highest I had been to so far. It was gratifying to pass a sign forbidding trailers or caravans to climb the road because of the steepness, while the bicycle was apparently perfectly welcome! At a vehicle park I donned all my extra clothing before transferring to a special tracked vehicle with other visitors for a ride on the bumpy surface of the glacier. In an area away from major crevasses we were also allowed to walk on the ice, a unique experience for everyone.

At the building beside the vehicle park, some foodstuffs were available to replenish my supplies. I was confident of now getting to Lake Louise without running out. After returning to the main road a gradual climb took me over the Sunwapta Pass, and from Jasper National Park to Banff National Park. A sharp descent followed after a few miles to the valley of the North Saskatchewan River, providing easy riding conditions. I arrived at the Alexandra River hostel at 4.45pm to find it deserted and locked. As the weather was still fine I continued 21 miles to Totem Creek hostel, arriving at 7.20pm after several miles of climbing. It was also deserted and locked. I just had time to improvise a shelter in the porch of one of the dormitories before darkness fell.

Progress was slow the next morning as I stopped to admire the incredible fluorescent green colour of Lower Waterfowl Lake, before starting a long climb over Bow Pass. Near the summit I looked down over Peyto Lake and some time later over Bow and Hector Lakes, all with the same fluorescent colour, due to silt suspended in the water. I dropped 1,700 ft on the way down to Lake Louise, where I replenished my food supplies at the store before proceeding to Corral Creek hostel nearby. It was deserted, but one door of the building was not bolted. I soon made myself a cup of tea.

I had some unexpected company during the evening when an engineering student at the University of Alberta in Calgary arrived. He said he knew hardly any adults who cycled and it was extremely difficult for the hostel organisation to find adults to accompany parties of schoolchildren on cycle tours during the summer. Before he left he gave me his key for the hostel chain in the mountain National Parks. Like many others he had a copy of one of the official keys. Since the officers in Calgary were about to change all the locks in full awareness of this situation, he had no further use for his key.

I could have turned west into British Columbia at Lake Louise, but the lure of Banff, 40 miles to the south-east, was compelling. It is in a gem of a setting, nestling between Mount Norquay, Mount Rundle and Sulphur Mountain. Arriving in Banff in the middle of the afternoon, I wanted to walk up Sulphur Mountain straight away to admire the view, but a lady in the Parks Information office cautioned me against it as I would run out of daylight before getting back down again. The rest of the afternoon was therefore spent in Banff before proceeding to the Spray River hostel nearby. My new key came in useful straight away, and I soon had some water on the boil for more tea.

Unexpected company arrived during the evening in the form of two student nurses from Montreal. One had spent three months cycling in England a year or two before. I awoke the next day to a very dull morning. As the sky cleared a little around midday I locked my bicycle up near the imposing Banff Springs Hotel and started a four mile walk, or rather climb, up Sulphur Mountain to an elevation of 7,500 ft. The 3,000 ft climb from the valley took me two and a half hours, but an alternative cable car ride was out of the question. It was a Sunday and the majority of visitors took this easy way upwards. As I ascended I met a number returning by foot, including Elizabeth and Lorraine from Montreal. There were commanding views at every stage of the walk. After refreshments at the Summit Tea House, the walk down took only half the time of the ascent.

The following day I returned to Lake Louise, enabling me to have another stay at the Corral Creek hostel before seeing some of the attractions in this area. I had postponed this on the journey southwards, knowing that I would be returning. The weather was glorious again as I saw the lake itself with another imposing hotel, the Chateau Lake Louise, beside it, and Lake Moraine, a further lake nearby with an incredible colour to the water.

It was then time to cross into British Columbia, the last province on my journey across the continent. A colourful sign at the border included cartoon drawings of two elderly, homely characters, Century Sam and Centennial Sue, and the message "Welcome to British Columbia - Centennial Years 1966-1967". The full significance of these dates escaped me for a while. I knew that the Confederation of Canada began in 1867, and learned later that 1866 was the year when Vancouver Island joined the mainland area of the colony of British Columbia to become the province of British Columbia.

Crossing into British Columbia took me from Banff National Park into Yoho National Park. Before turning off the main road to go up the Yoho valley, I stopped at a vantage point to look across a gap at the route followed by the Canadian Pacific Railway line as it disappeared into a tunnel. An impressive civil engineering feat involved the line climbing considerably over a short distance via spiral tunnels bored through the mountainside. I paused for half an hour in the hope of seeing a train disappearing into the tunnel or emerging from it, but it was the wrong time, and I set off up the Yoho valley to the Takakkaw Falls hostel. The journey to my final overnight stay in the mountain youth hostels was a memorable one, as I found myself having to travel eight miles on a gravel road, six of them uphill.

The return journey the following morning was correspondingly easy, but I came down the valley slowly to conserve my tyres on the gravel surface, and to take in some attractive views, including of the Takakkaw Falls where melt-water from the Daly Glacier plunged approximately 1,200 ft into the valley. A final detour off the main road took me up the Emerald River valley to Emerald Lake, to my mind the gem of the lakes in the mountain National Parks with its exquisite colour. The mountain views behind me slowly receded as I continued on the Trans-Canada highway, following the valley of the Kicking Horse River down to Golden. The Rogers Pass, hewn out of the mountainside only a few years before, took me on to Revelstoke. The air was often heavy with smoke from timber mills as the road continued between fir-clad hills. As I followed the valley of the Eagle River, the road, railway and river continually changed positions in the narrow valley. At Craigellachie a marker recorded the spot where the last spike was driven to complete the Canadian Pacific Railway line across the country in 1885, a major step in uniting the west of Canada with the east.

A few miles further at Sicamous there was an opportunity to get off the Trans-Canada highway. The traffic had not been heavy, but I had no wish to travel on main roads like this if there was an alternative. I turned southwards towards the Okanagan Valley, one of the finest fruit-growing regions in the world. From Vernon onwards I passed orchard after orchard of heavily-laden trees as the road followed first Kalamalka Lake, then Okanagan Lake, 80 miles long - so long it seemed to be a river. At Kelowna the road crossed from the east to the west bank, and for most of the continuing journey to Penticton the road ran high up the hillside, affording memorable views of the lake, the orchards and the hills beyond.

The hills were very light in colour, the area boasting a better sunshine record than Nassau or Bermuda! The annual rainfall was so light that the grass soon scorched in the hot summer sun. Some of this rain had chosen to fall when I was in Vernon. The houseparents at the youth hostel there told me that there had been hardly a drop of rain for two months. It was an almost eerie scene after all the greenery of the forests in the Rocky Mountains.

A ride over scrub-covered hills brought me to Keremeos in the Similkameen Valley, another thriving fruit-growing area. I stayed one evening at Hedley, a town which had known better times. Nearby were gold mines from which was taken, between 1904 and 1955, 47 million dollars worth of gold. I walked round the ruins of the mill in the evening, but unhappily failed to find a trace of the precious metal.

From Hedley to Princeton was a very pleasant journey, the road following the Similkameen River as it flowed gently down the valley between fir-clad hills. Turning south at Princeton the road climbed steeply for about two miles, giving attractive views of the valley as I looked back. After an easy stretch the road wound its way upwards for mile after mile as it climbed into Manning Provincial Park to go over the Alison Pass at 4,450 ft. The final descent then began towards Hope in the Fraser River valley, at an elevation of only 214 ft.

The descent was swift for many miles, taking me past some startling scenes of maple trees with their leaves turned all shades of red as autumn approached. As the road levelled out I came to a grim area called the Hope Slide where, early in the morning of 9 January 1965, an enormous chunk of the hillside fell into the valley. It was apparently triggered by a minor earthquake. Rock filled the valley to a depth of 275 ft, necessitating the building of a new road over the top of it. Four people were caught in the fall and never found. Passing by enormous boulders and piles of rubble, I had a firsthand impression of the frightening power of nature.

As the road swept downwards between high fir-clad hills, I wondered earnestly whether the adjacent hillside was stable. It would take a little time to relax and put this exceptional event in perspective. The ride downwards was cool as it required no effort on the pedals, but I arrived in Hope to find that all the towns in the area had been simmering in a heat-wave. Hope had it the worst with a maximum of 89°, quite a record for the near the end of September.

A change was under way though as I departed the following morning in heavy rain. I was now keen to get to my destination. Further, my relatives on the prairies had told me that when it rains on the west coast, it can rain for two months on end. The rain did clear up by midday as I rode along the fertile Fraser Valley, passing many prosperous-looking dairy farms. The following day I arrived in Vancouver. Some 6,100 miles lay behind me.

It was 24 September; time to settle down to some conventional work. I would be able to check the prairie dwellers' attitude to the big city on the west coast. They would never forsake their clear, blue, sunny skies during the winter for the dull, depressing skies of rain-sodden Vancouver, even if the temperature in the coastal city was 60° higher! I wondered at first how much of this was a defensive reaction to their cold winters. During November and December it rained in Vancouver for the proverbial 40 days and 40 nights. Actually, the weather man told us cheerfully, the number of consecutive days on which it rained was only 39!

When it wasn't raining, I discovered what an attractive city Vancouver was in which to spend the winter. From my hotel on Pender Street, I looked northwards from my room across Burrard Inlet to the city's mountain backdrop. A mile to the north-west was Stanley Park, an outstanding area which I visited a number of times. The high ground of Queen Elizabeth Park offered some of the best views of the city, and cycle rides out to the two University campuses of the University of British Columbia and Simon Fraser University allowed to me to get a feel for the area beyond the city centre. Back in the central area, it was a pleasure to be able to attend concerts and opera performances at the Queen Elizabeth Theatre. All these delights were, of course, of secondary importance to the requirements of work, but what a background in which to participate in these various activities.

Vancouver
Victoria
Olympic N.P.
WASHN
Seattle
Wenatchee
Mt. Rainier N.P.
Spokane
Yakima
Portland
Salem
Columbia River
Missoula
Helena
MONTANA
Calgary
Saskatoon
Regina
CANADA
NORTH DAKOTA
SOUTH DAKOTA
OREGON
Crater Lake N.P.
Boise
IDAHO
Yellowstone N.P.
Grand Teton N.P.
WYOMING
South Pass
Cheyenne
NEBRASKA
Reno
NEVADA
Salt Lake City
UTAH
Sacramento
San Francisco
Yosemite N.P.
Kings Canyon & Sequoia N.P.s
Fresno
CALIFORNIA
Death Valley
Las Vegas
Colorado River
Rocky Mountain N.P.
Denver
COLORADO
Colorado Springs
KANSAS
Fort Garland
Grand Canyon N.P.
Flagstaff
Taos
Santa Fe
OKLA.
Los Angeles
San Diego
ARIZONA
Phoenix
NEW MEXICO
Rio Grande
Tucson
Tombstone
El Paso
Carlsbad Caverns N.P.
TEXAS
PACIFIC OCEAN
MEXICO
0
200
400
Miles

Chapter 7

In Logging Country

Sunday, 9 April 1967

Today was meant to be the day when the next stage of The Grand Tour, a journey through the American West, was going to begin, but I awoke in Vancouver to a cloudy day and with a forecast of showers. Should I delay my departure? Heavy rain had fallen the day before while I arranged to post home a large parcel of all the maps, travel literature and photographs of last summer's journey. As I continued with packing in my room at The Parkway Hotel on Pender Street, home for the last six months, I stopped frequently to look out the window. The sun started to break through the clouds about 11 o'clock, and the decision was made.

I departed from the hotel at midday after saying goodbye to everyone I had got to know so well. There were so many young people in the hotel, especially emigrants from Britain, many hoping to make their fortunes in this attractive location. As I moved away I found myself swerving across the road: I had forgotten how to ride the bicycle with all the baggage on, and I now had much more. The majority of the weight was over the rear wheel, and I needed to lean forward slightly and hold the handlebars more firmly. It was a relief to get on top of the problem after just a short distance as I cycled towards Stanley Park and over the Lions Gate Bridge to the north shore. A few spots of rain fell, but the sky cleared considerably to the west as I headed along Marine Drive to Horseshoe Bay, arriving just in time to catch the 2pm ferry to Nanaimo on Vancouver Island.

The sky was now a brilliant clear blue as the boat sailed across the Strait of Georgia. Looking back to the retreating Vancouver skyline with which I had become so familiar, I experienced mixed feelings; of regret, that I was leaving one of the most beautiful cities in the world; of uncertainty, that I was once more giving up a steady job for the unknown; of excitement, in the anticipation of new adventures; and of guilt. Why shouldn't I still be working like everybody else? Why should I be allowed to disregard the rules of the game? For several days the feelings of guilt and uncertainty remained with me until I once more settled into my chosen role.

I could look back on a busy six months. I had been able to obtain work within two weeks of arrival in Vancouver, and had made up all the expenditure of the previous six months of travel. Romantic visions of working as a lumberjack had to be set aside, as I didn't have the build for it and found that Vancouver was a modern commercial and industrial city. If I was going to obtain work, I needed to make use of the skills I possessed. I responded successfully to an advert placed in the local newspaper by an electrical building services consultant seeking staff. My experience was with heavier engineering, but the underlying principles could be applied in any related field, and I threw myself into this new endeavour. I was able to obtain a conditional work permit, benefiting from Vancouver's location. There was a shortage of engineers in the city as so many were drawn to Boeing across the border in Seattle, attracted by high salaries. Provided a Canadian didn't apply for my job, the work permit could continue. The main income was supplemented by periods spent working as a desk clerk at my hotel during various evenings and at weekends. This was a new, illuminating experience as new guests arrived and departed all the time, adding to the considerable number residing in the hotel for longer periods.

A glance at the bicycle reminded me that I had spent a considerable number of hours during the winter sewing, to produce a new saddlebag. As I reached the Rocky Mountains last summer, I had realised that camping equipment was going to be essential on the next stage. I was going to be in the mountains a great deal, the distances between communities would often be considerable, and there were no youth hostels. I therefore purchased a tent and other equipment. Having bought all this extra luggage, security considerations made it very desirable to carry everything in a proper bag. But nobody produced one. Even the large saddlebag stolen in Chicago with the original bicycle would not have been big enough. I therefore had to make one, and two Army kit bags were purchased to obtain sufficient material for the bag now on the bicycle. It looked very professional, I thought, and a large new Union Jack advertised clearly to everyone where I came from.

The ferry journey took an hour and fifty minutes, the trip across the water helping to make the mental break with Vancouver. The rest of the day was spent in the small town of Nanaimo, before heading southwards through forested country. The weather was fine and sunny, although the temperature indicated it was not yet summertime. I passed through Ladysmith, without there being any possibility of realising a later claim to fame. A girl would be born there some two months later, on 1 July, who would later command the attention of half the world - the male half! Her name was Pamela Anderson. I followed the old highway where possible, and for long periods had the road to myself. Just after passing through Crofton a lady hailed me from her home and invited me to have a cup of tea. Her husband worked at a pulp mill nearby, and had spent two and a half years in New Zealand helping to set up a pulp mill there. She currently had a boarder from England, who was teaching in Crofton.

After this first experience of hospitality on this new stage of the journey I continued down the coast, with views over the Strait of Georgia on my left and snow-clad peaks to the right. As I approached Mill Bay a sign advertised a campsite, and I could not resist trying out my camping equipment. I was conscious of how long it took me to set everything up, but there would be plenty of practice in the future. The campsite owner would not accept any charge for my stay as the new season had not really started, and he told me of an older cycling couple from Quebec in their sixties who had stayed on the site the previous summer for four or five days. They were touring the country and often spent several days at a place to rest and regain their strength.

I was packed by 9am and caught the 10am ferry across Saanich Inlet to Brentwood for a visit to the Butchart Gardens. These incredibly beautiful floral gardens had been created many years before at an abandoned limestone quarry. It was just 13 miles to the provincial capital of Victoria, where I obtained a room in a small hotel with an atmosphere which made a lasting impact. Every room contained a few items of crockery, including a teapot, and I had soon made a cup of tea via a small kitchen along the corridor. The English atmosphere in Victoria was very strong, the city attracting, in particular, retired English emigrants from all parts of Canada, enjoying the opportunity to spend their later years in an area with milder winters. The pace of life was noticeably different to that of Vancouver; to the very progressive, the pace was seen as alarmingly slow; to others it was delightful and refreshing, a pleasant change to what most of them seemed to have to live with. Victoria was a city of beautiful homes, as I found when I followed a sightseeing tour through Beacon Hill Park to the coast, and followed the perimeter road for several miles. Everywhere was so clean, quiet and prosperous looking, especially around Uplands, the city's most exclusive residential area. If many of these homes were occupied by the retired from the east, it simply reminded one that it was inevitably going to be the more affluent who could afford to make the long journey west. An appreciable number of bicycles were to be seen on the streets. For what seemed to be my first time in North America, I saw a middle-aged lady on a bicycle. I almost fell off mine at the sight!

A long time was spent admiring the Parliament Buildings around the Inner Harbour, with an imposing statue of Queen Victoria at the front. Nearby was the large Empress Hotel, reminding one of a signal event during the Queen's reign. In 1870 the father-in-law of the Queen's eldest daughter, also Victoria, had become Emperor of Germany. The future prospect of the younger Victoria becoming an Empress one day while the Queen remained just a queen apparently concerned her greatly. After considerable difficulties with Parliament by the Prime Minister, Disraeli, the Queen was proclaimed Empress of India on 1 May 1876.

History came alive in locations like this, and I yearned to read so much more about Queen Victoria and this period in history. The conjunction of names and images in Victoria caused me to feel that I was on a tour of the former British Empire, an Empire which was approaching its zenith at the time when Victoria acquired her extra title. Many of the major public buildings which I had seen in Canada were built around this time, indeed most were built during Victoria's long reign. I toured the Parliament Buildings in Victoria with deepening interest. The sight of the buildings in the evening was a memorable one as a number of lights around the edge defined the entire facade.

On an earlier sightseeing tour I had looked out from Beacon Hill Park across the Juan de Fuca Strait to the Washington peninsula, 23 miles away. After three full days in Victoria it was time to make this journey. From the ferry terminal in the Inner Harbour looking directly at the Parliament Buildings, the sight of the diminishing buildings as the boat moved away leaves a lasting impression on the visitor departing from or arriving at Victoria by boat. The peaks of the Mount Olympus range were clearly visible as soon as the boat turned south into open water. An hour and a half later, on a fine, sunny morning, I reached Port Angeles, and was once more on American soil.

I had planned originally to turn eastwards towards Seattle, but the manager at my hotel in Vancouver advised me to avoid this heavily populated area and turn west towards the rain forests. I took his advice. The road west round the Washington peninsula quickly left the shore to climb into the foothills, and I quickly discovered I had lost some of my fitness of last summer. The fine weather didn't last as increasing cloud built up and it started to rain.

During the afternoon a young motorcyclist drew level with me, with a surprising story to relate. He had come from Surrey to Canada last October, travelled by train across the country and worked throughout the winter in Port Alberni on Vancouver Island. He was due to catch a boat back to England from Florida ten days later.

"Why are you going back so quickly?", I asked him.
"I have to get back to my wife and young son."

I would have to revise my thinking. I had always thought it essential to be free of such commitments in order to undertake such ventures.

I decided to camp at the west end of Lake Crescent, the rain thankfully stopping in the early evening so that I could erect my tent at the campground in the dry. It appeared to rain throughout the night, and the next morning I packed the tent away very wet. But it had proved its waterproofing quality. I travelled little more than two miles before sheltering from more rain, which quickly turned to snow. Watching the flakes falling, I meditated on the wisdom of turning west at Port Angeles as early as April. After three quarters of an hour the sky cleared and I continued on my way, to make eight miles before it rained again. When it came on heavily in the afternoon it did not look like clearing up for some time. I put on all my waterproof clothing to go as far as Forks, encountering heavy hail over the last three miles to round off the day's travels! I booked into a hotel for a dry night and to dry out my tent, packed away saturated in the morning.

The following morning I awoke to a brilliant blue sky, most welcome as I was close to the turning off to one of the main rain forests, in the Hoh river valley. The west side of the Olympic Peninsula has the wettest winter climate in America outside Alaska, with the yearly precipitation exceeding 140 inches in places, including the upper end of the Hoh valley. The road followed the river inland for 19 miles to a Visitor Centre within the boundary of Olympic National Park, presenting a panorama quite new to me. In this environment of wetness, an extraordinary forest growth had developed. The trees, mainly sitka spruce, Douglas fir, western hemlock and western red cedar, grew to a huge size, some reaching a height of 300 ft and diameters of over 8 ft. Vine maple formed an understorey beneath the giant conifers, with ferns carpeting the forest floor. Almost everything was covered in moss, which reached to the tops of the trees.

I stopped to photograph the bicycle beside one notable sitka spruce. A sign against it recorded: "Diam 11ft 8in above swell. Est. height 230ft. Est. age 500 years." After following two nature trails from the Visitor Centre, I returned down the valley to a campsite passed earlier on the way up. The next morning rain poured down before I was ready to take down the tent, with the result that it was once more packed away saturated. That afternoon I rode through a heavy storm which continued into the evening. I stopped for the night in a motel at Amanda Park, opening up the tent on the floor to dry it out. An unwelcome pattern seemed to be emerging, of camping one night and spending the next under a solid roof in order to dry out a saturated tent. But the pattern was broken directly afterwards, and I didn't need to take refuge under a solid roof for three weeks. By then I had covered a further 700 miles and was close to California.

As I journeyed down the Washington coast, I was introduced to another phenomenon in addition to the rain forests. I had crossed to Washington on a Saturday and found the traffic to be light. I recalled talking to the ranger at the Olympic National Park Visitor Centre beside Lake Crescent, and asking him what the traffic was normally like. "Well, on the weekdays you have the logging trucks." I inquired whether there were very many. "About 700 per day," he replied. He seemed to be right. Every few minutes logging trucks roared past me in one direction or the other. They seemed to have a signalling system which I was expected to understand. If a convoy of two trucks was coming up behind me, the leading driver would give two pips on the horn. Three pips advised me of a convoy of three, and on the winding road I would pull off onto the shoulder. My co-operation was often acknowledged by a wave of the hand when the trucks roared back down the highway towards me perhaps an hour or so later, now loaded with logs if they had previously been empty, or empty if they were previously loaded. At Raymond the road took me beside the log yard of the Weyerhaeuser Company, where I watched operations for some time, seeing the big machines with their huge arms lifting off in one operation the complete load of logs on a truck.

Approaching the Columbia River I encountered historical markers referring to the Lewis and Clark Expedition of 1804-6. Under the direction of President Jefferson, Captains Meriwether Lewis and William Clark set out with a party from St. Louis, Missouri, on 14 May 1804 to explore a route to the Pacific Ocean. After many hardships they succeeded in crossing the vast continental wilderness, reaching the Pacific at the mouth of the Columbia. With their return to St. Louis, they gave to the nation a route to the Oregon country - later the states of Washington, Oregon, Idaho and part of Montana.

I crossed the wide mouth of the Columbia River into Oregon via a new 4-mile long toll bridge, completed in 1966. Cyclists were allowed on it, although I was charged almost as much as a motorist. I surmised that I was paying for the time spent on the bridge, over half an hour, and involving a long steep climb to clear the water by over 200 ft. Soon I was riding beside some of Oregon's fabulous beaches, with mile after mile of clean, white sand. The beaches at Seaside and Cannon Beach were particularly noteworthy, especially the latter with its setting in a curving bay, and Haystack Rock rising from the edge of the water.

At Hebo I turned inland over the coastal range of hills towards the Willamette Valley. As I cycled through the Siuslaw National Forest on a Saturday afternoon I received a wave from a girl in a passing car. Shortly afterwards I caught up with the car, which had stopped. The girl had seen my Union Jack, and told me about her 10 months in Britain and Europe during 1965 and 1966, hiking with two friends and enjoying so much hospitality that she had been waiting for an opportunity to repay it. So here I was as the beneficiary. She told me more over a cup of tea at her friend's home nearby, and invited me to make contact with her in Portland where she lived. The following day I emerged from the forest into an area with an air of considerable prosperity as I approached the fertile Willamette valley. Passing a number of orchards, the blossom of the apple and cherry trees made an attractive picture.

I was looking forward to meeting further relations of my brother-in-law, who lived on a farm near Rickreall. Ruby and her son looked after me well during the next four days, taking me out to the local sights, visiting friends and also Salem, the state capital a few miles to the south-east. The relatively new Capitol building, replacing the original building destroyed by fire in 1935, had no dome like all the other Capitol buildings I had seen, and was so noticeably different. I sat in at sessions of both the House of Representatives and the Senate to take in the atmosphere.

When I left for Portland I resolved to keep off the main roads linking it with Salem. Heading north at Newberg to follow a minor road towards Scholls, I was soon winding my way up into a range of hills. A climb of over 1000 ft gave me some attractive views over the surrounding country, including the blossom in more orchards. An easy descent followed to Portland where I renewed my acquaintance with the girl met a few days before on the approach to Rickreall. Staying at her apartment over the weekend, I met her companions, and the boyfriend of one, summoned from Seattle to act as chaperone while a stranger was there: it was entirely appropriate. While in the city, I took the bicycle out to see some of the sights, climbing to Council Crest Park, the highest point in the city, before following the Westwide Scenic Drive, travelling along Skyline Boulevard for mile after mile. These scenic rides were all very well, but I was itching to get out of the city and up the Columbia River valley.

Chapter 8

Turn to California

Tuesday, 2 May 1967

The decision on which bank of the Columbia River to follow from Portland was straightforward. The road on the Oregon side was a freeway: the road on the Washington side was not. What was not straightforward was a decision on how far to go up the Columbia valley and beyond. The broad strategy for this summer's tour had developed during the year before coming to North America. On a trip to London I had collected an outstanding map from the offices of the United States Travel Service. I looked daily at the large map, mounted on a wall in my room in Stafford. Splashes of green emphasized the positions of the National Parks, and I therefore wanted to follow a route which would enable me to see as many as possible of these areas of outstanding natural beauty. From a position in the Pacific Northwest it looked logical to go across to the Yellowstone country, then travel south through Colorado and sweep round through the desert states to the Grand Canyon and on to California. After seeing the National Parks in the Sierra Nevada, I could move across to San Francisco and down the coast to San Diego.

Another factor now came into play - the weather. I had been carrying a small radio bought in Vancouver the previous winter. While beside the Oregon coast I heard with concern that the mountain states were experiencing some very wintry weather, with snow, high winds and very low temperatures. I should not therefore rush too fast across to the Yellowstone region. As I set off from Portland I was keeping my ear tuned for the latest weather reports from anyone I met.

The more immediate concern was crossing the Columbia River to the north bank as all my maps seemed to show the bridge as part of the local freeway system. However, I had no difficulty crossing the long bridge. Fort Vancouver National Historic Site on the north side preserved the site of a Hudson's Bay Company post, but I decided not to delay there but to continue into the countryside.

The sky was cloudy and the air misty, with the sun breaking through for short periods. East of Washougal the road wound its way up the hillside for some three miles. As I climbed about 1000 ft I could have done with better visibility to appreciate the views, the hills on the Oregon side rising sharply from the river and showing large areas of weathered sandstone on the vertical faces. At the end of the first day I camped at Beacon Rock State Park, named after a huge monolith of rock towering nearby beside the river. Everywhere was quiet apart from the singing of countless birds. I was conscious that I had deliberately left my radio behind at Rickreall, disgusted with the quality of music I had been able to tune into during the evenings while camping. I yearned for the BBC, and settled down to reading *Gone with the Wind*; it would keep me busy for most of the summer. I had an unexpected visitor early in the evening as a patrolling park officer stopped by to collect a nominal fee for my overnight stay.

The next morning I left the main road after four miles to have a closer look at the Bonneville Dam, one of several dams built on the Columbia to harness its power. There was more than a passing interest for me though, as the English Electric Company which I had worked for in England had supplied a number of transformers for the power station. But this equipment seemed to be on the south side of the river, and I decided against a long detour to see it. Some time later, while stopped by the roadside for my mid-morning break, a Highways Department employee stopped by and told me the weather was much better about 10 miles further east. Looking towards the eastern horizon I could see the cloud was much thinner. As I continued I soon found the sun beating down on me from an almost clear blue sky. The visibility had increased considerably, and a little later the cloud had disappeared completely.

There was a simple explanation for the rapid change in weather conditions; I had crossed from one side of the Cascade range of mountains to the other. On the drier, eastern side, the trees became fewer the further I moved east. I saw why the Columbia Valley is described as an outstanding scenic region, for I think I was now travelling along the most attractive stretch. Great walls of multi-coloured rock towered by the roadside on both sides of the river as it flowed through a deep gorge. The roadsides and the meadows were full of wildflowers such as I had never seen before. In many ways the scene reminded me of the Rhine gorge, and passing a small town named Bingen reinforced this impression.

In spite of the local improvement in the weather, I was stopping often to pore over my maps and think about the longer journey ahead. The weather reports from the Rocky Mountains were continuing to be unfavourable, with severe storms raging over the area. The relations near Salem had asked me to consider visiting them again after my sweep round through the west. If I did so, I would be completing a big clockwise loop. What would happen if I went the other way? The more I thought about it, the more logical an anticlockwise loop appeared. I would pass through Death Valley around the end of May, a far more suitable time than the end of July which would be the case travelling in a clockwise direction. I would also be in the mountain states in July and August, bringing me to Yellowstone Park around the end of August, a much more suitable time than the end of May.

By turning south at The Dalles a few miles further to the east, an attractive route presented itself for a journey south to California. The die was cast. It was one of those pivotal decisions which would affect my route for the rest of the summer, a decision which I would rejoice that I made as this new direction took me on a course which would for ever stand out as the most memorable of many memorable stages. Late in the afternoon on my second day out of Portland, I recrossed the Columbia into Oregon. The road climbed steadily away from the valley to reach a summit after two miles, presenting a panorama of rolling hills. But there were no trees, and I became aware that there was very little surface water in the region, a fact verified by observation of bone-dry gullies. I was by now wanting to stop for the evening, and the need to find some water was paramount. I descended into a deep valley to see a small stream running beside a meadow. When I approached the owner at a house adjacent, he had no objection to me camping beside the stream. It solved the immediate problem, but for the first time ever I needed to think ahead about water supplies.

There was a gradual ascent as the road continued southwards, broken at intervals by shorter sweeps downwards. From the rising ground there were views to the west over scrub-clad hills of Oregon's highest mountain, Mt. Hood, its perennially snow-capped peak rising 11,245 ft from the plain. It was a glorious day and as the sun climbed in a cloudless sky I changed to my shorts for the first time this year. Summer had arrived! Mt. Hood slowly receded and other mountains started to dominate the western skyline, first Mt. Jefferson, 10,495 ft, then the Sisters Range. Trees appeared once more as I climbed gradually, and south of Bend at about 4,000 ft elevation I entered the pine forest of Deschutes National Forest.

The first of the National Parks on my route, at Crater Lake, lay 80 miles to the south. I was determined to see what I could of this deep blue lake in the crater of an extinct volcano, and turned off the main highway towards it. Ignoring a "Road Closed" sign at a junction, it seemed to be clear why the road was closed. The surface was badly broken up in places, and the Highways Department clearly wished to repair the road with the minimum of inconvenience. Ignoring a second "Road Closed" sign some 12 miles on, I noticed far more snow around me than I had hitherto encountered. Soon I found myself travelling between two high walls of snow about half the full road width apart. After three miles of this I came to a full stop. Snow a foot deep covered the entire road for an indeterminate distance ahead: the snowplough had gone no further. I tried pushing the bicycle through the snow, but the surface was not hard enough and it sank straight in. It was no good: I didn't have snow tyres on! I had to turn round, but not before capturing the scene with my camera, recording the bicycle standing upright in the middle of the road, supported by the deep snow around it. Crater Lake had to be one casualty of the changed route round the American West.

I returned quickly to the main road as I was running out of time, and raced south to camp at Collier Memorial State Park, completing 76 miles on what had been an eventful day. The State Park proved to be a most interesting place to visit, with the largest Logging Museum in the country, and a fine collection of pioneering logging equipment. As I continued south to Klamath Falls I had to contend with a vicious crosswind from the west, particularly when I was level with Upper Klamath Lake and there was no barrier to mitigate the strength of the wind. I was glad of a wide shoulder to the road, allowing me to swerve at times as I was hit by stronger gusts without being forced into the path of passing lorries, but I had never felt so unsafe. Arriving in Klamath Falls at 3pm, I booked into a hotel, the first time it had been unsuitable for camping for three weeks. A heavy hailstorm occurred shortly after my arrival, followed by rain throughout the rest of the afternoon and for much of the evening.

I studied my maps during the evening to decide which route to follow the next morning into California. The direct route would have taken me to Weed and on to Redding, but I would have encountered sections of freeway with no alternative to take, and it was almost certainly a very busy road as it was the main road connecting California with Oregon. I decided to avoid the whole route and turned south-eastwards towards Canby. An inch of snow covered the ground everywhere as I set off, and I put my Balaclava helmet on for the first time during a number of snow showers. After two more nights under a solid roof I awoke the next morning near Susanville to find my tent covered with frost and a block of ice in one of my cans. But the weather was improving and a bright sunny day followed as I climbed over the Fredonyer Pass at 5,748 ft and descended to Lake Almanor, created in 1914 by building a dam at the south end to back up the waters of the North Fork and Hamilton Branch of the Feather River. The water had an unusually deep-blue colour. There were views northwards across the lake to the snow-capped peak of Mt. Lassen, rising to 10,457 ft 25 miles away in Lassen Volcanic National Park. The lower slopes were also covered with snow, and I saw no point in going closer to this smaller and lesser known of the National Parks. The red colouring to the terrain seen during the last two days reminded me all the time that I was travelling through a volcanic region. Mt. Lassen had last been active in 1917.

The setting of Lake Almanor was so unexpectedly attractive that I was reluctant to depart from the area. When I did eventually get under way, the road took me through Greenville. A few miles south I entered a deep gorge and started going downwards as I followed Indian Creek. Stopping for the evening at a campsite at Twain, I was invited to share a campfire by an older man from Concord near Oakland. He was glad of some company as his wife didn't always feel like accompanying him on his journeys into the countryside, and this weekend he was alone. The following morning he invited me to have breakfast with him. As a result of this generous hospitality, and a full breakfast of pineapple, pancakes and tea, I was later than normal leaving the campsite.

Some easy riding followed as Indian Creek joined Feather River, and the road went steadily downwards as it wound its way through the pine-clad hills of Feather River Canyon towards the great valley beyond. It made a memorable journey out of the hills, and a steady rise in temperature told me I was going downwards. A long climb over the Jarbo Pass was necessary when the valley ran out of space for a road, and from the summit I looked for the first time over the broad Sacramento Valley. The road swept down towards Oroville and avenues of palm trees. It seemed like a fairy-tale.

*****

A long day's run of 80 miles through the fertile valley brought me to California's most attractive capital, Sacramento. Moving slowly as the temperature rose to 90°, I went to see the outstanding Capitol building, one of the most beautiful of all the Capitol buildings, and in an unrivalled setting. The building was located towards one end of a large park, containing more than 450 varieties of trees and shrubs; palm trees lined the park perimeter. Another building attracted me as much, if not more, and I walked two and a half miles east to Sutter's Fort, perhaps the most famous building in California's history, and preserved as a State Historical Monument. My mind soaked up the story of how Sacramento had its beginnings in 1839 when Captain John Sutter chose the area to establish a colony for his countrymen from Switzerland. Granted 48,000 acres by the Mexican Government then controlling the area, he built his large fort between 1839 and 1846 to protect this land grant. The fort became a goal for large numbers of wagons coming from the Missouri River and the east, new arrivals seeking rest and shelter before staking out new lives in the surrounding country. When Mexico lost control of California to America during the conquest of 1846-48, it was to prove a cruel irony of timing for the enormous wealth which was now about to elude them.

During the latter half of 1847, James Marshall started building a sawmill for Captain Sutter beside the American River at a spot some 35 miles to the north-east of the fort. I headed out past Folsom Lake to this historic location at Coloma where, on 24 January 1848, Marshall discovered what he thought was gold while on his daily inspection of the mill tailrace. It was gold. The discovery could not be kept secret for long and, as news of the find spread, men started to head for California. So began the greatest mass migration in history. Such were the numbers, from all corners of the world, that they resulted in a substantial redistribution of the world's population. California became a state almost overnight, in 1850. For the gold seekers from the eastern states, there was the long journey across the Great Plains, and for month after month in 1849 lines of covered wagons a mile long were to be seen on the Oregon and Santa Fe Trails.

It was a riveting experience visiting the area, seeing firsthand this richly-storied region, and becoming acquainted with the methods used to mine the gold-bearing ore and extract the gold. I spent two hours at the Museum absorbing more history one morning before continuing down Highway 49; the Gold Chain Highway, passing through many places where the valuable metal was discovered as the gold-seekers spread from Coloma, the towns and camps being abandoned as quickly as they rose as the areas became exhausted. The names of the towns conjured up romantic stories of exciting days gone by - names like Placerville, Drytown, Mokelumne Hill and Angels Camp. The gold towns were strung out along the foothills of the Sierra Nevada Mountains, giving me a most arduous run. The road went up and down unceasingly, and the heat was intense as the temperature soared to 90° each day.

Early one morning I descended to the Tuolumne River south of Chinese Camp, to begin one of those pivotal rides which would long remain in my memory. I turned off Highway 49 towards Yosemite National Park, looking forward eagerly to visiting this outstanding area. I had read that the elevation of Yosemite Valley was 3,985 ft compared with about 700 ft at the river crossing, so I knew there was some climbing to do. The full extent slowly became apparent as I climbed up the hillside mile after mile, descending not to the main valley but to continue with further long climbs and descents. I decided to camp some five miles from the Park entrance when a suitable area presented itself. I found I had stopped at just the right time as the next morning started with a short descent to cross the Tuolumne River again, followed by a long climb to the Park entrance. The ranger at the entrance invited me to have coffee with him, and told me about the Golden Eagle Passport. For one payment of $7.00 it would allow me into all the National Parks without further charge for the rest of the summer, in fact until the end of the following March. It was going to be an incredible bargain.

The elevation at the Park entrance was about 4,800 ft, and the road continued upwards for several miles to reach the final summit at 6,200 ft. As a long descent began I stopped to have lunch at a spot looking over a level area below called Big Meadow. Lunch meant consuming everything edible in my bags to compensate for the energy expended on the climbs. Descending further, the road turned to look down for the first time on the main valley, of the great gorge and the peaks around it, including the dominant Half Dome at the east end of the narrow valley.

It was at times like this that you had a heightened awareness of the appeal of cycle touring, of the immense feelings of satisfaction as you looked back on the long climbs which had brought you into an awesome area like this by your own efforts, or "under your own steam" to invoke a phrase used by the Youth Hostels Association during its early decades. The pioneers of the organisation understood the virtues of exploring the countryside in this manner. The healthy exercise involved was entirely beneficial to one's health, both mentally and physically.

I felt exhilarated as I free-wheeled slowly downwards, one superb view following another, including the waterfalls which were now at their best as the warm weather melted the snow in the surrounding mountains. Down in the valley I stocked up with food at the store and headed for the campground nearby. Soon after I had erected my tent, several people came over to talk to me, curious to hear about my route and how I had succeeded in getting into the Valley at all. They wondered how I managed to carry everything on a bicycle and were fascinated by my tent, which was an attractive design and much larger than the size single travellers would normally use. The greater space and comfort desirable on a long journey had proved themselves many times. There seemed to be a special camaraderie at these major locations; maybe everybody was inspired by the surroundings, however they had travelled there. Later I walked round the crowded campground to meet other campers, and to admire the huge variety of caravans and camper trucks which had brought the majority of visitors there. People were flocking to the mountains to get away from the heat on the plain. I was told that the temperature in Fresno in the San Joaquin Valley had risen to 104°.

The following morning I had breakfast of bacon and eggs with two men from Livermore near Oakland whom I had met the previous evening. Bob and Charles expressed the view that it was good to get away from their womenfolk for a couple of days. Refreshed, I spent the day seeing the sights in the valley, including El Capitan - a vertical wall of rock almost 1,000 ft high - Half Dome at the east end again, and especially the waterfalls - Cascade, Ribbon, Bridalveil and Yosemite Falls, watching the water thunder down into the valley. In the evening I wrote out a large number of postcards to despatch from this landmark on my journey.

Leaving the valley I took the road on the south side of the Merced River, compared to the north side on the way down, and turned towards Wawona at the south-west corner of the Park. Further climbing was inevitable, and particularly when I turned off the main road towards the Mariposa Grove of Giant Sequoia. As I climbed steeply to about 6,800 ft using my bottom gear, there was snow all around me, but I was rewarded by some of the most memorable sights imaginable. Giant sequoia trees were all around me, the trees growing naturally in a narrow belt on the western slopes of the Sierra Nevada in central California at elevations of 4,000 to 8,000 ft. One tree would forever remain in my memory, the Wawona Tunnel Tree, through which a tunnel was cut in 1881. The tunnel was quite high, as it had to cater for horse-drawn stagecoaches. (Update: I was informed that the tree fell in a snow-storm during the winter of 1968-69.) I descended steadily to the main road, leaving the Park a mile further on and continuing downwards to a campsite in the adjoining Sequoia National Forest. The temperature seemed to be 30° higher at the lower elevation.

I had planned to cling to the foothills as I continued south to Kings Canyon National Park, but a change became necessary when I noticed a bad cut in my rear tyre while in Yosemite. The detour to Fresno to buy a new tyre involved a descent from about 5,000 to 287 ft. It meant I had it all to make up again as I headed for Kings Canyon. After many miles across the flat San Joaquin Valley, the land started to tilt upwards, and I learned that the 17 miles to the Kings Canyon entrance were all uphill. I decided to go just part of the way, finding a camping spot by the roadside about 10 miles from the entrance.

At a campground in Kings Canyon the following day numerous people spoke to me about passing me on the long climb or seeing me at my camping spot beside the road. In the General Grant Grove area I saw the California Tree and the General Grant Tree, the latter described as the second largest living thing. The major trees all had names for ease of identification. Much of this area was still under snow due to the high elevation, and I found myself cycling through cloud as I continued to Sequoia National Park to see the General Sherman Tree, the world's largest living thing at 272.4 ft high, 32.2 ft diameter, 101.6 ft circumference at the base and approximately 4,000 years old.

A long descent brought me out of the cloud, the road twisting and turning as it snaked down the hillside towards the San Joaquin Valley, leaving the trees behind to emerge to scrub-covered hills around Lake Kaweah. After camping nearby I found myself cycling past orange and lemon groves around the town of Lemoncove, such a contrasting experience with the previous day. Wanting to turn west I wound my way over scrub-clad hills to Springville. An arduous climb followed up the valley of the Middle Fork of the Tule River. When it started to rain, I put my cape on for the first time for six weeks. Climbing for 21 miles to a summit at 7,200 ft, it started to snow. There was a logging camp near Camp Nelson, and I was pleased to find a restaurant where I was able to have a good meal, before donning all my extra clothing, determined to get to a lower elevation. I found myself on a dirt road for seven miles as I descended to the Kern River, but at least it was warmer once again. When I continued down the Kern valley the next morning after camping, I found long stretches of gravel road. After a storm the previous winter the river had overflowed its banks and washed the paved road away. My maps couldn't begin to convey the road conditions, and I was relieved to rejoin the main road west near Weldon.

Back down at the lower elevation the hills were once more bare of trees and the ground was covered with sparse scrub. The whole area looked incredibly dry. I replenished my food supplies at the store at Weldon and bought a large sun hat. As I started to climb gradually, a new feature appeared on the scene in the form of Joshua trees. The road climbed to 5,250 ft to cross the Walker Pass. From the summit a desolate scene presented itself. Somewhere to the east lay Death Valley, which I needed to cross to get to Las Vegas and onwards to Arizona.

The bicycle rests at the intersection of Broadway and Fifth Avenue, New York, before setting off on the long journey.

The city of Montreal from Mount Royal Park, with the St. Lawrence River in the background.

Familiar scene in Wisconsin of fields of maize.

At the source of the Mississippi River in northern Minnesota, a shallow stream flowing north from Lake Itasca. The challenge is to cross it without getting your feet wet.

The Legislative Building, Winnipeg, Manitoba, from beside the Cenotaph on the Mall.

At the home of relations near Portage la Prairie, Manitoba.

Descending to the plain from the high ground of Riding Mountain National Park, Manitoba.

Characteristic scene on the prairies: grain elevators beside the railway line in Saskatchewan.

The Rocky Mountains and Athabasca River, Jasper National Park, Alberta.

The endless chain ridge in the Rocky Mountains, Jasper National Park, Alberta.

Pause in the Yoho Valley, British Columbia.

Emerald Lake, British Columbia.

The Okanagan Valley, British Columbia, with apple trees bent over under the weight of fruit.

Totem poles at the entrance to Stanley Park, Vancouver.

Vancouver from Queen Elizabeth Park.

In the Butchart Gardens north of Victoria.

Parliament Buildings and statue of Queen Victoria in the British Columbia capital of Victoria.

Impasse on the road to Crater Lake, Oregon.

The State Capitol, Sacramento, California.

A line of Giant Sequoia in Yosemite National Park, California, dwarfs a tiny bicycle.

Unusual elevation marker: in Death Valley, California.

Hedgehog and "teddy bear" cholla cacti on the rock-strewn floor of Death Valley, California.

At the south rim of the Grand Canyon, Arizona.

Breakfast time at the Grand Canyon Village Campground.

Mule train beside the Colorado River in the depths of the Grand Canyon.

Topping up the radiator in the land of the giant saguaro cacti in southern Arizona. With one pint lasting 4 miles in the extreme heat, the transport system thus had a consumption of 32 mpg.

Camping beside the Rio Grande in New Mexico.

In the foothills of the Rocky Mountains in Colorado.

"Please don't scratch the car!" the driver pleaded. The bears in Yellowstone National Park didn't often get the chance to inspect a Cadillac.

The Last Chancer tour train takes visitors round the Montana state capital of Helena, site of a major gold discovery in 1864.

The snow-capped peak of Mt. Rainier rises to 14,410 ft in Washington State.

Beside the California coast and the blue Pacific Ocean.

Chapter 9

The Desert Beckons

Friday, 2 June 1967

There was a pause at the top of the Walker Pass before I descended towards the desert. A lady came along in her car, one tyre of which was losing pressure. She was not experienced at changing wheels, and I volunteered my assistance. The wheel was soon changed, albeit with advice from another passing motorist. After this unexpected good deed for the day, I set off on a long descent towards a barren plain. I could see clearly the towns on my immediate route - Inyokern, China Lake and Ridgecrest. After lunch at Inyokern I speeded over the flat ground to Ridgecrest, a sizable town serving the nearby Naval Ordnance Test Station. In preparation for the days ahead, I bought a new bottle of suntan lotion, some salt tablets and a half gallon polythene container. I had left behind me on the west side of the mountains the last stream, and needed to carry more water than ever before.

The scene was barren as I headed towards the Panamint Mountains forming the western boundary to Death Valley. The brown hills were almost bare of vegetation, and the rocky, sandy ground was sparsely covered by either scrub or creosote bushes. I continued to Trona on the edge of Searles Lake for the evening. Borax was discovered in this dry lake in 1862, and it had since proved to be the world's richest chemical storehouse, containing half the natural elements known to man.

I was encouraged to learn that Death Valley was not too hot at the present time, with a temperature around 90°. Two weeks before the temperature had reached 117° both in the Valley and at Trona. From Trona to my next stopping place, Wildrose Station in the Panamint Mountains, was a distance of 41 miles, with no petrol stations, stores or communities in between. My half gallon container came into immediate use. Several motorists stopped by me as I pedalled along. "Got plenty of water?" they all asked. I thanked them for stopping and assured them I had plenty. In the heat I became conscious of the lack of almost anything to offer shade. Around 1pm when the sun was almost overhead and I was wanting to stop for my picnic lunch, I was fortunate to see ahead of me some road-grading equipment. Overhanging parts offered respite.

Near the boundary to Death Valley National Monument I picked up a leaflet entitled "Hot Weather Hints". I was disappointed as I read: "Do not deflate tyres". I had been looking forward to releasing air from my tyres in a dramatic gesture as soon as I reached sea level! For the moment I started a very long climb to Wildrose Station to camp there for the evening. The silence in the air was broken frequently during the evening and night by the braying of wild burros in the surrounding hills, descendants of others brought into the area by early mining prospectors. I found there was no store at Wildrose, but the lady there kindly let me have a little bread and a tin of meat to supplement my food supplies. I learned at the campground that the temperature at Furnace Creek in the Valley was no more than 90°. The journey was therefore on for the following day.

I recalled discussions with fellow campers almost two weeks earlier at the campground in Yosemite National Park. When I broached my intended plan to go east across Death Valley, it was greeted by a uniform chorus of disapproval. The unanimous opinion was that I would be committing suicide. "How much water are you drinking now, in the present heat?" I was asked. "About two gallons a day," I replied. "Man, you'll need three times that amount in Death Valley" was the spontaneous and vigorous reaction of one camper. The words dehydration and heat exhaustion were uttered a number of times and gave me something to think about. I recalled also an earlier conversation with a man whom I met in the Feather River Canyon. "They pull out all the services at the beginning of April," he said dramatically. "There is a ranger there, but he sits in his air-conditioned room and doesn't go out looking for trouble!"

Wildrose Station was at an elevation of about 4,000 ft, and I had another 1,500 ft to climb before starting the descent to the valley. The road descended very gradually for several miles and the roadsides were covered with a profusion of wildflowers, an unexpected pleasure. A speck of red appeared some yards off the road and on closer examination I saw my first cactus in flower, a small prickly pear cactus with large, delicate, crimson flowers. From that moment my eyes scanned the rocky terrain with a new intensity as I looked for splashes of colour which might indicate the presence of more beautiful blossoms. At about 4,000 ft the wildflowers ended and the road descended steadily. I passed through a gap in the hills and the valley lay before me, nearly 4,000 ft below and indistinct in the heat haze. I could feel the temperature getting higher and higher. There was a strong breeze from the valley and I kept being hit by waves of hot air which made me hold my breath. I reached Stove Pipe Wells Hotel to find the shade temperature 102°; I didn't think too much about what it might be in the open!

Over lunch I discussed my immediate journey with the proprietors of the hotel and other diners. I think I convinced them I knew what I was doing, and they did not try to dissuade me from continuing. However, they told me the "cool" spell was coming to an end and I had not arrived a day too early. It was 4th June, and normally the temperature was up to 120°. Safety was represented by Furnace Creek, a man-made oasis across the other side of the valley, a distance of 26 miles. I departed with a full supply of water and several cans of soft drink. I made headway quite slowly, fighting a crosswind so strong that it was uncomfortable with the sun-hat on. I took it off: I wasn't going to be troubled by the sun beating down on the back of my neck. The terrain undulated slowly, being just below sea level most of the time as I passed by sand dunes and the Devil's Cornfield, a large area of arrow-weed stocks.

Early in the afternoon I declined an offer of a lift by the driver of a small truck. Shortly afterwards I was surprised to see the same truck coming back towards me. The man's wife was concerned for my safety and I was offered a lift for a second time. "I was brought up in this area," the driver said, "and I know what the heat can do to a man." I declined as politely as I could, but I knew the couple were disappointed as they left me. I felt perfectly comfortable and could see the green oasis of Furnace Creek in the distance. As I headed towards it I was conscious of one phenomenon of travel in the desert, the illusion of distance. It is difficult to judge whether something is 5 miles away, or 10 or 20.

I reached Furnace Creek in the early evening with a salt-streaked face and half a pint of water left. The great barrier had been crossed. After buying groceries at the store I set about erecting my tent at the campground. The breeze was still blowing strongly and I needed to get all the tent pegs in the ground properly. The aluminium pegs bounced off the rock-hard ground as I hit them with a stone. I had to content myself with getting a few pegs in and using stones to anchor down the tent floor and most of the guy ropes. For the first time in my life I then slept below sea level, the elevation at the campground being about -100 ft.

The next morning I decided against going to the nearby Visitor Centre. It was advisable to seek the higher ground before the sun once more rose high in the sky, and I started a long gradual climb away from the valley. From the rising ground I looked back to the valley several times; it looked forbidding. At 3,000 ft I started seeing cacti again. The rock-strewn floor was covered with small cholla cacti and large clumps of hedgehog cacti. South of Lathrop Wells other types of cactus appeared, and more Joshua trees which I had seen earlier on both sides of the Walker Pass. The desert was turning out to be an area of extraordinary interest and beauty. I was now in Nevada and shortly afterwards left the cacti behind me for a few days as I arrived in Las Vegas.

*****

I found a small inexpensive hotel without difficulty and walked into the central area to have a meal. As I entered a larger hotel I was amazed to have to pass between two long lines of one-armed bandits to get to the restaurant. Fortunately I was carrying something in both hands! It was late in the evening by the time I had eaten, and I walked down Fremont Street in the heart of the Casino Centre. A more fantastic sight I had never seen before as my eyes were bombarded by an incredible concentration of neon lighting. Casino followed casino, all full of one-armed bandits and other gaming tables. It was interesting watching people's faces as with grim determination they deposited their coins in the machines and pulled on the handles.

The following day I went for a walk down "The Strip", a long stretch of Las Vegas Boulevard with one plush hotel following another on either side. All attracted the top names in entertainment, and all had a big casino. I decided to set aside $5.00 as I entered the casino at the Hotel Sahara. If I made a profit I would see a show in the evening: I did not go to a show. Instead, I had another walk round the Casino Centre to marvel at the neon lighting. I sent off a postcard featuring this to the electrical consultant I had worked for in Vancouver, with its printed comment on the rear that people said the entire output from the Hoover Dam was needed to light Las Vegas at night. He would be able to put this in context.

The Hoover Dam was just 30 miles to the south-east, and I was keen to get out of the city to see it. It was a most impressive sight, and I joined a party for a first-class tour of the whole installation there. I learned something of the power of the Colorado River, and of the devastation it caused almost every spring before the dam was built in the early 1930's, regularly flooding low-lying farmland along its route. As a former apprentice with an electrical equipment manufacturer, I was particularly interested to see close-to the electrical power-plant, including the large turbines, generators and transformers. The guide left us with the following words: "For those of you who are going to Las Vegas, the best of luck." "What about those of us who have just come from Las Vegas?" someone asked. "Better luck next time."

With these meaningful words ringing in my ears, I cycled across the top of the dam into Arizona. My entry into the desert state seemed to coincide with an increase in the amount of holiday traffic on the road, or maybe we were all heading in the same direction to one of the greatest attractions in North America on the only road available. In any event, there was a marked deterioration in the standard of driving as the motorists streaked over the desert. To my mind they were seeing nothing, but I had to recognise that none of them had the time which I was giving myself. I was travelling at perhaps the optimum speed to be able to take in properly the ever-changing scene around me, to see the details which were impossible to see at higher speeds. As I cycled south-eastwards to Kingman at about 10 mph, I couldn't get close enough to the edge of the road at times for my own safety.

Turning eastwards at Kingman my progress was slowed down as I stopped to look at large groups of prickly pear cacti in blossom. As the ground sloped upwards gradually I left the cacti behind to enter juniper pine forest, turning northwards just past Williams at an elevation of 6,770 ft to camp at Kaibab Lake campground. I felt a tension in the air the following morning as I performed the usual chores and got ready to leave. It was a beautiful morning, the breeze from the south-west was partly behind me, and I had about 55 miles to go. I travelled over a vast, gently rolling plateau dotted with juniper pine, a long gradual descent during the morning being followed by an equally long gradual ascent in the afternoon to reach 7,000 ft. At 4pm I entered Grand Canyon National Park, shortly afterwards having my first view of the Canyon at Mather Point. It was awe-inspiring.

However much one has read about the Canyon, however many pictures of it one has seen, it is a sight which cannot fail to impress. It was on a grander scale than one could possibly imagine. From an elevation of 7,000 ft at the South Rim, one looked across a span of 8 miles to the North Rim, 1,000 ft higher; and about midway across the span and one mile vertically downwards surged the Colorado River. I had to get myself established before seeing any more of this, proceeding to the Visitor Centre to gather information and continuing to the campground. While setting my tent up among the pine trees, I was under keen observation by a family from Portland, Oregon, and accepted an invitation to have dinner with them in their large caravan nearby.

A fine, sunny day followed for my first full day at the Canyon. After attending a talk during the morning on the geology of the Canyon, the afternoon was spent following slowly the West Rim Drive, stopping at a succession of lookout points and trying to take in as much of the breathtaking views as possible. After a meal at the campground it was time to return to Hopi Point, one of the lookout positions, to see one of the famed sunsets.

I rose early the next morning to be at Bright Angel Lodge by 8.30am when unclaimed tickets for mule trips into the Canyon were allocated for the day. I drove there with Steven and Dorothy, a young couple from near New Orleans, Louisiana, who were camping near me and had also put their names down for the trip. We were unlucky; the mules were booked up till the middle of September (it was now the middle of June), and we were unable to secure any unclaimed tickets. We might have stood a better chance if 12 mules hadn't been on the sick list, but they needed to be in perfect condition before being allowed on the trails. Steven and myself had come prepared to hike, while Dorothy had serious reservations. We dropped her off at the campsite and drove on to Yaki Point, setting off down the Kaibab Trail at 9.40am. The surface was extremely slippery, and it took us till 1.30pm to cover the 6.4 miles to the Colorado River on the winding trail, meeting several mule trains coming up. After a picnic lunch beside the river, we had to set off without delay, conscious of stern advice in the Canyon brochure; a Canyon trip is the reverse of mountain climbing, and the uphill grind comes at the end. We were also well behind our expected schedule. There was an easy walk of 3 miles beside the Colorado River, before beginning an 8 mile ascent up the Bright Angel Trail.

Within the Canyon we were able to see the peaks on the Canyon walls in truer perspective, as full-size mountains. The descent revealed the plant life of six climatic belts, ranging from the true desert scene down by the river to the forest of the cooler zones at the top of the rim. Stopping to read all the identifying markers gave a little respite to our weary feet. We continually looked upwards to the rim to seek reassurance that the vertical climb of one mile was reducing, finally reaching the top of the Bright Angel Trail at 7.30pm. It had been an experience we would never forget. We passed a number of people struggling on the ascent; in an emergency, telephone points at strategic positions could be used to summon assistance. There was then the ignominy of being hauled out by mule. Recovering at the top of the Canyon, we compared notes with people who had made the famed mule trip. It was by no means certain afterwards which was the more preferable means of descent into the Canyon. The end result in one case was sore feet; in the other case other parts of the anatomy apparently became very raw!

Most people who hiked into the Canyon took two days, staying overnight at the ranch by the Colorado River near the foot of the Kaibab Trail. Park Rangers told us that few people attempted the complete trip in one day; of those who did, many turned back before half way, while others had to be hauled out by mule. Steven and myself relived our experience over a campfire till late into the evening. Rest was then needed before setting off the next morning for the journey along the East Rim Drive. It was much less interesting than the West Rim Drive, with the road generally running some distance from the rim and there being just a small number of lookout points. I camped at the Desert View campground before leaving the National Park the following morning. The entire visit had been a truly memorable experience, providing inspiration to draw on for a very long time to come. I thought back to the words on a commemorative plaque at Mather Point where I had my first view of the Grand Canyon. Referring to Stephen Tyng Mather it read:

> "He laid the foundation of the National Park Service, defining and establishing the policies under which its areas shall be developed and conserved unimpaired for future generations. There will never come an end to the good that he has done."

I had ample cause already to appreciate the vision of dedicated individuals like Stephen Mather who saw the need to protect outstanding areas from commercial exploitation for all time. Other outstanding areas lay ahead on my route.

*****

The journey continued south by an area called the Painted Desert, an area which looked best after a storm when the rain brought out the colour of the rocks. No rain fell while I was in the area, but shortly afterwards I ran into a heavy storm as I approached Flagstaff. It cleared the air for the journey south between the vermilion cliffs of the Oak Creek Canyon. With its brightly coloured and dramatically shaped rock formations it was an area favoured by western film makers. I kept my head low in case any bullets or arrows should suddenly whizz over me.

In the Verde Valley I visited Tuzigoot National Monument, preserving the excavated ruins of an Indian pueblo inhabited from about 1000 to 1400. Close by and perched precariously high up on the steep hillside was Jerome, claimed to be the largest ghost town in America. Between 1880 and 1953 over £330 million worth of copper was taken from the surrounding hills. A one-time population of 15,000 was now down to two or three hundred. It was interesting to learn that coke for the smelter was imported from Wales.

As the road continued southwards towards Prescott through mountainous terrain, I had some arduous climbing in a temperature of about 85°. Early one evening at Yarnell a long descent began as I started going down to Phoenix. Waves of hot air hit me as the road swept downwards and I camped on wasteland near Congress. Prehistoric-looking lizards scuttled around my tent as I went about my evening chores. The descent continued the following morning into the "Valley of the Sun". With the temperature reported to be 105° in the state capital, it was time to ask myself what lessons I had learned in Death Valley. This time I was going down to a low elevation for several days, not just for an afternoon. A reassuring lesson learned was the knowledge that I could travel in such conditions. Without the experience of Death Valley I don't know what thoughts would have coursed through my mind. I needed to ensure that I always had plenty of water, and sipped almost continuously from my drinking bottle to stop my mouth drying up.

Just through Wickenburg I saw my first Saguaro cacti, the giants of the cactus world. They were to be found only in south-western Arizona, soaring to 50 ft high at full maturity with arms sprouting in all directions. It was fascinating moving along slowly and seeing Saguaros at different ages and stages of growth, some with no arms, some with just one or two and some with more than a dozen. The cacti gave way to enormous cultivated fields as I approached Phoenix, irrigation schemes allowing crops to flourish. I didn't reach the city till late in the evening, but the heat of the day still poured out of the pavements. Even the YMCA had air conditioning, which was a relief to return to after every sortie outside.

I visited the superb Desert Botanical Garden in Papago Park to help me better identify the tremendous variety of cacti and other desert plants which I was now seeing. It was a contrast to visit the Arizona Mineral Museum, containing one of the world's most complete ore and mineral collections, and reflecting the enormous mineral wealth of the state. One evening I cycled out to an address near Papago Park to meet a lady with a sister in my home town of Bury St. Edmunds. As I showed her and her husband photographs of my travels, they plied me with ice-cream and cold beer from the fridge, giving me a wonderful evening to remember.

I headed west out of Phoenix to go towards Organ Pipe Cactus National Monument. Some careful map study had been needed to choose a route which included points of interest and kept me off and away from the freeways. I was conscious at this time of not only the quality of the road maps collected from the petrol stations, which showed so well the topography of the area but also often included information on scenic tours. You could not do better than follow some of these routes. It felt unusually warm during the afternoon when I stopped at a petrol station north of Gila Bend to replenish my water supply. A thermometer on the station wall indicated a temperature of 112°. I stayed in the shade for half an hour having a cold drink. The proprietor, of Mexican origin, told me cheerfully that the previous day the area had the highest temperature in America at 113°. When I told him of a possible plan to cross the border into

Mexico the following summer, he advised me to be careful of the senoritas. "They are very aggressive," he said with a twinkle in his eye, "but you feel better the next morning."

The next day between Gila Bend and Ajo I had one of the longest stretches there is between petrol stations or any other places where I could obtain water, a distance of 42 miles. I left Gila Bend with nine pints of water and soft drink, and rationed myself to a pint every six miles. After a day's journey of 77 miles, it was late in the evening when I arrived at the campground at Organ Pipe Cactus National Monument to see a concentration of this special type of cactus.

There was an advantage in setting up the tent quite late, as it gave an opportunity for some of the heat which had accumulated in the ground during the day to dissipate. I remembered also to align the tent with the front facing towards the breeze. If I then slept with the main tent flaps tied back and with just the inner mesh doors closed, there was a chance of being able to sleep as the breeze wafted over me. In the extreme conditions I was evolving a regular plan for camping in the evenings. Because of the paramount need for water, I had to camp close to some community. As I covered the last mile to a chosen destination, the terrain would be studied carefully for suitable camping spots. If possible the spot should be in the shade in the early evening and the following morning. After buying groceries and stocking up with water and soft drink for the evening, the closest suitable camping spot would be returned to. I learned how to ration my water supply for washing and shaving - and making tea. The next morning more water and soft drink would be collected before continuing.

Around lunch-time the desire for shade dominated my thoughts. The problem was solved many times by making for a dip in the road ahead. An aqueduct was usually to be found, and it was usually a simple matter to ease the bicycle down the bank into the aqueduct, keeping a lookout for snakes which might also have found it offered respite from the burning sun. Many people asked me if I stopped during the hottest part of the day. I confessed I didn't; I wasn't even sure when the hottest part of the day was. It seemed to be hottest around 1pm when the sun was almost directly overhead, but several people told me later that the temperature reached its maximum between 5 and 6pm. For this reason it was inadvisable to erect the tent before 7pm. As I poured butter onto my bread for my evening meal, I would look forward to the later evening. After the last rays of the sun had sunk well below the horizon I could look up into the great dome of the clear Arizona sky and see thousands of stars shining in all their glory. I often laid on my back on the open ground gazing into the sky. After commencing the tour as a reluctant camper because of the increased weight to be carried, there was now not the slightest regret.

Whenever I laid on the ground at night to look at the stars, one experience reminded me to check that the ground wasn't covered with cactus spines. On the way out of the area enclosing Organ Pipe Cactus National Monument, I stopped to take a number of photographs, with one including myself. After setting up the camera on top of a short cactus I dived in front of a large cactus in readiness for the delayed shutter operation. During the next half hour I told myself it had not been a good idea, as I slowly removed hundreds of cactus spines from my anatomy. My shorts seemed to be paper thin as far any protection offered.

Cycling through the desert, I had to check in advance whether small places marked on my map represented the location of communities, where I could obtain water, or were deserted villages. This was particularly important when I crossed the huge Papago Indian Reservation. There were stores at both Wahak Hotonuk and Quitotoa, both operated by white families. The Indians did not identify with this Western role, and it was another sad reminder of the legacy of their treatment decades earlier when they were forced onto reservations. Some would always survive in the white man's environment, but the impression was formed that many were sunk into a state of lethargy, living on welfare payments or treaty money as it was widely understood, and with a major problem of alcoholism. I was reminded of what people had said to me earlier at the Red Lake Indian Reservation in Minnesota.

As I continued, the turn off to Kitt Peak National Observatory appeared on my right, reminding me of the ideal conditions at night for observing the stars. I was on my way to Tucson, or rather Old Tucson. In 1940, in the hills a few miles west of the modern city of Tucson, Columbia Film Studios built an exact replica of Tucson as it appeared in the middle 1800's for the filming of *Arizona*. Since that time, countless films and TV shows had been shot at the famous site, the films including *Gunfight at the O.K. Corral, 3:10 to Yuma, Walk the Proud Land* and *High Chapparal*. I was delighted to find some film-making in progress when I arrived. A Western series *Dundee and the*

Culhane starring our own John Mills was being shot for American TV. I learned later that it was not a commercial success. When lunch-time rolled around, the visitors watched a small group of actors perform, on the dusty streets, *The Reunion*, one of 45 shooting scenes in their repertoire and including some good stunt acting.

I left Old Tucson with happy memories, and south of Tucson detoured to see the mission San Xavier Del Bac, the "white dove of the desert". One of the most beautiful Spanish missions in America, it still ministered to the Papago Indians. I had now left behind the low-lying valley and the excessive temperatures I had been experiencing since going down to Phoenix. It was still extremely hot, but more tolerable. On the journey south to Nogales through the fertile Santa Cruz valley, I spent most of one morning seeing two historic attractions, Tubac Presidio State Historic Park and Tumacacori National Monument. The village of Tubac was the oldest inhabited European settlement in Arizona, and the Historic Park preserved the site of an historic Spanish frontier military post. There was an exceptionally fine museum, portraying the life of the first settlers to arrive in the region, first Spanish, then American, dealing at length with the life of the local Pima Indians - and of battles with the Apaches. The Tumacacori National Monument preserved the ruins of a typical frontier mission church and here again was a fine museum, telling the story of the Spanish missions, of what they brought to the regions they established themselves in, and how they fared among the local inhabitants.

These two museums just three miles apart drove home to me one feature of the West. It abounded in fine museums, portraying in depth and moreover, presenting attractively, the history of this most romantic part of America. At Nogales I turned away from the Mexican border to travel north-eastwards through hilly country. Yucca covered the roadsides near the Whetstone Mountains. Shortly afterwards there was a steady ascent from the San Pedro Valley to Tombstone. In the planning of my route through the American West, this famous town was an essential inclusion.

In 1878 a bearded prospector named Ed Schieffelin discovered silver in the San Pedro hills. Hundreds of men flocked to the area as news of the discovery spread. The town of Tombstone was to have one of the most turbulent histories of any mining town in the West. It seemed to attract more than its share of the lawless element. Such was the frequency at one time of murders, shootings and robberies that the town was threatened with martial law.

This was the Tombstone of Wyatt Earp, "Doc" Holiday, Bat Masterson, Luke Short, Curly Bill and Johnny Ringo. On 26 October 1881, at the O.K. Corral, occurred one of the most famous gunfights in history. On one side, representing the law, was Wyatt Earp, his brothers Virgil and Morgan, and his friend "Doc" Holiday; on the other side ranged the brothers Tom and Frank McLaury, and Billy and Ike Clanton. The resulting affray required the preparation of three more plots in Boothill Cemetery. Now that the bullets no longer fly, it was fascinating to visit places like this, and see the simple graves of an incredible number of men who "died with their boots on." I lapped it all up; I had, of course, just come away from Old Tucson where the famous film was shot in 1957, and I went along to see the real O.K. Corral. I took a trip down the "Goodenough" mine from which was extracted over one million dollars worth of silver ore. There were so many things to see and do in Tombstone; there was Shieffelin Hall, where you could see and hear the turbulent story of Tombstone portrayed with the aid of a superb diorama; the Court House, now a museum; the Crystal Palace Saloon; the Bird Cage Theatre; the Wells Fargo Museum; and the Wyatt Earp Museum. I considered the latter to be outstanding, and spent a long time there absorbing the story of the fighting Earp brothers; particularly the story of Wyatt Earp, the West's most famous marshal, whose exploits in Wichita, Dodge City and Tombstone made him a legend in his own lifetime. I was surprised to learn that he simply died in his bed in Los Angeles in 1929, as an old man of 80, after a life crammed with activity.

Leaving Tombstone my own journey continued south-eastwards to the thriving copper town of Bisbee, location of a huge open pit mine. At Douglas I approached the Mexican border again, to turn away north-eastwards as earlier at Nogales. Just north of the small community of Apache I came to the Geronimo Surrender Monument, describing how, on 5 September 1886, the feared Apache chief and a band of followers surrendered in the nearby hills to a detachment under General Nelson Miles. The surrender ended fighting between the Indian and the white man, ushering in a new era of stability in the West.

Shortly afterwards I crossed into the state of New Mexico to leave behind me a state of extraordinary beauty. So many people had discovered this in recent years that the population of Arizona was growing almost as fast as any state in the Union, many like myself, I felt sure, captivated by the desert.

Chapter 10

Return to the Rockies

Saturday, 8 July 1967

I entered the south-west corner of New Mexico with some concern. For the first time in North America I was heading straight for a freeway, with no alternative road available for 17 miles till I reached Lordsburg. In various sparsely populated parts of the West the growing interstate highway system was being created by upgrading existing roads. However, Interstate 10 passing through this area had only been completed in a number of separate sections, and it seemed that the restrictions were not being imposed until full completion. Inquiries at a petrol station at the road junction revealed I was free to use the freeway, but I received some questioning looks from motorists as I sped along, determined to leave the highway as quickly as I could.

It was a relief to get to Lordsburg, a stopping place on the old Butterfield stage route, and be able to turn off through rolling hills towards Silver City, Santa Rita and other towns very close together. The area was rich in mineral wealth, including gold, silver, copper and vanadium. At the higher elevations compared with a week or so before, I was now seeing different species of cactus and desert plant; "staghorn" cholla cacti covered several areas, their deep crimson blossoms now at the height of their glory, whereas they had long since died at lower elevations; century plants and groups of yucca in full bloom were rewarding sights, the yucca blossom being the state flower of New Mexico.

I was encountering more moisture than for some time, being surprised to learn that it was now the "monsoon" season. Almost every night since I had climbed away from the low-lying desert near Tucson there had been a tremendous storm. It was July, the month when this mountain area received its maximum rainfall. As I sheltered in my tent in the evenings, I would meditate on the beneficial effects on the tent material of an occasional dampening.

The descent to the Mimbres valley a few miles east of Santa Rita was followed by a long climb to the Emory Pass, taking me to 8,178 ft, the highest elevation so far. From the summit I looked towards the Rio Grande valley and over the hills beyond to the white sands of the desolate Jornado del Muerto - the Journey of the Dead - and the site in 1945 of the world's first atomic bomb test. In less than a year I would be able to see in Hiroshima the results of the atomic bomb explosion over the city which followed shortly afterwards.

It was a delightful run down to the Rio Grande, involving a descent of 4,000 ft, and I followed the rich, irrigated valley to El Paso. I had planned to stay just overnight in this big, industrial city and fit new tyres on my bicycle. However, leaving a grocery store I found myself in conversation with a barber who invited me to stay with him and his wife at their home on Montana Avenue. As a result I spent a whole day with them, enjoying their warm hospitality and being shown many of the sights of the city.

The next important destination lay 150 miles to the east, Carlsbad Caverns National Park. The journey involved two days of travelling through this northern part of Texas before re-entering New Mexico, a journey through desert terrain on either side of the Hulco Mountains. A long gradual climb was involved in crossing this range, and a much steeper climb through the Guadalupe Mountains close to the crossing into New Mexico.

The vast underground limestone caverns in the National Park contained some outstanding stalactite and stalagmite formations. I was curious to see them, not having seen anything like this since visiting the caverns at Hans-sur-Lesse in the Belgian Ardennes on my first cycle tour abroad four summers earlier. Buying groceries at the store in the late afternoon after a long, four hour tour, I found myself in conversation, first with a young lawyer from Big Spring, to the east in Texas, then a young couple from Amarillo in the Texas panhandle, who invited me to return to the caverns with them to see the bat flight which took place every evening at dusk. There was no time to lose. Arriving back at the caverns at 7.20pm, the bats started to leave 15 minutes later to seek food. I was glad to see this unusual phenomenon as the bat numbers slowly increased to about 5,000 per minute, an estimated million leaving the caves every evening to return later after feeding. Enjoying the company of this young couple, they asked me if I was married - as did an astonishing number of people at different times. The implication was that I must have left behind a very understanding wife as I pursued my sabbatical for an unknown number of years! I wouldn't forget this couple or where they came from; I felt Amarillo rolled so pleasantly off the tongue.

Returning to the campsite I found myself erecting my tent in semi-darkness. Two boys at a camping spot nearby were sent across with a lantern by their parents, and a mallet assisted in securing the tent pegs in minimum time. The boys were fascinated to watch the tent take shape and see how everything was arranged inside, including the sleeping bag, primus stove and all the cycle bags.

The route now swung northwards to Roswell through rather barren terrain, with scrub and creosote bushes covering much of the area. Near Artesia a farmer invited me to camp nearby on his land, an offer I gladly accepted. His son was as interested in my camping equipment as had been the boys at Carlsbad Caverns. The boy's mother remarked how independent I was when she received a negative reply to a query whether she could do anything for me. It was a dilemma: I needed to be independent all the time to live day by day, and couldn't suddenly become dependent on anyone else.

A short run of 40 miles followed the next day to Bottomless Lakes State Park east of Roswell, an area of rocky terrain. I reached the Park at 4.30pm, but wasn't going to set my tent up for another three hours following a very hot day with the temperature soaring to over 100°. The wind increased in strength during the evening, and I had to close the main flaps on the tent as it started to rain. A family from Oklahoma City were camping close by me, starting their first night's camping ever with a new tent recently bought. When I emerged from my tent the next morning, I was astonished to see the family in their car. The wind had ripped their tent to pieces during the night, while mine was undamaged. The family had experienced a most unfortunate introduction to camping.

I turned west towards Lincoln National Forest, and in the small town of Lincoln visited two museums, the main one being in the old Lincoln County Courthouse. I read about events concerning one of the Wild West's most infamous characters, Billy the Kid. He was a prisoner in the Courthouse awaiting hanging for murder when, on

28 April 1881, he escaped after shooting two guards. Less than three months later he was shot himself. He was just 21 and was said to have killed 21 men.

A marker east of Lincoln told the story of Smokey Bear, the National Forest Service's symbol of safety in the forest. The inscription read:

> "Time: May 1950. It was hot & dry when somebody traveling along Capitan Gap road flipped a lighted cigarette or burning match into the Forest. Fanned by strong winds the fire roared out of control. It took hundreds of firefighters several days to control the blaze that blackened 17,000 acres of prime timberland. Another victim was a badly burned bear cub found clinging to a charred tree. After receiving first aid, a Game Warden flew him to Santa Fe for treatment by a veterinarian. His story was flashed across the Nation & he was named Smokey, after the famous forest fire prevention poster. He recovered from his burns & was flown to Washington, D.C., where he now lives at the National Zoo. There he serves as the living reminder of the need for care with fire by everyone when in our Forests. Be sure to visit the Smokey Bear Museum at Capitan."

I stopped at the museum a few miles to the west before continuing to Valley of Fires State Park near Carrizozo, the Park being set in the midst of a lava bed. A truck delivering beer stopped by me on the run down to Carrizozo. The can of beer offered went down well with my evening meal. Then the Park officer declined any charge for my overnight stay when he appeared in the morning, an example which I hoped would be repeated. I turned north again to travel through undulating terrain, involving a number of tiring climbs through grass-covered hills with patches of pinion pine everywhere, the grass parched in the summer heat. Around lunch-time I caught up with a family from Omaha, Nebraska, who had passed me a few minutes earlier. They invited me to have lunch with them; these little gestures of hospitality punctuated my journey at intervals, and I never knew when the next one would occur.

I climbed a number of times as I continued north, reaching about 7,500 ft at the summits before going downwards. Late one afternoon I passed through the ghost town of Madrid, once a thriving coal mining town. It was startling to see row after row of identical timber-framed houses, all deserted and falling to ruin. A small community remained around the town centre. Three miles onward was Cerrillos, another town which had known better times when many minerals were being mined in the area.

The state capital of Santa Fe was just 20 miles away, and I was looking forward to a couple of days in this historic city. It was the oldest seat of government in the U.S.A. The buildings in the heart of the city were all in the Spanish style, lending to the city a unique atmosphere. Stretching along the north side of the central plaza was the Palace of the Governors, built by the Spanish for their capital building in 1610. Many artists were on the tree-shaded plaza daily, drawing portraits in chalk for anyone prepared to sit in the restful surroundings. I sat in the plaza for some time studying the latest batch of travel literature collected, and soaking up the atmosphere. I went to see the old Capitol building and the new one, joining a small group of visitors for a tour. I was not impressed with the external appearance of the new building, much preferring the Spanish style older building.

North of Santa Fe I travelled between rocky hills, coloured all shades of yellow and red, to Espanola on the Rio Grande. Looking down on the valley from near Velarde, it looked as fertile here as much lower down, north of El Paso. The road followed the river several miles before climbing steeply to give a commanding view of the Rio Grande gorge, a deep cleft in a flat grassy plain. Just north at the small town of Ranchos de Taos I admired the old mission church of St. Francis of Assisi, one of the finest examples of Spanish missionary architecture in the south-west. Construction took 45 years after starting about 1710.

I did not spend long there as I wanted to get three miles north to the town of Taos to visit the home of the famous frontiersman, Kit Carson. His home for 24 years in this picturesque town in the foothills of the Sangre de Cristo Mountains was now a museum. It was fascinating reading about the life of this famous trapper, hunter, Indian guide and agent, and fighter. His skills, knowledge of the surrounding country and understanding of the Indian tribes made him much sought after by official Government expeditions sent to explore the West. In charge of several expeditions was John C. Fremont, who became another of the idolized characters of the American West. The two men first met in 1842, forming a lifelong friendship.

There was a further item of interest in this scenic area. Along this stretch of the Rio Grande were to be found several unique Indian pueblos, or villages, which had been lived in continuously for hundreds of years. Some had changed little since they were first seen by Spanish conquistadors in the sixteenth century as they rode north in search of the Seven Cities of Cibola, where legend had it, untold wealth was to be obtained. Two miles north of Taos I visited Taos Pueblo, containing two large five-storied buildings unlike anything in any other pueblo; archaeologists judged that the pueblo had been inhabited for at least 800 years.

The following day I crossed into Colorado, reaching San Luis early in the afternoon. A sign in the town recorded that Manassa 30 miles to the west was the birthplace of the former heavyweight boxing champion Jack Dempsey; champion from 1919-26, he was known as "the Manassa Mauler". I continued north over a broad, flat valley, much of the terrain covered with sagebrush, to Fort Garland. It was built in 1858 as a military post to protect the new settlers, serving in this capacity for 25 years when it was abandoned, no longer necessary with the Indians on reservations. The fort had been restored and was now a fine museum depicting the story of a frontier post in the Indian days. Arriving at the fort as it was closing for the day, I told the curator I would return the following morning after buying food and camping nearby. I was invited to stay at the fort for the evening, using a room with no exhibits in, but with a table and chair. A memorable evening thus passed in historic surroundings before touring the fort the following morning. The commandant at the fort in 1866-7 was Kit Carson.

Leaving the fort I found a lady by my bicycle waiting to talk to me. Originally from London, she was married to an American and lived in Amarillo, Texas. She had been a keen cyclist and had cycled in Europe. It was always interesting to meet a fellow cyclist. After travelling nine miles west I turned north over a dirt road towards Great Sand Dunes National Monument. The area enclosed some of the world's tallest sand dunes, the sand piled to heights of over 700 ft. Lying along the western edge of the north-south running Sangre de Cristo Mountains, the dunes had formed slowly over centuries of time by the prevailing westerly wind blowing the light sandy soil of the San Luis Valley eastwards. The wind swept upwards as it reached the mountains, but the sand was too heavy to be carried on. I found it unbelievable walking on vast sand dunes in the Rocky Mountains. At the campground I met a family from England now living in Denver who invited me to call on them when I reached the state capital.

The immediate journey continued up the broad San Luis Valley at an elevation of about 7,500 ft, before climbing over the Poncha Pass at 9,010 ft and descending swiftly to the valley of the Arkansas River. From its source in the Rockies the river flowed south-eastwards across the Great Plains for about 1,000 miles to join the Mississippi near Little Rock. Following the river eastwards, it took me along one of the most attractive river valleys I had seen, first through green hills then very rocky hills as the river flowed through a deep gorge. I left the main road near Canon City to follow the Skyline Drive, which gave some fine views over the city and surrounding terrain. The road continued through Lincoln Park and Florence, the latter a most attractive little town with the main street lined with large trees, offering abundant shade from the hot summer sun. Someone's foresight long ago was now paying a handsome dividend.

I crossed the Arkansas River to continue over hills past Fort Carson to Colorado Springs. Before beginning a descent to the city, there were fine views over the huge, rolling plain of the Mid-West. I went to see the vermilion coloured rock formations in the Garden of the Gods, reminding me of the Oak Creek Canyon in Arizona. But I was annoyed with the weather; it was dull and cloudy and far from ideal for photographs. I realised how few days I had like this. Eight miles north was the U.S. Air Force Academy. I cycled round the vast grounds, stopping to take a close look at the modern architecture of the impressive Cadet Chapel. I heard many comments about the seemingly unlimited amount of taxpayers' money available for such projects, while other important projects had to fight for every cent. A prime candidate in my view would have been the road between Colorado Springs and Denver 70 miles to the north. I was astonished to find that the alternative to the freeway linking Colorado's two biggest cities, and running parallel a few miles to the east, involved 15 miles of dirt road.

That was soon forgotten when I arrived in Denver. It was time to renew acquaintances with two families met a few days before, first the Chavez family met on the approach road to Great Sand Dunes National Monument. They were so hospitable to me, and I somehow managed to show a large number of colour slides to them while the needs of seven lively children competed for attention. The following day, a Sunday, I went to have dinner with the Willson family whom

I had met at the campground by the sand dunes. While in the city I toured the Capitol building; from the dome there was a commanding view over the city towards the Rocky Mountains.

It was towards the mountains that I headed on leaving Denver, reaching the east entrance to Rocky Mountain National Park after two days journey in the foothills. It tuned me up for the journey ahead, which was going to take me to a higher elevation than I had ever been before. The Trail Ridge Road was going to take me over the highest continuous road in America. I was something of a phenomenon on this road as passengers in cars waved and stared round at me in disbelief, while cameras clicked and cine-cameras whirred. Up and up the road went. Around 11,000 ft the trees started to become very stunted. Soon I emerged above the timberline to see the Alpine tundra, a dense carpet of tiny wildflowers and plants which had adapted themselves to the climatic conditions at this high altitude. The road levelled out upon reaching the timberline, staying above 11,500 ft for 11 miles and reaching a summit of 12,183 ft. Climbs like this gave me an enormous sense of satisfaction. I stopped at the Visitor Centre nearby to celebrate with a cup of coffee, before putting on all my extra clothing for the long descent to the valley on the other side. The descent was interrupted by a short climb over the Milner Pass at an elevation of 10,759 ft, the Pass being on the Continental Divide which separated drainage to the Atlantic Ocean from drainage to the Pacific Ocean. The descent took me beside the infant Colorado River, which rose a few miles away.

I arrived at Ridge Creek campground in the early evening to find it full, but there was never going to be a problem in finding a vacant space for a small tent. With all the climbing, I was surprised to see that I had covered 47 miles during the day. Turning north at Granby after a good night's sleep, I had more climbing over the Willow Creek Pass, which was also on the Continental Divide. As the road descended into a broad valley, the pine trees were left behind once more. The terrain was now mostly covered with sagebrush, with a few isolated farms just as on my last day in New Mexico. This time it was my last day in Colorado.

Entering Wyoming south-west of Laramie, a vast area of rolling grassland and desert lay ahead. It was an astonishingly colourful area of red sandstone hills with their characteristic crests. A storm passed over the area every afternoon, causing the desert to erupt into a blaze of colour as wildflowers now covered the terrain. It was a sparsely populated area and, on the road towards Lander, I camped one night near Jeffrey City so that I could stock up with groceries the next morning. With the route I was planning to take, I did not expect to be able to buy any more for another 119 miles.

Two routes were available to me as I headed towards the north-west corner of Wyoming. The direct one would have taken me through Lander, but I chose the longer route via Farson on considerations of historical interest. Turning south-westwards off the main road seven miles from Larson, I crossed the Little Popo Agie River shortly afterwards to begin a long gradual climb to the South Pass. A number of historical markers in the area set the tone of this part of the Oregon Trail skirting the southern tip of the Wind River Range of mountains. One marker recorded:

> "The discovery of South Pass, an important segment of the Oregon-California emigrant trails, hastened one of the greatest mass emigrations in the annals of history when approximately half a million Americans channelled through here to claim the virgin west."

The years 1849-51 were recorded as the high tide of emigration, the gold discovery in California in 1848 helping to swell the normal emigration to one hundred and fifty five thousand people. The South Pass had been discovered some years before in 1812 by Herbert Stuart. As the numbers on the Oregon Trail increased, another informative marker recorded Government efforts to provide a better wagon road through the area, referring in particular to one diversion:

> "Oregon Trail - Lander Cutoff
> South Pass Area
>
> This is an old trail used by the Indians & the trappers of the fur period, a short cut to the Snake River country. It was proposed as an emmigrant road by mountain man John Hockaday in 1854. No emmigrant trails crossed the mountains north of here. It was improved as a wagon road for the Government by F.W. Lander in 1859 to avoid dry wastes of the roads to the south & provide more water, wood & forage. Here it commenced the crossing of the south end of the Windriver Mountains & the Continental Divide & on to the Pacific Northwest. Thirteen thousand people &

> thousands of domestic animals passed this way in 1859 & for thirty years thereafter was used as heavily, setting the destiny of an empire."

Surveying the scene around me, it was impossible to avoid getting caught up in the romance of this area. You needed to remind yourself that the journey on the Oregon Trail was a gruelling ordeal for many; many would perish on the trail, and many would die at the end of the journey before they had much opportunity to enjoy any rewards. For all those who survived, though, hard labour, continuous development and exploitation and harnessing of the immense natural resources of the West would eventually provide levels of prosperity which the pioneers could not have dreamed about. I felt in an expansive mood as I soaked up the atmosphere. It was a place in which to let the imagination soar. If you closed your eyes, you could see long lines of covered wagons trundling past, the oxen thankfully having no idea how many more steps they had to take before they could rest.

Before I could rest for the day I needed to get to Farson to replenish my food supplies. The lady at the store couldn't understand why I had made such a big detour from the direct route to the north-west of the state. I would draw on the memories of that journey over the South Pass for a very long time to come. As I turned north-westwards the road continued over rolling sagebrush-covered plains. A gradual climb north-west of Pinedale took me to a summit called The Rim at 7,921 ft, from which a long descent followed to the Hoback Valley. The desert was left behind near the top of the pass, and pine-clad hills were now all around.

Grand Teton National Park was just to the north beyond Jackson. As I moved slowly through the Park, my eyes were constantly drawn west to the craggy peaks of the Grand Teton Mountains. There were fine views across Jenny and Jackson Lakes. For a long time the wonders of this region remained known to just a few - the mountain men, who followed the streams and penetrated the valleys in pursuit of beaver. A marker by Jackson Lake told the story:

> "Along this route, during the western fur trade period (1807-1840), passed the 'mountain men', in search of beaver. These adventurers were responsible for much of the exploration of the far West. Jackson Hole was an important early center of the mountain fur trade, indeed, it marked the crossroads of

> the movements of the fur brigades. Trappers moving to & from the Yellowstone Country, or beyond to the three forks of the Missouri and the Northwest, passed this way. Donald McKenzie & his party, of the Northwest Company, were the first, in 1818. They were followed by such famous figures as Jedediah Smith, Jim Bridger, Thomas Fitzpatrick, Kit Carson, Joe Meek, & others. John Colter, credited with the discovery of Jackson Hole in 1807, crossed the valley and the Teton Range some distance farther south, but returned eastward not far from the northern end of Jackson Lake."

Hollywood had been to the region a number of times. In 1952 the Tetons featured in *The Big Sky* with a young Kirk Douglas; the following year they formed the backdrop in *Shane*, and in 1972 one of the mountain men was the subject of a sympathetic study in *Jeremiah Johnson*. The Tetons were still much in my memory when, a few miles north, I entered Yellowstone National Park, the first to be created, in 1872, and the largest, covering 3,472 square miles.

I had planned originally to be in this great park at the beginning of June, but with the change in route direction it was now the middle of August. The park rangers told me that the stormy weather in the region did not clear properly until the middle of July, so that the change in plan proved sound. I approached the park with some trepidation, having read all the guidance notes about not feeding the bears, and not approaching them closely; if they came close to your car, you should wind the windows up. I felt I had a slight technical problem! No helpful information about the dilemma resulted from discussions with several people.

Setting off along the Yellowstone roads somewhat cautiously, I quickly learned one or two very interesting things. If I rounded a bend in the road to see a bear no more than ten or twenty yards away, it invariably took one look at the strange sight approaching it and bolted off into the safety of the trees. It was not so with the cars and caravans. By long exposure the bears had come to regard the motorist as part of the natural scene; and they knew all too well where they could obtain food very easily. Not only was I such an unusual sight to the bears, but I was not looked upon as a supplier of food, and was left alone to pedal merrily on my way.

On my first evening in the Park I went for a walk round the Grant Village campground and to the nearby Visitor Centre, returning to be told that a bear had been roaming round my tent and bicycle. It was a good job the bicycle was chained to a tree, else I might have lost a second one in America, and the park rangers might not have approved of seeing one of their bears cycling along the park roads! It reminded me of the bears' acute sense of smell, and the need to leave all my food in the caravan of a fellow camper. The bears were not generally known to share Yogi's sense of humour, and certainly would have had no respect for my Good Companions tent if attracted by food inside.

The following morning I set off for the geyser area 18 miles away. I waited for Old Faithful to perform before moving slowly to the campground nearby, setting up the tent and collapsing inside it. I was suffering from food poisoning and wasn't going any further that day. I couldn't work out what food had been contaminated. Feeling a bit better the next morning, I recovered gradually during the next three days as I went to admire the Grand Canyon of the Yellowstone, the two Falls on the river and the colourful area around Mammoth Hot Springs. By the time I arrived at the Madison Junction campground, my appetite had returned - and at just the right time.

There had been a desperate situation at all the campgrounds in Yellowstone and at the Grand Tetons for many days. Every campground was full by 10am in the morning, as vacated sites were immediately occupied by new campers waiting to come on to the site. I moved slowly round the Madison Junction campground in the early evening, and approached the site of an Airstream trailer. The small area adjacent for any tent was vacant, and the elderly couple in the trailer had no objection to me using it. They watched with interest as I set the tent up. An offer of fried bacon and eggs was accepted gladly. The couple, who came from north of Denver, showed me over the trailer, the first time I had seen inside this special type of caravan. I learned of the Airstream owner clubs and the frequent expeditions made by groups all over the world. It seemed an enviable lifestyle.

It was time to leave Yellowstone and Wyoming. During five memorable days in the Park, I had seen 28 bears, but there had been no sign of Yogi or his little friend Bobo. Yogi was smarter than the average bear and had probably realised that I wouldn't be carrying a picnic hamper. He was almost certainly directing his attention towards other travellers where there were potentially greater rewards. Several travellers told me that they had seen vehicles from every state of the Union, and it was easy to see why Yellowstone was the most popular of all the National Parks.

Chapter 11

Closing the Loop

Thursday, 24 August 1967

Leaving Yellowstone National Park via the west entrance, I emerged into Montana, "The Big Sky Country" as proclaimed on a large sign. Just to the north was another reminder of the power of nature as I rode beside Earthquake Lake, created on 17 August 1959 when a violent earthquake caused a huge slide across the Madison River. The flow of the river was completely blocked until a channel could be cut through the earth slide. The visit to the area resulted in just a pause before continuing north-west through rolling grassland to Virginia City, nestling in Alder Gulch in the Tobacco Root Mountains. Gold was discovered in the gulch in 1863, leading to the creation of the city. Walking down the main street past the restored buildings, it was easy to imagine oneself transported back through time to the romantic but earnest days after the gold discovery. Virginia City had a much quieter charm than Tombstone in Arizona, but had its own Boothill Cemetery, where I was able to see the graves of five "road agents" hung at the same time by The Vigilantes. A memorable evening was spent at the Playhouse watching The Virginia City Players perform *Rip Van Winkle* by Washington Irving.

The visit to the nightly melodrama during the summer was marred by finding one of my gear cables cut as I left the theatre. I had to replace the cable with a spare one before setting off the following morning towards the state capital of Helena. Following Ruby River and Jefferson River through fertile valleys with many farms, I was now on the route travelled by Lewis and Clark. An historical marker set the scene:

"Jefferson Valley

> The Lewis & Clark Expedition, westward bound, came up the Jefferson River in August, 1805. They were hoping to find the Shoshone Indians, Sacajawea's tribe, & trade for horses to use in crossing the mountains west of here. Just south of here the River forks, the east fork being the Ruby & the west fork the Beaverhead. They followed the latter & met the Shoshone near Armstead.
>
> On the return trip from the coast in 1806, Capt. Wm. Clark retraced their former route down this valley to Three Forks, & then crossed to the Yellowstone. Capt. Lewis left Clark in the Bitter Root Valley, crossed the Divide via the Big Blackfoot River & thence to Great Falls. They met near the mouth of the Yellowstone, arriving within nine days of each other."

Heading up the Boulder valley past many more farms, the road climbed steeply north of the town before descending through a number of small towns, all one-time gold mining camps, to the capital. Helena also owed its existence to the discovery of gold. A party of four who had left Virginia City to prospect further north became discouraged, and were about to give up when one of the party suggested they explore a small gulch on Prickly Pear Creek passed the previous day. It would be their "last chance", another of the party remarked. It was 14 July 1864, they were lucky, and over £80 million worth of gold was to be taken out of the winding gulch. The camp which sprung up was named Last Chance Gulch. As a large town gradually came into being and a shorter name became desirable, Helena was chosen. The main street, still named Last Chance Gulch, had several bends in it. Old-timers said this was deliberate so that in the event of a shooting affray not more than three people would be shot at once!

Visiting the imposing Capitol building, I was struck by a number of outstanding paintings depicting scenes from the Lewis and Clark expedition. I resolved to do some deeper reading on this great voyage. I spent several hours in the State Historical Museum, which I considered one of the best for its coverage of the history of the West and of the Indian tribes. It was appropriate that the Museum should have a notable coverage of the Indians due to all the associations with Lewis and Clark, and the conflicts within the state boundaries as the frontier advanced westwards. In 1876 the Little Big Horn River in eastern Montana was perhaps the scene of the most famous conflict during this era. As I read various notices in the Museum, I became immersed once more in the story of the buffalo:

> "For countless centuries the great shaggy animal was the Indian's staff of life. It served him completely as food, clothing & shelter. It entered into his religion, his societies & his migrations, & when the white man came, buffalo was not only food & sport, but very soon was the key weapon for suppressing the red man. The wanton slaughter of this majestic beast - to clear the ranges for cattle & for farming & to make the Indian subservient - is a tragic chapter in Montana's history.
>
> The diet of the Northern Plains Indian was predominantly one of meat. It included virtually all edible wild animal & dog. But buffalo meat, marrow, intestines & suet, in volume & frequency, exceeded all other food. This shaggy animal was more than equivalent to the butcher, baker & candlestick maker. He was grocery & drug store, meat market & even bakery - for the substance found under the hump along the spine was eaten like bread. Sun & air dried in strips, or pounded with berries & dried into pemmikan, buffalo meat could be preserved & stored for long, lean periods. No modern military ration has the nutritious value or staying quality, per highly concentrated ounce, than had dried buffalo meat.
>
> There are those practical people who say that the westward march of civilization & the early development of Montana required extermination of the buffalo & subjugation of the Indian. Undoubtedly the buffalo's near extinction was inevitable. And ultimately the Indian's way of life would have changed to more closely parallel that of the white man who had usurped his vast grassland & mountain domain.
>
> Nevertheless the methods, heavy handed, inhuman & unjust, which characterized the banishment of the Indian & his staff of life, constitute a tragic chapter in American history.

> The Indian was caught in the crushing vortex of the intruder's manifest destiny. History records few parallels for such complete upheaval in the well-formulated life of a race of people. Culture, custom, religion & livelihood, all were brutally assaulted & forced into abrupt change.
>
> Our Indians, like others before them, saw the clear mountain streams muddied by the frenzy of gold placering, the prairies were fenced & the grass turned upside down. The primitive forests were desecrated.
>
> The intruder's government involved sly treaties. Some were made in good faith, most were not. This restricted the movement of the various tribes & narrowed their horizon. Cavalry & infantry enforced the edicts. It was the opening wedge to destroy & conquer the Indian.
>
> The final means was the government reservation. Usually this represented land least desired for white settlement. Here the Indian became a captive, a public ward, & an abused & abject outcast of a once-proud society. He was transfused quickly from proud huntsman to inexpert farmer; clothed in the white man's garb; disciplined in his schools & by the device of rations & dole.
>
> A proud people was broken & humbled during the reservation period of the last half of the 19th Century.
>
> But the Indian has survived & re-adapted himself. He has become, generally, a competent livestockman, careful farmer & good citizen, after heartbreaking adjustment to the white man's will & way."

I had read essentially the same story earlier in the State Museum in Denver, but repetition did not make it more palatable. The text quoted, which at least ended on an optimistic note, contained the words "manifest destiny" which came to represent an explanation, defence and justification for events concerned with the advance of the western frontier and general territorial expansion. It captured the confident mood at the time when a New York editor, John L. O'Sullivan, wrote in 1845 that it was "the fulfillment of our manifest destiny to overspread the continent allotted by Providence for the free development of our yearly expanding millions."

The small city of Helena, with a population of about 25,000 in 1967, was packed with history; among so much of interest, there were the arts and crafts centre at Reeder's Alley, the gothic cathedral and, most memorably, the Last Chancer Tour Train. There was something about the city which caused me to leave it with the fondest of memories as I climbed 2,000 ft over the McDonald Pass just to the west before beginning a long descent to the valley of the Little Blackfoot River. Near Avon an historical marker provided some interesting information on the Mullan Road, a former military road built along the route I was now following:

"The Mullan Road

> From this point west to the Idaho line U.S. No. 10 follows the route of a military road located & constructed during 1855-62 by Capt. John Mullan, 2nd Artillery, U.S.A. The road was 624 miles long & connected Fort Benton with Fort Walla Walla. An average wagon outfit required a minimum of 47 days to travel it.
>
> The Captain, aside from his engineering ability, was a man of considerable acumen as evidenced by the following excerpts from his final report. He prophesied 'the locomotive engine will make passage of the wild interior at rates of speed which will startle human credulity.'
>
> Also he advised parties chaperoning pack mules to 'never maltreat them, but govern them as you would a woman, with kindness, affection & caresses, & you will be repaid by their docility & easy management.'"

Captain Mullan was a very wise man I told myself several times as the journey continued, the Little Blackfoot River joining the Clark Fork at Garrison. The journey beside it to Missoula was a delightful run between grass-clad hills with a scattering of pine trees, the grass parched yellow in the hot sun. I was at about 3,300 ft, the lowest elevation for some time. The sun felt unusually hot, and I reached Missoula to learn that the temperature had climbed to 99°.

I kept hearing more and more about the forest fire danger, particularly in the neighbouring state of Idaho. The whole of the Northwest had experienced one of the longest, driest and hottest summers on record. The fire danger was extreme in Montana, Idaho,

Washington, Oregon and British Columbia, Canada, and all travel off the main roads was temporarily forbidden. Major fires raged almost every day in some part of this region, most started by lightning storms at night. It was not without interest that I visited just west of Missoula the Aerial Fire Depot and Smokejumper Centre at the Northern Region Headquarters of the Forest Service. After seeing what is done to combat the menace of forest fires, I turned northwards over hills towards Ravalli in the Flathead Valley.

I was suddenly startled by a sight on the road ahead. Coming towards me was the first long distance cycle tourist I had met in North America. I had heard of one or two at different times, but this was the first time I was meeting one; and this one was exceptional. A student at the University of Minnesota at Minneapolis, he had cycled up to Alaska during the summer, returning south by the coastal ferry. We exchanged experiences for a considerable time before continuing in our different directions. A slight detour from my direct route allowed me to visit the mission church of St. Ignatius, built in 1854 to minister to the Flathead Indians. Two wheeled vehicles were banned on the next route I wished to follow, a 19 mile tour round the National Bison Range established at Moiese in 1908, and containing some 500 bison, or buffalo, in addition to other wildlife. After locking the bicycle up beside the Visitor Centre, I accepted a lift from a generous couple from Pittsburgh, Pennsylvania. It was reassuring to see this significant herd of buffalo after reading in the museum in Helena about the slaughter a hundred years earlier.

Returning to the bicycle, I followed a river for the remaining 100 miles in Montana, first the Flathead then the Clark Fork. The sun beat down from a bright blue sky on the parched hillsides and placid waters of the river, mirror smooth for miles due to damming of the river for irrigation projects. It was an incredibly picturesque journey, a superb finale to the "Big Sky Country." The scenery remained similar as I entered Idaho, although I lost the crystal clear air. Crossing the state at its narrowest section, where it was only 45 miles wide, I was in the state for just one day, but it was one day more than in Utah. I had realised earlier on entering Wyoming that my journey was taking me into all the western states except Utah, which I was completely encircling. I had absolutely nothing against the residents of the Mormon state: it was simply the way the route had worked out.

The scene beside me in Idaho changed as the Clark Fork River flowed into the vast Pend Oreille Lake. Following the northern shoreline through Sandpoint, I picked up the Pend Oreille River flowing out on the west side. Entering the state of Washington at Newport for a third period, a turn south-west brought me quickly to Spokane, the "Heart of the Inland Empire."

I would remember Spokane for two things in particular, the first being a fine statue of Abraham Lincoln. Few cities seemed to have a statue of this most revered of all the American Presidents, so that it was a surprise to encounter this one so far from the federal capital. Erected in 1930, one face of the plinth contained an inscription which I had not encountered before. A mother had written to the President during the Civil War to seek solace, advising him that all five of her sons had served the Union cause and been killed. Lincoln wrote to her: "I pray that our heavenly father may leave you only the solemn pride that must be yours to have laid so costly a sacrifice upon the altar of freedom." I was profoundly impressed by this extract from a fuller letter, as inspirational as so much of his writing.

I went round the shops looking for a number of items on a list, and was successful in obtaining a plastic two-egg container and some close-up lenses for my camera. At the photographic shop I was delighted even more to see a lightweight tripod. This could be a boon for taking pictures of myself on the bicycle using the camera's time delay feature. I had been dependent up to now on setting the camera up on such items as posts round the edge of the road; I could now set the camera up in the middle of the road!

I headed west through terrain which rolled very gently, past wheat-fields recently harvested, to the Grand Coulee Dam on the Columbia River. It was fascinating visiting this enormous structure and the associated power-plant, comparing everything with the Hoover Dam seen three months earlier. The route continued south-westwards beside Banks Lake through farmland very productive as a result of the irrigation schemes associated with the vast Columbia Basin Project. The scenery changed around Quincy as fruit orchards started to appear; there were more as I followed the Columbia to Wenatchee.

Camping just outside the town I had a fright as I lit the primus stove. A spark ignited the grass adjacent, and I had to stamp it out very quickly. I thought for a moment I was going to set fire to the whole

Northwest. The incident drove home to me the need for extreme caution. Being unable to buy a newspaper very often, I had taken to buying *Time* magazine; the issue the previous week referred to the exceptionally hot weather in the Northwest this summer. Portland had endured its 63rd day without rain, the last 12 with a maximum temperature above 100°. When I bought some fruit at a roadside stand, the lady told me Wenatchee had experienced temperatures up to 114°, which was the highest I encountered in the Arizona desert! Meanwhile the eastern states had been having a washout, with continual rain.

I cycled up the Wenatchee Valley for 20 miles, passing orchard after orchard, the trees all heavily laden with fruit - apples, pears, peaches and plums. Turning south, the road climbed over 3,000 ft to cross the Swauk Pass before descending to Ellensburg and Yakima. I was on a slightly tortuous route to put me on the road for the east entrance to Mt. Rainier National Park. A long climb began from Yakima up the Naches Valley for 40 miles before turning to follow the American River over the Chinook Pass, an ascent of almost 4,400 ft from Yakima. From the top of the Pass, there was a glorious view of the snow-capped rounded top of Mt. Rainier, rising to 14,410 ft. A succession of memorable views followed as the road skirted the southern slopes. There was much more climbing before a final, long descent began to the lowlands. It was now much greener at the lower elevations; I was once more on the west side of the Cascade Range of mountains, and splashes of red on the hillsides signalled the approach of autumn. As the road passed through gently rolling farmland, I turned south at Vader to cross the Columbia River into Oregon at the lumber town of Longview.

The continuing road southwards beside the river brought me back to Portland on 17 September to close a great loop of 6,350 miles started four and a half months earlier on 2 May. It was a journey I would never forget; it encompassed nine National Parks, excluding Crater Lake, and a variety of terrain which I could not have imagined beforehand. I had met countless generous Americans, and arranged to go out to the eastern side of Portland to see again the Riley family whom I had camped beside at the Grand Canyon. After dinner they wanted to see all the slides I had brought with me, including those that enabled us to relive the moments when we stood on the Canyon's rim.

I was still far from my planned destination for the winter. Before leaving Portland I needed to use the resources of a larger city; after some difficulty I managed to purchase some lengths of aluminium rod from a metals distributor to make some new tent pegs. So many of the original pegs had not survived the punishment of the last few months; more than 100 nights had now been spent in the tent, and there were many more to come.

Chapter 12

Coastal Journey

Wednesday, 20 September 1967

Leaving Portland I retraced exactly the route followed in the spring, giving me an opportunity to enjoy again the hospitality of the family relations near Rickreall. It also enabled me to form into tent pegs the aluminium rods bought in Portland. The change in the scene was now very noticeable. In contrast to the green of the growing corn in the spring, there were now large areas of brown following ploughing after the harvest. The almost bare branches of the trees in the coastal range of hills were now replaced by the brilliant reds and yellows of autumn.

Conditions were not always ideal as I headed south down the Oregon coast. Mist rolled in from the Pacific Ocean at intervals, but when it cleared there were memorable views, particularly when the road ran higher up the hillside. There was something hypnotic about watching the rollers crashing on the shore as the road followed the shoreline for mile after mile. As I approached the border with California the weather deteriorated, and I retreated into a motel at Brookings to escape the rain. The last time I had stayed in a motel because of rain had been the day I travelled to Flagstaff, Arizona, three months before: I couldn't complain.

After 250 miles down the Oregon coast, I crossed into California the next morning with improved weather. It was most welcome, as I entered an area of the redwood trees. The trees soared to a greater height than any other tree, up to about 350 ft. The giant sequoia of the Sierra Nevada, which had impressed me so much, were considered the larger trees by virtue of the volume of wood in the trunk, but did not reach quite the same heights. Most of the finest stands of coastal redwood were protected in a series of state parks, and I moved slowly through the region, trying to take in as much of the grand scenes as I could.

There was a setback to progress as I reached Fields Landing south of Eureka. Camping a mile to the south, a ferocious storm blew up during the night. After packing the tent away with difficulty the next morning, I retreated the mile north to Fields Landing and booked into a motel for the day. It proved to be just an interlude, but there was another problem in travelling through the area. Several stretches of the road had been upgraded to freeway status, with no alternative road available. However, as in south-western New Mexico, no restrictions seemed to be in force until these separate stretches were joined together. It was a worrying sign for the future.

The road took me inland through Humboldt Redwoods State Park, past hundreds of the giant trees. At Leggett the road divided to provide a main road, Highway 101, running approximately 20 miles inland to the south and a true coastal road, Highway 1, the roads coming together again at San Francisco. The weather improved dramatically as I followed the quiet coastal road hugging the coast, travelling through a succession of small communities and past some fine beaches. The grass everywhere - by the roadsides, in the meadows and on the hillsides - was parched brown after a hot dry summer, which continued. The Pacific never looked bluer and the ocean horizon was incredibly distinct, the deep blue of the ocean contrasting with the lighter blue of the sky. This was the California I wanted to know, and four glorious days after leaving the redwoods I crossed the Golden Gate Bridge into San Francisco.

As the roads converged at the bridge I found myself on the wrong side of the road for the one pavement for cyclists and pedestrians. It was now impossible to cross the road with the volume of traffic racing past in both directions, three lanes for each direction. I had to lift the bicycle over barriers as I proceeded. With my progress followed on CCTV cameras, a policeman was waiting to give me a dressing down at the far end. I made for the YMCA, only to be told there was nowhere in the building to store the bicycle. This had occurred at just one or two other YMCA's, and I sought out a small hotel in the central area. I realised after obtaining a room that the hotel concerned was full of retired people; many were interested to suddenly find a guest 60 years younger than themselves!

I left the bicycle in the hotel for a time to explore the central area and to ride up and down the steep streets of this beautiful city in the cable cars. As I sat in Union Square studying literature collected at the Visitor Centre, my eyes were drawn to an advertising board above one building proclaiming "BOAC has a sleeper to London." I was overcome by feelings of homesickness. I needed to move away from the Square: I was not planning to return home for some considerable time. A walk through Chinatown transported me into a different world, San Francisco having the largest Chinese community outside Asia. The city also had the largest hippie population in the country, congregated in the Haight-Ashbury district; it was 1967, the height of the "flower power" era. There was an extraordinary atmosphere in the area, as a vast number of young people attempted to live a different way of life to their parents, who were seen to be on a headlong rush into soulless materialism as the country enjoyed the highest level of prosperity ever. In a way, I had left this route behind myself to experience something different, but I was light years away philosophically from the way this particular group of young people viewed the world.

One evening after darkness had fallen I walked up to the North Beach area, the night club district. It was the home of topless shows, topless waitresses and almost everything else topless. Almost every show advertised topless performers, one show purporting to feature the world's only topless all-girl band. I noticed one place where a topless shoe-shine could be obtained, and high above the pavement a shapely girl gyrated in a cage. I had seen nothing like this while travelling through the deserts of Arizona - or anywhere else for that matter! It made an interesting visual commentary on the advancement of cultural life in the city.

While in the San Francisco area I phoned Bob at Livermore, whom I had met at the campground at Yosemite National Park in May with Charles, a colleague at work. Bob decided generously to take a day off work, collected me in San Francisco one evening and introduced me to his wife and family. He spent the following day showing me round his home area, the research centre laboratories where he worked and the nearby Del Valle power project and recreation area. We met Charles while travelling round the area. A notable feature of the Livermore district was the widespread use of bicycles by adults in the town for transport to work and for recreation. I was impressed.

A boat trip round San Francisco Bay provided some fine views of the city and the two bridges connecting it to the north and east, the Golden Gate and Bay Bridges. Returning to dry land, I took the bicycle out on part of the 49 mile Scenic Drive and spent some time admiring the graceful Golden Gate Bridge from Lincoln Park and Baker's Beach. I needed to cross the other bridge, the 8-mile long Bay Bridge, when I left the city for Oakland. The local Highway Patrol office confirmed that cyclists were not allowed on the bridge. After depositing myself at one of the approaches and removing the bags from the bicycle, 45 minutes elapsed before I was able to obtain a lift on a truck.

A swift crossing of the bridge followed. I was deposited on University Avenue, convenient for the nearby Berkeley campus of the University of California. Berkeley was receiving world attention at this time due to vociferous political activity by many of the students. Approaching the campus I met a recent emigrant from London who told me I had missed a good demonstration the day before, during which eight men burned their draft cards, two of them students at the University. There was much publicity in the newspapers in connection with plans to have an anti-draft "teach-in" on the campus three days later, and to attempt to block entrance to the Oakland Induction Centre the next day.

The Berkeley campus had some attractive buildings to see, with the site dominated by the 307 ft tall Sather Tower, popularly known as the Campanile. It was modelled on the Campanile of St. Marks in Venice. Ascending the Tower gave some fine views over the campus and allowed me to see the carillon of 12 bronze bells which had been cast in Loughborough in 1915. There was an extraordinary atmosphere on the campus at midday when classes stopped for lunch and thousands of students milled everywhere.

Early in the afternoon I left the campus to continue south through Oakland. A lift over the San Mateo Bridge brought me to Belmont to visit Burt, a former employee of English Electric, the company I had left in England. I had first visited Burt in Vancouver during the previous winter, and he moved south to San Francisco before I left Canada. I had spent an evening with him a few days before, Burt and his family welcoming me again so warmly. Now it was time for Burt to take me into the city to sample some culture. The first show was hilarious, featuring a number of female impersonators; this was followed by a visit to one of the topless shows, featuring topless girls dancing on the tables, topless waitresses and a topless fashion show.

After this improvement to my education, it was a relief to return to the countryside. I headed out from Belmont to Half Moon Bay on the Pacific coast to continue the ride down Highway 1. It was the middle of October and the weather was still extremely hot. Around Santa Cruz I cycled past enormous fields of Brussels sprouts, before reaching Watsonville, the "Apple City", and Castroville, the "Artichoke Capital of the World". Camping one evening near Seaside, the lights of Monterey appeared in the distance as the sun went down.

Monterey served in succession as the capital of Spanish, Mexican and American California. Historic buildings from each period were spread over the town. On Fisherman's Wharf I saw the home of the sardine fishing fleet, and cycled up Cannery Row immortalized by John Steinbeck in his novel of the same name. Following the 17 mile Drive round the Monterey Peninsula, there were scenes of sandy beaches and wind-swept cypresses; just off the beaches, surfers rode towards the shore in an unrivalled location. The Drive brought me to Carmel, a resort town and artists' colony, and the location of the Mission San Carlos Borremeo del Rio Carmelo.

It was the second in a chain of 21 Missions stretching along the California coast from San Diego to San Francisco, and was the favourite of Father Junipero Serra who founded the Mission chain in San Diego in 1769. The chain was built over a period of 54 years to minister to the Indian tribes in California, and to serve as a buffer against advancement from the north of British, French and Russian explorers and land-seekers. History was to result in all of this area falling to America, but there was the lasting legacy of the Spanish style Mission buildings, which I found very attractive.

The Monterey Peninsula divided the coastal scenery dramatically. To the north the land sloped gently to the sea: to the south was the Big Sur coast, containing some of the most spectacular coastal scenery in America. The terrain was rugged and the road was like a roller coaster, going up and down continuously. The gradient was so steep at times that I had difficulty in keeping the front wheel of the bicycle in contact with the ground as I pulled on the handlebar in reaction to pushing down on the pedals. I remained in bottom gear for long periods; as I swept down to the next valley there would be just a short time before the next steep gradient upwards commenced. I expected to climb in the Rocky Mountains, but the Big Sur coast took me by surprise. The views were at times spectacular.

The scenery changed abruptly as I entered San Luis Obispo County. The hills receded from the shore, leaving an area of gently rolling meadow-land, and progress was easier. There was a succession of Spanish Missions to visit, including San Luis Obispo, founded in 1772, La Purisma Concepcion (1787), Santa Ines (1804) and Santa Barbara (1786). The latter was the only one remaining under the control of the Franciscan Fathers. All the others were abandoned following Mexican independence from Spain in 1821, and the new Government's decision not only to stop supporting the Missions but to secularize them. They fell into decay but have been restored, providing a lasting reminder of a rich period of history.

I turned inland slightly as I left Santa Barbara to take the quieter roads towards Los Angeles. Huge lemon and orange groves were all around me near Ojai and Fillmore, before my route zigzagged south-westwards through Moorpark and Chatsworth. After a long climb to Woodland Hills, the road swept down Topanga Canyon to the coast. Santa Monica was just a few miles away, where I called on Alvin, whom I had met in Yosemite National Park in May. He was a cyclist and invited me to stay the night.

I looked forward to renewing another contact the next day. Malcolm, a fellow passenger on the *s.s. Bristol City* to New York, was at the University of California at Los Angeles a few miles away. It was a delight to see him again, to meet his wife and daughter, and to find that his research work had gone well. He was coming to the end of his assignment and was about to return to England. After lunch on the campus, I left him for a time to cycle through Beverly Hills and Hollywood nearby, and to visit Sid Grauman's Chinese Theatre, to gaze at the foot and hand prints in the concrete paving stones of so many famous stars.

After a visit the following day to the Hollywood Bowl and a tour of Universal Studios, I headed south to Long Beach through a vast built-up area. I wasn't enjoying things very much; for several days since approaching Los Angeles my eyes had been stinging with the smog in the air. Thankfully it cleared a little the next day when I cycled a few miles to Anaheim, where I spent an enchanting day at Disneyland.

It was just two days easy riding to San Diego, my destination for the winter. I stopped at the northern end at La Jolla, hoping to see Dr. Clifford Graves, one of America's most well known cyclists. President of the International Bicycle Touring Society, this surgeon was a testament to the health-promoting virtues of cycling, and had cycled in many countries. Dr. Graves was at work, but I was able to speak to his secretary for some time.

I continued towards the centre of San Diego. I felt it would be a good place to spend the winter. It was now the end of October, and I had completed 8,600 miles in seven months from April. It had been an even longer stage than the first one across the continent. San Diego was a big naval port, but it was also an historical city. In 1542 Juan Rodriquez Cabrillo, a Portuguese navigator in the service of Spain, discovered the California coast and claimed all of what is now California for Spain. I went out to the Cabrillo National Monument at Point Loma at the southern tip of a promontory to the west of San Diego Bay to learn more about the history of this period. San Diego was of course the location of the first of the chain of Spanish Missions up the California coast, and there was much history to see in Old San Diego several miles west of this location. Close to the city centre was Balboa Park, which I went up to on many Sunday afternoons to hear the concert on the Spreckels Outdoor Organ, the world's largest.

*****

The primary reason for being in San Diego was to earn some money. I settled down to conventional work after getting my suit sent on from Vancouver, quickly securing a post with a building services consultant, thus continuing with the same kind of work as in Vancouver the previous winter. But I wasn't able to settle down as long as I had hoped, as I now got caught up in problems with the draft. I looked back over a sequence of steps and the circumstances which brought various matters to a head.

In order to be able to work in America I had to satisfy the requirements of an emigrant. This imposed an obligation to register for the draft after six months in the country. I had done this while in Santa Fe, giving the address of family relations in Oregon as a mailing address. I arrived there to find mail awaiting my attention. But as far as the system was concerned, this mail should have been attended to earlier, and I was judged to have deliberately flouted the rules. This was a curious judgment since I had attempted at every stage to find out everything I ought to know, and I had not been advised of any time restriction for dealing with mail. By breaking a rule I could be drafted up to my 35th birthday, not the 26th as previously, and which I had passed.

I appealed on a matter of principle. How could I have deliberately broken a rule which they had declined to tell me about? I expected my appeal to be upheld, but I got nowhere. I could consider the response to my special circumstances to be heavy-handed, but there was a hardening of official attitudes around this time as public servants attempted to administer the Selective Service System in the face of the most massive opposition throughout the country to America's involvement in Vietnam and growing questioning of the moral justification for being there. It would culminate in President Johnson announcing to the nation on 31 March 1968 that he would not seek a second elected term in the White House.

Whatever the rights and wrongs of the situation, I was in a mess: the main question was how to extricate myself from it. I was conscious of being just a small pawn on a very large chessboard; but I didn't need to continue playing the game. With my travelling in America completed, I planned to remain only a few months longer before starting the next stage of my journey. If I wasn't going to be able to continue working, there was no point in staying at all. I had no intention of getting involved in America's conflict in Vietnam. As time started to run out, a contingency plan conceived a long time before for such an event was put into action. I stopped work and travelled up to Canada by coach, sending the bicycle ahead as freight. The tour could be continued from there as soon as arrangements could be finalised.

I resolved not to let the episode damage the feelings of enormous admiration which I had for America as I looked back on 11,000 miles of cycling in the U.S.A. during the summers of 1966 and 1967. As I left the country towards the end of January 1968, I recalled the words of Abraham Lincoln as he departed from Springfield, Illinois, in February 1861 for the White House: "I bid you an affectionate farewell."

JAPAN

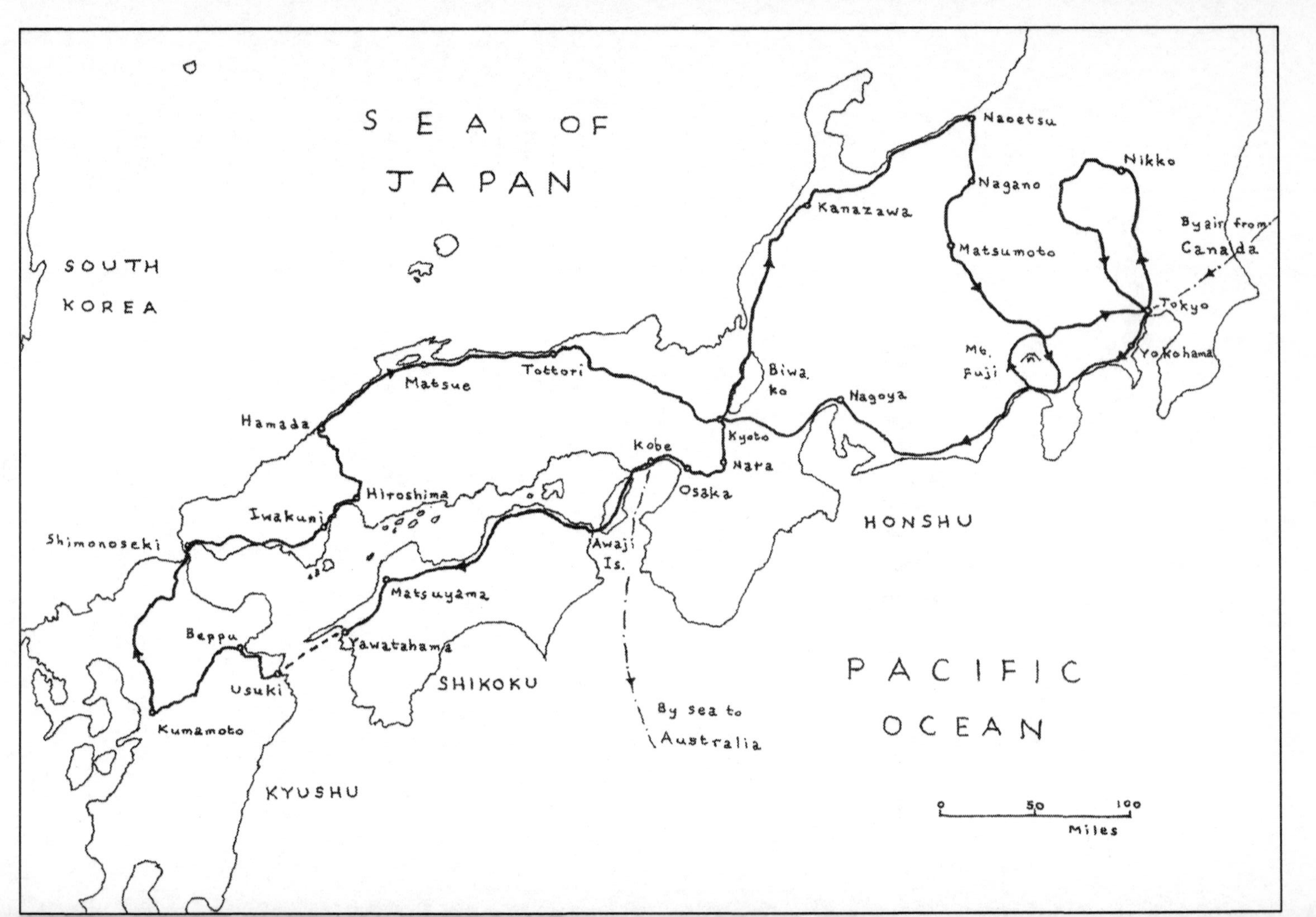
SEA OF JAPAN
SOUTH KOREA
Naoetsu
Nikko
Nagano
Kanazawa
By air from Canada
Matsumoto
Tokyo
Mt. Fuji
Yokohama
Tottori
Matsue
Biwa ko
Nagoya
Hamada
Kyoto
Kobe
Nara
Osaka
Hiroshima
Iwakuni
HONSHU
Shimonoseki
Awaji Is.
Matsuyama
Beppu
Yawatahama
Usuki
SHIKOKU
PACIFIC OCEAN
By sea to Australia
Kumamoto
KYUSHU
0
50
100
Miles

Chapter 13

To the Capitals

Tuesday, 9 April 1968

It was a glorious day in Vancouver as I left the city for a second time, to fly to Japan to start the next stage of my journey. It had taken longer than expected to finalise arrangements, but I was finally under way as the plane took off just after 2pm for a 10 hour flight to Tokyo. However, it would not be midnight when I arrived in the Japanese capital but 5pm the following day with Tokyo 17 hours ahead of Vancouver. It was all very confusing as I made my first flight, crossing the International Date Line in mid-journey; Tokyo would otherwise have been 7 hours behind Vancouver. We followed the afternoon sun as the plane, a McDonnell Douglas DC-8, effectively flew just a little slower than the speed of the earth's rotation. It was thus a long afternoon as the plane flew on a northern arc over the Queen Charlotte Islands and then the Aleutian Islands. With considerable breaks in the clouds, I regretted that my camera was in one of my bags in the baggage hold as I looked down from my window seat on scenes of mountain ranges, valleys, meandering rivers, forests and lakes.

The bicycle was also in the baggage hold, dismantled and enclosed in a cardboard box obtained from a cycle shop. I had hoped to make the journey much more slowly, and a few weeks earlier had looked down from higher ground in Vancouver on a number of Japanese ships in the harbour, pondering the possibility of a working passage across the Pacific. But even if I had been able to approach the ships, there was the major problem of language. How could I make contact with any ship captain to discuss my wishes when I didn't speak a word of his language? I resigned myself to flying, conscious that the problem of language was going to be a very real one during the coming months as I was expecting to travel outside the familiar tourist locations.

More immediate problems had to be considered as the plane descended to Tokyo International Airport at 5.45pm, a little later than scheduled due to strong winds in the upper atmosphere. The bicycle was retrieved with little delay and assembled outside the airport building, watched by a fascinated group of onlookers. One of the airport staff took away the redundant cardboard box, and I set off for Ichigaya youth hostel in the centre of Tokyo at 8pm on the first tentative miles of cycling in Japan. The route between the airport and centre of any major city is always going to be a challenging journey, this one more than most as mile after mile of the road resembled a construction site. Large steel plates formed a temporary road surface. Somehow I navigated the 19 miles to the hostel, arriving late in the evening to find it swarming with foreigners, young Englishmen, Germans, Swiss, Canadians and Americans. Those from Europe had invariably hitch-hiked through Europe and Asia, reaching Japan by ship from Southeast Asia.

I set about getting to know the huge city. I had to slow down to take in so many new images, so many sights different to anything previously encountered. I must commit to memory the sight of many women in kimonos; the many styles of geta or footwear worn with the kimono; mothers carrying their babies in a harness on their back; the sight of a significant number of people wearing small facial masks to filter the air; and the refreshing sight of so many bicycles on the streets. I marvelled at the enormous loads carried on wide, sturdy carriers: my baggage no longer looked quite so exceptional.

I wasn't concerned at this stage with seeing all the sights of the city, as I would be returning after an excursion into the countryside. With a visa for 60 days, I made inquiries about a boat passage to Australia early in June, and scoured the bookshops for the best maps available which showed place names in Roman letters in addition to Japanese characters. I was fortunate to find a series at a scale of 1:250,000, or just under 4 miles to the inch; 4 maps purchased would be invaluable throughout my travels, supplemented by a comprehensive official guide by the National Tourist Organisation, and a series of booklets obtained in Vancouver.

The sun rose in a bright blue sky on my third morning in Tokyo, following two dull, rainy days, and I felt compelled to leave the city. I knew that I shouldn't delay any longer than necessary if I wanted to see as much as possible of the major attraction of the countryside during spring, the cherry blossom. It appeared first in the southernmost islands in March, advancing northwards with the warmer weather to come out in Hokkaido in May. There was a good chance of me seeing at least some of this as I travelled in the opposite direction towards the historical cities of Kyoto and Nara.

I had made a valuable contact a few weeks earlier in Vancouver, meeting a Canadian architect who had been lecturing at the University of South Australia in Adelaide. He had travelled through the south of Japan on his way home, and the slides he showed me of the historical buildings in Kyoto convinced me that this city had to be incorporated in my travels. Unfortunately, the area between Tokyo and Kyoto was the most densely populated part of a densely populated country, but I was determined to make the journey once. The first part of the journey to Yokohama was an excellent baptism, probably as interesting as any journey between two large industrial centres 20 miles apart! The roar of the traffic was deafening, and it seemed that the whole of Tokyo and Yokohama were on the move.

A few miles out of Yokohama I saw my first countryside. Crossing the Miura Peninsula, I reached the coast road south of Fujisawa and followed the road westwards beside sandy beaches. It was a Sunday morning, and the road and the beaches were crowded with weekend vacationers. There was the heart-warming sight of dozens of cyclists on the road, both male and female. I generally had my eyes focused into the distance, trying to penetrate the haze for a clearer view of the snow-capped cone of Mt. Fuji. At Odawara I climbed into the Hakone hills, being rewarded by the glorious sight of many cherry trees by the roadside in full blossom. After a short descent to Lake Ashi, there was a fine view across the lake of the sacred mountain 20 miles away. Leaving the lake shore, the road climbed to a summit of 2,870 ft before starting a long descent to the coast to complete the journey across the Izu Peninsula. On the sweep down between rolling hills, with many more cherry trees by the roadside in full blossom, I had a first glimpse of the intensive cultivation of many hillsides.

Flat land was at a premium. This basic fact of the geography became all too evident as I continued westwards. The terrain was generally so mountainous that there was just one road, following the coast closely. There was an unrelenting battle with the traffic as I cycled along this narrow strip, seeming to be forever going through large towns and cities. One feature of the road construction was disconcerting; I looked down frequently on an open, rectangular, concrete rainwater channel at the road edge. If I rode too close to it, there was a danger of veering into it, and a sudden vertical drop would do neither myself nor the bicycle any good. If I rode some distance away from the channel, there was a danger of being mown down from behind by car drivers, an alarming number of whom seemed to have been taught to drive as fast as possible at all times. Yet the control seemed to be there, and I never saw an accident.

There were interesting stretches of countryside between the towns and cities, including orange trees on the hillsides around Yui, and large fields of mulberry bushes around Toyohashi, a large silk and cotton textile manufacturing centre. Progress was punctuated at intervals by one of the bullet trains of the New Tokaido Line streaking past; I never seemed to have time to stop and get my camera out for a photograph.

My first choice for accommodation at the end of each day's travel was the youth hostels. There were over 500 of them, all established since 1951, and I left Tokyo with a copy of the latest handbook listing information on every hostel, including location details. The information was in both Japanese characters and Roman letters. If I ever became stuck in interpreting the information - which meant frequently - an approach to any local person invariably resulted in a sympathetic response. If the person was a student, an unexpected opportunity suddenly presented itself to practice a few words of English. If the student was on a bicycle, he or she often cycled with me towards the hostel as a way of guiding me on a route difficult to describe. I welcomed these opportunities for personal contact, brief though some of them were, as I realised I was not going to get beyond learning a few words and sentences in Japanese during my stay. I felt these interactions were mutually beneficial as the students in particular were suddenly confronted with a chance to try out their English. It was happening, as well, to students who might rarely meet a Westerner; not many Western cyclists travelled the route I was on.

The hostels varied considerably, and I was never quite sure what I was going to find. Just a few were purpose built, resembling the hostels in western countries; for the benefit of foreigners, they might incorporate very small rooms marked "Western Style." A hostel was more frequently a private house, a Japanese inn or ryokan, a temple or a shrine; I then lived Japanese-style. I tried to remember to remove my shoes at the entrance, and to change slippers upon entering and leaving the smallest rooms. Forgetting this on one occasion the sternest of looks received from the houseparent meant that I never forgot again. I concluded early that I was not constructed to sit cross-legged on the floor in comfort for any length of time. At night the bed would be laid out on the tatami mats on the floor; for the Westerner who finds the mattress a little hard, the secret is to use two, if available. I was introduced to the Japanese method of bathing, and to so many other things which constituted the Japanese way of life. It was all an interesting and refreshing change to Western living.

I remembered in particular the hostel at Fukuroi near Hamamatsu. It seemed to be a temple or meditation centre, and there was an extraordinary air of calm throughout the building. I saw few people there, but those I encountered appeared at peace with the world, and seemed to know exactly where they were going. I don't know what they made of people like myself rushing round the world.

The food at all the hostels was invariably Japanese, and I found myself eating many things the identity of which remained a complete mystery. Rice was the staple food with every meal, to be eaten with chopsticks. Initially, in Tokyo, it took me twice as long to eat a meal as any of the Japanese around me, and I was determined to lower the ratio before departure. Somehow, whatever was consumed, the necessary nutrition was obtained for the next day's journey.

If I ended a day far from a hostel, the plan was to camp. However, wanting to camp and being able to were two quite different matters. The search for a small, flat piece of ground sometimes became almost an obsession. If I saw a piece of uncultivated ground, it was invariably very rough and unsuitable for anything. In other countries you would be able to find a spot in the corner of a field, but you cannot camp in the corner of a rice paddy! There were countless little grocery stores for buying items of food for camping and for picnic lunches. Bread was sometimes available in packets of a few slices, and a range of groceries was available in many stores. Some delicious cakes were available, but some had to be turned down after considering how to carry them in my bags. The location of a store along the road was often heralded by a large sign on the side of the building exhorting one to "Drink Coca-Cola".

It was fascinating to see an abacus used for totalling a bill, and the simplest way to convey the total to me was to show me the arrangement on the abacus. It was useful in the stores to know numbers, and I familiarised myself with the system after getting a student to write translations in my notebook. Other students were prevailed upon to write down various key words and phrases to supplement what I had in a phrase book.

By the time I reached Kyoto a week after leaving Tokyo, I felt well immersed in the Japanese way of life. Kyoto was the capital from 794 to 1868, when it lost the position to Tokyo. You could spend many days here, visiting the large number of imposing shrines and temples attesting to the glory and splendour of earlier days, and presenting some of the finest examples of Buddhist architecture. The settings of the buildings were often as important as the buildings themselves. I had to see the Kinkakuji Temple, or Gold Pavilion, surrounded by a lake, and the Kiyomizu Temple, with its massive structure leaning over a steep tree-clad hillside. By contrast there was the 5-storey pagoda of Toji Temple, and the rock garden at Ryoanji Temple, considered a masterpiece.

I had the fortune of being in Kyoto when the cherry blossom was at its height. Some of the finest blossom was to be seen in the gardens surrounding the Old Imperial Palace, and there was always the possibility in this historical environment of seeing some Japanese girls in kimonos, a most delightful sight. Walking in the grounds of Nijo Castle close to the Old Imperial Palace, I approached two Westerners, so meeting a young Swiss cyclist, Kurt, whom I had been told about in Tokyo. Kurt was following a different route to myself, and we had much to discuss. I met another Swiss cyclist at the youth hostel, or rather a one-time cyclist who had sold his bicycle in Iran on the way to India; he had found the cycling too hard, a judgment that I personally found difficult to accept! Two English girls were also at the hostel, travelling on one year air tickets and having just spent six months in Sydney. I learned from other hostellers of an intriguing return route to Western Europe, the Trans-Siberian Express from Nahodka. The youth hostels were wonderful information exchanges.

With its wealth of history, Kyoto was nevertheless a large, noisy city, and I much preferred the little town of Nara 30 miles south. It preceded Kyoto as the Japanese capital, holding the position from 710 to 784. It was the first permanent capital, as before 710 it had been customary to change the seat of government on a change of ruler. The view of the 5-storey pagoda of Kofukuji Temple across Sarusawa Pond was, for me, one of the most beautiful scenes I saw during my stay in Japan, and seeming to embody so many of the elements which I associated with the country. It was impossible to forget the largest bronze statue of Buddha in Japan in the Todaiji Temple, and the astonishing sight of 800 or so tame deer in Nara Park, right in the heart of the town. Everywhere swarmed with parties of young school children, and I guessed that Nara was considered a much more suitable location for such groups than Kyoto.

I battled my way through Osaka, Japan's second largest city 20 miles to the west, and on through a continuously built-up area to Kobe. At the offices of the shipping company, I confirmed my passage by passenger-carrying freighter to Australia in June, but departure from Yokohama was now scheduled for 13 June, a number of days later than planned earlier. The built-up area continued for several miles west from the centre of Kobe. Soon the houses lessened, the road ran beside the water, and small fishing boats were numerous. At Akashi I had an opportunity to leave the mainland and headed for the ferry terminal. I was dismayed to learn that the ferry to Awaji Island took cars, lorries and pedestrians, but not cyclists. The problem was solved by a sympathetic lorry driver gesturing to me to lift the bicycle onto the back of his lorry.

The ferry took just 25 minutes to cover the 4 miles to the little fishing village of Awaji. I seemed to enter another world as I left behind a thick smog over Kobe, to look up at blue sky. I had also escaped from the traffic, and enjoyed a quiet, peaceful atmosphere as I cycled down the east coast to Sumoto. Fishing boats chugged along off the coast, and on the land many people were busy in the fields. The whole area seemed to be a giant market garden, with vegetables of all kinds being grown. At Sumoto I turned inland to cross the island to the south-west corner, travelling in a broad valley which was intensively cultivated. After staying overnight at the youth hostel at Fukura, I left early in the morning for the ferry terminal nearby. But neither the passenger nor vehicle ferries to Shikoku Island were running because of fog, and I could only wonder how long everything would be delayed. While we all waited a young Japanese girl came to my aid, informing me that the passenger ferry was more likely to leave first, and I could take the bicycle on this ferry. As the sun rose higher the fog cleared and I was soon on my way on the 8-

mile 50 minute crossing to Naruto. (Update: In April 1998 a new suspension bridge was opened to traffic between Akashi and Awaji to complete a chain of bridges and tunnels connecting the main islands. The peace I found on Awaji Island was probably lost forever!)

As I started a journey along the north coast of Shikoku, the smallest of the four main islands, I soon had my shorts on as the temperature rose. The road sometimes ran beside the water's edge, sometimes inland with intensively cultivated land all around me. There was the pleasant sight of girls riding side-saddle on the carriers of boyfriends' bicycles, and they seemed to balance easily. During the afternoon I had just passed one such couple when a group of policemen was encountered who were checking motorcycles. A long finger was pointed past me, prelude to a ticking-off for the act of chivalry. When I looked back the couple were moving again - walking! The weather deteriorated as I approached Takamatsu, and I was glad to reach the youth hostel to escape the rain.

I met more cyclists two days later as I took a direct route towards Matsuyama. I was suddenly overtaken by a group, followed by a second group. Three rode beside me, telling me they were from Ehime University Cycling Club in Matsuyama, the latter being the capital of Ehime Prefecture and location of the University. There were some twenty of them altogether, including eight female students, enjoying a National Holiday as it was 29 April, Emperor Hirohito's birthday. I was invited to share their picnic lunch, and found that between them they carried stoves, fuel and water for boiling rice. While the female students prepared the meal, the rest of the party practised their English, having many questions to ask me about England. I set off again before them, knowing they would soon catch me up as I started on a long gradual climb over the hills before dropping down to Matsuyama. They did so, but I met them all again at the summit as they stopped to deal with a puncture on one bicycle.

As I approached Matsuyama, I started seeing the Japanese flag outside homes in honour of the Emperor's birthday. One of the University cyclists turned up as I arrived at the youth hostel to invite me to go with him in the evening to the public baths nearby. This was an interesting experience which I would not otherwise have had, finding myself with some 40 men and boys all bathing together. Our clothes were looked after by a number of women, who surveyed the surroundings with an apparent air of boredom. It was a noteworthy day in one further respect as a car turned up at the hostel, and I met again two Londoners, Peter and Nigel, and a German, Heinz, whom I had met at the hostel in Tokyo. A French Canadian, Bernard, from Montreal filled the fourth space in the car.

On this special day I was reminded that my youth hostel card alluded to the Emperor on every date stamp. Today's stamp for 29 April 1968 read "43.4.29", the first part indicating that 1968 was the 43rd year of Emperor Hirohito's reign. I wondered how widespread this practice was with date stamps - and how much confusion had been caused over the years.

From Matsuyama south-west to the ferry terminal at Yawatahama I had my first long ride in Japan on an unpaved road. As it wound its way over the hills, I looked down from the higher ground on a patchwork of fields which continued up the hillsides in terraces. After camping outside the town I went along to the ferry terminal at 8.15 to find that the ferry had left at 7.30. With the next sailing at midday, I took a slow walk round the shops, and attempted unsuccessfully to solve a looming financial crisis. Being almost out of money, I needed to cash a traveller's cheque, but it quickly became clear that this service was not available in the smaller towns. I had somehow to manage for one more day until I reached the larger centre of Beppu on the island of Kyushu.

The 44 mile ferry crossing to Usuki was smooth, taking three and a quarter hours. When I camped after 20 miles, there wasn't the previous difficulty of finding a suitable spot as the land opened out, and I started to see terrain quite different to anything previously encountered in Japan. Leaving the hot spring resort of Beppu, the road began a long steep climb to cross Aso National Park, containing Mt. Aso, the world's largest active volcano, and last active in 1965. For about 50 miles a fine toll road wound its way over the mountains at an elevation of 3,000 ft and above. It was unusual to see so many almost bare hillsides, clad only with grass. I looked down from the high ground on a patchwork of fields and what seemed to be hundreds of miniature houses before making an abrupt descent to the Aso valley and on to Kumamoto.

Stopping at a cycle shop in the city to seek directions to one of the hostels there, the proprietor's daughter kindly offered to accompany me on her bicycle as it was some distance away. Her father suddenly appeared after half a mile, and led the way to the hostel door. I would not quickly forget gestures like this. I was meeting touring cyclists almost every day now, and also racing cyclists on lightweight machines, with heads down invariably protected by crash helmets. It was in fact a major holiday week, the "Golden Week", containing three National Holidays including the Emperor's birthday on Monday when I reached Matsuyama. Today, Friday, was Constitution Memorial Day and on Sunday it would be Children's Day.

The schedule I had worked out was not going to allow me to travel further south on Kyushu, and I turned north through gently rolling country, travelling through a vast market garden with communities at regular intervals. The second day after leaving Kumamoto I found myself in a built-up area, and realised that I was in the suburbs of Kitakyushu. Heading for the tunnel crossing of the Kammon Straits, it was fascinating to find two tunnels, an upper one for cars, buses and trucks, and a lower, smaller one for cyclists and pedestrians. Emerging from the tunnel the youth hostel at Shimonoseki was visible on the hillside overlooking the Straits. I had come to the end of the first stage of my travels in Japan, having covered just under 1,000 miles during the previous four weeks. From the western extremity of the mainland of Honshu I now needed to return to Tokyo.

Chapter 14

Country Return

Monday, 6 May 1968

The plan was to return to Tokyo via the north coast of Honshu, but there were a few places to see in the south-west before crossing the island. I hoped for a rapid improvement in the weather as it rained throughout the afternoon on the first day back on the mainland. There was an unexpected event during the evening at the youth hostel at Yamaguchi when a knock on the door heralded the arrival of the two Londoners, the German and the Canadian whom I had met at Matsuyama a week before. They had travelled in their hire car on a similar route to myself, but had spent two days in Nagasaki.

A dry day followed as I turned inland near Tokuyama to cross a small bulge in the coastline, climbing gradually most of the morning before descending to the Nishiki River. Following the river downstream a few miles towards the coast brought me to the Kintai Bridge, where I gazed in wonder at the five graceful arches. The bridge I was looking at was, in fact, relatively new, dating from a faithful rebuilding in 1953 to the exact original shape. Three years before, the original bridge of 1673 had been washed away in a flood. The houseparent at the youth hostel nearby made sure I would not forget my stay there by stamping my card with three different stamps featuring the famous bridge.

It was just a few miles to the island of Miyajima just off the coast, the scenic location of the Itsukushima Shrine thought to date from the Seventh Century. When the tide was in, the vermilion lacquered shrine buildings and massive torii appeared to float on the water, creating a magical effect. I spent a morning there before proceeding a few more miles to Hiroshima, feeling somewhat apprehensive about the reception I would get as a Western visitor. But I need not have worried; all visitors seemed to be welcome. A vast park covered much of the former central area, and the grim scenes in the Peace Memorial Museum put everyone in a sombre mood as they reflected on the events and aftermath of the dropping of the atomic bomb on 6 August 1945. As I looked round at the parties of school children, I wondered what they, in particular, were being taught about the history of the period.

Contrasting scenes were provided in the Shukkeien Garden, one of the most attractive landscape gardens in Japan, and first laid out early in the Seventeenth Century. I met a number of Westerners at the youth hostel north of the city, including an interesting Swede seeing something of the world before going to University to train as a doctor. He had travelled through Asia, with visits to Thailand, Cambodia, Taiwan, South Korea and Japan, planning to return to Scandinavia on the Trans-Siberian Express. He told me his father had paid all his costs, having enjoyed a period of travel himself as a young man and wanting his son to have a similar experience before committing himself to his career. I could only concur with the spirit behind this arrangement.

Heading inland as I left Hiroshima, most of the traffic was left behind at Kabe as I turned north-westwards to meet the north coast at Hamada. The road followed closely the Ota River as it wound its way in a number of great loops between high green hills, giving me some of my most enjoyable travelling so far in Japan. Everywhere was so green. With every bend of the river another memorable view appeared, but I had to keep looking at the road as the surface changed to gravel for most of the journey across the mountains.

At least the weather remained dry until after I had reached the coast and was once more on a paved road. A price had to be paid for all the greenness around me. The weather was all I expected it to be, and hoped it would not be. Every three or four days since I had arrived in Japan, I had to unpack my waterproof clothing. But didn't I recall telling so many people that cycling in the rain was an exhilarating experience? My views were sorely tested many times.

The abundant water supply meant that the farmers had no problem filling their rice paddies, and I found myself travelling along the Japan Sea coast at a most interesting time. It was the middle of May and everywhere transplanting of rice seedlings was proceeding at full speed. There was not the variety in the agriculture previously encountered, and nearly all the flat land was given over to the growing of rice. The rich green rectangular strips of young rice seedlings were slowly disappearing as women gathered the seedlings into small bundles. It was fascinating to see the different methods employed to transplant the seedlings in straight rows in the paddies. A particular frame design seen in one area would not be seen a few miles away. All the transplanting which I saw was being done by women, with a man pulling the frame behind them; and everybody was knee deep in mud. I wondered if mechanisation would come to everyone's aid before many more years and eliminate most of this back-breaking work, and inevitable problems such as rheumatism.

On the journey along the coast rice planting scenes interspersed with views of the Japan Sea and of fishing villages. With traffic so light, there was time to take in all the images around me. Near Tottori I turned inland to make a second visit to Kyoto, climbing over hills initially before the road followed a number of river valleys. There were more rice planting scenes, and I started seeing some of the very large thatched farmhouses characteristic of central Honshu.

The return to Kyoto enabled me to attend a programme presented at one of the theatres on the traditional Japanese arts. The programme comprised the tea ceremony, flower arrangement, court music, Japanese-style dance and puppet play. This introduction to some of the Japanese arts was beautifully presented, and made me realise how different Eastern and Western cultures were. I was glad to have had this experience, having regretted not staying longer in Kyoto the first time in my eagerness to get away from the mostly densely populated region of Japan.

The second visit enabled me to see some of the historic temples again before returning towards the Japan Sea coast, cycling beside the western shore of Lake Biwa, easily the largest lake in the country. Each day's travel for the next few days was arranged to fit in with a string of youth hostels about 50 miles apart. This was convenient as I had to contend with a considerable amount of rain, far from ideal conditions for camping, and I seemed to ride for hours with my cape on. Rice transplanting continued regardless of the weather as the coastal route took me through a wide, flat band of land which was given over almost exclusively to the growing of rice.

Contrasting scenes were provided at Kanazawa. After staying at the youth hostel there, I delayed my departure from the town by going for a walk in Kenrokuen Park, considered one of the most beautiful landscape gardens in Japan. Built in 1819 by Lord Maeda, a daimyo or noble at the time, it covered a huge area. After these refreshing scenes it was back to the rice paddies. I was able to get off the main road for several stretches, but the price for a quieter route through this area with a considerable population was a gravel road. The roads came together near Asahi as a range of hills suddenly loomed up. The one road hugged the coast and climbed up the hillside, reminding me of California's Big Sur. After several miles conditions became easier, but there was little flat ground and the road often ran close to the water, taking me past a number of fishing villages.

At Naoetsu I left the coast for the last time, turning south to return towards Tokyo. The land sloped upwards almost imperceptibly at first, the gradient then increasing to give me some sweeping views over the surrounding terrain. I was travelling through a major skiing area, and snow was visible on the higher hills. After a number of days of poor weather, the sun rose in an almost cloudless sky as I left the youth hostel at Lake Nojiri. Stopping often to admire the views, there was a long descent to the Nagano Valley. The rice paddies were suddenly left behind as I entered an apple growing area.

There was a choice of routes southwards from Nagano; the one south-westwards towards Matsumoto took me up a winding river valley on a most peaceful journey. A number of dams built for power generation resulted in some superb reflections in the still waters which backed up behind them. A few miles south of Matsumoto I climbed steadily to the Shiojiri Pass at 3,276 ft. On the way up there were memorable views due to vivid splashes of red from japonica bushes on the hillsides, contrasting with the view of Okaya and Lake Suwa from the top of the Pass which was marred by a haze. After sweeping down to Okaya, the road started to climb again almost directly to cross a line of hills on the route south-eastwards.

After climbing for several miles, a long gradual descent began to Kofu. I suddenly found myself with unexpected company in the form of a young female University graduate from Kofu. She had only recently completed a degree in English literature at Tokyo University, and was enjoyable company as she rode beside me on a new bicycle; she was just leaving a café as I ambled past and quickly caught up with me after seeing my flag. Stopping for drinks and ice-cream a few miles from Kofu, she phoned her mother with the result that I was taken home to be treated to some Japanese delicacies, biscuits and tea. As with all meetings of this nature, the element of surprise and the warmth communicated meant that I would remember this Sunday morning for a very long time. I could not expect encounters like this due to the problem of language, and the approach by a young woman signalled that education would allow the diffidence of an earlier generation to be set aside.

As we departed I began a long steep climb to the Misaka Pass. The top of the Pass was shrouded in cloud, but a new tunnel almost two miles long meant that I didn't need to climb into the cloud. Near the entrance to the tunnel were roadside stands with burners selling corn on the cob. The stands which seemed to do the most business were staffed by the prettiest girls; it was the same all over the world!

The sky was dark on the south side of the mountain as I descended to Lake Kawaguchi. With Mt. Fuji just to the south, I had entertained high hopes of seeing the celebrated mountain clear of cloud. During the next four days I cycled slowly round the base of the mountain in a clockwise direction, a distance of about 90 miles. I stayed at Gotemba on the east side for a whole day, hoping the cloud would lift. At the youth hostel the warden took two of us staying there outside and angled his hands to show how I would have seen Mt. Fuji if the cloud disappeared. There were glimpses of the full cone as I travelled up the west side, but not the kind of views shown on the postcards. It was probably best not to know how often these ideal conditions occurred.

I set off for Tokyo, which was just a day's travel away. It was the beginning of June. After checking that my boat departure was further delayed from the 13th to the 17th, I arranged an extension to my visa and set off on a brief excursion to the north. The extra days gave me an excellent opportunity to visit one of the most attractive areas in the country, the area around Nikko. There, in a setting of outstanding natural beauty were temples and shrines with a richness of ornamentation and decoration exceeding those anywhere else in the country, even Kyoto.

After what seemed an eternity I left the last suburb of Toyko behind me as I headed directly north. In the countryside I travelled beside many fields of corn, much of it ripe and being harvested. But there were no combine harvesters; the corn was being cut with short sickles and laid on the ground in rows, to be later bundled up by hand into sheaves and secured with string. Japan's rapid strides in industrialisation and introduction of technology had not yet affected this aspect of agriculture any more than it had affected the rice growing areas which I had seen in recent weeks.

At Koga some 40 miles north of the capital I turned off the main road to follow a quieter parallel road to the west. It brought me to the youth hostel at Ohira, but there was the usual penalty for leaving the main roads. There were many miles of gravel road and I stopped at Kanuma to buy a new rear tyre. A few miles north of the town I encountered for the first time the cryptomeria trees which lined the sides of the road on three approaches to Nikko. I stopped for several minutes to take in the story behind these trees, presented on a large sign in both Japanese and English, and the first such sign I had seen in Japan:

> "Nikko Cryptomeria Avenues
>
> These magnificent trees were contributed to the Toshugu Shrine by Masatsuma Matsudaira, one of Daimyos, about 300 years ago, who spent over twenty years in planting saplings along the three highways which are separated at Imaichi about 4 miles away from Nikko. The whole extension of the cryptomeria avenues is estimated about 22 miles long, & the originally planted trees are about 17,000 but nearly 25,000 trees are now standing on the both sides of the roads, including the supplementally planted ones. These trees have been under special protection of the Government."

The small grammatical errors on the sign added to the charm of the area. I wondered, as so many other travellers must have wondered, if the daimyo could have envisioned the scenes which would result as these Japanese cedars grew to maturity. I didn't mind being slowed down by the gravel surface as I moved along a 10 mile avenue of the trees on this enchanting approach to Nikko.

I spent a day walking slowly round the richly decorated temples and shrines, centred on the Toshugu Shrine and dating from early in the Seventeenth Century. The area thronged with visitors, including coach parties of Americans and Australians, and one from India.

Before leaving the youth hostel in the morning to see the sights, I put the new tyre on the rear wheel of the bicycle. The old tyre bought in San Diego had covered 2,300 miles without a puncture, though inspection of the tyre and inner tube revealed an interesting story. Glass or stones had pierced the tyre at a number of places, but not sufficiently to pierce the inner tube, the wall thickness of which was about 3mm, twice the standard thickness. I learned of these tubes for the first time in the desert states of America, the tubes having been produced to deal with the problem of thorns from cacti and other desert plants. How I wished I could purchase these tubes everywhere, but it raised complex questions about the appropriate quality of components for products to produce a replacement market of the size needed to maintain a commercially healthy operation for the manufacturer. The balance between quality and price was far from correct for the long distance cyclist, and I searched continually for higher quality tyres and tubes.

The essential work on the bicycle early in the day had focused my thoughts on some American products. During the evening, while talking to the son of the houseparents at the youth hostel, my attention was drawn to America again. "Do you know Robert Kennedy?" he asked me. After replying that I knew who he was, the son went on to tell me that Robert Kennedy had died today as a result of being shot earlier in Los Angeles. It was 6 June 1968. Just two months earlier another leading figure, Dr. Martin Luther King, had been assassinated. It was difficult to believe, and impossible to contemplate all the consequences for the political life of America.

Nikko was located on the edge of a very mountainous area, as I discovered upon leaving the town to return to Tokyo by a circular route. It involved me in the most incredible journey I made in Japan, in what was meant to be just a brief interlude before departing. A steady climb westwards for six miles brought me to the start of Irohazaka Driveway No.2. A series of 20 hairpin bends took me up to Lake Chuzenji at an altitude of 4,169 ft. While on the climb I not only looked down on the road I had just come up, but also looked across the valley to the older Irohazaka Driveway No.1, which involved 30 hairpin bends and was now used just for the descent. Driveway No.2 was confined to the ascent since its completion in 1965.

After stopping to see the Kegon waterfall, the road followed the north shore of Lake Chuzenji for two miles before climbing to the

Senjo Plain and on to Yumoto. With grey cloud covering the sky and the possibility of rain, I decided not to stay at the youth hostel there, but to buy some groceries and proceed over the Konsei Pass while it was still fine. From the summit at 6,638 ft a long descent began. Several miles of gravel road were encountered, but a new road was being built and it seemed that a paved road would be available for this western approach to Nikko before very long.

I was awoken the next morning by the sun beating down on my tent, one of few times in Japan when this had occurred. The temperature rose quickly as I continued down the valley to a lower elevation. A thick haze quickly developed in the heat, restricting visibility over the plain. I returned towards Tokyo via Numata, Maebashi and Ota. After camping one more night, the early cloud and haze the following day cleared quickly, and I rode into Tokyo in brilliant weather. It had been a fascinating six days away.

There were still several days before my boat sailed, an opportunity to see leisurely the beautiful parks and gardens in Tokyo, the temples and shrines, the museums, the shops and amusement areas, and the glittering lights at night in the Ginza and other amusement areas. Some very attractive kimono-clad girls were seen scurrying to work as hostesses in the bars, and I had to fend off offers to have "Just one drink" and inquiries as to whether "You want nice girl?"

Leaving Tokyo for Yokohama, a circuitous route was followed to keep away from the roaring traffic as much as possible. I left early to be able to spend a day seeing the temples and shrines at Kamakura, omitting this area two months earlier in my eagerness to get away from Tokyo. I was able to stay again at the youth hostel at Fujisawa nearby. The houseparent, a lady, remembered me from my stay two months before on my first overnight away from Tokyo. I had since covered 2,400 miles on the bicycle to bring my cycle tour of Japan to an end; it had been an experience which I would look back on fondly.

*****

My boat, the *s.s. Eastern Star,* looked most impressive as I approached it in Yokohama harbour. It looked as if it had only recently been repainted, and was larger than the boat to America. There were already four passengers on board, one man and three middle-aged ladies from Australia who were making the round trip, seeing something of Japan whenever the boat stopped at a port. I would be meeting other passengers when the boat took on its last cargo at Kobe, but I had arranged with the shipping company to embark at Yokohama. There was no way I wanted to cycle to Kobe a second time.

The boat berthed first at Nagoya as we sailed west, a stop of 36 hours allowing the passengers considerable time to see the city. Apart from stopping one night there on my way to Kyoto two months earlier, I had seen little of the city. Following inquiries about tours, I accompanied two of the ladies on an interesting afternoon visit to the Noritake china factory and the Ando Cloisonne enamel ware factory. The following day we reached Kobe, where we stayed for several days as the boat took on cargo at different times, interspersed with long periods when nothing seemed to be happening at all. I took the train to Nara on one of the days, with the two ladies I had toured Nagoya with, in order to show them the sights of this historic city. Another day was spent a few miles north-east of Kobe at Takarazuka, the location of an all-girl musical revue troupe started in 1914. The high-quality productions at the theatre there had to be seen to be believed.

The boat finally left Kobe on 29 June on a 10 day voyage to Brisbane. There were now five further passengers, including a Canadian couple from Vancouver and two young Japanese, one male and one female. The Japanese girl, Midori, a University student studying languages, proved delightful company. She was on her way to see Australia and New Zealand, having spent three months in America the previous summer. We knew many places in common, and she spoke English well. She was able to tell me so much more about the Japanese attitude to various aspects of life than I could ever have read in a book.

As we sailed southwards the temperature rose and the crew erected a swimming pool on the deck. It was welcomed by all the younger passengers particularly. Land was seen for the first time as we passed by Gaferut Island in the Caroline Islands. A day or so later we crossed the Equator, the event being celebrated by a special Chinese dinner. There was a memorable sunrise as we sailed by Rabaul on New Britain Island to enter the Coral Sea. We were now on the last stretch, heading directly southwards to Brisbane, where I was looking forward to beginning the next stage of my journey.

AUSTRALIA

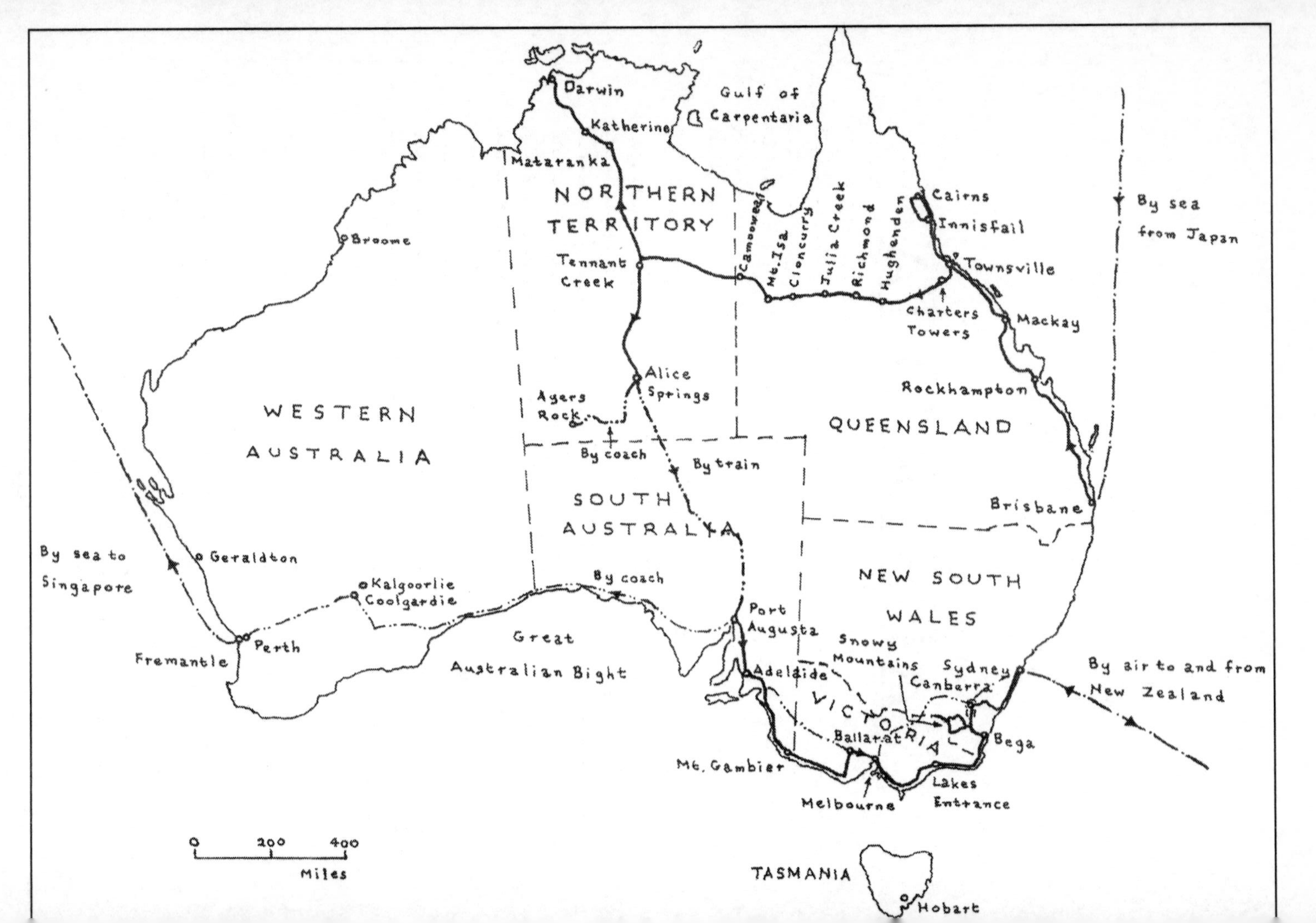

Darwin
Gulf of Carpentaria
Katherine
Mataranka
NORTHERN TERRITORY
Broome
Tennant Creek
Camooweal
Mt. Isa
Cloncurry
Julia Creek
Richmond
Hughenden
Cairns
Innisfail
Townsville
Charters Towers
Mackay
By sea from Japan
Alice Springs
Ayers Rock
By coach
By train
WESTERN AUSTRALIA
QUEENSLAND
Rockhampton
Brisbane
SOUTH AUSTRALIA
By sea to Singapore
Geraldton
Kalgoorlie
Coolgardie
By coach
Perth
Fremantle
Great Australian Bight
Port Augusta
Adelaide
NEW SOUTH WALES
Snowy Mountains
Sydney
Canberra
By air to and from New Zealand
VICTORIA
Ballarat
Bega
Mt. Gambier
Melbourne
Lakes Entrance
0
200
400
Miles
TASMANIA
Hobart

Chapter 15

Up the Bruce Highway

Wednesday, 10 July 1968

The *s.s. Eastern Star* turned into the mouth of the Brisbane River about 6am. There were some fine, clean views of Brisbane as we sailed upstream and it became light. Just before 8 o'clock we berthed at Dalgety's Wharf above New Farm Park, only two miles from the city centre. After clearing Customs and Immigration it was time to say farewell to my fellow passengers; it was just a temporary parting with most of them, as I hoped to see them again when I reached their particular home areas in the south.

I was conscious more than anything at this time that, by arriving in Australia in the middle of winter, it would give me an opportunity to see something of the north and also the interior. Travel in parts of the interior looked viable provided that I could make the most of the cooler conditions during the next three months. All the reading I had done a few months earlier, allied with conversations with a number of valuable contacts made, told me that conditions could be hazardous for cycling in the interior during the middle of the Australian summer. Not only would the temperature be very high, but the distances between communities would pose problems concerning the ability to carry sufficient water.

All these considerations were never very far from my mind as I collected literature on Brisbane and Queensland, and looked for good maps to assist in planning the first part of the route. But there was the city to see before leaving, and I explored the central area, touring the City Hall and ascending its clock tower; there were some fine views over the city from this tall tower. Walking round the Botanic Gardens, the plants reminded me that I was virtually in the Tropics. A cruise 15 miles up the river to the Lone Pine Koala Sanctuary gave me an opportunity to see some of these lovable creatures; there would be few opportunities apparently to see koalas in the wild.

In addition, I had a number of people to visit. The English Electric Company I had left in Stafford had an overseas factory in Brisbane, in the Rocklea district. George had emigrated here before I left in March 1966, Keith shortly afterwards, and Jack a few months later. It was wonderful to see again all these people I had worked with, to see their new environment, and to catch up on news concerning everyone we knew in common. Keith took me round the factory one afternoon, and at the weekend showed me some of the sights around the city.

After the weekend in Brisbane, it was time to start on the journey north up the Bruce Highway. It was 900 miles to Townsville, and 2,500 miles to Darwin, but I was no longer daunted by these long distances. First I posted home all my literature and slides on Japan, lightening my load by 8½ lb; the space in my handlebar bag was needed for a growing collection of literature on Queensland. I was soon out of Brisbane and cycling past eucalyptus, or gum, trees and fields of pineapples. The undulating terrain made for a tiring run; I needed to build up stamina again after doing little cycling for a month. Stopping to buy fruit during the morning, the lady in the shop heaped advice on me. She had lived in Darwin for five years, and told me to be careful in the area because of snakes and wild animals. I was advised to burn a fire at both the front and back of the tent to keep the snakes and animals away.

It had been cool at night in Brisbane, but I was pleased to have a warm night for my first night's camping in Australia. It had resulted from a cloudy sky, which continued throughout the next day as I passed by a number of fields of sugar cane. I camped the next three evenings at Rest Areas constructed by the state's Main Roads Department. It was pleasing to see the large number of such areas, reflecting Queensland's designation as the "Holiday State". Caravans passed me at intervals, their registration plates indicating that some had come from the southern states of New South Wales, Victoria and South Australia. Dull, cloudy weather continued for a couple of days as I continued through undulating terrain, and with a lot of rain falling. There were demonstrations of Australian bush-craft at the Rest Areas, as campers set about lighting camp fires. I watched as petrol was poured onto piles of damp wood, and lighted matches dropped from above!

Approaching Maryborough I met a young motorcyclist, originally from England, and stopped to have a cup of coffee with him and his wife. They were also travelling up the coast, but had taken a cabin for a day in the hope that the weather would improve and to dry out their tent and sleeping bags. I arranged to contact them again at Mt. Isa where they planned to work. The following morning they passed me as the road cut through thick gum forest.

The weather did improve and the sun was shining as the gum forest suddenly ended a few miles south of Childers, and large canefields were all around. The canefields continued a few miles north of the town, when the gum forest reappeared. I was startled by one aspect of the sun as it made its presence felt; I was travelling north, yet the sun was in front of me. I had to get used to being in the southern hemisphere.

Travelling in the middle of winter, the days were relatively short. With darkness falling around 6pm, I needed to stop about 5pm to pitch camp and have a meal before the light faded. As the sun went down in a clear sky, I could look forward to studying the stars of the southern sky. There was an immediate penalty for these conditions as the temperature dropped during the night. The nights were often not as quiet as I expected, as kookaburras let out raucous cries. It started to get light about 6.15am, and for the moment the sun climbed no higher than 45° above the horizon. I could look forward to longer and warmer days.

There were more canefields around Wallaville and Gin Gin. Approaching Gin Gin I spoke to a hitch-hiker from Adelaide who was travelling round Australia in a clockwise direction and finding things difficult along the east coast. He told me that when he left Perth there were ten others trying to get northwards; it took four days for the first ones to obtain a lift. This encounter gave some indication of the number of young people trying to hitch-hike round the country at any time. The sheer size of Australia represented a great challenge.

I travelled through grassland for miles as I approached Rockhampton, with a scattering of gum trees on the gently rolling terrain. There was generally a line of low hills miles away to the west. Six miles south of the town I crossed the Tropic of Capricorn, an impressive aluminium spire beside the road marking the position of this boundary between the Temperate and Tropical Zones. An informative plaque reminded visitors of the significance of this line drawn on so many maps:

> "The Tropic of Capricorn
> Latitude 23°27'30"
>
> Because of the tilt of 23°27'30" of the earth's axis of rotation to its orbital path, the Tropic of Capricorn is the southernmost latitude at which the sun reaches the zenith. This happens only once each year on the Summer Solstice (about 22nd December).
>
> Capricornus was, in Roman mythology, the sea goat into which Pan was changed to escape from the terrible giant Typhon. It is also the name given to the constellation resembling it, and when the December Solstice was first observed the sun was situated in this constellation, hence this Tropic was named Capricorn."

Conditions were hardly tropical around me. I learned the reason when I bought a newspaper in Rockhampton. As a result of a weather disturbance off Tasmania, the south was in the grips of some of the coldest weather ever for this time of the year. North of Sydney the Pacific Highway was blocked in several places by snow, and there had been power cuts in Brisbane due to an unprecedented demand for electricity for heating due to the cold weather there. I wondered for a split second if my former colleagues at English Electric were concerned about the temperatures I was experiencing. But I was now 400 miles north of Brisbane.

While in Rockhampton I had a shower at a petrol station. This unusual, free facility was available at a number of petrol stations for the travelling public, recognising the limited presence of amenities like this in the outback where there were often huge distances between communities. There were no facilities like showers at the Rest Areas provided by the Transport Department. I travelled slowly through the town, the third largest in the state, and the distribution centre for Central Queensland. I stocked up with food as ahead of me was a barren stretch of 150 miles with no communities where food could be purchased.

This was still a day's travel away, but I could not be sure whether I would be able to purchase much at Marlborough, 66 miles to the north. My map cautioned me that localities shown were no indication of the facilities available at any of them. I bought more bread at Marlborough before starting the barren stretch to Sarina. There was a welcome change to the terrain for a short time as the road curved inland to climb over the Boomer Range, allowing some sweeping views over the plains to the west. The plains were covered by gum trees and low bushes as far as the eye could see. Bottle trees with their characteristic shaped trunks appeared for a time, and I was astonished to pass clumps of giant prickly pear cacti. These were all welcome diversions on the journey through the wilderness. When the scrub gave way to pasture, small herds of cattle appeared. They were not used to seeing cyclists and, when one started running to take a closer look, a stampede was quickly under way.

I was filling my water container from the creeks but, on the second day in the wilderness, I noticed they were all dry. For the first time I replenished my supply from a large tank in a field; a windmill nearby pumped the water up from an artesian bore. The experience signalled a problem which would become more pronounced in the future. I was needing a significant amount of water as the days were getting warmer. One result of the sun going down in a cloudless sky was that there was often a frosty night, and it was startling to wake up in my tent to find ice in the water bottle.

The road eventually turned towards the coast, starting a sharp descent to Sarina as it passed through the Colston Gap in the Connors Range. The most difficult part of the Bruce Highway was behind me. I swept down to Sarina where I was able to replenish my exhausted food supplies. Having reached civilisation again, I took the opportunity in Mackay to the north to have a shower and get all my washing done at a launderette. I entered the launderette wearing just my shorts and a jacket; with camping all the time I had to make the most of these opportunities to catch up with such chores.

A fascinating journey had begun at Sarina through a major sugar growing area. For mile after mile I passed by canefields, which alternated with wooded areas. A lot of cane was being cut, some by hand but the majority by machine. After crossing the O'Connell River about 20 miles south of Proserpine, the terrain suddenly opened out and I found myself crossing a vast, flat, grass-covered plain before meeting more trees. I was soon among canefields as I approached Proserpine, and went to the mill to see if there was a chance of a visit. My guide book informed me that the mill could be inspected on Tuesdays, which today was. No guided tours were scheduled, but I was invited to walk round by myself. I was astonished at this ease of access and wandered slowly round, seeing the various stages the cane went through to extract the sugar. My mind worked overtime as I tried to recall all the details of a related visit several years before as a schoolboy to the sugar-beet factory in my home town of Bury St. Edmunds. There was no literature at the mill, but I was told some was available at Mackay; it was 80 miles away in the wrong direction!

At one of the Rest Areas several days later I met a young Australian from Melbourne who had worked at one of the mills. He was able to provide me with the kind of background information I was looking for to put all the images I was seeing in some perspective. There were many varieties of cane, some of which were ready for cutting when the blossom at the top was full, others when the blossom had died. During a growing period of one year, the root system of 1 ton of cane must absorb 150 tons of water. 16 tons of cane produced 1 ton of sugar and other products and 15 tons of waste, which thankfully was a good fertilizer.

A few miles north of Proserpine the canefields gave way to forest again. Approaching Bowen there was a fine view of the town across Denison Bay, and I had my first view of the coast from the Bruce Highway since leaving Brisbane 750 miles to the south. Camping outside the town, the peace of the evening was disturbed when fire engines raced past with their bells clanging. There seemed to be a fire at the large meat processing works in the town. Outside the town I passed by a large market gardening area noted for its tomatoes, mangoes and tropical fruits. After travelling through an area covered by volcanic rock, the terrain changed to pasture. With the ground almost flat, the road disappeared into the distance in a long straight line. There were more canefields around Home Hill and Ayr, and a wallaby bounded across the road in front of me as I approached Home Hill. It was one of few I had seen so far in the wild.

A few miles south of Townsville the road climbed gradually. From the top of the rise there was a fine view towards the town, dominated by Mt. Cutheringa or Castle Hill rising 1,000 ft behind it. I spent just a few hours in the town, as I would be returning after a detour to the north. It was long enough to purchase a new tyre for the rear wheel of the bicycle and to look for one or two items I needed to purchase on my return. The tyre bought in Japan had been no better than average, with the tread erased after just 1,000 miles.

*****

A detour to Cairns was going to give me an opportunity to see part of the Great Barrier Reef, which came close to the coast in this area. It was now the beginning of August, and it was getting warmer. There were no more frosts at night, and there was just a trace of dew on the tent in the morning. As I started the journey north from Townsville, it felt very hot as a result of a following breeze equal to my cycling speed. The air felt dead, and I stopped at intervals to feel the breeze. The road through gum forest was long and straight, with canefields around the communities along the road. A climb for a few miles north of Ingham allowed some fine views of the Hinchinbrook Channel and Island.

Gum forest continued to a few miles south of Tully, when a large cane area started. As the terrain became undulating, the small elevations enabled one to look over rolling fields of cane, making this a most attractive journey which continued through El Arish, Silkwood and Cowley. The weather was deteriorating for a short time, though; it rained during the night and continued for most of the next day as I passed through Innisfail. I kept going as I had read that Tully had an annual rainfall of 180 in; it was the wettest place in Australia. Work continued in the canefields. With most of the cane-cutting machines brought to a halt by the muddy conditions, cutting proceeded by the time-honoured method using sickles - and dirty work it was. Before the introduction of machines just a few years before, it had been a much more labour-intensive industry than it was now. The mills operated for six months of the year, from June to December. Much of the work was casual, and I passed a number of the accommodation blocks provided for migrant workers. Some were now falling into decay.

I put the tent up in steady rain, which continued throughout the evening and night. I was pleased when it left off before I got up. As the sun rose, the cloud lifted and broke up, resulting in a warm ride into Cairns just 25 miles away. After walking round the central area of this most attractive town, I went along to the Caravan Park; it was crowded, reflecting the number of people travelling in the north at this most suitable time. It was the first time I had camped in a town or city, but camping had now become part of my way of life. I had also packed the tent away in the morning saturated; I rationalised that the best way to dry it out was to camp again.

A glorious day followed as I took the boat journey to Green Island, a lush coral cay 17 miles from Cairns. I could hardly wait to transfer from the launch to one of the glass-bottomed boats in order to view the coral all around. The Underwater Observatory provided another opportunity to inspect the coral in a very interesting area. With films to see on the Great Barrier Reef, a visit to the Marine Zoological Gardens and a one and a half mile walk round the perimeter of Green Island, it was a memorable day.

Leaving Cairns the following morning, I could have simply retraced my route from Townsville. But I was intrigued by the area just inland from Cairns, the Atherton Tableland. The travel literature described it as a tropical wonderland, and curiosity had to be satisfied. Heading north up the Cook Highway, the road started climbing after turning off for Kuranda and making its way up the Macalister Range. The elevation allowed some attractive views of the canefields on the plain below and the mountains beyond. Travelling west to Mareeba, the road passed through gum forest much of the time, with a few homesteads along the road by the creeks and tobacco fields around Mareeba. There was a gradual climb southwards towards Atherton, 2,456 ft above sea level, when the scenery became more interesting as thick jungle appeared on both sides of the road. There were interesting features to see to the east of Atherton, including the Curtain Fig Tree, the Giant Cedar Tree and Lake Barrine; close by the lake were two giant kauri trees. From the higher ground along the main road there were glimpses of Lake Tinaroo, a huge lake created by the building of the Tinaroo Falls Dam to store water for irrigation. The road south to Millaa Millaa through dairy country took me through very undulating terrain.

Turning east towards Innisfail on the final part of the detour, the road generally went downwards. After a short climb near Campbell's Hill, the road descended sharply into thick jungle. It was late in the afternoon, and I decided it was an interesting area in which to camp. A clear piece of ground soon appeared, and I camped surrounded by giant ferns. As the light disappeared, it became pitch black; for half an hour I had the company of a swarm of fireflies which produced flashes of light as they flew around. The following morning I was surprised to wake up to find the tent dry, expecting the opposite in the jungle. From my camping spot the road climbed gradually for three miles, then beginning a long gradual descent. As I emerged from the jungle there were extensive views over the rolling terrain.

Arriving back in Innisfail I was delighted to have a clear blue sky, which remained throughout the return journey to Townsville. It was an interesting experience retracing my steps, approaching every location from the other direction. I knew where I wanted to stop to take photographs, the bright conditions contrasting with cloudier skies just a few days earlier. I camped at the same spots as on the way north, the final one being a Rest Area seven miles north of Townsville.

The following morning I cycled up The Strand towards the Caravan Park, planning to get my tent erected and baggage unloaded before making the steep climb up Castle Hill to survey the city from its commanding vantage point. The plan was suddenly thrown into disarray when I saw the Volkswagen camper van of the Vancouver couple who had been with me on the *Eastern Star*. Laurel was inside writing. When Ken returned at lunch-time I joined them for a picnic lunch, before leaving my bags in the van and cycling up Castle Hill for some glorious views over the town and surrounding area. I had no difficulty getting into the Caravan Park a little later than expected. In the evening a second trip was made up Castle Hill, this time with Ken and Laurel to see the lights of the town.

There was just one more day in Townsville, or rather the Townsville area, before starting the next major stage of the journey. From the top of Castle Hill I had looked northwards to Magnetic Island five miles away. I took the bicycle with me for the 40 minute journey on the launch to this very picturesque island, as there were several miles of good road to follow. The scenery was about to change for me when I returned to the mainland.

The snow-capped peak of Mt. Fuji viewed across Lake Ashi.

Cherry blossom in Imperial Park, Kyoto.

The 5-storey pagoda of Kofukuji Temple viewed across Sarusawa Pond in Nara, the first permanent capital of Japan.

The delightful Kintai Bridge spanning the Nishiki River at Iwakuni.

The massive torii of the Itsukushima Shrine off-shore near the southwest corner of the main island.

In the fertile Ota River Valley north of Hiroshima.

Transplanting rice seedlings along the north coast of the main island.

At the start of one of the cryptomeria avenues lining the approaches to Nikko.

In sugar cane country up the Queensland coast.

Camping at Bohle River Rest Area north of Townsville.

Looking towards Hinchinbrook Island from the Bruce Highway north of Townsville.

West of Townsville near the start of the Flinders Highway across Queensland to the Northern Territory. Now I could start setting up my camera tripod in the middle of the road.

Between Julia Creek and Cloncurry. "Have you come from the dirt, or are you going towards it?" I was asked earlier.

A welcome sight in the outback: the author goes to fill a gallon container at the artesian bore storage tanks.

View from the saddle while heading west in the Northern Territory.

On the long road across the Northern Territory.

Cattle road train on the road north to Darwin.

Termite hills: an unusual feature in unique terrain.

Memorable campsite at the Devils Marbles in the Northern Territory.

The city of Adelaide from Light's Vision, the statue of Colonel William Light, Adelaide's celebrated planner.

Temporary road obstruction in Victoria: reminder of a major industry.

Trams on Collins Street, Melbourne.

Idyllic view from the lookout at Lakes Entrance, eastern Victoria.

The magnificent harbour and twin symbols of Sydney: the Harbour Bridge and Opera House.

The Buller River near Murchison, South Island.

The Southern Alps dominate the view down the west coast of the South Island.

Lake Wanaka, one of several large lakes in the south of the South Island.

Heading south, and a long way from home: in the south of the South Island.

Pastoral scene near Mossburn, South Island.

Breakfast time at Blind River Rest Area near Seddon, South Island.

Morning view of Mt. Egmont, North Island.

Lake Waikaremoana, North Island.

Chapter 16

Into the Interior

Sunday, 18 August 1968

As I left the Caravan Park in Townsville, I was joined for a short time by two boys who had a thousand questions to ask. They left me before I reached the Charters Towers Road, where I stopped at a launderette before heading for the outback. I wasn't sure when I would next encounter a facility like this. From Townsville it was 570 miles to Mt. Isa on the Flinders Highway and a further 430 miles to Three Ways in the Northern Territory on the Barkly Highway. The three way road junction there stood out as a beacon on my maps, seeming at times in my mind to be the only such junction in the vast area.

Leaving Townsville behind me, I travelled through rolling pasture. It was a beautiful day and, with a following breeze, it felt very hot. Stopping at a small store at Woodstock during the middle of the afternoon, I bought an ice-cream and a cold drink. I also wanted to top up my water supplies. "Is there a tap outside where I can help myself?" I asked. "There are no taps here, just tanks," was the reply. I had run into the dry area a little earlier than expected.

I knew that when I turned inland I would generally be leaving all surface water behind me, and would need to carry more than at any time before. There had been a similar problem in the desert areas of America but, except for isolated instances, the distances between communities were not great. Now the distances between communities were often going to be considerable, allied to which was a general uncertainty about what might be available at locations marked on the map. I left Townsville with an additional gallon plastic container supported in a wire cage in front of me on the bicycle crossbar. The cartoonist, Heath Robinson, inspired me with the design, making use of a few lengths of wire which I had collected for the purpose. The new container supplemented the half gallon container carried in a pannier bag. The extra capacity would not be enough for the Gibson Desert, but I wasn't going there and felt confident about the route I was following. There were many sizable communities along the route. The strategy was therefore to arrange each day's milage as far as possible so that it involved passing through one of these communities, where food and drink supplies could be replenished as necessary, and I could continue camping to minimize expenditure.

The pasture around me as I continued to Charters Towers, the first town on the route, was burned yellow. There was a gradual slope upwards to this former gold mining town, its elevation being 1,000 ft. Traffic was very light, with just a few caravans compared with the large number encountered daily on the Bruce Highway. West of Charters Towers the terrain became much more colourful, with considerable numbers of wattle trees with their brilliant yellow blossom. There was an immense amount of yellow from other bushes, and everywhere there were the ubiquitous gum trees. I stopped many times to take photographs, not knowing how long this colourful scenery was going to last.

On a hot day, I also stopped early in the afternoon for a drink at a motel at a small community along the road. A motorist arriving at the same time, very impressed with what I was doing, offered to buy me a drink, and started to tell the barman about my adventures. The barman was not impressed. "Some people do the stupidest things," he retorted. "The car of a local man broke down some time ago," he went on, "so that he had to walk twenty miles to get help. He talked about it for a year as if he had accomplished some incredible feat." My cycling adventure was not discussed further with the barman. I had experienced a well-known feature of the Australian character, the inclination to knock down anyone who might have a reason to talk about some achievement. This was the land of the anti-hero, the underdog.

My reception was generally more sympathetic, however. Later on the same afternoon, I was pleased when two good Samaritans stopped ahead of me, and offered me a cold beer from their ice-box. The young men worked on a property at Clermont some 230 miles to the south-east, and we talked for some time. After entreating me unsuccessfully to take a lift with them for 25 miles as far as Pentland, they offered me a second beer as we departed. It went down well later with my evening sandwiches.

The road climbed considerably near Pentland to cross the Great Dividing Range, and I looked back over a sea of gum trees. The trees gradually thinned out, giving way to large stretches of open grassland. At the store at Prairie east of Hughenden, a lady asked me if I had "come from the dirt" or was going towards it. With my map showing three long stretches of dirt road between Hughenden and Cloncurry, I could only wonder what condition the surface was in. Approaching Hughenden I was surprised to cross a cattle grid in the main road. Shortly afterwards there was the unusual sight of a goods train moving slowly along the line which ran parallel with the road, the train was preceded by a hand-propelled track maintenance vehicle with two men pumping furiously to stay ahead of the train and presumably get to a siding further along the line.

Arriving in Hughenden during the middle of the day, I stopped for a steak meal to show my identification with a major industry of Northern Queensland, and had a haircut so that I could brush out more easily dust thrown up by vehicles on the dirt road ahead. I also bought a sun hat as a precautionary measure in case the temperature rose much further during the coming weeks.

There were just two miles of hard surface before the dirt road started. In places the dirt was packed hard, but generally it was loose. Progress was correspondingly slow as the wheels slid on the surface and the rear wheel attempted to find some traction. I could have wished to be able to travel a little faster to lessen the problem of the flies, which swarmed round my face most of the day. Vast areas of grassland were all around me, with patches covered by spinifex bushes.

After camping by an artesian bore run-off, I sailed into Richmond the next day with a following breeze. The last six miles of dirt road were hard and smooth before meeting paved road again. I was disappointed as I left Richmond after lunch at a café to find the dirt road starting again just outside the town at the turn-off to Winton; my map showed some 14 miles of paved road. Winton lay about 140 miles by road to the south. I wasn't going there but it was in my consciousness, for in 1895 in the surrounding district "Banjo" Paterson wrote the words to a famous song which I sung to myself often on the long stretches of open road. The song was *Waltzing Matilda*.

As I travelled the 92 miles between Richmond and Julia Creek, I heard from different people about a cyclist who had passed along the road three years before with a sail attached to his bike. He had travelled north like myself from Brisbane, and featured in reports in the Brisbane and Townsville newspapers. At the small store at Nelia, the storekeeper told me how the cyclist had spent a whole day coming 16 miles from Nonda, another small location to the east, pushing his bicycle most of the way. It must have been an ordeal on the dirt road, with all the extra weight, and the cyclist apparently turned back at Cloncurry after another 120 miles, mostly on dirt road. The episode reminded me that news was sparse in the outback, so that anyone travelling through the region by unusual means received attention.

Before reaching Nelia a car stopped by me. While enjoying a refreshing cup of tea, the driver told me he knew the outback well, years before having surveyed the road from Mt. Isa to Camooweal, a little further along my route. He informed me that there were artesian bores every 10 to 15 miles along the 118 mile section, thus dealing with any water supply problem. He then surprised me by asking me if I carried snake-bite kit, knew judo and was armed. A number of people had warned me to be on my guard, not holding a very high opinion about some of the aborigines in the area.

Arrival at Julia Creek completed the second section of dirt road, involving 89 miles on the stretch from Richmond compared with 56 miles between Richmond and Hughenden. I bought a newspaper to catch up with what was happening in the outside world. The fourth cricket Test Match between England and Australia at Headingley, Leeds, seemed to be heading for a draw at the end of the fourth day. On the political front, I read about the crisis in Czechoslovakia as the USSR clamped down on the liberalization campaign launched by Alexander Dubcek. Closer to home, the paper reported that the temperature was 31° yesterday in Mt. Isa to the west. It seemed to be similar here. My sun hat was in frequent use as the weather became increasingly hot.

I stocked up with food and had a drink in one of the hotels before setting off for Cloncurry 89 miles away and the third and final stretch of unpaved road. Once again my map was in error, showing a paved road for the 25 miles to Gilliat. The unpaved road started after just a mile, and lasted for 80 miles. It was by far the roughest stretch, being a dirt road at first, then changing to gravel. But it was coming to an end, and I could look forward to a paved surface for a considerable time. From Gilliat I lost whatever company the railway provided as the line now ran a few miles south of the road. There were few signs of habitation, so that I was pleased to see half a dozen wild horses for a short time. There were other companions closer to the ground, signalled by the appearance of termite hills on the red soil around me as I approached Cloncurry.

The town was relatively quiet, having been a flourishing copper mining town in earlier decades. It was an old town, celebrating its centenary in 1967, and I stopped at the monument to the Flying Doctor Service, the first base of the service having been established here in 1928. I stocked up with water and groceries before departing. Progress was slow as I stopped to take photographs in the colourful, rocky terrain. I was also experimenting with a new purchase, a multi-coloured umbrella with a G-clamp on the end of the handle. By fixing it to the handlebar, I surmised that it could provide me with some welcome shade from the hot sun. However, there were problems with the clamp, which would not stay tight, and a bigger problem of stability in the breeze. It was worse when a vehicle passed me, especially any large vehicle.

Six giant road trains passed me west of Cloncurry, comprising the main lorry and two equally large trailers. The road trains reminded me of the vast cattle stations in the hinterland around me. The east-west railway line from Townsville finished at Cloncurry, being supported by a few branches, but the road trains took over in the hinterland.

After crossing the Corella River I stopped at an obelisk nearby which commemorated the expedition of Burke and Wills. This famous expedition passed through here on 22 January 1861 on their journey across the continent. The founding of Cloncurry just six years later demonstrated the pace of settlement following these pioneering journeys and reports back to the organisers.

A much newer settlement lay to the west of the Corella River. Uranium was discovered in July 1954 at the location of Mary Kathleen. I found a ghost town in 1968, following fulfilment of a contract with the United Kingdom Atomic Energy Authority a few years before. A caretaker staff looked after the fenced site pending possible further operations. I pushed on to Mt. Isa, a town very much alive and a landmark on the journey. Someone notified the press that I was on the way, and a reporter came out to meet me while I was still several miles from the town.

The discovery of lead in 1923 resulted in the mining of copper, lead, zinc and silver by Mount Isa Mines Ltd, Queensland's largest single industrial enterprise. I spent an interesting morning on a tour of the mine, adding to the swelling number of visitors for the year. A few days before, the newspaper I had bought in Julia Creek reported a record 889 visitors to the mine during the previous week. That made 8,008 before the end of August, compared with a total of 9,613 for the whole of the previous year.

I went along to the Flying Doctor Service base and spent an interesting period listening in to the School of the Air. This imaginative development from the Flying Doctor Service had first started experimentally at Alice Springs in 1951. At the newspaper office I was given copies of the day's paper, which contained an article on my trip. As a result, there were looks of recognition when I returned to the Caravan Park, which was full. I attended to all my washing before talking to my fellow travellers. Several I spoke to had come up from the south and been up to Darwin, enabling me to form a picture of what lay ahead. Some of the travellers had just managed to get up from the south before being affected by unusually heavy rain in the Alice Springs area. The paper told me that the road from Port Augusta was temporarily closed, leaving many travellers stranded. Many younger travellers arriving in Mt. Isa hoped to find work at the mine or in the town, but there were few vacancies at the time. Collecting films at the Post Office, I enquired in vain about the young couple I had met near Maryborough on the Bruce Highway. They had clearly been unable to find work and moved on.

*****

Before moving on myself along the Barkly Highway, I stocked up with food for the 118 miles to Camooweal. I sold my umbrella to a lady at the Caravan Park, deciding I had no further use for it. On the outskirts of Mt. Isa I passed two hitch-hikers, later meeting one again, who came from Gloucester. He had travelled to Darwin from

Indonesia, worked in Darwin and was returning there, unable to obtain work in Mt. Isa.

There was little to stop for as the road continued through gum forest, alternating with areas which were suddenly devoid of trees. The man I met between Richmond and Julia Creek was right about the regular distribution of artesian bores. I was able to replenish my water supplies without difficulty. The only problem with the bore water was that it always had an unpleasant bitter taste, but there was no real choice between survival and dehydration. I masked the taste in the evening and early morning by boiling the water to make tea. For a time I had a packet of "billy tea", which I felt masked the bore water taste particularly well. During the day I added varying amounts of sugar to the water in my drinking bottle, but these experiments were never very successful. In addition the water soon became warm as the temperature rose. When anyone stopped by me on the road and offered me a cool beer, it seemed like nectar. A good Samaritan appeared almost every day.

A few miles west of Camooweal I crossed into the Northern Territory. This time I had stocked up with food for the 205 miles to Frewena, the next main place where I expected to be able to buy groceries. A couple of cooler, cloudy days followed; with a breeze from the south-east I sped along, recording over 60 miles a day compared with a target figure of 50. The situation was helped by the lengthening days, as it was now early September. I also had extra daylight each day, after finding out that Northern Territory time was half an hour behind Queensland time. Topping up with water at Avon Downs, an aboriginal policeman there helpfully went over the points along the route where I could obtain water.

Seven road trains passed me the same day, all with two trailers or "dogs"; each could carry 20 cattle. The biggest trains with three "dogs" could thus carry 80 cattle. I was told that the cattle were inspected at regular intervals, particularly after very rough stretches of road. Near Soudan I saw some large herds of cattle, but most of the large stations in the area were well away from the main road. Unfortunately cattle did sometimes get knocked down when they ventured onto the road. If cycling into the breeze, a carcass beside the road ahead would be smelt before it was seen as the stench was indescribable.

As the cloud disappeared after a couple of days, the temperature started to rise again. Replenishing food and water supplies at Frewena, I learned that no more water would be available before reaching the junction with the Stuart Highway 82 miles west. The continuing breeze from the south-east helped to maintain a good daily milage. The last stretch to Three Ways was a memorable one, with the roadsides covered with colourful wildflowers and undulating terrain allowing sweeping views from the crests of the road. Arrival at the junction was delayed by a car stopping ahead of me. I was offered a cup of coffee by a man travelling up to Darwin to work for the Missions.

A spiritual element reappeared again at the junction as I admired the "Flynn of the Inland" monument, now bathed by the golden glow of the late afternoon sun as I arrived at 5.45pm. A plaque recorded the achievements of one of the outstanding figures in the history of the outback:

"Commemorating
"Flynn of the Inland"
The Very Rev. John Flynn O.B.E., D.D.
Of the Presbyterian Church of Australia
1880 – 1951

> His vision encompassed the continent. He established the Australian Inland Mission and founded the Flying Doctor Service. He brought to lonely places a spiritual ministry and spread a mantle of safety over them by medicine, aviation and radio."

This strategic location in the middle of the Northern Territory seemed a fitting location for this memorial. From this position I could turn north to Darwin or south to Alice Springs. Before moving in either direction I went along to the Three Ways Road House for a drink to celebrate completion of another stage in the journey.

Chapter 17

Along the Stuart Highway

Tuesday, 10 September 1968

At the Three Ways Road House there was little food to purchase to take away. My simple life style would have to be simpler still for a short while, but I could manage on biscuits, crisps and chocolate. Two giant road trains, each with three trailers, arrived at the Road House before I left my overnight camping spot nearby. One carried nine cars in addition to three sealed containers; the road trains were awesome to behold. They had probably started their journey at Alice Springs, and were taking their cargo to Darwin. The cargo would have been able to come up by train from the south to Alice Springs, where the railway line ended. The road then took over; it was a good road, having been paved during the Second World War for troop transportation.

I was looking forward to cycling the 600 miles to Darwin. As I set off, I listened for traffic coming up behind me. It wasn't long before the two giant road trains at Three Ways caught up with me. I took to the side of the road to allow them to pass without deviating from their course, and for my own safety. I did this whenever a road train came along; the majority carried cattle, but there were a number of petrol tanker trains. I wanted to get off the road in any case to take photographs of these vehicles, which were unique to this part of Australia. I began to worry that my own transport wasn't fitted with giant kangaroo bars like every road train, in case a kangaroo suddenly bounded out of the bush in front of me!

The gently undulating terrain changed little for many miles, covered by a mixture of gum trees, bushes and areas of grassland. The road north wasn't going to be quite as dry as the road from the east. At Gibson Creek 17 miles north of the junction I was startled to see water. A further 12 miles brought me to Attack Creek, where I paused by a monument to one of Australia's most famous explorers. A plaque recorded details of the first attempt by John McDouall Stuart to reach the north:

> "On 25th June 1860, John McDouall Stuart and his two companions William Kekwick and Benjamin Head reached Attack Creek, their most northerly point on that expedition. Hostile natives and illness forced the party to return. This plaque was unveiled by the Honourable Paul Hasluck M.P., Minister of State for Territories, 25th June 1960."

Early in 1860 the South Australian Government had offered a bonus of £2,000 to the first man to cross the continent from south to north. John McDouall Stuart led the first party to get under way, leaving Adelaide in March 1860. The race was joined in August when a party under Robert O'Hara Burke left Melbourne to follow a route towards the Gulf of Carpentaria. As I stopped at Attack Creek, I recalled the memorial to Burke and Wills at the crossing of the Corella River by the Barkly Highway, where I had been 11 days earlier. Stuart's route from Adelaide was thus about 400 miles west of Burke's route. History records that Burke made the first crossing, reaching tidal waters near the Gulf in February 1861. Stuart eventually reached the north coast east of Darwin in July 1862 on his third expedition.

As I came face to face with history, I wanted to read more about the exploits of these brave explorers, whose journeys were the essential forerunners of future settlement and development of the country. These developments would allow cyclists like myself to traverse the country on reasonable roads within a hundred years. The distances and nature of the terrain were such that we would still consider we were having challenging journeys, but the challenges were on a different scale to those facing the explorers as they ventured into unknown terrain, with no stores ahead, unknown water supplies and the constant risk of attack from the natives whose land was being invaded. These comparisons helped to put matters into perspective. Thus when my rear tyre failed three days after I had been at Attack Creek, I knew that I would be able to purchase some kind of replacement in Katherine to the north. I would experience just some temporary inconvenience.

Leaving Attack Creek, I was able to buy more foodstuffs at Renner Springs and Elliott during the next two days travel. North of Elliott Creek I stopped at a further memorial, this one connected with the overland telegraph line, the northern and southern parts of which were joined nearby in August 1872. The project had started within eight years of Stuart's crossing of the continent. Via submarine and overland cables, telegraph communication then became possible for the first time between Australia and Britain. Such was the pace of progress.

My progress came to a halt south of Daly Waters the next day when my rear tyre went down. I stuck a large patch over a slit in the inner tube, but it held for only a few miles. Unfortunately it was my last spare inner tube, which I had fitted three days earlier. I could only smile when I looked in my diary: it was Friday, 13 September. After camping in a dense area of gum trees, I locked the bicycle to a tree well away from the road, and walked to the road at 7.30am to attempt to get a lift. Forty-five minutes later I was racing the 175 miles to Katherine in an empty petrol tanker at 60mph, reaching Katherine at 12.15. Following lunch and the purchase of a new tyre and two inner tubes, the return journey was made in a small pick-up truck with two young men from Perth on a tour of Australia in five weeks. They were in a hurry to get to Alice Springs, and the miles were eaten up as we talked and raced southwards. Arriving back at the campsite at 5.30pm, there was just time to set up my tent and fit a new tyre and tube before darkness fell. It had been quite a day.

The following morning I started the journey northwards at a gentler pace, travelling through gum forest. South of Mataranka, there were some unusually large termite hills, one or two over 10 feet tall, and I passed the cemetery of the old Elsey Homestead, where Mrs. Aeneas Gunn wrote *We of the Never-Never*. I had not heard of the book before, but it was apparently a classic of outback life known to generations of young Australians. I must look out for a copy. At the store at Mataranka, I was told of a young man and woman who had cycled through the town in 1962, starting in Brisbane and travelling south right round the coast through Western Australia. I was always interested to hear about other cyclists, but wondered how this pair had managed to get across the Nullarbor Plain or to negotiate the hundreds of miles of rough gravel road in the north of Western Australia.

For several days, as I travelled through an area with considerable numbers of termite hills, selection of camping spots presented a real problem. The termite hills might appear picturesque, but you looked down on a ground surface with numbers of the little creatures moving in all directions. Sometimes it was impossible to find a clear area on which to erect the tent. I awoke one morning hearing the faintest of sounds in the tent: something was different. Inspection of my food bag revealed a slab of cheese swarming with termites; the cheese could not be seen at all. I threw it out of the tent as far, and as rapidly, as possible. As I made a sandwich, I inspected my slices of bread carefully in case I entrapped unwanted nutritional material. I was going to have to wrap up all my food much more thoroughly in plastic bags.

The weather was really warming up now as the days passed and I approached the north. The temperature had risen to 35° in Mataranka early in the afternoon and the humidity was increasing. My clothes were starting to stick to me as they became damp, whereas a few days before they remained bone dry throughout the day. Arriving in Katherine at midday the following day, I had lunch at a restaurant, my first cooked meal since leaving Mt. Isa two weeks earlier. As I left the restaurant and consulted my map about a nearby attraction, I found myself in conversation with a former farmer from Proserpine in Queensland, who had sold his farm to embark on a new career making travel films for sale to TV. He offered me a lift out to the Katherine Gorge 18 miles away. I was glad I didn't cycle out as the road was extremely rough. In no time I was travelling in a small motorboat up the broad Katherine River, framed by sandstone cliffs which plunged vertically into the deep blue water. I hadn't seen so much water since I left the Queensland coast, and was astonished to discover such terrain again.

Returning to Katherine, the road north-westwards passed through rolling rock-strewn terrain, with the usual covering of gum trees. By contrast, a large clear area three miles south of Pine Creek contained the largest termite hill I had seen, rising about 14 ft without taper; in fact it was larger at the top than at ground level. At the store at Pine Creek a short time later, I listened to a most unusual story recounted by the elderly owner as I enjoyed a cold drink.

When he found out I was from England, he told me that he was brought out from Hull to Australia by his parents when he was 15 months old. While serving in Europe during the First World War he received injuries. At the War's end he was presented to King George V, who made him a King's Corporal. He was then about 18. He later served during the Second World War, receiving further injuries. He told me that it was one of his proudest experiences to attend the

Queen's coronation in 1953, receiving an invitation as a result of his special rank. During the royal tour of Australia the following year, he was presented to the Queen in Darwin. It was a wonderful story to hear, from a man with justifiable pride. (Update: Correspondence in *The Daily Telegraph* in February 1972 discounted the existence of the rank of King's Corporal. I wrote to the Editor with details of my experience: the letter was not acknowledged.)

Two days later, at Adelaide River, a further military note encroached on the journey, when I visited the nearby War Cemetery containing the graves of service personnel and civilians, both men and women, who had been killed in the Darwin area during the Second World War. A tropical tone appeared as I travelled towards Adelaide River, with the growing appearance of fig and palm trees. There were further large termite hills, and I saw my first wallaby in the Northern Territory. I wondered whether all the kangaroos and wallabies I had been told were in the area were frightened to show themselves to cyclists.

The number of cyclists on the road doubled shortly afterwards when the unusual sight confronted me at Adelaide River of a cyclist coming down the road towards me. He was the first cycle tourist I had met in Australia, and was an exceptional one by any yardstick. We adjourned to a café nearby to compare notes over a pot of tea. Ian Hibell was another Englishman, leaving England five years before, spending three of them working in Alaska. He had been to Japan and to almost every country in Asia, coming to Australia from Indonesia. On the day we met, he had left Darwin earlier in the morning to begin a long ride to Sydney via Brisbane. I went over my maps to give him the benefit of my experience. We talked for a very long while about so many aspects of our common interest, eventually parting with the expectation that we might meet again as we could be in the same area a few months later.

The following day I reached Darwin myself, gratified to see four kangaroos on the final run as they had so far been eluding me. Finding the Caravan Park by Mindil Beach close to the city centre was solely for caravans, I took a room in a lodging house. It brought to an end an unbroken run of 68 nights spent camping since leaving Brisbane. The decision to arrange a solid roof over my head, rather than seek out a more distant Caravan Park, seemed a sensible one as I had to shelter from a brief storm while near Mindil Beach. More rain was threatening, resulting in a heavy storm during the early evening, lasting for an hour. The previous evening there had been a downpour while I camped south of Darwin. Was this the start of "the wet"?

There was no further rain while I explored the sights during two days in the capital of the Northern Territory, seeing the tropical flora in the Botanical Gardens and the principal buildings. The location on the coast meant that a sea breeze tempered the energy sapping effects of the high humidity as I travelled round. Darwin's position meant there were diverse memorials to inspect, including one south of the city centre overlooking Lameroo Beach, to the naturalist and explorer, Friedrich Wilhelm Ludwig Leichhardt. On a 2,000 mile journey between 1844-5, Leichhardt led a successful expedition from Brisbane to Port Essington north-east of Darwin, discovering valuable pastoral country. A few miles north, overlooking Fanny Bay, the Ross Smith Memorial commemorated the landing of the first aerial flight from England in 1919 by Capt. Sir Ross Smith and a crew of three. Nearby was the Fanny Bay Gaol with its green, corrugated sheeting. It was apparently known as "The green hotel on the hill", and generally contained a considerable number of aborigines following problems with drink. The native population struggled to survive in the populated areas.

I was particularly interested to see a cairn in the city, describing events associated with the landing of a submarine cable in 1871 which allowed communication between Australia and Britain. On the journey north I had stopped at the cairn adjacent to the position where the overland telegraph line was joined the following year, enabling communication with the south.

As I contemplated the return journey south to Three Ways, I looked at my schedule for the coming months: it was tight. While prepared to cycle the return journey, I decided I would endeavour to obtain a lift. Any time saved could be put to better use in the south. Leaving Darwin at 9am one morning, I arrived back at Three Ways the following morning at 8am. (Update: When I left Darwin in September 1968, it was impossible to imagine how it would change a few years later. On Christmas Day 1974 the city was struck by Cyclone Tracy: 65 lives were lost, 150 other people injured, and 90% of all buildings devastated. An immense effort was required to rebuild the city.)

I could hardly believe it as I looked back on one day's events. The day started with departure from Darwin past all the freight terminals and warehouses. I had hardly reached open country when a truck stopped, taking me some 60 miles as far as Adelaide River. I continued cycling to find a spot which was both shady and suitable for a vehicle to stop at. After an hour without success, I was about to set off again when another truck stopped. It was going all the way to New South Wales. I think the young 23 year old driver appreciated some company as we raced down the Stuart Highway, reaching Katherine at 6pm. We stopped for a meal, along with the driver's boss and a friend, who were following in a car. Leaving Katherine at 8pm, we were south of Daly Waters by midnight, when the driver's boss took over in the truck, and the young driver transferred to the car to get some sleep. I didn't see all the road as we journeyed on, continually dozing off to be awoken when the truck bounced over the next uneven piece of road. I tried to stay awake as the light started to break, and an increasing amount of the surrounding terrain became visible. It always seemed a magical time as the sun popped above the horizon, and the long shadows slowly receded. As the truck dropped me off at Three Ways to continue east along the Barkly Highway, I offered my profound thanks and pushed the bicycle into the trees to attempt to get some sleep. I had experienced first-hand the enormous distances covered by the trucks as they traversed the Australian continent.

*****

It was difficult to sleep in the trees as a result of a strong breeze blowing from the east. After a leisurely meal, I set off on the 330 mile stretch south to Alice Springs at 12.30pm. It was pleasant to have left behind the high humidity in the north. Just before I reached the gold mining town of Tennant Creek 16 miles away, my rear tyre started to balloon up. I realised immediately that a thousand shock loads at the same position on the tyre during the previous 24 hours on the truck had taken their toll. I bought and fitted a new tyre in the town before proceeding a few miles south and camping for the evening.

As the trees thinned out, the road continued through open grassland to bring me late the following afternoon to the Devils Marbles. It was a memorable location in which to camp. Before setting up camp, I spoke to two men who stopped to admire the setting. They told me they had met another cyclist at Three Ways a short time earlier. Ian Hibell was thus making good progress since we met at Adelaide

River, covering about 100 miles a day. This was almost twice what I liked to do, demonstrating that we were all individuals who needed to determine by experiment what was a comfortable day's travelling for each of us.

By spending the evening at the Devils Marbles, I had ample time to explore the astonishing arrangement of gigantic granite boulders around me. The corners of all the boulders were well rounded as a result of erosion and spalling over millions of years. The majority resembled rectangular loaves of bread; on top of some of these were almost circular boulders. One could only wonder how long ago the boulders first acquired their positions, and about the conditions prevailing at the time.

It was difficult to think about a past Ice Age and a vast inland sea as the sun rose to produce another hot day. As I now travelled southwards with the sun behind me, I felt the need to wear my hat to shield the back of my neck. The terrain was an astonishing riot of colour for mile after mile, produced by wildflowers which I guessed had sprung into bloom following heavy rain three weeks earlier, and which I heard about while in Mt. Isa. The road passed through a gap in a line of low hills which dominated the open scene for many miles north of Barrow Creek. Some 40 miles south of this old telegraph station site, a mountain came into view a few miles to the west. I stopped at a cairn beside the road, at what is considered the geographical centre of Australia. A plaque informed me of events in the exploration of the continent involving McDouall Stuart and his two companions, attempting to reach the north:

> "John McDouall Stuart and William Kekwick ascended and named Mount Sturt on 23rd April 1860. Later the name Mount Sturt was changed to Central Mount Stuart in honour of the explorer. Stuart's other companion on this expedition was Benjamin Head. This plaque was unveiled by the Right Honourable John McEwen M.P., Minister of State for Trade and Acting Prime Minister of the Commonwealth of Australia on April 23rd 1960."

I was reminded of the similar plaque at Attack Creek, recording McDouall Stuart's most northerly point on this first of three expeditions to reach the north. It was interesting that both plaques were unveiled on the exact centenary of the earlier events. The older plaque introduced the name of Sturt, one of Australia's greatest explorers. In 1829-30 Captain Charles Sturt led a party which rowed 1,000 miles in a whaleboat down the Murrumbidgee and Murray Rivers to the sea, leading to the opening up of vast new areas to colonists. Fifteen years later Sturt led expeditions to the Centre; a member of the party was a young McDouall Stuart. I applauded the erection of all such monuments: they helped to set the scene for all travellers, adding meaning to the landscape.

The colourful, wildflower-covered terrain continued all the way to Alice Springs. Twenty miles north of the town a large sign beside the road advised "You are entering the Temperate Zone", as I crossed the Tropic of Capricorn. Approaching "the Alice" I stopped at the site of the old Telegraph Station there, expecting to spend just a few minutes. The few minutes extended to nearly two hours, as I became absorbed in the history of the overland telegraph line and associated events. I saw the water-hole in the Todd River found by the line surveyor W.W. Mills in 1871, and named by him "Alice Springs" after the wife of Charles Todd, the Postmaster-General and Superintendent of Telegraphs of South Australia. A wildlife enclosure adjacent enabled me to see a large number of kangaroos, wallabies, emus and other birds, compensating for the dearth of wildlife seen so far in the wild.

*****

The following morning I was on the coach from Alice Springs to Ayers Rock, a journey of 270 miles to the south-west. When the paved road ended after 10 miles, it quickly became apparent why few people took their own vehicles on this journey. The road surface was the red soil of this part of the Northern Territory; in places it was firm, but it was often loose, and the coach wheels moved along parallel trenches full of loose soil up to a foot deep. For the first 117 miles to Erldunda Homestead the road was the same one used by cars travelling between Alice Springs and Port Augusta, and I could only admire the courage of the drivers who exposed their vehicles to these conditions. At the homestead a turn-off led to Ayers Rock 153 miles due west. As the coach churned through the loose soil and bounced over frequent corrugations, we looked forward to lunch and afternoon breaks at homesteads along the road. Aboriginal settlements nearby exposed all the young Western travellers to the primitive conditions still lived in by many of the native population. There were lots of dogs and, at Curtin Springs Homestead, the first camels I had seen in Australia. Many camels had been imported to the continent during the early years of exploration.

My fellow passengers included an American girl, two American men, one from Luxembourg, four Australian girls and three from London. The road to the Rock was a severe test for every element involved with the coach's mechanical strength. The scheduled arrival time of 5pm disappeared as two leaf springs were broken, plus a spring in the accelerator linkage. We admired the calm demeanour of the driver, Kurt, a recent migrant from Germany, as he arranged emergency repairs. This was not his first journey, and he seemed prepared for almost anything.

The terrain was quite open, generally covered with grass or scrub. Wildflowers frequently produced a splash of colour just as on the journey south to Alice Springs. When there were bare patches or slight rises in the ground, the bright red soil was to be seen to advantage. At a high point on the road a few miles from the destination, there was a fine view of Ayers Rock, and the Olgas beyond, as the sun went down.

Many of us were up early to see the sunrise at the Rock from a vantage point a mile from the campground. We had heard about the changes of colour at the ends of the day; having missed yesterday's sunset from a close position, we were determined to make the most of the following sunrise. However, atmospheric conditions were such that there were no unusual colours, and we returned to the campground for breakfast.

It was fully light when we all left to inspect the amazing Rock, to see all the folds and contours, and the aboriginal paintings in a number of caves. The Rock was a sacred place to the aborigines. It must have been an awesome sight to the explorer William Gosse in 1873 when he became the first white man to see the Rock, naming it after Sir Henry Ayers, Premier of South Australia at the time. The region was then under the control of South Australia. It was 5½ miles round the base of the enormous sandstone Rock, which rose 1,143 ft above the surrounding plateau. The majority of the coach party were young, and the challenge to climb the Rock from the west end where the slope was gentler could not be set aside. From the top of the Rock there were sweeping views over the surrounding terrain, and to the Olgas 20 miles to the west. Kurt drove us out there for a closer look at this unusual group of sandstone hills before returning to the Rock for the sunset. Once again the atmospheric conditions were unsuitable to produce bright colours. We were told at the motel nearby that photographers often spent weeks at the Rock waiting for the right conditions.

The scheduled departure at 10pm was delayed while Kurt attempted to wire up three further leaf springs of the coach's suspension system, broken on the trip out to the Olgas. With the springs in a doubtful state, Kurt stopped early the following morning. The decision met universal agreement as everyone could then get to sleep. Setting off again after sunrise we returned in daylight to Alice Springs to complete a memorable excursion. There was unexpected news at the campground: while I had been away, a murder had occurred. After deciding there was no point in over-reacting to the situation, I stayed, set up my tent and left to see more of the town.

A short coach tour the following morning took me to Simpson's Gap and Standley Chasm, two passages in the MacDonnell Ranges. On the way out, the coach stopped by the grave of Rev. John Flynn of the Flying Doctor Service. An 8 ton granite boulder from the Devils Marbles rested on a plinth, making a unique memorial. I would have needed a full day to cycle out there, but needed to be back early to catch a special train.

*****

The train, which would take me to Port Augusta, and which I had heard about a few days earlier, was a goods train with one carriage attached. An important criterion was that the fare was just over half the fare on The Ghan, the main passenger train. The 770 mile journey would take 43 hours compared with 29 hours on The Ghan, but that was potentially 14 more hours to see the unique terrain on the journey. Departure was scheduled for 5pm. We started to move at 7pm, but nobody was complaining in view of the bargain package entered into.

The carriage was crowded, the passengers including the three London girls who had been on the coach to Ayers Rock. It was wonderful to have their company for so many more hours. The terrain was often very bare, with scrub and low bushes being the main vegetation. The train swayed and jerked considerably on the narrow gauge line for the first 530 miles to Marree, south-east of the dry salt-pan of Lake Eyre. We were on this train for 29 hours, the first evening and the whole of the next day. There were a number of short stops. I set up my primus stove and "boiled the billy" a number of times, spilling a little water whenever the train jerked. Arriving at Marree, I learned that I might have been upstaged by another passenger, who had fried eggs and bacon on a 2-ring gas hob.

At Marree we transferred to another goods train with carriages, which departed at 2.30am for the 240 miles south to Port Augusta. It was much easier for sleeping now that we were on a broad gauge line. As the sun rose, the Flinders Ranges to the east were visible for mile after mile, while some 20 miles to the west was the dry salt-pan of Lake Torrens. I had finally reached the south of Australia after three months in the north.

Chapter 18

Southern Loop

Monday, 7 October 1968

The train from Marree pulled into Port Augusta station just before midday. I bade a temporary farewell to my compatriots from London, looking forward to seeing them again in Sydney, where they had lived since emigrating. First, there were a few miles to travel in the south. I was eager to get back on the bicycle after the journeys by coach and train through terrain utterly unsuitable for bicycle travel. From Port Augusta I was not only back on good roads, but there was a choice of roads, an element which I had not had to contend with for a number of weeks. A key factor now that I was in the more populated south was to try and keep off the main traffic routes as far as possible. The first choice confronted me a few miles south-east of Port Augusta. The right fork south to Port Pirie was clearly the main highway: the left fork took me slightly inland on a gradual climb towards the Horrocks Pass. From the rising ground there were some fine views looking back towards Port Augusta. I stopped early to fit two new tyres bought in the town before leaving, hoping they would ensure reliability for many miles on this next stage.

I felt I had chosen the scenic route south, the road through Gladstone and Clare taking me through prosperous farming country. On the smaller farms, I quickly saw as many cattle and sheep as I had seen all the time in Queensland and the Northern Territory. The buildings in all the towns and smaller communities I passed through were all so clean and attractive. There was bright colour everywhere, from the growing crops in the fields and from wildflowers by the roadsides, by field borders and the banks of creeks. Or was my mind having to adjust to the changed conditions? At least it was incredibly bright whenever the cloud dispersed to show the area at its best. When cloud obscured the sun, I was reminded that spring was just coming on in the south; the temperature was markedly lower than in the centre and the north. I had come down to the south at a suitable time, and could look forward to rising temperatures as summer advanced.

Progress was slow as everyone I met wanted to talk at length, and everyone seemed to have time to talk in this prosperous region. The proprietors of the store at Wilmington told me of someone travelling round the world by tractor. A cyclist had been on the TV sometime previously, so they wondered at first if it was me. There was so little waste ground for camping on that I spent two of the four overnights on the way to Adelaide at caravan parks. The charges were nominal, and had the advantage of bringing me into contact with more people. As I was quizzed about my experiences by different people, thoughts were entertained about compiling an information sheet for distribution.

Around Gawler were a number of fields of vines as I was on the edge of the wine growing region of the Barossa Valley. I travelled slowly through the new town of Elizabeth a few miles to the south-west, from which it was just 17 miles to Adelaide. After collecting literature at the Tourist Bureau, I headed south to the youth hostel on South Terrace. Finding it full I returned northwards to the YMCA. Its central location proved convenient during the next four days as I explored the sights of the city.

There was something about Adelaide which commended the city to me, causing me to feel I would not see a more attractive state capital. The view was strongest at Light's Vision, a high point north of the central area from which there were commanding views towards the centre, the Adelaide Oval nearby and towards the Mount Lofty Ranges a few miles to the south-east. I stood for some time admiring the views beside the statue of Colonel William Light, Adelaide's celebrated planner and first Surveyor-General. A plaque recorded an extract from his journal, answering powerfully the heavy criticism directed at him on his siting of the city:

> "The reasons that led me to fix Adelaide where it is I do not expect to be generally understood or calmly judged of at present. My enemies, however, by disputing their validity in every particular, have done me the good service of fixing the whole of the responsibility upon me. I am perfectly willing

> to bear it; and I leave it to posterity, and not to them, to decide whether I am entitled to praise or to blame."

Posterity has conferred on Adelaide the description as one of the most beautiful cities in the world, its location and layout praised many times. On the way up to Light's Vision a walk through the park beside the Torrens River brought me to a cricket match in progress at the University Oval.

Adelaide was a city of statues, including one of Queen Victoria in the heart of the central area. I was pleased to see the statues to Sturt and McDouall Stuart, two of the country's greatest explorers; Adelaide was the starting point for Sturt's journeys to the centre and for McDouall Stuart's journeys to the north. This particular day of sightseeing was rounded off by a visit to the Scott Theatre on Kintore Avenue for a performance of two operettas by the Gilbert & Sullivan Society of South Australia. After seeing a poster in the YMCA on my arrival, I was delighted to be able to obtain tickets for *Trial by Jury* and *H.M.S. Pinafore* for the very next evening. The Saturday evening was especially memorable, as I had little opportunity to hear any music on my solitary journey. A lump came to my throat as the boatswain sang:

> But in spite of all temptations
> To belong to other nations
> He remains an Englishman!

The following Monday was Labour Day, a national holiday, and another memorable day. I was collected at the YMCA early in the morning by the Frankhams, who lived at Clarendon to the south of the city. They had invited me to contact them after meeting on the road north of Alice Springs two weeks earlier. On the way to their home in the country, I was shown Happy Valley Reservoir and Mt. Bold Dam. The roads were crowded as a result of the holiday. It was a change to spend a relaxing day in family surroundings, to talk about the places we had both seen in recent weeks, but mostly just to share each other's company.

There was a temporary heat-wave as I left Adelaide two days later, making for a warm ride as I climbed about 2,000 ft to pass over the Mt. Lofty Ranges. I looked back many times, unsure when I was going to see my last view of the city on the plain below. Crossing the Murray River at Murray Bridge, the road followed the great river southwards on the last miles of its long course before it flowed into Lake Alexandrina, named by Sturt, after the first name of the princess who became Queen Victoria, after his epic voyage down the Murrumbidgee and Murray rivers in 1830.

Most of the traffic was left behind at Tailem Bend as I headed south down the quieter coastal road, the Princes Highway. South of Meningie, the Coorong came into view, a 90 mile long lagoon between the mainland and a strip of sand-hills bordering the ocean. The Coorong was visible from the road for just part of the long journey beside it, thick bushes preventing any view at other times. A few sheep stations and fishermen made up most of a light population in the region. My main company was the rich bird life, including ibis, ducks and seagulls. A flight of ducks in almost perfect V-formation flew overhead, pointing the way south. As I felt cut off from the rest of the world, one incident brought me back in touch, when a newspaper was thrown out of a passing car. I was able to read of the forthcoming marriage of Jacqueline Kennedy to Aristotle Onassis. It took place two days later on 20 October.

A detour off the main highway at Kingston brought me at the end of one day to the old fishing port of Robe, one of the earliest settlements in South Australia, and at one time its only port. In 1857 Robe was the chief port of entry for Chinese on their way to the Victorian gold-fields. It was a fascinating place to visit before continuing towards Millicent through rich pasture. Pine forests were visible to the south as I approached a diverse area in the south-east corner of the state.

At Snuggery I found myself on tours of both a cellulose mill, where paperboard was manufactured, and a tissue mill, seeing the manufacture of toilet paper and tissues. Near Mt. Gambia the following day, I watched operations at the coralline limestone quarries, seeing slabs being cut for countless future office buildings. I never expected to be witnessing so much commercial activity. Returning to the traveller's more traditional role, I cycled to the nearby mountain which gave the city its name. The mountain was an extinct volcano with four craters containing picturesque lakes. From the slopes there were fine views over the surrounding pastoral area. It was then just a few miles from Mt. Gambier to the state border with Victoria.

*****

Arrival in Victoria coincided with deterioration in the weather. I had been very lucky throughout my time in South Australia. A cloudy day followed as I continued along the Princes Highway towards Portland, stretches of pine and gum forest near the border quickly giving way to pastoral country. Mt. Richmond was to be seen to the south, then Portland Bay came into view as the road turned towards the coast. It rained heavily during the night, leaving off thankfully half an hour before I took the tent down. Near the former volcano of Tower Hill, pastoral country gave way to market gardening, the lava-covered soil of the surrounding area being rich and fertile. The sun shone for a short time as I passed through Warrnambool late in the afternoon, followed by a stormy night after I had turned off the main road at Allansford for the quieter Ocean Road. The road remained some distance inland until I approached Peterborough, when the ocean remained constantly in view. The surf was impressive to see in the high wind from the south-west, partially assisting me. Another stormy night and day followed, causing me to turn northwards earlier than planned as I reached undulating country and rugged coastline near Cape Otway. With visibility reduced at times to 200 yards, I wasn't going to see much of the Otway Ranges to the east as planned.

A direct turn north through Colac brought me to the historic city of Ballarat, which I was determined to include on my itinerary. This former gold mining town must be in all the history books as the location of Australia's only civil war when, on 3 December 1854, fighting occurred between the miners and police and soldiers. It was the culmination of many grievances, the central one involving the payment and inspection of the miners' licences at a time of falling revenue by the government and widespread evasion of payment for licences. I studied all this history again as I stood beside a memorial at the Eureka Stockade, the site of the fighting in which 22 diggers and 6 soldiers were killed. At another memorial, to the discovery of gold in Ballarat in 1851, I admired an imitation of the "Welcome Nugget", one of the largest pieces of natural gold ever found. I had arrived far too late to make my fortune there.

I rode along Sturt Street to the west of the city to see an impressive memorial to more recent fighting. An imposing Arch of Victory straddled the road at the start of a 14 mile long tree-lined Avenue of Honour on the western approach to the city, in memory of the soldiers, sailors and nurses of Ballarat who took part in the First World War. Fixed to each tree was a plate with a name from one of these groups. North-east of the Arch of Victory was large Lake Wendouree, location of the rowing events during the 1956 Olympic Games centred on Melbourne. On the north side of the lake in a quiet, ordinary road, Lindisfarne Crescent, I marvelled at the mosaic work of Arthur Pickford, who had died in 1962. Using glass and shells he created a unique wall and fencing at the front of his bungalow. The masterpiece, set in the middle of the front lawn, was a model of the Imperial Crown about five feet high, the entire surface richly decorated with glass and shells. Mr. Pickford's widow showed me all this work with justifiable pride before I left for a nearby camping ground.

Earlier at the Arch of Victory I suddenly found myself in a short and unexpected interview with *The Courier*, the local paper. When I saw the following day's issue, I wasn't surprised to see a mistake in a couple of lines below a photograph of me as a result of the abrupt interview. The caption referred to me being on the way to Adelaide, while I knew I was on the way to Melbourne, which I reached after a long day's ride of 70 miles along the Western Highway. Sunshine early in the morning allowed me to see Ballarat at its best before I left this attractive city. Thick cloud quickly covered the sky as I travelled through dairy country. West of Bacchus Marsh I looked down over a vast plain to the east, before descending to it through the Pentland hills. Fruit grew all around in the valley, and the departure from Bacchus Marsh was made along another attractive tree-lined Avenue of Honour. As the road climbed to the top of a small rise 17 miles from Melbourne, tall buildings in the city centre came into view, illuminated by some welcome late-afternoon sun. A few miles onward, Deer Park proved to be the start of the western suburbs.

I was aiming for Footscray, another western suburb, to meet once again Stan, a passenger on the *Eastern Star* to Brisbane. Though living in a small flat after remarrying a short time before, Stan and his new wife extended warm hospitality to me while I visited the city. They were also playing hosts to Keiichi, the young Japanese man on the boat, who had just spent 2½ months at the farm near the Victoria - New South Wales border of another passenger. He didn't seem to have the confidence to explore Australia by himself. Stan took us to call on a further passenger in the nearby suburb of Williamstown.

In the city centre, after admiring the trams running on Collins Street, I had a tour of the massive Parliament House. In this location, various strands came together to remind me once again of fundamental historical associations of the area and its immense growth during the Victorian era. I was in the state named after the Queen, and in the city named after her favourite Prime Minister, Lord Melbourne, who held power when Victoria ascended the throne in 1837 and guided the young Queen during the early years of her reign. Near Parliament House was a fine statue of General Gordon, whose death at Khartoum in 1885 was reported to have caused Queen Victoria much grief. The statue resulted from the admiration of Gordon by the people of Victoria. Another statue nearby reminded all of the expedition led by Burke and Wills to attempt the first crossing of the continent from south to north, setting out from Melbourne in August 1860. My earlier travels in the north had acquainted me with some of the details of their tragic journey and the competing journeys by McDouall Stuart, starting from Adelaide, to complete the journey first.

Visits to the new Arts Centre and the Planetarium brought my mind back to the modern era. How I wished that the Planetarium had been in Brisbane so that I could have had an earlier understanding of the southern sky prior to all those nights below the stars in the north. During a Sunday in the parks, I was amused to see Captain Cook's cottage in Fitzroy Gardens, transferred lovingly from Yorkshire as a centenary gift, Melbourne having been founded in 1835.

I followed the shore of Port Phillip Bay through endless suburbs as I left Melbourne, turning east at Frankston to pass north of Western Port, another deep indentation in the general coastline. Leaving the suburbs behind me, I entered dairy country. Near Tooradin the quieter road I was on converged with a more direct route to the south-east, which was crowded with traffic. It was Tuesday, 5 November, Melbourne Cup day, the most prestigious day in the country's horse-racing calendar. It seemed that everyone not at the races was trying to get out of the city into the countryside. Meanwhile, in America, it was voting day in the Presidential election, which would be won by Richard Nixon. Most of the traffic left me after a few miles, heading south down the Bass Highway, possibly to a wildlife centre at Cowes on Phillip Island. I continued south-east on the South Gippsland Highway towards Leongatha and Yarram, the road climbing into hills. As it followed a line of crests, there were wide views all around over rolling dairy and sheep country.

From a summit near Foster, there was a fine view to the south-east over Corner Inlet to Wilsons Promontory, its many peaks contrasting sharply with the surrounding flat land. Travelling was easy as a following wind from the south-west blew me along. The road joined the Princes Highway, the main coastal road, at Sale, but traffic was light as there were no large towns on this route. The road turned to the coast at Lakes Entrance, a holiday and fishing resort. There were stunning views over the area from a lookout at high ground at Jemmy's Point; with the ocean an incredibly deep blue. I stopped to visit the Antique Museum, which fellow passengers on the *Eastern Star* had told me about. Along with a number of vintage cars, motorcycles, buggies and many miscellaneous items were two penny farthing cycles in excellent condition; my fellow passengers guessed correctly that I would be interested to see these veteran machines. The museum was the creation of one man, and all the more interesting to see in this relatively remote location. The road quickly turned inland again, the journey through the south-east corner of Victoria characterised by mile after mile of gum forest in undulating terrain. There were some particularly fine stands, many preserved in Lind and Alfred National Parks.

*****

A showery day followed as I crossed the border into New South Wales, but there was little rainfall. Black clouds moved overhead during the afternoon, followed by lightning and great peals of thunder, the first I had heard for a long time. With all the pyrotechnics in the sky, I expected a downpour but there was none. The local population were praying for a number of downpours as the region was suffering a serious drought.

I became very conscious of this the following day when I arrived at a station south of Bega where Mrs. Solomons, a passenger on the *Eastern Star,* lived with her husband. They made me welcome despite the enormous difficulties they were experiencing. I was amazed to find Keiichi there, having arrived from Melbourne three days earlier. The Solomons had lost a number of stock, and I went round the station helping to distribute bales of straw to the surviving emaciated animals. The straw had been transported many miles from healthier regions. As the farmers united to organise feed supplies and to assist each other through the crisis, I learned that there were approximately 1,000 dairy farmers and 70,000 head of cattle in the Bega Valley. I was taken to see the local coastal resort at

Tathra and a cheese factory at Kameruka. A meal at a club in Eden, followed by a visit to the Returned Servicemens League club in Merimbula, introduced me to the extensive range of facilities at these social clubs, which were apparently only in New South Wales.

As I left the Solomons, hoping that there would soon be an improvement in their conditions, I turned off the Princes Highway at Bega for the Snowy Mountains. On the climb towards Nimmitabel many trucks passed me coming in the opposite direction, loaded with straw and hay for the drought-ridden valley. Reaching a summit at 4,310 ft about 11 miles from the town, it was easily the highest I had been to for some time. After a brief descent, there was more climbing in the undulating terrain. North of Nimmitabel, at the top of a ridge, a line of snow-capped peaks came into view for the first time about 60 miles to the north-west. The wind whipped across the open pasture, with sheep stations on both sides of the road. Large granite boulders were strewn over many of the paddocks.

At Cooma I collected literature at the Snowy Mountains Authority Information Centre, confirming that the roads I intended to travel on were clear of snow. I wanted to see something of not only the mountain scenery in this highest region on the continent but also of the Snowy Mountains Scheme. This was one of the largest and most imaginative civil engineering works ever, providing for the east-flowing waters of the Snowy River and its tributary, the Eucumbene, to be impounded and diverted through long trans-mountain tunnels to the west-flowing Murray and Murrumbidgee Rivers and their tributaries. The primary object was increased irrigation along the long Murray and Murrumbidgee Valleys. Power generation was of secondary importance, but the project involved some spectacular schemes. With my engineering background, I was keen to see something of them.

An Avenue of Flags in Centennial Park in Cooma helped to set the tone for the massive works which followed the establishment of the Snowy Mountains Authority in 1949. The flags were unfurled on the tenth anniversary in recognition of the men who came from more than 50 countries to work on the project. I headed west along the Alpine Way towards Jindabyne after deciding to make a clockwise circuit of the mountain area. The weather was warm and sunny as I travelled through sheep farming country to Berridale, the sparse terrain covered with groups of granite boulders just as I had seen near Nimmitabel. A long climb away from Berridale was followed by a descent to Jindabyne, where the road ran across the top of the new dam which impounded the waters of the Snowy River. There were several boats on the deep blue water of the lake created.

A succession of long climbs and descents followed, the climb beside the Thredbo River taking me over Dead Horse Gap at an elevation of 5,190 ft. I was back among the trees, the mountain slopes covered with thick gum forest, and with patches of snow near the tops of the crests of the Ramshead Range to the north. The road turned northwards to skirt Mt. Kosciusko, the country's highest peak, rising to 7,314 ft. I found it ironic that Australia's highest mountain was named after a Polish patriot after being climbed for the first time in 1840 by a self-styled Polish Count, Paul Edmund de Strzelecki, while exploring a route through Victoria which became known as Gippsland. Strzelecki was in Australia for less than 10 years, yet left a lasting legacy.

After admiring the views from Scammel's Spur Lookout, I started a long descent shortly afterwards to Murray 1 Power Station near Khancoban. No guided tours were in progress when I arrived, but a maintenance engineer kindly agreed to show me over the station. I was pleased to see the generator hall and transformer bank at close quarters, though disappointed to observe that none of the equipment was supplied by the company I worked for in England. I looked up the mountainside at the three enormous pipelines which brought water down from the mountain tunnels, and down at further pipelines to serve Murray 2 Power Station, under construction. Following the road down past this Station, I stopped by at the Murray Control Centre. It was all very impressive.

The maintenance engineer had told me that the Alpine Way which I was travelling on was closed by snow only two months earlier. Much rain had fallen since, and the recent fine, dry days were about the only ones. It was warm in the mountains, but I read in a newspaper later in the day that much of New South Wales was simmering in temperatures above 100°F. Fires were breaking out in many forest areas.

I turned off the Snowy Mountains loop north of Khancoban, detouring to visit another passenger on the *Eastern Star,* the final passenger on my schedule. Mrs. Gadd lived with her family on a farm just 45 miles away down the Murray Valley on the Victoria side of the river. I was pleased when she first gave me her address to find that it was close to my planned route. Crossing the Murray near Bringenbrong, I followed the river through rich sheep and dairy country, with hills on both sides of the valley. The grass was thick and green, in contrast to the arid conditions in the Bega valley which I had left a few days before. I reached the Gadd's property at Mount Alfred at 12.30 one day, just in time for lunch before going out to one of the paddocks with Mr. Gadd where he was cutting hay. The following day I found myself assisting with baling. Work was proceeding apace in the fine weather, as it was uncertain how long it would last. A change was known to be under way. Although I had arrived at a busy period, there was time to talk, to look at photographs, to meet other members of the family, and to see a little of the attractive, surrounding area.

The weather was still fine and sunny as I returned up the Murray Valley to the mountains, but heavy rain fell during the night. It presaged cooler weather as I climbed over the Jagumba and Toolong Ranges before crossing Tumut Pond Dam south of Cabramurra, the highest town in Australia at 4,880 ft. Two power stations nearby were closed to inspection. I stocked up with food and had a warming cup of tea before seeking lower and warmer ground. The climbing was not over, however, as a long descent was followed by a long climb over the Great Dividing Range. The road descended to the old gold mining town of Kiandra and to the Eucumbene River before climbing again.

I camped in trees just over the summit to get some shelter from the wind. Rain and sleet fell during the evening and night, continuing in the morning. It was time to get out of the mountains, but getting the bicycle ready was a long operation. After fixing each baggage strap, I had to stop and thaw out my fingers before going to the next one. Eventually I got under way with all my extra clothing on, including my cape, which not only kept me dry but dealt with the wind chill factor. The sleet changed to rain and the temperature rose a degree or two as I descended the Snowy Mountains Highway, the rain finally lessening and leaving off as I approached Adaminaby. I was back to the plains and on my way to Cooma to complete a 260 mile loop round the Snowy Mountains.

The federal capital of Canberra lay just 80 miles to the north of Cooma. After a run through gently undulating pastoral country east of the Murrumbidgee River, I arrived in the capital during the middle of the morning after camping overnight near Royalla. With the approach from the south running close to the Diplomatic district, I detoured to see some of the Embassy and High Commission buildings and the Prime Minister's Lodge before crossing Lake Burley Griffin via Commonwealth Avenue Bridge to the city centre.

A short time later, as I looked for somewhere to eat, I was startled to see a bicycle which I recognised. Entering a café nearby, I was delighted to see Ian Hibell again. It had been two months since we met on the road at Adelaide River south of Darwin. After lunch we cycled south to Parliament House to listen to Question Time in the House of Representatives, joining a large number of visitors in the Public Gallery. During an entertaining hour, we heard both the Prime Minister, Mr. John Gorton, and the Leader of the Opposition, Mr. Gough Whitlam, speak. We went to the youth hostel later, this stay being my only one in a hostel in Australia.

A glorious day followed during which I walked up Mt. Ainslie to obtain some fine views over the city, particularly the view looking down on the Australian War Memorial and straight down Anzac Parade to Parliament House across Lake Burley Griffin. It was a vantage point which allowed one to appreciate the city layout, designed by the American architect Walter Burley Griffin following the winning of an international competition. Descending Mt. Ainslie, I made a long visit to the War Memorial.

After two days seeing the sights, I set off for the famous city of Sydney. Ian set off with me, but it wasn't long before we separated. He travelled a lot lighter than myself, and his daily milage was double mine. He went on during the next 15 years to cycle from Cape Horn to Alaska, from the Norwegian Cape to the Cape of Good Hope, and across South America at its widest section.

I made for the coast via Braidwood, guessing that this would be a far quieter and more interesting route than the direct one via Goulburn and the Hume Highway. The road took me through undulating dairy country, the grass parched yellow due to the dry weather. In the tinder-dry conditions, I read of more bush fires around Sydney, resulting in closure of the Hume Highway for a long period yesterday. The slopes of Clyde Mountain were covered with gums, and there was increasing gum forest as I approached the coast at Bateman's Bay. Considerable areas of the forest were in a distressed state due to recent fires. There was smoke in the air as patches continued to simmer. Not wanting to camp in such an environment in case another fire flared up, I was pleased to find myself beside the ocean south of Ulladulla at the end of the first day along the coast. Camping among sand dunes along the edge of the beach, it was pleasant to be able to go for an evening swim.

More forest to the north had been ravaged by fire. There was increasing development along the coast as I became within a day's car drive from Sydney. With a weekend, the road was busy. Many cars had surf boards strapped to the top, and the standard of driving was the worst I had encountered for a long time. There were fine views of the ocean from high points on the road. It was a relief to get off the Princes Highway at Sutherland in the outer suburbs of Sydney, proceeding towards the centre via Captain Cook Bridge at Botany Bay.

It was Tuesday, 3 December 1968. Reaching the centre at midday, I collected mail at the P.O. before later walking up Macquarie Street to see Parliament House, and on to Bennelong Point to see the Opera House. It was at an advanced stage of construction, and at great expense, as teams of architects and engineers attempted to translate into practical form the inspiring concept of Jørn Utzon, the Danish architect whose design had won an international competition. There was a fine view of the Harbour Bridge from this location. Having seen the new and older symbols of Sydney, I made my way out to Bondi, keen to renew acquaintances with the three London girls I had first met on the coach trip to Ayers Rock. They had been back at work for some time, and it was wonderful to share their company again and discuss everything that had happened in the intervening two months. I reached Sydney not a day too early, as the weather changed dramatically. It rained heavily during the night, continuing for most of the following day. The rain was apparently moving down the coast, thus bringing relief to the farmers in the Bega Valley.

The southern loop from Port Augusta which I had just completed had involved 2,250 miles, including the detour inland to the Snowy Mountains and Canberra. More particularly, arrival in Sydney completed my cycle touring in Australia. Since arriving in Brisbane early in July, the bicycle had covered 5,700 miles. I thought back to several people I had met before coming to Australia, and who had told me that I would find little to see as regards scenery. I wondered where they had been. But, then, they hadn't been using the right transport for a start to see the wonders and unique terrain of Australia at its best.

NEW ZEALAND

Auckland
NORTH ISLAND
Rotorua
L. Taupo
Taupo
L. Waikaremoana
Wairoa
TASMAN
SEA
Mt. Egmont
Napier
Hastings
Wanganui
By air fromand
to Australia
Wellington
Picton
Blenheim
Westport
Kaikoura
SOUTH
PACIFIC
OCEAN
Greymouth
SOUTHERN ALPS
SOUTH ISLAND
Christchurch
Mt. Cook
Haast
Timaru
L. Hawea
Milford
Sound
L. Wanaka
Wanaka
Oamaru
Queenstown
L. Wakatipu
L.
Te Anau
L. Manapouri
Dunedin
Invercargill
0
100
200
Miles
STEWART I?

Chapter 19

Round the South Island

Thursday, 5 December 1968

The southern latitude of New Zealand persuaded me to spend the two peak summer months there if possible. Arriving in Sydney with December already under way, I therefore lost no time in immediately booking a flight to Wellington. The heavy rain of the previous day had cleared up as I left for Kingsford Smith Airport north of Botany Bay at 8am. Arriving at 9.15 for a scheduled departure at 11.45, it gave me plenty of time to deal with dismantling the bicycle. Opinions differed at the Air Cargo Terminal as to how much I needed to do, but I removed the wheels, seat and handlebars. I tried to remove the pedals, but they wouldn't budge. Thankfully, there was no insistence on this and I consigned the bicycle to the airport staff. It was convenient that there was no requirement to enclose the bicycle in a box, as on my only other flight so far from Vancouver to Tokyo, since it allowed me to cycle out to the airport.

After all this work, I reached the Passenger Terminal at 11am to learn that the plane departure was delayed for more than two hours, from 11.45am to 1.55pm. Ominously the plane, an Air New Zealand Lockheed Electra turbo-prop, had been delayed by bad weather at Wellington on the earlier morning flight to Sydney. I was in optimistic mood that this poor weather was only temporary as I adjourned to the Observation Deck to watch other arrivals and departures, and contemplated seeing a new country.

There were some attractive views over Botany Bay as the plane eventually took off to climb quickly above the cloud layer. A blanket of cloud was below us all the way on the 1,400 mile flight over the Tasman Sea, breaking up as we approached Wellington at sunset after a flight of just under four hours. My watch told me it was 5.40pm, but an advance of two hours was required to correspond with New Zealand time. The approach was exciting, with the runway just fitting on a neck of flat land between Evans and Lyall Bays, with steep hills on either side. I told myself that the pilot had made this journey many times, understanding the wind conditions and the precise length of the runway so that we would not end up in the water. He didn't fail us, and I was soon on my way by bus to the city centre and the YMCA.

The following day, a Friday, "Windy Wellington" lived up to its reputation, with the weather fouler than in Sydney two days earlier. During a respite around midday, I left the YMCA to gather some travel literature and introduce myself to the city. Early in the evening I collected the bicycle at the Cargo Terminal building nearby, assembling it there before riding back to the YMCA. I decided to spend the weekend in Wellington to give myself a chance to settle into the new environment, to see something of the capital before departing for the countryside, and to hopefully allow the weather to recover.

During a break in the rain on Saturday, I toured the Parliament Buildings. A following visit to the Dominion Museum allowed me to steep myself in New Zealand history and Maori culture. On an altogether better day on Sunday, I took the bicycle out to see some of the sights in the capital's scenic location. At the Overseas Passenger Terminal in the harbour, Shaw Savill Line's *Northern Star* was berthed, having recently arrived from Britain via South Africa and Australia, a reminder that jet travel was in its infancy and many people still wanted to travel in a more leisurely manner. There was a fine view south-east across the harbour to the densely packed frame houses on the hillside. A steep, winding climb up this hillside brought me to the lookout on Mt. Victoria at 640 ft, from where there were commanding views over the city and towards the airport.

I looked forward to making this journey again in a few weeks time when I returned to Wellington. As I watched the news on the TV during the Sunday evening, dramatic pictures of landslides on the main highway between Wellington and Auckland seemed to confirm the correctness of my decision to be heading south. The highway was cut in eight places after the recent, heavy rain. I wanted to tour the South Island first in any case, its shape as a leg of lamb lending it to a circular tour, which would reveal more continuous dramatic terrain than in the North Island; and there were particular features on the South Island which I didn't want to miss on any account in the limited time I had.

After the weekend in Wellington, I was full of excitement as I caught the ferry for Picton at 10am on the Monday morning. The water was deep blue and smooth as we set off down the harbour on a fine, sunny day with some cloud. But we were in the shelter of the harbour and the waves became bigger and bigger as we approached Cook Strait and the open water separating the North and South Islands. There was a grim reminder of the power of the sea as we passed close to the wreck of the ferry *Wahine*, which had capsized on rocks eight months earlier during some of the worst weather ever in the region. 51 lives had been lost, including 3 children, out of 734 passengers and crew. We were in open water for about 1½ of the 3½ hour journey of 52 miles to Picton, and I was soon feeling seasick. The sea suddenly became calm again as we entered the shelter of the long channel of Queen Charlotte Sound, protected by islands on each side, for a most attractive introduction to the South Island.

As I climbed westwards away from Picton, I was able to watch the ferry sail back up the Sound. The turn west started an anti-clockwise circuit round the South Island, so that I would have the sun behind me on the long, scenic journey down the west coast close to the Southern Alps. First, a pleasant afternoon's ride brought me to the youth hostel at Havelock. The hostel was formerly a school with a very distinguished pupil, Lord Rutherford, who was pre-eminent in the field of atomic research and split the atom for the first time at the Cavendish Laboratory in Cambridge in 1918.

The road towards the west coast continued through mountainous terrain, following river valleys and climbing over saddles. So much of the terrain was picturesque, with snow-capped peaks visible at some time during the day, pine forest covering the higher slopes and colourful wildflowers lining the roadsides. Everywhere was so green with the considerable rainfall. It was difficult during these early days not to keep making comparisons with Australia, where I had seen some picturesque terrain in the south, particularly in South Australia and in the Snowy Mountains. Now it was all around me, and there were no large distances to cover to experience changes. There were pastoral scenes in the valleys, and the sheep did not look up as I passed, having so much green grass to consume.

At Kawatiri the road started to follow the Buller River all the way to the coast as it surged between high hills. There was little flat land near the river, and west of Murchison the river started to flow through the Buller Gorge, a deep canyon. An earthquake had struck the region seven months earlier in May, causing many landslides and closing the road until September. I had a rough ride on gravel as construction of a new road proceeded. At a notable feature called Hawkes Crag, a massive slab of granite mountainside plunged vertically into the river, requiring a slot to be cut into it for the road. I prayed for stable conditions before commencing the ride along the mountain overhang.

The coast was reached at Charleston, south of Westport, a region which enjoyed a surge of interest after the discovery of gold around 1860. As the road ran close to the coast for many miles, there were fine views over the Tasman Sea. I camped close to the Pancake Rocks at Punakaiki, so that I could spend the maximum time at this unusual location where wind and rain had eroded the limestone headland so that it looked to have been created from thousands of pancakes laid on top of each other. There were already glimpses of the Southern Alps 60 miles away to the south, and they came increasingly into view from Greymouth onwards, as the main ridge converged towards the coast. The Alps now came almost constantly in view, my eyes being drawn towards them as they dominated the scene for mile after mile. I could concentrate on the ever-changing vista as the road was almost empty of traffic. A few hitch-hikers I met were having a lean time.

Short detours from the main road to Franz Josef and Fox Glaciers reminded me that I was directly in line with New Zealand's highest mountains, Mt. Cook at 12,349 ft and Mt. Tasman at 11,475 ft. There were stunning views of the main peaks across Lake Matheson as I followed the forest walk round the lake. Returning to the main road, there were long stretches through sub-tropical forest and long stretches of gravel road as I approached the Haast Pass. On the coast at Arnott Point I paused at the monument commemorating the opening of this stretch of road on 6 November 1965 by the Prime Minister, Mr. Holyoake. It enabled a circular tour to be made of the South Island for the first time. As I followed this route just three years later, I could therefore have no reasonable complaint about the gravel road: I needed to be grateful that there was a road.

The main road turned inland to cross the Haast Pass, while the coastal road terminated after a few miles as increasingly rugged terrain commenced, and the sea made huge indentations in the coastline at the start of the fjord area which covered the south-west corner of the island. The scenery seemed to get better and better as I descended the Haast Pass to an area of huge lakes and spectacular mountain terrain. The road ran first beside Lake Wanaka, then Lake Hawea, the water an incredibly deep blue. At the town of Wanaka, I replaced my rear tyre, which was badly cut after the many recent miles of gravel road. It had covered 1,400 miles since fitting in Bega, virtually the same distance as the earlier tyre of the same type bought in Port Augusta. The new tyre was a type new to me; it looked reasonably sturdy, but only time would tell. I fitted it in the shade of the petrol station where it was bought as the weather was now extremely hot. Meanwhile, the North Island was having a spell of poor weather.

The bare hills and parched grass in the broad Clutha Valley signalled how dry this area was, as the prevailing westerly winds deposited most of their moisture on the coastal mountains. Just before turning west at Cromwell, I crossed the 45° parallel line. Inspection of the miniature maps in a small diary confirmed that South America was the only other land mass where it was possible to do this in the southern hemisphere. Heading west up the Kawerau Gorge, I camped beside a creek near Gibbston. It seemed an idyllic location, right beside the babbling waters of the small creek as it tumbled over the stony bed. My experience told me that it would not be quite so simple, as I learned quickly that thousands of flies and mosquitoes had already chosen the same location. Insects were even more of a menace in New Zealand than they had been in Australia.

It was just a short run to Queenstown on the north shore of the 52 mile long Lake Wakatipu. Gold was discovered in the area in 1862, but in more recent times Queenstown had developed into a major holiday centre. I didn't see the area at its best, though, as the weather had to change sometime, and did so as I approached the town. In the circumstances I decided against a cruise on the lake, but relaxed at the caravan park, having a chance to talk to a few of the many visitors there. After a dull day, rain started to pour down early in the evening, continuing throughout the night. When it left off at 9am, I decided to make the most of it and move south out of the area.

There was snow on the mountains little more than 500 ft up as I followed the eastern shore of Lake Wakatipu before emerging from the mountains into good pastoral country inhabited by thousands of sheep. The weather improved steadily over two days, during which I reached Lake Manapouri. The following day was Christmas Eve and a glorious day, ideal for the launch trip on the lake to admire the views of the surrounding mountains and to see something of the major hydro-electric project then under construction. At West Arm at the end of the lake, a presentation of slides with a recorded talk informed us of the work going on to divert the outflow from Lake Manapouri through tunnels to an underground powerhouse, 6¼ miles away at Deep Cove at the head of Doubtful Sound. A coach took us over the Wilmot Pass down to Deep Cove to see the site where the tailrace emerged. Nearby was the former passenger liner *Wanganella,* providing an imaginative solution to the problem of arranging accommodation for 500 construction workers. It was all very impressive, taking me back mentally a month to when I was seeing similar work on the schemes in the Snowy Mountains.

The journey over the Wilmot Pass gave me my first sight of one of the fjords, Doubtful Sound. The next destination was another one, Milford Sound, which I had heard so much about. It was reached by a one-way journey of 73 miles northwards from Te Anau over a challenging road. Starting the journey late in the afternoon on Christmas Eve, the whole of Christmas Day was spent reaching Milford Sound. I would never forget this Christmas. It was difficult for a traveller from the northern hemisphere to accept that, here in the south, it was the middle of summer and the peak holiday period. As I left Te Anau, the hotel bars were full as Christmas celebrations got under way.

There were many miles of rough, gravel road ahead, but there was little doubt that resources would be found in future years to pave the road. With the anticipated growth of travel, it was too important a route to remain much longer as it was. For the present it was a gruelling ride as the road climbed and descended as it followed the Eglington River up the mountain valley. In the middle of the evening, I reached the ¾ mile long Homer Tunnel, involving a descent from 3,200 to 2,800 ft on the passage through the tunnel, which was unlit and unlined. Water seeped through the rock at intervals, creating a stream of water down each side of the road. After switching on my dynamo, I set off with the brakes on to counteract the gradient and to reduce the chances of riding into the wall. After a hundred yards I couldn't see a thing. Retreating to daylight, I removed the torch from one of my bags which I used while camping and tried again. After a tense journey I reached the other end of the tunnel to begin a swift, winding descent to Milford Sound a few miles to the west. Arriving at a camping area I couldn't get my insect spray out fast enough when I stopped, to be attacked immediately by swarms of flies and mosquitoes also here for Christmas.

It all seemed so unreal as I embarked on the launch trip down Milford Sound on Boxing Day morning. It was a dull morning, but conditions were calm with the water as smooth as a millpond. There was no certainty what conditions would be like if I waited until the afternoon. Rudyard Kipling described Milford Sound as "the eighth wonder of the world". As the launch moved slowly down the deep canyon towards its mouth, it was easy to share his vision, seeing the high mountains plunging vertically into the water on each side.

Back on dry land I had lunch at Johnston's Hostel with considerable company. There were several coach parties there, and every person seemed to be at least 30 years my senior. I was overwhelmed with attention as they discovered the unusual circumstances of their young visitor. The cloud was breaking up as I departed on the first stage of the return journey, to get within a day's travel of Te Anau the next day. This time I had my torch ready for the ride through the Homer Tunnel.

On the journey to Te Anau the weather was even better than on the journey north. On the last stretch of gravel road two cars heading north stopped by me. I was asked the same question from each: "How much more have we got of this?" The road was extremely rough and trying even for motorists. Another car stopped, the driver, who was the station owner at Te Anau Downs station nearby, inviting me to stop by for a cup of tea. There I met his wife and four young children. As I enjoyed a piece of Christmas cake and a mince-pie in addition, I was surprised to find myself being shown the children's schoolroom in the house. With the road often blocked by deep snow during the winter, there were problems in getting the children the 19 miles south to Te Anau township each school-day. The mother, who was a teacher, therefore instructed them, following a correspondence course. This warm gesture of hospitality rounded off an unusual Christmas for me.

I emerged from the mountains to gentler terrain as I turned southwards towards Invercargill. I was now looking at sheep again, thousands of them. After a visit to the main park and museum in Invercargill, I set off on the coastal route through gently undulating farmland and over a number of hills. I had been away from the coast for many days since leaving it at Haast. The road passed close to a number of shearing sheds, reminding me that it was shearing time now in the middle of summer.

On New Year's Day I arrived in Dunedin as the whole of the city's population seemed to be coming the other way. Almost everywhere was closed on this national holiday, but I managed to find a restaurant open for lunch before walking round the central area to see the principal buildings in this city founded by Scottish settlers in 1848. There were superb views from Signal Hill of the city, with its fine location at the end of the long Otago Harbour and surrounded by hills. When I left Signal Hill, I descended to the main road down the steepest hill I had ever encountered. I had to have both brakes fully on all the time just to hold the bicycle back to a safe speed. If I lived in Dunedin, I could see myself endeavouring to fit gears to the bicycle even lower than my present ones to meet this new challenge.

Back at the lower level, I cycled to Duke Street to an address I had been given by a fellow guest at the Parkway Hotel in Vancouver. Clyde had left New Zealand to see something of the world, and we had spent many hours talking together. His mother and stepfather could not have made me more welcome, inviting me to stay with them straight away. Since I last saw Clyde nine months earlier, he had moved north to the Queen Charlotte Islands off the British Columbia coast.

I left Dunedin via the Mt. Cargill road, the old highway, a long gradual climb for five miles being followed by an equally long descent to Waitati. From the high ground there were fine views of Port Chalmers and the entrance to Otago Harbour. At Evansdale I was able to get off the main highway again for a few miles to follow the scenic, coastal road, which went up and down like a switchback. North of Palmerston at Shag Point the road started to run beside the coast for several miles, beside a long wide sandy beach bordering the blue ocean. The beach was deserted, reflecting perhaps the country's small population. As the road turned inland to pass through farming country, I suddenly came to an abrupt halt four miles south of Oamaru as my rear tyre suffered a blow-out. It had covered less than

700 miles since fitting at Wanaka: it was not as strong as I had hoped, but might have been weakened on the very rough road to Milford Sound. After locking the bicycle up, I obtained a lift into town. I was just in time to catch a cycle shop owner as he was leaving for home at the end of the day. He not only declined payment for a new tyre, but drove me out to the bicycle. I could never forget such generous consideration.

Following a stay at the youth hostel, I re-crossed the 45° parallel north of Oamaru. The road passed through an almost flat market gardening area, with views over the wide plain towards the snow-capped Southern Alps to the west. They were closer here in this region where the island narrowed. The youth hostel at Timaru enabled me to have successive nights in the hostels and meet further young travellers. A few miles north at Winchester, I took the opportunity to leave the main highway for a longer but quieter sweep round the edge of the fertile Canterbury Plain, crossing the Rakaia River near Windwhistle after descending into a wide, deep gorge. There were fine views of the Malvern Hills just to the west.

I was looking forward to visiting Christchurch, this most English city on the banks of the river Avon. Founded in 1850, two years after Dunedin, it was an incredibly attractive city to visit, with its well-maintained buildings and beautiful parks and gardens. There were fine views north over the city and the Canterbury Plain from the Summit Road along the top of the Port Hills to the south. The high ground looked south down on Lyttelton Harbour. From the city's port in the harbour, Captain Scott embarked on his last fateful voyage to the Antarctic in 1912. Back down in the city in the main park was a fine statue of Captain Scott. Also in the park was an equally fine statue of Captain Cook, who circumnavigated the North and South Islands of New Zealand on his first voyage of discovery in 1769-70.

Returning my mind to current voyages, a guest at the youth hostel told me that Ian Hibell had crossed to the South Island two days earlier. If he came down the east coast, I might see him; but this was unlikely as Ian liked the mountains as much as myself, and almost certainly set off for the west coast. While on a walk in the city, I was delighted to encounter Keiichi, whom I had met at the homes of other passengers on our ship to Australia. He seemed finally to have plucked up courage to do some travelling on his own, and we had a long chat over a cup of coffee. Before leaving Christchurch I bought two new tyres, replacing the tyre on the front wheel of the bicycle and deciding to carry a spare tyre for the very first time ever. I had contemplated for some time whether to start carrying a spare tyre, as concern grew about the deteriorating quality of the tyres available. I was reluctant to do so, since a tyre was a bulky item and more weight to carry. Nevertheless, carrying one immediately relieved me of anxiety over availability in the event of a blow-out or failure for some other reason. In a similar vein, continuing to carry my large water container reduced concern about the availability of the next water supply. The negative side again was the burden of extra weight.

There was considerable traffic on the main road north from Christchurch, making it desirable to take an alternative route if there was one. A short detour was available between Kaiapoi and Amberley, then a longer one between Waipara and Kaikoura, taking me over the Weka Pass through rolling, limestone hills. North of Waiau there was gravel road for 27 miles, but the reasonable surface did not impede progress on the way to the youth hostel at Kaikoura.

The one road north from Kaikoura ran close to the coast, constrained by the Seaward Kaikoura Range, before turning inland south of Seddon over hills. The grass on the hills was yellow due to the hot, dry weather. By contrast the floral gardens in Pollard Park in Blenheim provided the most colour I had seen for some time, arranged as part of an imaginative garden design including a stream winding its way through the Park. This served almost as a final, outstanding memory of the South Island, as a short time later I rode into Picton to complete the circuit round the island.

During five weeks the bicycle had covered 1,750 miles through some of the most outstanding and varied scenery to be found anywhere in the world. After a long winter, it had been a brilliant summer so far, at least on the South Island. I rode up Queen Charlotte Drive to watch the arrival of the afternoon ferry, before going down to take my place on it. The crossing of the Cook Strait was beautifully smooth. Darkness fell before we entered Wellington harbour, the lights of the city and surrounding area creating a memorable return.

Chapter 20

North Island Interlude

Monday, 13 January 1969

It was a delight to be back in Wellington for a couple of days. I took the bicycle up Mt. Victoria for a second time to admire the views over the city, before descending to ride out to Point Halswell at the northern end of the Miramar Peninsula. The impressive Massey Memorial there to a former Prime Minister had been clearly visible from the ferry on the journey to the South Island. A third visit to Mt. Victoria in the evening showed me the lights of the city laid out below.

Before departing from Wellington again, I was not only planning the immediate journey ahead, but needing to focus increasingly on the overall strategy. I considered I had sufficient savings for all the travelling in Australia and New Zealand, and for the return journey home, without needing to work in either country. If I did work, it would have to be for a whole year, or two years, to get the timing right for the journey through Asia. This would have extended artificially the duration of the tour: I decided against it, and had started enquiries on boat passages from Australia to Singapore on arrival in the south of Australia. Following these up at intervals, I was now booked for a passage departing from Fremantle on 20 February. While in Wellington I paid the balance on my ticket, had my first cholera and typhoid shots and renewed my smallpox vaccination. The following day I retired to bed just after midday, feeling totally worn out as the vaccinations took effect.

After a long sleep I felt better as I set off northwards from Wellington on a warm, sunny day on a tour of the North Island. It would not be a complete circuit as for the South Island. I would have to turn across the Island before getting anywhere near Auckland and the long peninsula to the north-west, but I ought to be able to see a reasonable amount of the Island during the next three weeks before returning to Australia and preparing for the final stage of the journey. There was a steady climb through the hills to Johnsonville, then an undulating run on the old highway to Porirua. At Pukerua the road reached the coast for some attractive coastal scenery for a few miles before turning inland slightly.

As the road continued through pastoral country, the snow-capped top of Mt. Ruapehu became visible 70 miles to the north from rising ground south of Sanson. A few miles further at Bulls I was glad to get off the main highway north as I turned north-westwards to Wanganui. I stopped for a cup of tea and a walk round this attractive city, which was a thriving Maori centre centuries before the first white settlers arrived in the late 1830s. A succession of long climbs and descents followed as the road crossed river valleys. On this third day out of Wellington I was feeling quite exhausted after a sleepless night, causing me to look for a quiet camping area near Waitotara. Although it was only late afternoon, I had hardly erected the tent before falling asleep as the recent vaccinations took further effect.

I awoke feeling much better. A run through gently undulating terrain brought me to Hawera, where I turned north, already seeing Mt. Egmont at this prominent bulge in the coastline, the upper slopes of the mountain shrouded in cloud as I viewed it across the rich green Taranaki plain. But I wasn't seeing the mountain in the best light as I looked into the afternoon sun. Setting my tent up in a meadow directly east of the mountain and facing it, I held out great hopes for the following morning. I was not disappointed as I opened the tent flaps to behold a clear view of Mt. Egmont's conical peak rising to 8,260 ft, the morning sun now behind me. It was a magnificent treat for my 28th birthday. Moving northwards slowly, my eyes were continually drawn to the west to take in further views before cloud moved in.

Turning east on reaching the coastal road near Waitara, I approached an unusual area. Leaving the pastoral country behind, I entered a very hilly area with sub-tropical vegetation all around, including huge ferns. It all suggested an area with a high rainfall. I left the coastal road at Ahititi to start a zigzagging course across the widest part of the North Island in order to join together a number of points of interest. There was suddenly a most undesirable change in the state of the road as I hit rough gravel. It lasted for 25 miles as I travelled up the Kotare Gorge, climbing to a summit of 1,710 ft. At the higher elevation, the hillsides were even more thickly covered with ferns and jungle foliage. I emerged from the jungle near Ohura to rolling grass-clad hills.

A turn south near Ongarue brought me to a picturesque area south of Taumarunui. Following a long climb, there were fine views looking down on the deep blue Wanganui River. I seemed to have the road to myself, causing me to wonder how well the area was known. The road remained high on the hillside, and Mts. Ngauruhoe and Ruapehu came slowly into view to the south. The cone of the active volcano of Mt. Ngauruhoe, rising to 7,515 ft, was clear of snow, while the upper slopes of Mt. Ruapehu, which rose 1,660 ft higher to 9,175 ft, were white.

At a community called National Park I turned north-east to take the road running north of the mountains. I sped along under a strong, following breeze as the road gradually descended. A long ride beside the eastern shore of Lake Taupo brought me to Wairakei, an area of unique interest just north of the lake. It was the start of a large thermal area, with boiling mud pools and clouds of steam rising from the scarred surface of the ground. My mind went back to Yellowstone National Park, where I first encountered features like this.

It was particularly interesting at Wairakei to see how the huge energy reserves presented by the underground hot water and steam had been harnessed to produce a significant proportion of the North Island's electricity. The first large-scale project to harness geothermal steam to produce electricity had taken place at Larderello, in Tuscany in Italy, the first plant starting operation in 1913. Drawing on this experience, the first shallow bore was drilled at Wairakei in 1950, and the first generator brought into operation in 1958. The banks of pipes leading from the boreholes to the power station were an impressive site, accentuated by huge expansion loops. I arrived at the power station just in time to join a party for another interesting visit.

A long ride through pine forest brought me to the thermal areas at Waiotapu and Waimangu for more amazing scenes. It was just a few miles further to Rotorua, a centre of Maori culture. It was the most northerly point on my journey in the North Island, and an area I did not want to miss. The great majority of place names on my maps were of Maori origin, reminding me constantly of the people who came to New Zealand long before the *pakehas*, or Europeans. Yet I was conscious of having hardly seen any Maoris on my travels so far, and certainly few in the South Island.

Rotorua provided an opportunity to correct this imbalance to a small degree, particularly at the Ohinemutu and Whakarewarewa Maori villages. Business required attention first. After collecting mail at the Post Office, I made contact with a doctor, who was able to give me my second doses of cholera and typhoid vaccination without any formality. During the evening I attended a Maori concert at the Municipal Chambers, feeling far from well. A restless night followed. I left the youth hostel during the middle of the next morning to see one of the Maori villages and adjacent thermal area, but staggered back to the hostel two hours later, finished for the day. I was glad that I had attended the concert the night before; the singing provided my most abiding memory of Rotorua. I was enchanted.

Before leaving Rotorua, I replaced the rear tyre on the bicycle, using the spare which I had been carrying since Christchurch. The tyre removed had covered less than 1,000 miles, but bulged due to a bad cut. I moved south slowly, trying to regain energy as I climbed slowly away from Rotorua. I knew I was in for a long climb as I had descended the same road two days before. Turning south-east near Waiotapu, there was further climbing as I approached pine forest near Kaingaroa to cross the hills to Hawke Bay. I was glad I had replaced my rear tyre as I was soon on gravel road again. It was interesting that the few settlements along the road in this area were occupied almost exclusively by Maoris. As I passed through Te Whaiti early in the morning, a large group of Maoris sat in the open in front of a meeting house listening to a Maori speaker. It was an Anniversary Day in Auckland and throughout the surrounding area.

Climbing continued as the road passed through exotic forest in Urewera National Park, reaching a summit of 3,050 ft at Taupeke Saddle. A descent was followed by a climb high up the hillside to 2,150 ft to suddenly reveal superb views over Lake Waikaremoana some 400 ft below. As the road remained high on the hillside for several miles, a succession of glorious views occurred. A long general descent towards the coast eventually began, and the paved road returned. Three hydro-electric stations in the valley used the water from the high lake. There had been 84 miles of gravel road, but the scenery had been outstanding, all the more so since it had not been expected.

The road from Wairoa round Hawke Bay went up and down unceasingly as it tried to find a route over high grass-clad hills and across a number of rivers. There would have been some fine views over Hawke Bay in different circumstances, but I encountered heavy rain during the next two days. Arriving in Napier, I just managed to get a photograph of the bronze statue of Pania, a maiden of Maori legend, before the next downpour occurred. As I hovered around deciding on a position for a photograph, a lady walking past muttered to her companion: "Why is it men spend so much time in taking photographs of this statue?" It was the most beguiling statue of a girl that I had seen anywhere, reflecting the beauty of the women of the Polynesian races. While the rain continued to pour down, I spent some time in St. John's Cathedral, the new Anglican cathedral built following the destruction of the earlier one in the earthquake of 1931. I retreated later to the youth hostel, glad to have a solid roof above me for the night.

A brighter day followed as I travelled a few miles to Havelock North, hoping to make contact with someone who came from the same village of Hartest in Suffolk as myself. Although our paths separated after primary school, Chris and I saw each other once or twice in future years, with our families continuing to live in the area. I couldn't pass by his present home without attempting to make contact. When I reached his house, he was out working, presenting me with the task of explaining to his New Zealand-born wife who the odd person was who had suddenly turned up on a bicycle and appeared to know her husband from the past. It wasn't difficult in the end since she had recently returned from a visit to Europe with Chris, and was as familiar with the family background and home environment as myself.

Chris recognised me straight away when he returned home a short time later. I was taken on an exhilarating flight over the area in his small plane, flying over Hastings, Havelock North, out to the gannet sanctuary at Cape Kidnappers, and seeing the rich agricultural land in the area, much of it intensively cultivated. Chris was engaged in aerial spraying, small aircraft like his being used extensively for seeding, fertilization, and the spraying of insecticides and weed killers. I had to admit I was relieved when we descended to *terra firma* again. It was the first flight I had ever made in a small plane: it was my third flight ever. Chris generously invited me to stay with his family for a couple of days, but I needed to continue to Wellington.

The road south-west continued through grass-clad hills, the grass quite brown, indicating the area had experienced some hot, dry weather, even if it eluded me for the present. There was heavy rain for half an hour early in the evening before I stopped to camp near Waipawa, and more the following afternoon as I followed the road through Dannevirke to Woodville. I kept to the main road through the centre to avoid likely gravel on a winding road closer to the east coast, reaching the youth hostel at Mangatainoka during the evening. It was my first evening in a house hostel, the home of an elderly lady who had been taking in hostellers for three years following a family loss. While having a meal, we listened on the radio to the final episode of "The Gilbert and Sullivan Story". I had listened to an earlier episode at the hostel at Timaru a few weeks earlier, this all taking me back home mentally, where I had heard the whole series just before leaving.

After this pleasant evening in homely surroundings, I sped along as the road generally found a level route through the green hills. Leaving the main road for 20 miles south of Eketahuna for a parallel road to the east, I was disappointed to run onto gravel for a few miles. As this detour rejoined the main road at Opaki and the hills receded, the road started to travel across a wide plain, an area of much fruit growing, principally strawberries, raspberries, loganberries and similar fruits. After a break in Featherston early in the evening, I turned to cross the Rimutaka Range to the west in order to reach the youth hostel at Kaitoke for the evening. The wind had been increasing in strength, with sudden gusts causing me to stop several times and lean into the wind to avoid being blown over.

On the climb to a summit at 1,817 ft, a car pulled up ahead of me. I met Julie again, a Scottish girl first encountered at the youth hostel in Rotorua, and then on the road to Lake Waikaremoana when she passed me on a bus. She had stayed at the youth hostel at Clive, where Ian Hibell was acting as warden. She told me that Ian wanted to get in touch with me. I found it ironic that I had stayed at the hostel at Napier just seven miles to the north, unaware that Ian was so close. I thought he was still going round the South Island. If it hadn't been for the heavy rain in Napier, I might well have proceeded to Clive that day.

At the hostel at Kaitoke, I was delighted to meet another cyclist, not presently cycling but with a long background involving tours over most of Europe and Scandinavia. David was of Scottish origin and visiting a married daughter in Auckland. He had been given extended leave of absence by his wife, and was travelling round New Zealand in a mini-van, youth hostelling and camping. He was thoroughly enjoying his new-found freedom. Leaving Kaitoke, there was farming country for a few miles before I reached the outer suburbs of Wellington at Upper Hutt.

It was a fine, sunny day as I returned to the capital on Monday, 3 February 1969, after a most satisfying interlude on the North Island. On the three week circuit I had covered 950 miles, getting a fair introduction to the attractions of the Island, so different in many ways to its competing southern neighbour. I was able to book a return flight to Sydney for the following day. As the plane took off just after 8am, there were fine views of Wellington on another beautiful morning. The Southern Alps could be seen piercing the cloud way down to the south, while to the north the cone of Mt. Egmont made for a wonderful view as we moved away from this earthly paradise.

OVERLAND

Chapter 21

Asian Preparations

Tuesday, 4 February 1969

The plane from Wellington arrived at Sydney after a flight of just over four hours. My watch said it was 12.15pm, but it required turning back two hours to correspond with Eastern Standard Time in Australia. With the bicycle on the same flight, I was able to ride away towards the centre of Sydney about an hour after arrival. The temperature hit me straight away, as the area was experiencing a heat-wave, quite different conditions to two months earlier.

As a result of being able to obtain the return flight to Sydney so easily, I now had a little longer than expected before needing to leave the city, just over a week. It provided ample time to deal with various preparations, while visiting some of the sights of the city and seeing again the girls I had first met on the way to Ayers Rock. They looked after my literature and films on Australia while I went to New Zealand. Things had not been standing still while I was away, as I returned to find that one had got married.

I was looking forward in a few days time to crossing the continent by train, to experience in particular the 300 mile section across the Nullarbor Plain representing the longest stretch of straight railway track in the world. It was therefore disappointing to learn at the railway station that so many other people were planning to make the journey at the same time that there were no spare seats for a number of days. It would be possible, however, to transport the bicycle by train. I was directed to the coach station, where I was able to make a booking. A few days later I left the YMCA to be confronted by headlines on the newspaper advertising boards about a strike threat on the railways. As I made inquiries about sending the bicycle to Perth by air, I reflected on how all my travel plans were being turned upside down once I involved myself with other agencies instead of travelling independently.

I went to a pharmacy to buy water purification tablets and anti-malarial tablets. The water tablets would be needed throughout Asia, while I would need to take anti-malarial tablets until I reached the Khyber Pass. In the drier conditions to the east, malaria was not considered a problem. I came away with a quantity of chlorine tablets to last for a number of weeks, but was told that anti-malarial tablets were a proscribed drug: I would need to see a doctor. A short while later, a doctor explained to me that young people had discovered that consumption of the drug in large quantities could induce a hallucinatory trip. We were in the middle of the psychedelic era: sale therefore had to be controlled. After discussing the very different kind of trip I was embarking on, the doctor wrote out a prescription for all the tablets I would need. I returned to the pharmacy with the valuable piece of paper.

The bicycle needed far more of my time to prepare it for the journey ahead. It was due for a complete overhaul, just as had been carried out between the two summers in North America and before departing for Japan. During the last 10 months in Japan, Australia and New Zealand, some 10,700 miles had been covered without major maintenance. Certain equipment now needed replacement, or at least detailed inspection, to prepare for the similar cycling distance separating me from England.

Over several days, the tyres and tubes were replaced, the hub gear dismantled and inspected, rear sprockets and chain renewed, and all bearings dismantled, inspected and regreased. These and other operations took many hours, but it was a sound investment of time in order to reduce the likelihood of serious problems while on the road. Following a letter a few weeks earlier, my cycle dealer in Stafford sent new sprockets out to me: I had doubts about being able to buy them in Sydney. Considerable help was provided by an elderly cycle dealer; John, originally from Redruth in Cornwall, could not have been more obliging over the temporary loan of special tools.

Respite was provided by a memorable free concert at the Town Hall on the Sunday evening, performed by the Sydney Symphony Orchestra. A programme featuring works by Mozart, Smetana, Handel and Dvorak provided the first classical music I had heard for a long time. There was no question that it was appreciated all the more after an absence.

When I made my final visit to John on Broadway to return a couple of tools the day before I left the city, I had to have my rain cape on. During the previous four days, six inches of rain had fallen, building up from thundery showers in the late afternoon on earlier days. The weather during my two periods in Sydney was not allowing me to see the city at its best. Time suddenly ran out. On this last full day in Sydney, the newspaper boards announced that the railwaymen were going on strike at midnight. How relieved I was, in one sense, that I had been unable to book a train seat a week before.

*****

Thursday, 13 February 1969

Awakening to a blue sky, for the first time for several days, I posted a parcel home containing most of my travel literature and films on Australia and New Zealand; I still needed some of the literature, as I hadn't left Australia yet. After depositing my bags at the coach terminal, I cycled to the Air Cargo terminal and consigned the bicycle for a flight to Perth. Feeling much lighter, I headed downtown to Australia Square Tower, the country's tallest building at the time, to take a few photographs looking over the city and the harbour from the 600 ft elevation. Cloud was already building up, but the views helped to give me a better, final impression of what had been a very damp city.

The coach departed at 3.15pm on a 2,787 mile journey to Perth, which would take almost three days. More correctly, the first coach departed, as the long journey would be split between three coaches, the first travelling the 605 miles to Melbourne via Canberra, the second 472 miles from Melbourne to Adelaide, and the final coach covering by far the longest stretch of 1,710 miles across the immensity of Western Australia. I looked forward to comparing parts of the journey in the east with the route I had followed, plus seeing completely new terrain west of Port Augusta.

As the coach headed out along the Hume Highway towards Goulburn, where we stopped for an evening meal, it was abundantly clear that the coastal route which I had followed from Canberra to Sydney was by far the more interesting route for a cyclist, or for anyone wanting to see the country. It was getting dark as we reached Canberra late in the evening, so that I saw nothing more of the first stage until daybreak the following morning. Arriving at Melbourne behind schedule, there were just 20 minutes before the next coach departed at 8.15am. There was a fascination about the first and last parts of this second stage to Adelaide, as the coach travelled between Melbourne and Ballarat, and Tailem Bend and Adelaide, on the same road I had cycled on some three months earlier. The relatively ordinary terrain on the long stretch between Ballarat and Tailem Bend on the Western and Dukes Highways made me glad I had followed the coastal route.

The stage to Adelaide was made entirely in daylight. Arriving at 7pm, there was time for a leisurely meal in this beautiful city before the final coach commenced its long journey at 8.45pm, 30 minutes behind schedule. We heard that the rail strike had ended. The coach was full, including a party of women bowlers on their way to Perth for a tournament. Since I was going to be on the coach for a day and a half, I looked forward to some conversation with the person sitting beside me. I found myself sitting next to an elderly man from southern Europe who did not seem to speak a word of English. It was a reminder of changing times as an increasing number of emigrants to Australia were drawn from all over Europe.

When the coach reached Ceduna on the edge of the Nullarbor Plain at 7.30am, we stopped for breakfast. There was a longer break later in the morning at the small community of Nullarbor while a rear wheel was changed and a puncture mended. The sealed road had ended at Ceduna, giving way to dirt, which was smooth most of the way, but tested the strength of the tyres. The dust thrown up penetrated into the coach without too much difficulty. As the road ran close to the coast, compared with the rail route at least 50 miles inland, there were slight undulations in the terrain most of the way, and a considerable amount of vegetation, with stretches of gum forest and bush and long stretches of scrub.

We crossed into Western Australia at 5.15pm South Australia time, 4.45pm Western Australia time. Every time change served to confirm that we were moving west. There were only 50 miles of dirt road to travel in the new state compared with 300 miles which had been covered in South Australia. Some time during the second night on the coach, we finished crossing the Nullarbor Plain. When I woke up, we were some distance west of the gold mining town of

Kalgoorlie. After breakfast at Merredin, the coach started to cross a vast wheat belt. As we passed through the small town of Meckering, eyes gazed at piles of rubble resulting from an earthquake four months earlier. West of the town we passed over a long ridge created by the earthquake.

It was just 50 miles to go from Northam, where the road started a winding run over the Darling Range. From several miles away, the city of Perth came into view, spread out on the plain some 1,000 ft below. We arrived on schedule at 10.45am, emerging into a furnace with the temperature up to 106°F. I booked into a hotel after being unable to obtain a room at the YMCA, relieved to find a room as a result of the 4,000 women bowlers in the city for their tournament. After a rest and a shower I collected the bicycle at the Air Cargo terminal. It had beaten me to Perth, and equalled again the number of flights I had made, making up for my flight over the Hastings area in New Zealand.

After the heat of the day, it was a delight to walk down to the Supreme Court Gardens in the evening for an open air concert performed by the West Australia Symphony Orchestra at the Orchestral Shell. On a warm, clear evening, with many stars visible, the light orchestral music wafted over me, taking me back mentally to open air concerts in Detroit and Chicago two and a half years earlier. I had arrived in Perth on a Sunday, thus attending concerts on consecutive Sunday evenings.

There was business to attend to as I began two full days in the state capital. Collecting my boat ticket at the travel agency, discussion occurred as to whether I would be allowed to land in Singapore. Regulations had been introduced a month before requiring future visitors to have either a return ticket or a ticket to an onward destination. It was an attempt by the Government to deal with an increasing number of young Westerners arriving in Singapore after hiking through Europe and Asia, hoping to obtain cheap boat passages to Australia. The result of there being few such passages was that many quickly became destitute, imposing themselves on the generosity of the Singapore Government and its people. But Singapore was not like India: it was not a charitable society, with a religious framework imposing an obligation to welcome and support all travellers, regardless of circumstances. Singapore was developing into a harsh, commercial society dominated by the work ethic. After discussions with the shipping company, it was felt that my circumstances should not present a problem. The combination of heavily laden bicycle and money for the onward journey indicated that I would not become a burden to Singapore.

I left to see some of the sights of the city. The views from the parks, from Riverside Drive and from the Legacy Lookout on an upper floor of the new 17 storey State Government Offices building caused me to equate Perth with Adelaide as the most attractive of the state capitals. When I entered Parliament House, I was delighted to be taken on a personal tour by one of the staff. Returning to the hotel, I heard on the evening TV news that my ship, the *m.v. Australasia,* had berthed at Fremantle during the morning. There was a buzz in the lounge when it was reported that Judith Durham of *The Seekers* had arrived in Perth to give two concerts.

On my last evening in the city, I took the bicycle out after darkness had fallen to see the city lights. There were fine views from the Legacy Lookout, which I was pleased to find open in the evenings. Back at ground level, I crossed the Narrows Bridge to admire the city from across the Swan River. Bright bands of light reflected in the still surface of the water made an enchanting picture before I returned to the city via the Causeway to the east. The next morning I followed the north bank of the Swan River for a leisurely ride downstream to Fremantle, to spend the rest of the day in this port city, and my last full day in Australia.

*****

Thursday, 20 February 1969

There was an air of excitement at the north wharf of the harbour as passengers arrived throughout the morning to take their places on the *Australasia*. This was going to be a different kind of journey for me compared with the passages across the Atlantic to New York and down through the Pacific to Brisbane. While the ships on these voyages carried just a few passengers, the *Australasia* could carry 173. The present voyage listed 110, of which 85 were on the round trip: most would be Western Australians. While some of us were having lunch, a transformation occurred at the side of the ship. When I next looked over the port side against the wharf, I was amazed to see hundreds of coloured streamers blowing in the breeze. Increasing numbers of streamers were released by passengers towards families and friends on the quay, waiting to wave farewell to those on board.

The *Australasia* moved away from the quay at 2.30pm to begin its 2,260 mile voyage to Singapore. It was just a short run up the harbour before we emerged onto the open sea of the Indian Ocean and turned northwards. A following wind from the south-west created a slight swell on the ocean, with the result that many of us were soon feeling less than 100 per cent. It was an opportunity to meet my cabin mates. I had been allocated to a 4-berth cabin, one berth being unoccupied. Charlie, an Australian about 45, had been working as an electrician on the north coast at Dampier. Henri was German, aged 23, and had been in Australia for two years as he travelled the world. He had started a return trip home some time earlier, but had succumbed to the charms of various young ladies in Thailand. The result was that he had to return to Australia to replace deleted funds. As he told me about his experiences, and how much he was looking forward to returning to Thailand, I didn't rate very highly his chances of getting back to Germany.

Life on board ship quickly settled into a routine dictated by mealtimes. There was interesting friction as, although the ship was not a passenger liner, the number of passengers was such that the ship's officers and crew attempted to maintain similar standards. With reasonably formal dress desired at dinner, the modern world found itself in conflict with the conservative world of the ship's officers. A number of the younger passengers, especially those travelling to Asia, were not in the habit of wearing a conventional shirt, yet alone anything smarter, while the passengers on the round trip seemed to have come prepared for the more formal life.

The *Australasia* had an unusually long and colourful history as it began its nineteenth year. It had been built in 1950 in Belgium for the Belgian Government to be run on the Congo run. After the uprising, she was sold to a British company and operated for a short period on the company's Amazon River run, before being transferred to another company and converted to carry refrigerated cargoes on a South America run. In 1965 the ship was transferred to Austasia Line Ltd. of Singapore and given her present name.

As we sailed north across the Tropic of Capricorn, the humidity gradually increased, and it was easier to sit down and either talk or read rather than contemplate anything more onerous. I had time to review the factors which resulted in me approaching Singapore at the end of February, rather than at any other time of the year. With about 9,000 miles to cycle, it was going to take me about eight months at the speed which I travelled at. Starting at the beginning of a year would therefore result in me getting through Western Europe before the onset of winter. However, too early a start would involve me in heavy rainfalls up the Malay Peninsula, while I needed to get across India before July prior to the start of the monsoon season there. These and other conflicting considerations left me concluding that I ought to have arrived in Singapore a month earlier, but that would have upset all my travel plans for Australia and New Zealand. The long journey had to involve compromises; only time would reveal whether my plans were at all sensible.

An information sheet on the *Australasia* told me that she normally ran at 15 knots for fuel economy reasons, though she could run slightly faster. A bulletin posted every day at noon gave the distance covered during the previous 24 hours. It was interesting how close this figure was to 360 miles each day as we sailed through remarkably calm seas. The 2,260 mile voyage would therefore take a little over six days if the rate was maintained.

On Monday morning, as we sailed past Christmas Island, I had to look at a map to clear up some confusion in my mind. It confirmed the existence of another island of the same name in the Pacific south of Hawaii, and well known as the location for a number of nuclear tests. Early the following morning we started the turn through the Sunda Strait between Sumatra and Java. The 4,203 ft peak at the south-east corner of Sumatra dominated the view after breakfast on the penultimate day of the journey. At noon on Wednesday there were just 115 miles to go as we passed a succession of small islands. Many bamboo-roofed houses were to be seen by the water's edge, supported on stilts, and small fishing boats were everywhere. The last stage of the great adventure was about to begin.

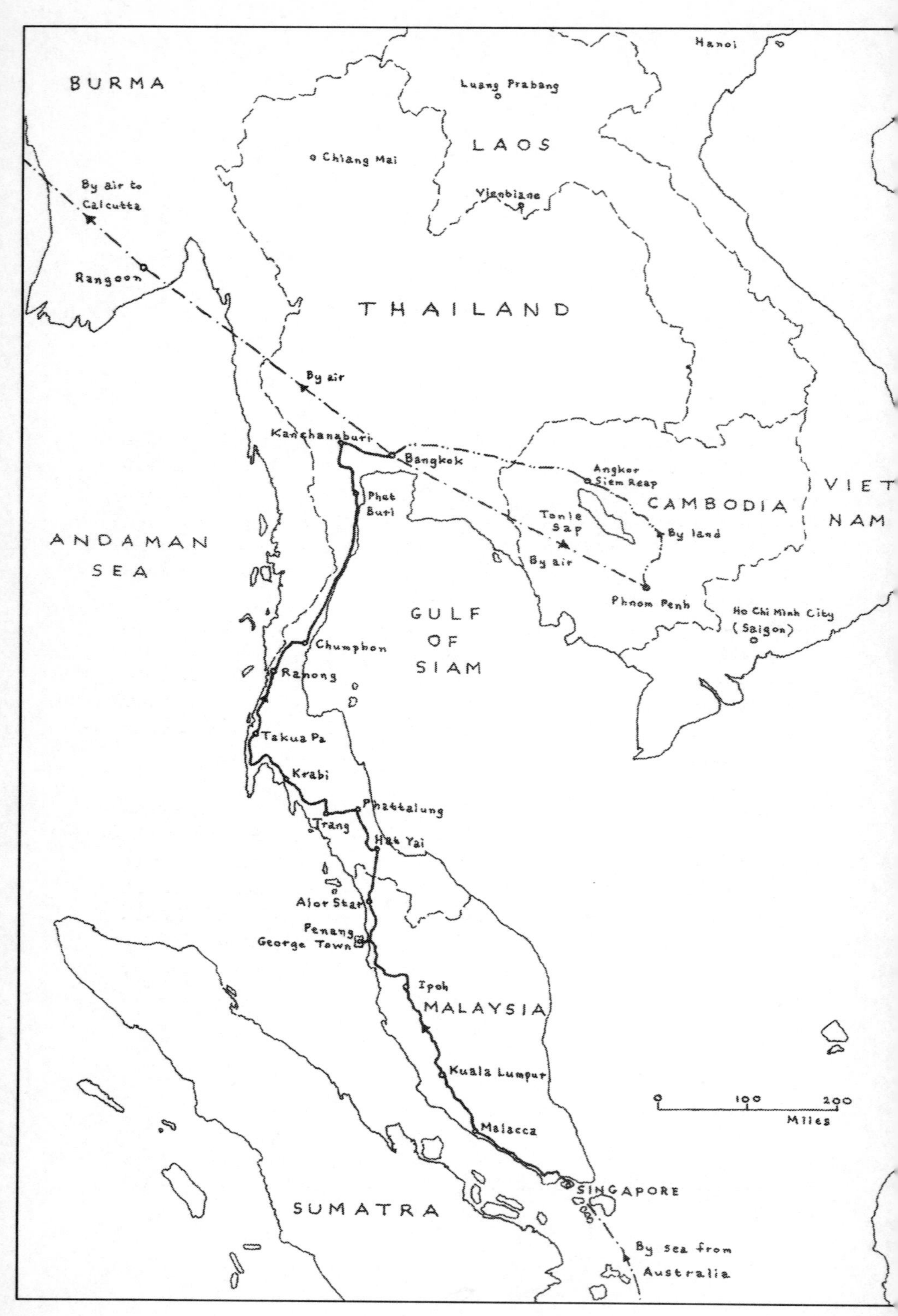

BURMA
Hanoi
Luang Prabang
LAOS
Chiang Mai
By air to
Calcutta
Vientiane
Rangoon
THAILAND
By air
Kanchanaburi
Bangkok
Angkor
Siem Reap
Phet
Buri
CAMBODIA
VIET
NAM
Tonle
Sap
By land
ANDAMAN
SEA
By air
Phnom Penh
GULF
OF
SIAM
Ho Chi Minh City
(Saigon)
Chumphon
Ranong
Takua Pa
Krabi
Phattalung
Trang
Hat Yai
Alor Star
Penang
George Town
Ipoh
MALAYSIA
Kuala Lumpur
0
100
200
Miles
Malacca
SINGAPORE
SUMATRA
By sea from
Australia

Chapter 22

Up the Malay Peninsula

Wednesday, 26 February 1969 Singapore

The overland journey through Europe and Asia has had an appeal for Western travellers for many years. The sheer distance would be a challenge on its own, but when you add to it the number of different countries along the route, each with their own geography, history, culture, languages and climate, you have the elements for a journey of endless fascination. There is, of course, no set route; and the route taken by an individual traveller will depend on a number of factors - the mode of travel, the time of year when the journey is undertaken, the person's particular interests, and the background which the individual brings to the venture. Not the least important factor is the political situation prevailing in any country along the intended route. It is a prerequisite that a country on the route will not be at war, or seriously affected by war in neighbouring countries.

The route I planned to take was a fairly direct one, but one which seemed to involve as many points of interest as alternative routes through the vast region. As the *Australasia* entered the Empire Dock at 7pm in fading light, I was poised to start my overland journey. Clearing Customs and Immigration without any problem, I cycled towards the centre of the city. I was pleased to obtain a room at the YMCA, as everything around me seemed alien. After unpacking my bags, I set off in the relative cool of the evening to see a little of the teeming life of Singapore. I was soon conscious of the three predominant races; the Chinese, Malays and Indians; the Indian Sikhs, with their beards and turbans, all looked so distinguished. Every few seconds a taxi blasted its horn to try to get one's custom. Other residents were also after my custom and, during a short walk, I was accosted by a prostitute, a pimp and by a young boy. I got used to dealing with the inquiries: "You want pretty girl?" "No, you want boy, then?"

I walked further than expected, returning foot-weary to the YMCA after midnight. The following morning Henri and Charlie, my cabin mates on the *Australasia,* booked into the YMCA after a night in a hotel. We walked round the city together during the next three days, seeing the principal buildings, the shops and the famous Raffles Hotel. Walking beside the Singapore River which ran through the heart of the city, there was so much activity to observe. Small boys dived and swam in the muddy-looking water. In an older, quieter part of the city, I was delighted to encounter trishaws for the first time; the vehicles here involved a side-car attached to a standard bicycle without further modification. I resolved to obtain one at some time in the future.

It was a continuous struggle to move very far or for long periods. The heat and humidity were oppressive at this location just north of the equator. How long would it take to get used to these conditions? The local people seemed to be moving around without concern, while Western visitors were in a state of exhaustion. On a bright Sunday morning, after three days in Singapore, I left the city to start the long journey north. As I crossed the island via Thompson Road and Mandai Road to keep away from the main traffic as much as possible, I was surprised to see how much open land there was once away from the city. Reaching the north side just after midday, I looked across the Johore Strait to the city of Johore Bahru in Malaysia.

*****

Sunday, 2 March 1969   Malaysia

I crossed the Causeway into a new country. It would not have been the case four years earlier but for the speed of political developments. Malaysia had been created in September 1963 as a federation of the States of Malaya, Singapore, Sarawak and Sabah, formerly North Borneo. Just under two years later, in August 1965, Singapore broke away from this young federation to become an independent country.

The road ran beside the Johore Strait for a few miles before turning inland, taking me beside rubber plantations, the first I had seen. It was fascinating watching women workers going from tree to tree collecting the latex which dripped into a small bowl just below the latest sloping cut on the tree bark. As I rode later past oil palm plantations, I could not help feeling what a wonderful education I was continuing to receive.

When I stopped to buy bread at Kulai in readiness for my first night's camping in Malaysia, I found myself surrounded by a group of interested onlookers. One went off to obtain badges of Singapore and Malaysia for my saddlebag, after seeing the others which recorded the countries travelled through so far. The collection had been growing very slowly, but was now increasing at a faster rate as the time in each country came down. This collection of badges provided a growing focus of attention, indicating to everyone I came into contact with an outline of where the bicycle had been. There was a lot of interest as, particularly in the countryside and smaller towns, people cycled themselves and had an understanding of what I was doing. I would have to sew on the new badges at the first opportunity.

The following day, my first full day in Malaysia, was extraordinarily full of interest, far surpassing anything I ever imagined. The scene was now getting familiar, with the rubber and oil palm plantations, and a number of rice paddies. Water buffalo moved slowly along the flat road pulling heavy carts, while bicycles laden with pineapples passed more quickly. There were trishaws in the towns, and everywhere there were people. In the countryside I passed groups of women washing clothes at special places beside the road. Everywhere there were people on the move. Countless times during the day I was hailed with the greeting: "Hello, Joe". I had yet to discover why every Westerner was called Joe. A few greeted me with the question: "Around the world?" Whenever I stopped, there was considerable interest in myself, the bicycle, in its gear system and all the baggage. In a group, there was usually someone who spoke a fair amount of English; he automatically took on the roles of spokesman and interpreter.

Among all these people on the road, I picked up a useful tip from one cyclist. I noticed him pour water onto a cloth wrapped round his neck. Some time later I stopped to remove the face-flannel from my toilet bag. After placing it at the back of my neck and inside my shirt, I poured water from my drinking bottle onto it. The beneficial effect was amazing. As the water evaporated due to the hot sun, but very slowly due to the humidity, it drew heat from my neck, producing a feeling of comfort which I found surprising. As the flannel dried out, I would add further water to it as I cycled along. Drawing on my reservoir for this additional purpose, I did not have to worry about replenishing my water supply in this rich, tropical region.

After crossing the river at Batu Pahat late in the afternoon, the road passed between unending oil palm plantations, with a house every 50 yards. Luckily, when I wanted to stop for the day, a rubber plantation came into view; with no houses in sight, I pushed the bicycle into the trees. No sooner had I erected my tent when the first visitor arrived! It was almost dark. The man spoke little English, but it didn't matter. He had come primarily to look, and stayed for about 15 minutes. He must have reported back to his community, since he was followed by a dozen more visitors later, with the odd torch between them to flash all over the bicycle, tent and baggage. It seemed to them the most natural thing in the world, while nothing like it had ever happened to me before. Camping once or twice in Japan, a few people slowed down to have a look as they travelled past, but they clearly considered it rude to approach me.

The Malaysian boys used their torches to light their way as they cycled along the road in the dark. With no lights on their bicycles, white-shirted men and boys moved past throughout the evening like phantoms. I was awoken at 6.30am by the arrival of a man come to collect latex, as he marched straight in front of the tent. I had just the mosquito net doors of the tent closed, so was aware of all the activity around me. A couple of women arrived to collect latex; they were the only ones of all the visitors during the previous 12 hours who showed some inhibition about coming close to me. As I started to pack my bags and take the tent down, the man arrived with two pails full of latex. Setting them on the ground, he watched me pack everything away and prepare to move. It was like a dream. I would not be surprised by any attentions in the future.

I felt flattered by what was genuine curiosity, and attempted to learn a few more words and phrases in Malay in order to be able to communicate more with all the people I was meeting. I could not depend on everyone speaking English. Words and phrases were added in my notebook at every opportunity. I didn't camp among the rubber trees the next evening, since I reached Malacca in the late afternoon. Various rules on a card in my hotel room needed noting so that they could be respected:

> "No gambling, bringing in of prostitutes, opium smoking or anything that goes against the law is prohibited.

> All lodgers are requested to inform personally or write to the manager of any disobedience on the part of the boys."

Malacca had a rich history. It was only a small city, so that a walk round for a few hours enabled me to see many of the principal buildings and feel the unique atmosphere created by various events. The ruins of St. Paul's Church and the statue of St. Francis Xavier at the top of Residency Hill overlooking the city served as a reminder of the start of a long period of European incursion, when the city was captured by the Portuguese in 1511. Visiting the ruins, I noted Henri's name in the Visitor's Book; my cabin mate on the *Australasia* had been here two days earlier. Down in the city centre, a number of major buildings attested to a long period of Dutch rule, following seizure in 1641. Christ Church, built in 1753, dominated the centre, involving a number of buildings using salmon pink bricks, brought from Middleburg in Zeeland. The covering of red laterite created a lovely, warm tone. In the shade provided by mature trees, I watched as a man sat at a table typing a letter for another resident: I could not imagine more agreeable working conditions. The Dutch remained in Malacca for 184 years, exchanging it with the British in 1824 for their settlement of Bencoolen on Sumatra.

Before leaving Malacca, I bought a hat, attracted by some pith helmets on a market stall. This form of headgear, symbolic of the British presence throughout this part of the world, seemed appropriate as I continued my tour of the former British Empire. The contrast between Malacca and the country's capital of Kuala Lumpur 90 miles to the north could not have been more striking. While Malacca experienced centuries of development under various rulers, Kuala Lumpur was little more than a village until late in the Nineteenth Century when tin was discovered in the area. I visited a city undergoing modern development at an astonishing pace, as new buildings sprang up to reflect the city's importance following the creation of the Federation of Malaysia in 1963.

Entering the city past new sports stadiums, I came to the attractive, older Moorish-style Railway Station. While photographing it, I found myself in conversation with a young Malaysian of Indian origin, who told me he was planning a second trip to Thailand. "The girls are very beautiful there," he told me. It was not the first time I had been advised of this. He then used an expression which perhaps came close to describing how many men felt about them. "They are very loving," he said. I left him to continue into the city and up the

Ampang Road to the Thai Embassy to obtain a visa for myself. As I left with forms to complete, another young Malaysian spoke to me. He was obtaining a visa to renew his acquaintance with Thailand's fair sex.

The following day, a Saturday, I decided to relax in the afternoon by watching a cricket match on the large grass area in front of the Federal Secretariat building. Inquiring at the pavilion who was playing, I was pleasantly surprised to be asked if I would like a game. The players were expatriates, getting their first game of the season under way on the Selangor Club ground. They told me that the season could not be started earlier due to regular afternoon rains. This suggested that I had started my journey up the Malay Peninsula at roughly the right time. I doubted if I would ever play cricket again in a location to rival this one, beside the Moorish-style Federal Secretariat, with palm trees around the edge of the green area.

Over the weekend I took the bicycle out to visit the National Parliament, National Mosque and National Museum in the spaciously laid out city. On a walk round the centre during my final evening, I bumped into Henri, who had been in the city for a number of days before going to the Cameron Highlands. Charlie, our cabin mate on the voyage to Singapore, was also in Kuala Lumpur.

After collecting my visa at the Thai Embassy on the Monday morning, I headed north. The Batu Caves a few miles away were impressive for their size, and for the climb up the hillside to the Caves entrance via a long flight of steps. A Hindu shrine in the Caves resulted in a strong religious atmosphere pervading the whole area.

I was now being confronted starkly by tin mining operations, introducing me to one of the country's two basic industries. While the rubber plantations were picturesque, the opencast tin mines created ugly scars in the countryside as powerful jets of water broke up the hillsides to release the tin-bearing ore. The adjacent plains and river valleys were covered in a white deposit. After passing through each mining area, it was a relief to get back to greener scenes of rubber and oil palm plantations and rice paddies.

There was an air of prosperity in Ipoh, due to the tin industry, as I passed through it on the third day after leaving Kuala Lumpur. I saw for the first time trishaws with a carriage at the front of the vehicle.

Back in the countryside, heavy rain fell at the end of each day. As I sought camping spots in the rubber plantations, I needed to ensure that I was not on ground liable to flooding. I was awoken one morning just before daylight by the voices of women come to collect latex. While I had breakfast, they stopped for a break, sitting on their buckets in a circle some thirty yards from the tent. As soon as I started to take it down, a rearrangement occurred, since two had their backs to me, making it difficult to follow operations. They were soon all in a semicircle facing me.

The following morning, at another plantation 60 miles north, I had an interesting visit by the estate manager, summoned by one of the workers. The manager told me that the trees I was among were 10 years old, and had been tapped for 3 years. The trunks, which were 8 in. in diameter, would be twice the size after another 5 years, by when they would have ended their useful life. The trees, which gave the highest yield so far as a result of research, had a name like B67: such was the price of progress.

I was now close to the island of Penang, my next major destination. Arriving at Butterworth directly opposite the island at midday, I was able to go straight on to a ferry. After collecting welcome mail at the Post Office in George Town, half the afternoon was spent obtaining an extension to my Visitor Pass. It had been restricted to two weeks when I entered Malaysia at Johore Bahru, while three weeks would have avoided the problem. The large youth hostel provided convenient accommodation for the next three nights, bringing me into contact with a number of European travellers. It was my only hostel accommodation in Malaysia, and would be the last for some time.

Penang Island, and in particular its capital of George Town, was a place of extraordinary and varied interest. It was the kind of place I enjoyed visiting. Penang was the location of the first British contact with Malaysia when, on 12 August 1786, Captain Francis Light of the British East India Company established a settlement there to assist in the company's trade with China. George Town, named by Captain Light after King George I, grew rapidly as a naval base for the East India Company's warships and as a centre for trade between Britain and South East Asia.

I was fascinated to learn in the George Town Museum that Captain Light was born in my home county of Suffolk, his birth registered at

Dallinghoo near Woodbridge in December 1740. Educated at Woodbridge, he was the father of William Light, the celebrated planner of the city of Adelaide in South Australia. At the end of the promontory containing George Town was Fort Cornwallis, built by convict labour between 1808-1810 to replace the wooden stockade built by Captain Light soon after landing in 1786. On the streets I was fascinated to see a large number of trishaws with the carriage at the front, in very good condition. If the predictions were correct that the trishaws were slowly disappearing, I wanted to save one for my own use before this regrettable stage was reached. I had read in the Museum how the last hand-pulled rickshaw had appeared on the streets of George Town less than a year before my visit, following over 2,000 in 1941.

As I approached the long building of the Wat Chayamangkalarum Thai Temple in Burmah Lane, I was startled by what was inside, a statue of the third largest reclining Buddha in the world, 108 ft long and covered with gold leaf. Outside George Town to the west, in a dominating position on a hill near the village of Ayer Itam, the Chinese Kek Lok Si Temple was stunning to behold, with sections of Burmese and Thai design, all with ornate, lavish decoration. A ride round the island brought me to another temple, the Snake Temple, a refuge for these alarming creatures. It was hot seeing all these attractions, but relief was obtainable by taking a trip on the Penang Hill funicular railway built in the 1920's. It was delightfully cool 2,500 ft higher, from where there were views over the city and towards the mainland.

There was a pleasant run past more rubber plantations and through rice country after I returned to the mainland. Early in the afternoon on the second day I approached a large sign beside the road reading: "Selamat Jalan - Pleasant Journey". I was about to leave Malaysia after a journey of 600 miles during just over two weeks, completing the first part of the journey up the Malay Peninsula. It had exceeded all expectations.

*****

Tuesday, 18 March 1969 Thailand

I approached the border with Thailand with some apprehension, travelling through no-man's land between the border post for Malaysia and the post for Thailand. It seemed an eternity as I cycled through uncleared jungle on both sides of the road. Were there still guerrillas lurking in the jungle from the time of the Communist Emergency during the 1950's? It was a relief to reach the border post on the Thai side to begin a long run up the narrow part of the peninsula to Bangkok.

The journey through Malaysia had divided into stages, with stopovers in Malacca, Kuala Lumpur and Penang. The longer journey through Thailand did not seem to involve any major centres; or was I simply unaware of them at present? I knew about the cities in Malaysia: it was all part of a knowledge of the history of the British Empire. Thailand was not only an independent country, but it had somehow escaped the attentions of all the European contenders during the Empire building period.

I was soon seeing one of the country's major attractions, its women. Passing through a village every few miles, there were beautiful women and girls all along the route. They nearly all smiled as I went along. It was an intoxicating experience. Everywhere there were lots of young children. The people seemed so happy, yet it was clear from many of the houses that the standard of living in much of the countryside was low. The scenery in the south of Thailand was unexceptional, with rubber plantations, rice paddies and much untamed bush. There were touches at intervals to remind me that I was in Thailand, as I travelled past a Buddhist wat with its characteristic roof of coloured tiles, or encountered elephants on the road, used to haul timber from the forests. Outside some of the humblest houses was a spirit house, in the shape of a miniature Buddhist wat, to protect the occupants from evil. If the houses could match the brightly coloured spirit houses, the occupants would be rich indeed.

The road surface in the far south was generally poor, but a welcome feature was a decrease in the amount of traffic compared with Malaysia. This was partly offset by an increase in recklessness, about which I had been warned. The weather continued very hot, but the humidity seemed to have dropped; alternatively, I was getting used to it. A slight change of diet was necessary while camping, since I could no longer buy loaves of bread; but I could get various small buns. Stopping to camp at the end of my first full day in Thailand, in what I thought was a quiet spot, I had visitors before I had finished erecting the tent. At least 15 people arrived altogether, mostly young boys, but including a couple of girls and some older men and women. The following morning I had my first visitors while I was shaving; from breakfast to when I was ready to set off my every movement was watched by about ten people. It was the same scenario as in Malaysia.

Coming into contact with the local people like this, at the refreshment stalls, and in the towns, I was endeavouring to add to my Thai vocabulary, adding words and phrases in my notebook as opportunities arose. I could see this becoming a regular procedure in each new country visited, where I would be for just a few weeks, too short a period to be able to learn much of the local language. This would be the case especially in countries like Thailand where the written language looked impossibly complicated. As earlier in Japan, I kept a lookout for students to translate words for me, pronouncing the words so that I could write them down phonetically in my notebook, then getting them to write the words in the actual script.

In Hat Yai, the first position where the peninsula became very narrow, I saw for the first time trishaws with the carriage behind, and many with a carriage on the side as in Singapore and Malacca. Close to the east coast at this position, study of my map suggested hill climbing ahead as the main road crossed from one side of the peninsula to the other to run within a few miles of the coast. There was a winding climb over hills between Phatthalung and Trang to bring me back to the west side of the peninsula where it started to widen again, while the railway line kept to the east side. Trang was the largest town on my route so far. I passed an attractive park on my way into the town, and some very attractive girls.

North of Krabi the road went up and down like a switchback, as I entered very hilly country, the hills characterised by rounded tops and sheer sides. With dense tropical vegetation to the edge of the road, a weird atmosphere was created. There was a considerable air of prosperity at Thapput, where I arrived during a colourful Sunday market. So many of the people were brightly dressed, and numerous lightweight Japanese motorcycles were parked all around. They were a frequent sight on the roads, a reflection of growing affluence. I was in a tin mining area, this probably explaining the relative wealth on display.

The market at Thapput provided an opportunity for me to purchase some fruit, especially bananas, which were becoming a major part of my diet in this region. Whenever I stopped or passed through a village or town, I attracted considerable interest. It was only natural, since not many long-distance cycle tourists followed the route I was on. There were plenty of people to see in the afternoons especially, when a siesta was taken, and only mad dogs and Englishmen were out in the midday sun. When I passed a pool containing a number of water buffalo keeping cool, I could not help but feel that they probably had more sense than me.

After crossing the hills, the road ran close to the coast north of Khok Kloi. Following a short climb, I had my first view of the ocean from Thailand. Proximity to the sea produced a gentle breeze, so that for once I didn't need to wear my hat. I camped by a stream in order to get some washing done; in no time 10 people were watching me. An undulating run continued through jungle and past rubber plantations. I was glad when the terrain levelled out, as it coincided with a first attack of dysentery. I felt exhausted, leaving the road a number of times to collapse under the shade of trees and attempt to get some energy back. I had some tablets to take to deal with this affliction which affects so many Western travellers, and put my faith in a diet exclusively of bananas to put me on the road to recovery.

Apart from numerous local people on bicycles, I was pleased to meet scouts in this area on longer rides. I first met a group of three from Songkhla in the south on their way to Bangkok. The ride of approximately 900 miles seemed to me a considerable challenge, since they were only 15 years old. Two days later I met two more scouts, who had recently set off from Ranong to cycle to Chiengmai in the north. They had stopped at a refreshment stall close to a waterfall. Mention of Chiengmai reminded me once again of what numerous young travellers had been keen to tell me, that the most beautiful girls in the country were to be seen in the Chiengmai area. It was hard to believe that they could surpass the beauty of the girls I had been seeing all the way up the peninsula. The lush, green scenery and ever-smiling, beautiful girls combined to create a tropical paradise.

As the peninsula narrowed again, the road crossed to the east side again at Chumphon. The peninsula was now shared with Burma. The line on my map defining the road suggested an easy route north, but it was an illusion. The road was like a switchback for most of the next 100 miles. There was surprisingly little to buy in the stores for some time. My desired staple foods while camping were bread, butter, cheese, tomatoes, apples, oranges, jam and tinned meat. With none of these available, eggs, fish and bananas formed my main diet, supplemented by meals of rice and vegetables if I was passing through a small town at lunch time.

Boiling water for eggs, for making tea and for washing, I found that my primus stove functioned perfectly well on ordinary petrol, though with some black smoke while warming up. It had been a problem for some time finding white spirit, the lead-free version sold for camping stoves. It was a relief to find out that I would be able to use the stove throughout Asia and Europe, without needing to bother too much whether white spirit was available, or whatever it was called in different languages.

A huge market garden area slowly opened up from south of Thap Sakae, almost certainly to serve the burgeoning city of Bangkok. I was seeing areas devoted to bananas, coconut and oil palms, rice, sugar cane, pineapples, papaya and other tropical fruits. Early in the morning, there was the sight of women scurrying from the fields to the road, with baskets laden with produce, to catch the trucks to market.

I approached the old town of Phetburi along a tree-lined avenue, following a trishaw with a carriage behind. It was a delight to see a large number of these vehicles in the town. I walked round for a time to feel the atmosphere and to get a closer look at a large Buddhist temple which dominated the scene. At Ratchaburi to the north, I turned west off the main road to Chom Bung, intending to turn north there to reach the main east-west highway at Tha Muang. I soon found myself on a dirt road and completely lost, in spite of reassurances from the local people that I was going in the right direction. Prudence would have told me to turn back and follow the busier main road, but I decided to continue going forward. I eventually reached my destination after a puncture and with a broken rear carrier.

I had been making for Kanchanaburi, not sure of what to expect. It was the location of the bridge made famous in the film *The Bridge on the River Kwai,* which captured the ordeal endured by Allied prisoners of war and civilian populations brought to the area from adjacent countries to build the Thai-Burma Railway during the Second World War. I found myself visiting the location at the same time as many others. There was a sombre mood everywhere as we looked at the actual bridge, so different from the one presented in the film; at a traction car and wagons used during construction; and at a steam locomotive used for troop and supply transportation upon completion. A large sign presented the background to the events, a story which has become well known.

I went along to the War Cemetery nearby, one of three established in the region to hold the remains of some of the 16,000 prisoners of war who died building and maintaining the railway. A short distance away was a memorial built by the Japanese Army in 1944 to all who died in building the railway, prisoners of war, impressed labourers and Japanese. It was an attempt to atone for the appalling suffering and loss of life caused, and to appease world opinion in its harsh condemnation of the Japanese. I could not be in an area like this without thinking about my earlier visit to Hiroshima. As a young Western traveller born during the Second World War, I had to feel extremely grateful that I had not been born 20 years earlier. I felt justified in visiting the countries of former war enemies, as we now attempted to build a different world, competing in trade only and rejecting military supremacy. Contacts now could only help to improve understanding. I could understand how some who had been directly involved in the conflict would see matters differently.

I was glad to have made the detour to the River Kwai; it was a visit I would never forget. As I left the area to travel past more scenes of rice paddies, fields of sugar cane, and palm and banana plantations, it helped to bring me back to the modern world. The traffic was building up all the time as I headed the 80 miles east to Bangkok. Just over half way there, I was taken back mentally to an earlier era as I reached Nakhon Pathom, the oldest city in Thailand, and where Buddhism was first introduced into the country. I wanted to see the Pathom Chedi, the largest pagoda in South East Asia, rising to 377 ft in the shape of an upturned bell. It was an impressive sight, having been built during the Nineteenth Century by King Mongkut, immortalized in the Hollywood musical *The King and I*.

After two and a half weeks in the countryside, I arrived in the capital late on a Friday afternoon. As I left the Tourist Organisation office in the centre, an unexpected event occurred which shaped my entire stay in the city. A Thai soldier, who had seen my bicycle locked up nearby, approached me and invited me to stay with him and his family. Preecha had learned some English while on secondment to the American forces, and was trying to learn more. He seemed perfectly genuine. I was soon meeting his charming wife, who could speak no English, and their three young children, at their home a mile or so away. They made me so welcome, giving me a wonderful opportunity to experience Thai family life. In exchange, I spent many hours talking to Preecha and recording several passages of English on his tape recorder. I slept on the verandah on his army camp bed, over which he rigged a mosquito net; I probably had the coolest area in the house, a lucky circumstance in the hot weather.

On my first evening, Preecha volunteered to show me some of the sights of the city. As we walked towards the centre, he stopped to talk to an older woman. From the environment, I rapidly became aware that he was trying to arrange a treat for me, setting me up with a young prostitute. It was going to be a 12 year old virgin to eliminate the possibility of catching any undesirable diseases. I had come face to face very quickly with Bangkok's sex industry. As soon as I realised what was going on, I made it clear that I was not interested. I was appalled at the whole prospect of taking advantage of any young woman. It was contrary to everything I ever believed in. But the young women in this situation didn't want respect: they wanted money, driven into the profession by an underlying problem of poverty in parts of the countryside. How long would it take for the Government to solve this problem? But I was being naive. It was seen not as a problem, but as an established phenomenon, a reality which attracted millions of tourists to Thailand every year, bringing huge sums of foreign exchange into their vibrant, capitalist economy. It was a factor which could not be ignored.

During the next five days in Bangkok, I clocked up 99 miles on the bicycle in the big, noisy city, sightseeing and making travel arrangements for the period ahead. Trishaws had long since departed from the city, supplanted by three-wheeled motorized cabs which belched out exhaust fumes into the polluted air. The women were no longer smiling, since life in the city was altogether more serious than for their cousins in the countryside. An exception was provided at the Pakhavali Institute, where I went one evening for a performance of Thai classical dancing. It was beautiful; I wished I could watch something like that every evening. There were some fantastic sights to see in the city, including a vast number of richly-decorated Buddhist temples and palaces. A boat trip on the Chao Phraya River provided a quieter, relaxing tour. I was up very early one morning to see the Floating Market on the canals. During these early hours, many saffron-robed monks were on the streets with their begging bowls, seeking food for their two daily meals. The city dwellers coming out with their offerings did not expect thanks; on the contrary, they were being provided with an opportunity to gain merit, so that their souls might possibly attain a higher position in the next life. It was a compelling aspect of Buddhist philosophy, causing the Westerner to question how he viewed such matters.

I proceeded with arrangements to make a short visit to Cambodia, getting caught up in complications arising from the conflict in Vietnam. As a result of Thailand providing support for the Americans in South Vietnam, and Cambodia supporting North Vietnam, there were no diplomatic relations at the time between Thailand and Cambodia. The Indonesian Embassy was providing "good offices" for the issue of visas to intending travellers. After obtaining a visa for a maximum stay of six days, I went along to the Thai Ministry of Foreign Affairs to obtain a re-entry visa. It was also not possible to enter Cambodia overland, so that I booked a flight to Phnom Penh.

*****

Thursday, 10 April 1969 Cambodia

As I packed my bags prior to departing for the airport, I became aware that my camera was missing from the cupboard where the family had told me to put it for safe keeping. It was nowhere to be seen. I felt disappointed as the family had been so good to me, and everything else had gone so well. There was no time to do anything further at this stage. After completing my packing, I left Preecha and his family at 8.30am to cycle to the airport 15 miles to the north, completing 1,000 miles in Thailand. Upon arrival I consigned the bicycle for a direct flight to Calcutta in three days time. I would be following a few days later, but with a brief stopover in Rangoon; it was advisable not to have the bicycle with me.

My flight to Phnom Penh was due to depart at 11.00am. We went out to the plane at 11.30, to be told by the pilot that there would be a further delay as an aircraft was blocking the runway after an accident on landing. It was encouraging news! We were in the air at midday for an hour and a half flight. I had wondered earlier if I would be seeing a little more of Thailand and Cambodia as we flew over the countryside, but a blanket of cloud prevented anything being seen until we descended to land. It was an opportunity to think about what I hoped to see in a very short while.

I was looking forward immensely to seeing the great temples at Angkor. I had first read about them a year or so earlier in a weekend magazine with my daily newspaper. An article in the magazine reported the visit to Angkor in late 1967 by Jackie Kennedy with a party including Lord Harlech, Britain's Ambassador to Washington during the Kennedy Presidency, while on a tour of Asia. The report was accompanied by a number of photographs which caught my imagination. If I ever managed to get to the area, this was a location not to be missed. The time had almost arrived.

Phnom Penh was pleasantly quiet after the noise and bustle in Bangkok. It was, of course, so much smaller, with a population of 600,000 compared with 2 million in the Thai capital. The French influence in Phnom Penh was strong in their former colony, reflected in the architecture and the outdoor restaurants on the street corners. Booking in to a hotel on arrival, I found myself on a rapid recall of my schoolboy French. I hadn't used the language since travelling across Belgium on my first cycle tour in Europe six years earlier in 1963. It was a pleasant surprise to find a few words and phrases coming back to me. The educated Cambodians could generally speak both English and French, but some only one of the languages.

I checked the bus departures for Siem Reap, the town adjacent to Angkor, for the following day before taking a walk round the city to soak up the atmosphere. I could not resist one alternative to walking, a ride in a "cyclo-pousse", the local type of trishaw with a carriage at the front. How I would have loved to have been able to send one of them home to England. I was up early the next morning to get a seat in one of the recommended taxi buses, leaving Phnom Penh at 7am. The taxi buses took 6 hours to complete the 200 mile journey north-west, compared with 10 hours for the ordinary buses. It wasn't that the ordinary buses travelled more slowly, but they stopped frequently to pick up and drop off passengers and goods. When moving, they raced along as fast as the driver could make them go, often with unfortunate consequences. We were little more than 10 miles from the capital when a group of people by the roadside drew our attention to a bus which left the road the day before. A few miles further there was a second one. It was apparently a regular occurrence; the taxi buses were considered safer, a perspective I needed to put total faith in as we raced up the road. There was a long delay at the ferry crossing of the Tonle Sap River, but no further hold ups. I was fortunate to have sitting beside me a young Cambodian student, who attended an English speaking school in

Phnom Penh. The miles sped by as we talked about our countries, and raced past scenes similar to those in Thailand. There was a great deal of traffic on the road as it was the Cambodian New Year; many people were travelling during the holiday.

I was astonished to find us approaching the market town of Siem Reap just before 1pm, scenes of rice paddies giving way to increasing amounts of forest. With the whole afternoon ahead of me, I couldn't wait to set off for Angkor, about five miles to the north, after being able to hire a bicycle at my hotel. There was a pleasant approach to the main temple of Angkor Wat along a winding, shady tree-lined avenue, revealing slowly the vast monument. The outer walls were about a mile in length; the combination of immense distances and rich decoration throughout the building complex made an awe-inspiring sight. I could only wonder how all this must have appeared to a wandering French naturalist, Henri Mouhot, who stumbled through the area in 1862 to discover the ruins of the former capital of the Khmer Empire. Soon the world would learn of his discovery, involving some of the most monumental architecture ever.

Angkor became the capital of an Empire created at the beginning of the Ninth Century by a Cambodian prince proclaiming himself King Jayavarman II. The Empire lasted for six centuries, reaching its zenith in the Twelfth Century. In 1432 Angkor was suddenly abandoned for Phnom Penh, to become increasingly enveloped by the jungle. Angkor Wat was simply the largest of a vast complex of temples which I tried to see as much of as possible, including Angkor Thom. One of the most interesting temples was Ta Promh, left almost as it was discovered, with giant trees twisting their branches and roots throughout the walls and windows. It seemed impossible to remove all this growth without causing a collapse of so much of the stonework. A gem of the Angkor temples was located at Banteai Srei, some 13 miles to the north-east of the main complex. Outside my hotel, Cambodians with motorcycles competed to take young visitors there, involving a journey on very rough roads through the jungle. It was an exhilarating ride, but worth it to see the small temple in red sandstone. It had the most exquisite decoration, and all in a superb state of preservation.

A performance of Cambodian classical dancing on the floodlit forecourt of Angkor Wat made for a pleasant evening. It lacked the vitality of a similar performance in Bangkok a week before, but what a memorable setting. There was a memorable moment of a different kind the previous evening when one of the hotel staff came along to fill a thermos flask with cold water. He was smiling broadly as he introduced other services which could be provided. "Would you like a pretty girl?" he inquired. He did not seem to lose face when I declined politely.

I had a host of memories as I started the return journey to Bangkok. It was a peculiarity of the time that the traveller had to fly from Thailand to Cambodia, while a journey in the opposite direction could be made overland. There was no question about which course I was going to follow. It was only 90 miles from Siem Reap to Arah Prathet across the Thai border, but it turned out to be the longest 90 miles I had ever travelled. While the 200 miles from Phnom Penh to Siem Reap three days earlier had taken six hours, the shorter journey took all day, involving a bus, two taxi buses and a remorque - a motorcycle driven trishaw pulling an open carriage. I was not very pleased with all the unwanted detours along the route, as I was suffering with another attack of dysentery! It was a relief to reach the border during the evening, and catch a bus for Arah Prathet a few miles to the west.

*****

Tuesday, 15 April 1969 Thailand

The train departed from Arah Prathet at 6am. As the journey progressed, everyone became aware that it was the time of a water festival. The children all seemed to have come prepared, and bags of water appeared from nowhere to be thrown at passengers at stations along the route and through the windows of stationary trains. It was a treat for children living close to the line; with the train running on schedule, they were ready. It was unfortunate that the wrong people were hit quite often, elderly women and very young children. The station guards seemed to be singled out for special treatment. It was a supreme test of patience for everyone, as the game continued all the way to Bangkok, which the train reached early in the afternoon.

I returned to Preecha and his family to hear some welcome news. My camera had been found, the older son having moved it from one cupboard to another one as he thought it would be safer. I could not possibly be angry with him. After the flight to Phnom Penh, I now had to concentrate on the next flights, to Rangoon and on to

Calcutta. At the Burmese Embassy, I was pleased to meet Jenny, an Australian fellow passenger on the *Australasia* to Singapore. We were on the same mission to obtain visas. She had spent two weeks in Indonesia before returning to Singapore and arriving in Bangkok before me, where she had met my cabin mate, Henri. While I had been in Cambodia, she had travelled up to Chiengmai. It was interesting how our paths crossed at different times. At the BOAC office, I was able to confirm that my bicycle departed for Calcutta a few days earlier; it was indeed a privileged bicycle.

On the Saturday I left by taxi for the airport with Preecha, after saying a heartfelt goodbye to his wife and family, who had been so hospitable to me. Preecha wanted to accompany me on this last journey. By flying with Union of Burma Airways, I was going to be able to visit Rangoon for a maximum of 24 hours. It was the only kind of visit allowed at this time to a country with a troubled history since achieving independence from Britain in 1948. As it chose its own way forward, it cut itself off from the rest of the world. There was a major problem in allowing visitors, with the Government in Rangoon having only limited control over much of the country beyond the capital. I was aware of only one overland journey which had taken place in recent years, the expedition during the mid-1950's by a joint team from Cambridge and Oxford Universities. It was therefore not too difficult to accept that a complete overland journey could not be made, though there was a constant gnawing in the mind over this one link in the long chain of countries straddling the route. At least, I was being allowed a glimpse of Burma.

*****

Saturday, 19 April 1969 Burma

The passengers on the Union of Burma Airways flight which took off at 4pm were nearly all young people, mainly hitch-hikers and back-packers from Europe, Scandinavia, Australasia, North America and Japan. There were no conventional Western middle-aged travellers. Rangoon perhaps conjured up too many troublesome questions. The plane landed at 5.30pm local time after a two hour flight, but it then took an hour for everyone to pass through Customs and Immigration. We all queued nervously: nobody could afford a problem at this stage. I was glad I didn't have the bicycle with me, otherwise I think I would have been having visions of my cycle tour coming to a premature end.

The light was fading as we boarded a bus for the 10 mile journey from the airport to a hotel arranged for the whole party in the heart of the city, but we were able to see a little of the countryside before the light failed. With everyone on the same timetable, rooms had already been allocated at the hotel. I found myself sharing a room with Ingmar from Sweden, while the Australian girl, Jenny, was sharing with an English girl, Valerie. I was delighted to meet her as she came from my home county of Suffolk. During dinner, she told me that she had met Ian Hibell in Indonesia a year earlier.

I would never forget that dinner, entering the dining room to the sounds of a string trio playing beside a group of potted palms. It was a scene straight out of *Grand Hotel*, a programme I listened to at home on the radio every Sunday evening for years while growing up in the 1950's. I wanted to ask the members of the trio if they had heard of Jack Byfield, Reginald Kilbey and Max Jaffa, but felt it was inappropriate. The music seemed to be wasted on all the young hitch-hikers in the dining room, while I was enchanted. It was curious that the trio were playing at all, since the type of music they played, light orchestral and dance music, was suited to a kind of audience which they surely never had while visitors were restricted to a 24 hour stay. It was as if I had entered a museum, to witness a re-creation of an era which must have ended in Rangoon during the Second World War.

If time seemed to stand still, it made no difference regarding the major attraction in Rangoon, the huge, gold-covered Shwe Dagon Pagoda. As a group of us took a taxi for an hour's guided tour of the city, this was the important destination. We strained in the limited light to take in as much as possible of the form of this sacred Buddhist shrine. There were many local people in all parts of the shrine, and a calm, peaceful atmosphere pervaded the area. In fact it was calm and peaceful throughout the city. The few cars on the streets moved relatively slowly. Leaving the Pagoda for a market area, people watched us with curiosity. Living under the pressures of a strong, military dictatorship, one wondered if they envied the freedom of the temporary Western visitors.

The evening was over all too soon. I had to be up at 5am the following morning to catch the bus to the airport half an hour later. We were in the air at 7.30, on our way to Calcutta. The way the flight schedules worked out, we had spent only 14 hours in Rangoon. I would be spending much longer than this in the next country on my route. The departure from Rangoon meant that I was finally leaving South East Asia after almost two months since arriving in Singapore. It had been the most inspiring beginning possible to the long, overland journey.

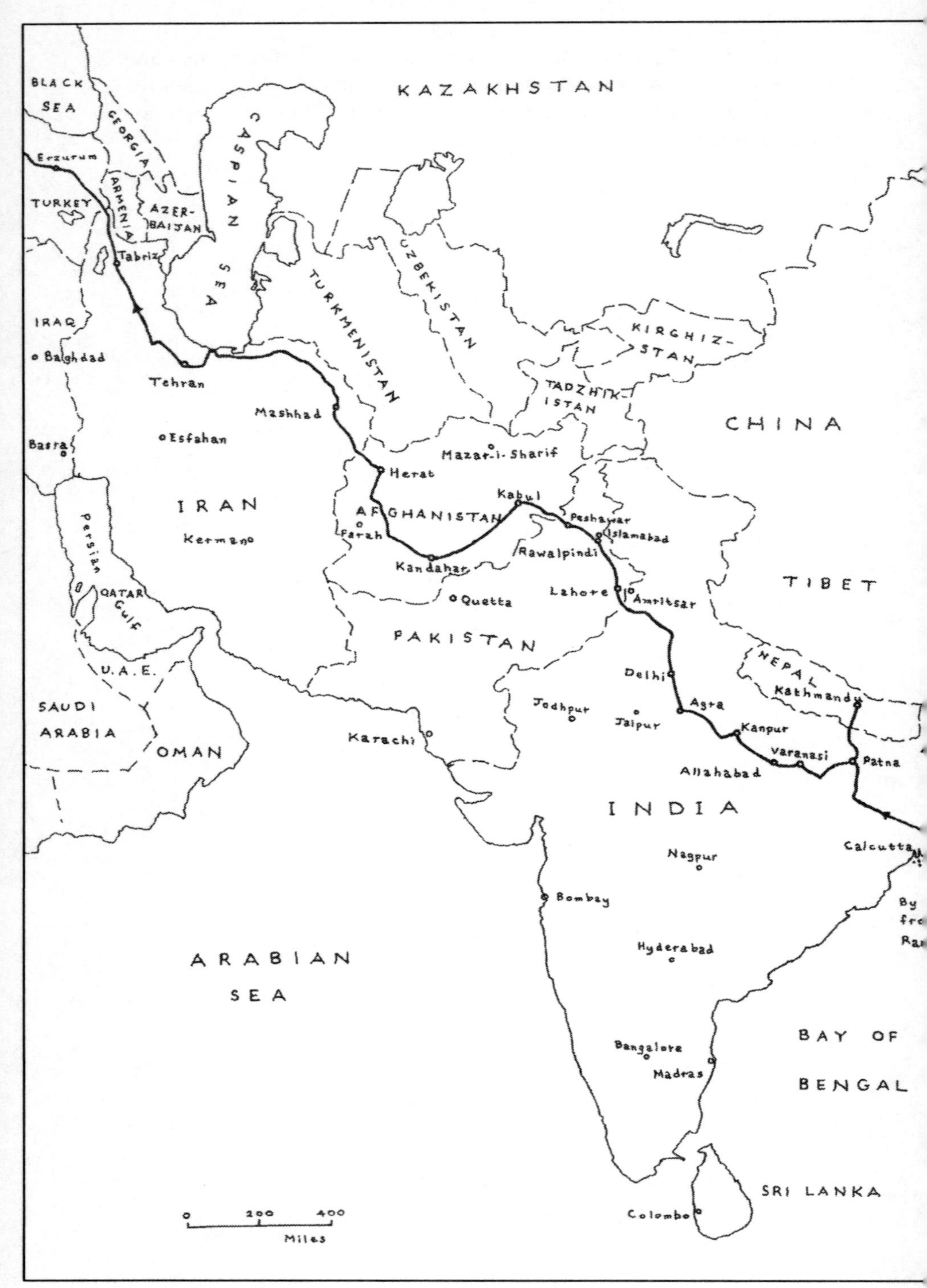
KAZAKHSTAN
BLACK SEA
GEORGIA
CASPIAN SEA
Erzurum
TURKEY
ARMENIA
AZERBAIJAN
Tabriz
UZBEKISTAN
TURKMENISTAN
KIRGHIZSTAN
TADZHIKISTAN
IRAQ
Baghdad
Tehran
Mashhad
CHINA
Basra
Esfahan
Mazar-i-Sharif
Herat
Kabul
IRAN
AFGHANISTAN
Peshawar
Islamabad
Farah
Kerman
Persian Gulf
Rawalpindi
Kandahar
TIBET
QATAR
Quetta
Lahore
Amritsar
PAKISTAN
U.A.E.
NEPAL
Delhi
Kathmandu
SAUDI ARABIA
Jodhpur
Jaipur
Agra
Kanpur
OMAN
Karachi
Varanasi
Patna
Allahabad
INDIA
Calcutta
Nagpur
Bombay
Hyderabad
ARABIAN SEA
BAY OF BENGAL
Bangalore
Madras
SRI LANKA
Colombo
0
200
400
Miles

Chapter 23

Along the Grand Trunk Road

Sunday, 20 April 1969 India

As the plane flew north-west from Rangoon towards Calcutta, I looked ahead to the next stage of the journey. The air flights which had been necessary, to Cambodia and across Burma, were coming to an end. All being well, I should be able to cycle the entire distance from Calcutta to England, except for ferry journeys across the Bosphorus and the English Channel: it was an intriguing prospect.

After a three hour flight, the Union of Burma Airways turbo-prop aircraft descended to Dum Dum airport. I set my watch back an hour as it was still only 9.30am in Calcutta. I was keen to collect the bicycle, but it was not at the airport. I was advised to go to the BOAC office in the city the following morning. A bus took us all into the city, the 10 mile journey giving us our first views of India. The well-known poverty in parts of Calcutta was reinforced as we passed some squalid shelters on the journey towards the centre. When the bus stopped at a small hotel, four of us decided to take a room, including Ingmar, who shared a room with me in Rangoon. We walked round the city together after settling in.

The following morning I was given a form at the BOAC office to take to the Customs House. I was approached on arrival by a young, articulate Indian, who offered to help me with the formalities. It was soon very clear that I would not have got very far unaided, as we went from one office to another, from one official to the next, and back to earlier ones, gaining signatures on forms after what seemed interminable delays when nothing seemed to be happening. I was seeing the famed Indian bureaucracy at work, a bureaucracy bequeathed by the British, but tailored since to suit the native population and to provide as many jobs as possible in a country with so many people. Huge piles of buff files covered every desk. The procedure seemed to stall a number of times. A glance from my assistant, Sukhendhu, indicated that a period of quiet patience was required. I could only presume that the purpose was to allow the planets to arrange themselves in a particular alignment, since no movement occurred at the desk in front of me, and there was no discernible mental activity. Sukhendhu indicated the need to give him a reserve of money, from which he drew at intervals. Unless so many rupees were passed to a particular official, the needed signature was not forthcoming and the procedure ground to a halt. After what seemed an eternity, the signature would be given, and we would proceed to the next official. Nothing was ever said, but Sukhendhu knew where to go. After three hours I emerged from the Customs House dazed and bewildered, but I had the bicycle. I expressed my deep thanks and agreed a final payment to Sukhendhu. As I rode away, I wondered how many others had benefited from his help. It had been a remarkable experience.

Ingmar left early the following day to catch a train to Nepal, obtaining a visa while I was recovering the bicycle. I proceeded to the Nepalese Consulate to obtain a visa for myself. The direct journey home was going to be long enough, but I wanted to include one detour to Nepal to see something of the Himalayas. They had captured my imagination a decade and a half earlier when Mount Everest was climbed for the first time during the Coronation Year of 1953.

I scoured the bookshops and petrol stations for maps, but could find surprisingly little. It seemed that a number of maps had been withdrawn following the war with Pakistan in 1965, maps which showed the border position as it had been; there was continuing disagreement over details as to where it was now. I regretted not being able to find one of the famous Bartholomew maps of the Indian sub-continent before leaving Australia. It was an academic matter as to whether possession would have caused problems if my baggage had been inspected.

With the essential business completed, I could concentrate on seeing the sights and life of Calcutta, the teeming life everywhere with poverty never far away. I needed to adjust to it quickly if my stay in India was not to be marred. Escape was provided by a visit to the Victoria Memorial, built of white marble and modelled on the Taj Mahal. Opened in 1921 by the Prince of Wales, later to become King Edward VIII for a brief period, I was overawed by its superb collection of paintings of royal scenes. Considered to be the finest collection of British paintings of India existing, they evoked the great days of the Raj, reminding me vividly that I was in the next country on my continuing tour of the former British Empire.

I went to have a look at the Howrah Bridge spanning the Hooghly River, one segment of the River Ganges as it divided near Calcutta to form an enormous delta. The cantilever bridge with its 1,500 ft span was an impressive design, but what was equally impressive was the amount of life on the bridge. I had never seen so many people on a bridge before, with both pavements lined with vendors selling fruit. On the slight rise to the centre, rickshaw drivers toiled, but not as much as those pushing bullock carts, laden with sacks of rice. An even bigger effort seemed to be required on the descent to stop the carts rolling away.

I had to cross the Hooghly River to the west bank to begin my journey towards Delhi along the main highway, popularly known as the Grand Trunk Road. Midway through the afternoon I reached Sahaganj, where Dunlop had the largest tyre factory in Asia. I stopped by to see if there was a chance of touring the factory, and to check whether they produced heavy duty tyres suitable for the bicycle. Arriving too late for any tour, I was invited to stay at the Guest Lodge, where I was looked after superbly by the General Works Manager and his wife. The following morning I saw the many stages in the manufacture of car, truck and bicycle tyres, most of the latter going to Raleigh's factory at Asansol. I came away with a tyre for myself.

For the first time since leaving Calcutta, I emerged into open country, flat, rice-growing country with a village every three miles. There were more trucks on the road than cars, with bullock carts and bicycles encountered at regular intervals. Selecting a site for my first night's camping in India after a quiet stretch of road, about 20 people appeared from nowhere to watch my every movement. After a couple had told me it was not safe to camp where I was, I told them that if they all stopped shouting and went away, nobody else would know where I was. They left as darkness fell, leaving me to eat some roast chicken generously given to me by the manager's wife at Dunlop; it tasted especially good in the circumstances, as I was well aware that I could not expect to eat so well again for some time.

After passing through the steel city of Durgapur, I reached Asansol later the same day. Stopping for a cup of tea, I met an Anglo-Indian with an interesting line of work, which he proceeded to tell me about with relish. It involved smuggling goods from Nepal to India, and had been a lucrative venture. Since it was Sunday, I contemplated staying in Asansol in order to go to the Raleigh factory the next day, but decided to press on. I wanted to get clear of the industrial area, which included a coal mining area to the west of Asansol.

As the days progressed and the temperature rose, I recalled discussing my daily strategy with the staff at Dunlop, how I divided a general day's travel into four periods, two in the morning and two in the afternoon, interrupted by 15 minute breaks with an hour at lunch time. The strategy came in for a quick review as I felt the heat become particularly intense; it was not going to do me any good to travel during the middle of the day. It seemed a different kind of heat altogether to what I had encountered in the south-west of America and in the north of Australia. There was the added factor that I was having to contend with an inferior diet and questionable water supplies. With Western foods unavailable, I was having to buy whatever Indian foods were available, and judge how safe they were.

A revised plan evolved very quickly. By getting up at 5am as the light broke, two periods of travel could be completed before the heat built up. An extended lunch break from 10.30am to 3pm could be followed by two further periods of travel as the burning sun descended in the sky. It would still be hot when I set off in the middle of the afternoon, but cooling down perceptibly with every hour. By riding till dusk, I could still achieve a reasonable daily milage close to 45 miles. The strategy had a sound, safety bonus; by riding until the light started to go, and leaving the road at the last minute for a camping spot in an area with trees or bushes, there was the maximum chance of nobody knowing where I was during a particular evening. An important task each day as the time of the long afternoon break approached was to keep a look out for a suitable shady location, stopping earlier or later according to the solution which appeared.

After 250 miles on the Grand Trunk Road, I turned north at Barhi to start the detour to Nepal. The road wound its way over hills surrounding Tilaiya Reservoir. A few miles further north, I was surprised to find myself riding through undulating, bush country similar to that in northern Australia. The bush ended just before Rajauli, the undulating terrain giving way to a vast, flat plain covered by rice paddies. The majority were parched brown, but it was a refreshing sight to see areas of green where irrigation was allowing a further crop to be growing. There were further irrigation schemes to the north. The villages looked so much more prosperous than others in the area, suggesting a successful co-operative venture.

A fierce storm blew up before I reached the town of Bakhtiarpur just south of the Ganges. With mud on the road and the wind so strong, my tyres started to slide. For half an hour I stood beside the bicycle, pointed towards the wind. Leaning almost horizontal over the machine, I just managed to avoid being swept away over the open plain. When the rain left off, I could not continue for another half an hour because of the continuing high wind. I moved to the shelter of a pile of bricks, watching the local people emerge from whatever shelter they had been able to find to hurry home across the fields in case the storm started again.

I proceeded to Bakhtiarpur to find it looking the most miserable town I had seen in India, or anywhere. The potholed streets were awash with mud and water, every building looked filthy, and I saw not a scrap of food to buy. Turning west towards Patna, I managed to find a little food in one of the villages, including the first eggs bought in India. Another storm blew up during the night, allowing a leisurely breakfast. From the moment I got up, my movements were closely watched by a small group from a local village, receiving a thorough soaking in the process. The rain and wind suddenly stopped. By the time I was ready to take the tent down, the numbers watching had swelled to about twenty, perhaps the entire male population of the village. Before parting I was offered a couple of mangoes, which I accepted gratefully. This generous action was all the more noteworthy since the area was relatively poor. I had long left behind the more prosperous area near Rajauli, with its extensive irrigation schemes.

After lunch in Patna, the capital of Bihar state, I went direct to the ferry terminal, arriving just in time for a departure. The crossing of the Ganges to Hazipur on the north bank, and several miles upstream, took 1¾ hours. The Ganges was very broad at this location, where it was joined by the Gandak River from the north-west. I travelled north through productive farming country, seeing much more to buy. In addition to fields of potatoes, maize and onions, there were tomatoes, cucumbers, bananas, tangerines and mangoes. Stopping for a cup of tea at Muzaffarpur, I met a Canadian couple travelling by car. The tea I was drinking at all the roadside stopping places was very refreshing, made by boiling milk, sugar and water together in a pan, adding tea, and pouring it all through a strainer. The Canadian couple augmented my food supply with a tin of ravioli: I looked forward to the evening meal.

As I prepared to leave India for a few days, I contrasted the situation with that in South East Asia. India presented a very masculine world to the traveller. The tea and eating places were invariably operated by a man, and women were not seen in them. I had yet to see a woman or girl on a bicycle. Speaking the word of greeting to an Indian along the road was invariably met with a blank stare. Continuing over the plain, there was no suggestion of hills to the north. The earlier storm had the desirable result of cooling the air, making it unnecessary to stop during the middle of the day for the time being. In the fresher air, I looked forward to the journey ahead.

*****

Monday, 5 May 1969   Nepal

I reached the border early in the morning, with the towns of Raxaul on the Indian side and Birganj in Nepal. Stopping about 14 miles north of Birganj, I noticed with dismay that my jacket had worked its way out of the saddlebag somewhere along the bumpy road: my passport was in a pocket. I returned to Birganj without seeing the jacket, all inquiries along the route proving fruitless. The police at the border station gave me a statement to take to the Immigration Office in Kathmandu. As I retraced the journey north, my mind kept returning to the unexpected incident, and its possible consequences. How long would it take to obtain a new passport? How much would a new jacket cost me in this region? I told myself I needed to be more careful about securing my baggage, but it could do nothing to solve the present problems.

The concern diminished as a range of hills showed faintly on the horizon through the haze. As the farmed land gave way to bush, a gradual climb started. Stopping for tea just before larger hills loomed ahead of me, an English-speaking Nepalese told me firmly that it was impossible to cycle to Kathmandu: the roads were too steep. I assured him that I was intending to cycle the journey, and would look for him to report to when I returned a few days later.

Shortly afterwards I met the start of the Tribhuvan Rajpath, a fantastic road over the Himalayan foothills to Kathmandu, and named after the reigning monarch who died in 1955 while it was still in construction. The 72 mile road had been completed little more than a decade before my arrival, constructed by the Corps of Indian Engineers between January 1953 and December 1956 with money given by India under the Colombo Plan. It started in the most dramatic way possible, with the road zigzagging up the hillside in a succession of loops. About eight small boys ran to catch up with me as I started the climb, amused that they could keep up with me without difficulty. They needed only to walk, since I was moving at only 2½ mph in my lowest gear. The speed was something I had been interested to calculate from the time of fitting the low gears a few years earlier; it was a straightforward calculation based on the number of pedal revolutions per minute. After two miles, the boys decided they had better return to their village as the road crossed to an adjacent hillside, doubling back to look down over the switchback ascended earlier. It was enormously satisfying. If the entire Rajpath was like this, it was going to be an amazing journey.

It had to change, of course, otherwise the road could not move forward. I was fortunate to find a reasonably flat, clear area when I wanted to camp. During the next two days I completed the remaining 68 miles to Kathmandu, climbing first to the main summit at 8,162 ft, dropping 2,400 ft before ascending to a second summit at 6,662 ft. A long descent followed to 3,170 ft before the final climb to 4,802 ft. Kathmandu lay in the valley seven miles away at 4,128 ft. Markers recorded the elevation at every significant point along the route.

I hadn't realised how much I missed the mountains. The bare statistics could not begin to convey how enjoyable such a journey could be, with the inspiring and ever-changing vistas opening up from the higher elevations. With numerous villages and towns along the road or close to it, it was fascinating to look over endlessly varying patterns of terraced hillsides, at the clusters of solid houses built to withstand the ravages of winter, and to see the refreshingly cheerful countenances on the faces of the Nepalese hill people encountered along the route. This was a contrast to general, sombre expressions in India.

Stopping at a small store and tea place on the first climb, I was astonished to see bars of Cadbury's milk chocolate in a cabinet. No further indication was needed that I was in a civilized area. I had lunch later close to a couple of houses, watched by six Nepalese, including three children. They were fascinated as I made tea on my primus stove. After winding upwards for 18 miles since the start of the morning, I reached the first and main summit. The sign recorded 8,162.93 ft: I could only admire the surveying accuracy of the Indian Engineers! I stopped for a couple of cups of tea before descending for 10 miles to a valley. After climbing to a second summit six miles further on, I stopped to camp just beyond, leaving 33 miles for the next day.

Awaking to a bright morning, I rounded a bend two miles after setting off to see the most incredible sight. From the elevation of about 6,000 ft, I looked north over endless ridges towards the main Himalayan range. In the clear light of the early morning, the peaks of Gamesh Himal at 23,361 ft and Himalchuli rising to 25,801 ft were free of cloud some 25 miles away. This was what I had come to see. In another part of the world, the terrain around me would be described as mountains. The real mountains to the north drove home how I was just in the foothills. Cloud moved over the Himalayan peaks shortly afterwards, preventing any further view; in any case, the distant view became cut off by the ridges of closer hills as the road made a long descent to the second valley just 15 miles from the Nepalese capital. After a final climb, the road descended towards Kathmandu in a broad valley, past a number of communities along the road. Wheat was being harvested at a number of locations.

Arriving in the capital, I saw many young Westerners as I approached the centre. Stopping to talk to one, he walked with me to a small, simple hotel where I was able to obtain a room. It would be perfectly satisfactory for a few days stay. Walking round the city later, I saw an astonishing number of Western hippies. Kathmandu represented the end of the hippy trail through Europe and Asia for young, Western travellers hiking overland. The big attraction was the legality of drugs like cannabis. Cafés and shops sold tea, coffee, cakes and biscuits containing hashish, derived, like cannabis, from the Indian hemp plant. Some of the restaurants thronged with hippies, using them as social meeting places.

Traffic in the Malay countryside, with, in the background, women performing their washing at a stream beside the road.

Christ Church, Malacca, built by the Dutch in 1753 - a fine legacy to their period of occupation.

The Moorish-style Federal Secretariat, Kuala Lumpur - one of the most attractive of the older buildings in the city.

Trishaw rank in George Town, Penang.

Inspecting a rubber plantation in northern Malaysia.

Market scene in Thapput, southern Thailand.

Trishaw rank in Phetburi, southwest of Bangkok.

Busy street scene in Calcutta.

The Victoria Memorial, the noblest building in Calcutta - a tribute to the Victorian years of Imperial greatness.

Start of the Tribuwan Rajpath, the most fantastic road over the Himalayan foothills to Kathmandu.

Pause on the Rajpath to admire the main Himalayan range to the north, with Himalchuli, 25,801 ft, to the left, and Gamesh Himal, 23,361 ft, to the right.

Procession of bullock carts on the plain in northern India, with mango trees in background.

Scene in Varanasi, the Hindu holy city on the banks of the River Ganges.

Market scene with piles of mangoes a reminder of the author's principal diet in India.

The great cannon at the front of Panjab University, Lahore, Pakistan, immortalised as "Kim's Gun" by Rudyard Kipling.

At the start of the Khyber Pass.

Inspecting plaques of British regiments near the top of the Khyber Pass.

With young Afghans by the Amir Abdul Rahman Tomb, Kabul.

Retreat from the midday sun in Afghanistan.

A slimmer author surveys the Afghan desert west of Kandahar after a number of attacks of "Delhi belly" and the "Kabul trots". Note distance to road in background and bicycle supported in front of tent.

Afghan tea-house with washing-up in progress beside stream, while one man's personal transport awaits his master.

The Great Mosque at Herat in western Afghanistan.

Climbing over the Alborz mountains between the Caspian Sea and Tehran.

Camping west of Istanbul by the Sea of Marmara.

Procession of carts in the Yugoslav countryside, showing common scene of line of farmhouses at right angles to the road.

Language lesson at Virovitica, Yugoslavia.

The snow-sprinkled Erzberg peak rising to 5,031 ft dominates the scene near Kallwang, Austria, as winter arrives.

Rothenburg ob der Tauber, perhaps the loveliest of the medieval - looking towns along *die Romantische Strasse* in southern Germany.

Bird's eye view.

The heart of the bicycle, showing the hub-derailleur gear combination to give a wide range of gears.

Close-up of mapcase, invaluable on a long tour.

The saddlebag at the end of the journey, showing a badge or miniature flag for each of 21 countries travelled through, plus a large Union Jack and the badges for the Youth Hostels Association, International Youth Hostel Federation and the Cyclists' Touring Club.

There was important business to attend to the following morning. I went first to the British Embassy, where I was extremely pleased to hear that my jacket and passport had been handed in to the police at Birganj at the border. It was the best possible news. At the Immigration Office, I arranged for a pass for the return journey. In the city later I noticed an overland bus which had passed me a few days earlier. Speaking to one of the passengers, an English girl, she told me that the bus carried 17 passengers. It was meant to be arriving in London mid-June, but was well behind schedule, since it was now early May. She had been on another kind of trip as well, as she told me of a restaurant where she had bought a biscuit containing hashish the day before; it "turned her on" for the whole afternoon. It did not encourage me to go there: I derived my kicks by riding a bicycle! I saw one of the passengers from the *Australasia* emerge from a café. He had been in Kathmandu for two months, and looked in a sorry state. I tried to tell myself that all he needed to do in order to return to normal life was to decide firmly to give up the drug-crazed lifestyle, but I had serious doubts as to how easy this was going to be at some unknown time in the future. (Update: A report in my newspaper four years later in July 1973 informed me that the Nepal Government had closed the shops and restaurants selling cannabis and hashish-containing foods, part of a larger anti-drugs campaign.)

After walking round the temples in Kathmandu, I rode out a few miles south to Patan, another ancient city with a wealth of temples. A Tibetan refugee village was nearby, with the people hard at work gathering in the harvest. On the way to the village, I encountered Danish and Dutch couples who had motored through Europe and Asia. A cup of tea with them provided an opportunity to glean information on the route they had followed, while I was able to tell them something about South East Asia, where they were bound. An excursion two miles west took me to the Swayambhunath Temple in its dominant position on a small hill. On each face of the square, central tower, the all-seeing eyes of Buddha seemed to watch the approach of visitors or worshippers from which ever direction they approached. Returning towards the city, I stopped for an hour at a fascinating museum. There were the customary statues of Buddha and other religious artefacts, but more interesting to me was a formidable collection of weapons, mainly rifles and kiri swords, reminding me of the close association between Britain and Nepal concerning enlistment of its men into the British Army. On another floor was a fascinating collection of paintings and photographs, including several photographs of King George V and the then Prince of Wales on tiger and rhinoceros shoots in Nepal. There were evocative pictures of the royal personages riding howdah.

After four days in Kathmandu, I started the return journey over the Himalayan foothills. This was one return journey I looked forward to immensely. In mountainous terrain it was going to feel like a completely new journey, but giving me a chance to savour once more the outstanding vistas along the road. I camped at the same spot as on the outward journey. As I made the final descent towards the plain, the distant view looked forbidding in the heat haze. The temperature had risen again to the level near Calcutta. I looked for the man who had voiced his opinion a few days earlier that it was impossible for anyone to cycle over the Tribhuvan Rajpath, but he was not around. I wondered how many cyclists had made the journey, as it was surely one of the most outstanding cycle rides that anyone could make.

I braced myself against the heat as I returned to Birganj without stopping during the middle of the day. I couldn't wait to get to the Police Office to collect my jacket and passport. I wanted to arrange a reward for the boy who had picked it up, but the officer seemed disdainful of the whole idea. I was surprised by this attitude, and wondered many times later about the reasoning behind it. Was there an element of Hindu philosophy here? Should the boy be rewarded for performing an action which was only a correct action in the first place? What I was very much aware of was that the course of events which had taken place was counter to the prevailing conception of what could normally be expected to occur. I could only have respect for everyone involved in the return of the items to me.

I had a second reason for wanting to get back to Birganj quickly. For the very first time, a problem had developed with the bicycle's hub gear, leaving me without the higher gears. Thankfully, the omission was in the right direction, as it was the low gears I needed to return over the mountains. After booking into a hotel, I dismantled the gear to find that the rivet securing the sun pinion on the axle had dropped out. It had been slightly loose when I overhauled the gear in Sydney. I cursed myself for not taking remedial action at the time. I took the axle with me as I walked round the market place. At a machine shop a length of rod was cut to produce a new rivet and carefully hammered into position, so as not to damage the small teeth on the pinion wheel. I returned to the hotel to reassemble the gear. Machine shops similar to the one I had been to could be found in every town in Asia to provide support for bicycles, trishaws and all kinds of mechanical equipment.

*****

Friday, 16 May 1969 India

I rose early while it was still cool. After changing remaining Nepalese money at a street counter, I headed for the border two miles south. Getting through both Nepalese and Indian Customs and Immigration quickly, with no baggage search, I celebrated the last stage of the journey with two cups of tea in Raxaul before setting off. The 295 miles covered during the previous 11 days in Nepal would stand out forever as a highlight on the overland journey. As I returned south, I met four Indian youths from Allahabad on bicycles, bound for Nepal. Their Indian bicycles had no variable gears, and I shuddered to think what kind of journey awaited them; they were going to be doing a lot of walking. When I met them, they were not moving at all as one had a puncture, and their tyres generally looked worn out.

I tried to find out at the border how many cyclists had passed through in recent years, but the officials were mostly new. However, an official at Indian Immigration told me of an Indian who passed through several years before on a trishaw. It had been modified considerably, including the provision of some variable gears. I was fascinated. If I ever obtained any of these machines, the fitting of some gears would be the first action to be considered. I wondered how this particular Indian fared on the long hills, as he dealt with the considerable weight of the trishaw.

I had plenty of time to think about such matters as the intense heat on the plain necessitated a long stop during the middle of the day. Later, a middle-aged man rode beside me for several miles on his upright bicycle. He told me that he cycled 25 miles every day, 12½ miles from his home to work and then back again. I observed that it was very good exercise, suggesting that he felt very well. "I am never ill," he replied with pleasure.

As I returned through Muzaffarpur, I noticed orchards of lychee trees, this being a major growing area for the delicious fruit; I had been introduced to it in Calcutta, and it was now at its prime. To the south of the city were many mango trees, this fruit now ripening quickly. The ferry across the Ganges from Hazipur to Patna was crowded after waiting for a train to arrive. I bought an English language newspaper, *The Sunday Searchlight*, published in Patna earlier in the day. It was full of insights into Indian life. A further insight was provided on board the packed ferry. Looking round at the mass of passengers, I became conscious of the enormous patience of the Indian people, as they rested on the deck, quietly, with dignity and without complaint.

The newspaper brought me up to date with some current events, including a report on riots in the Malaysian capital of Kuala Lumpur. Reassurance was being sought concerning the safety of the Indian population there. Since they did not seem to have been directly involved in the disturbances, it could only highlight friction between the native Malays and the Chinese population. I was reminded of a conversation I had there two months earlier with a Canadian student, who felt that the apparent racial harmony in the country was only skin deep. He went on to develop his thesis, making reference to the striking public buildings going up all over the capital. The buildings had to be paid from taxes. Since most of the business was run by Chinese, their taxes were contributing in large measure to pay for buildings like the National Mosque, which they would have no interest in. The Government's many statements about developing a Muslim state would hardly please the Chinese community. With the newspaper report offering no explanation for the cause of the riots, it remained to be seen whether there was substance in the views expressed to me.

The paper brought me up to date with the American space programme. Apollo 10 was due to be launched the following day, involving the flight of three astronauts round the moon to prepare for a later moon landing. On a lighter note, a brief report informed me that a new bicycle belonging to an assistant of the Civil Courts had been lifted from the Civil Court building, although locked in a stand. "It may be recalled that cycle lifting from the Civil Court building has become the regular feature and incourse (sic) of the last two years several locked cycles were lifted from the building." It was a timely reminder to take special care of my machine.

It was early evening when the ferry reached Patna, too late to proceed into the countryside before darkness fell. After a ride round the city centre, I took a room in a small hotel. It allowed me to catch up with some washing before heading south-west the following morning towards Arrah in order to rejoin the Grand Trunk Road at Sasaram. Once into open countryside, large areas were a rich green in colour as a result of extensive irrigation. Rice was growing mainly, with some sugar cane, but a suggestion of plentiful food did not materialize in the villages passed through: there was virtually nothing to buy. Although I was hungry, I could at least enjoy the unexpected delights of a narrow gauge railway running close to the road from Arrah to Sasaram. There were contrasting scenes of a train with a large number of passengers travelling on the roof of the carriages, and another train with passengers travelling in an open goods wagon, representing a class of travel which I had not heard about. These scenes helped to distract me from a problem which was causing considerable discomfort: I was getting saddle-sore after all the miles on inferior roads. I was used to the inevitable jokes which arose when anyone learned my name, but the actual problem was not a laughing matter. Foam rubber strips inserted inside my shorts provided some relief; I had to hope that the main road would be a little smoother.

A fine mausoleum at Sasaram to Sher Shah, described as one of the noblest specimens of Pathan architecture in India, provided a memorable scene as I returned to the main road. The overall setting of the tomb in the middle of a lake contrasted so much with the arid terrain beyond. I focused on the next important destination of Varanasi, or Benares as it was known during the period of the Raj, a day's travel away. The crossing of the Ganges via the long, high Malaviya Bridge provided a first view of the Hindu holy city, a centre of pilgrimage for more than a thousand years. I went direct to the Government Tourist Bungalow close to the railway station, hoping to sample this unique form of accommodation provided for Western travellers. I was in luck and soon relaxing in the cool surroundings behind the thick walls of one of the units; other Western travellers were in adjacent units. Having arrived mid-morning, I rested in the shade till late in the afternoon, emerging for a walk round the city and to replace depleted food supplies.

The walk provided an introduction to the city, before continuing early the following morning with a conducted tour. I was at the Ganges at 5.30am to embark with other visitors on a small boat, which took us up and down the river close to the principal ghats, or flights of steps, leading down to the water's edge. Already large numbers of pilgrims were bathing in the sacred waters before sunrise and before daily prayers. The ghats, the mass of pilgrims and the large number of temples and other buildings along the steep river bank created an extraordinary atmosphere. Every Hindu was obliged to try, at least once in his lifetime, to make the pilgrimage to Varanasi. Most would stay as long as they could, while some older ones stayed to die there. The boat went close to the cremation area downstream of the central bathing area, but not too close as the crew were aware that many Westerners were upset by such open sights.

After the boat trip we returned to the Tourist Bungalow for breakfast before setting off on the second part of the conducted tour, staying on land to visit the main temples along the river bank and the Shiva Temple in the grounds of Benares Hindu University. It was a thought-provoking tour. Every visitor to India quickly becomes aware of the dominant force of religion in every facet of daily life. It had been a privilege to be able to visit one of the major centres where this force expressed itself so strongly.

The terrain west of Varanasi was arid, but large mango trees often lined both sides of the road. They provided welcome shade when I stopped for the daily siesta as the temperature soared to about 107°. The mango fruit now came to my salvation as I continued along the Grand Trunk Road. In the absence of other food worth buying, ripe mangoes were now readily available, with the result that I often had mangoes for breakfast, mangoes for lunch and mangoes for my evening meal! Thankfully, I found the fruit so delicious that I could have continued with this diet indefinitely. It solved one problem, but I had to be careful with another. I learned that 90 per cent of the wells in the area were dry as a result of little rain having fallen during the last three monsoons. I needed to make sure that my water supply did not run down to a critical level.

Whenever the supply was replenished, the first operation afterwards was to sterilize it. My initial supply of chlorine tablets had long run out. As further tablets became difficult to obtain, someone recommended potassium permanganate crystals to me to perform the same function. As any schoolboy is aware from chemistry lessons, the addition of the crystals to water turns it purple in colour. Only the smallest amount was required in my gallon container on the bicycle crossbar to turn it pink in colour, resulting in numerous amusing incidents whenever I stopped at roadside stalls or eating places for food or drink. As a crowd gathered to inspect the bicycle and all its baggage, one person usually came forward to act as spokesman for everyone else. Pointing at my water container, the word "benzene" would be uttered, the bicycle being considered some kind of motorized vehicle: It took a little time to correct this impression. There was huge interest in the gear system as no gears were manufactured in India, and the Government would not allow any imports to save foreign exchange. A dealer told me that a bicycle I had seen with a hub gear must have been smuggled into the country.

There was an incredible level of interest whenever I stopped, as the local people used bicycles in great numbers. In this environment, I never felt unsafe along the road or when camping. I was not flaunting any wealth, a criticism levelled at many travelling by car or larger vehicles. I wasn't seen as having anything significant to steal; any thoughts in this direction were compounded by an innate empathy with my method of travel, with an element of admiration in seeing someone putting in so much effort to see their country using a method which they understood. Whether or not my reasoning was faulty, I derived considerable strength from the argument, a strength which I drew on with undiminished belief throughout Asia.

There was little to relieve the tedium of travel through the parched terrain. From time to time I would hear the tinkling of bells in the distance, signalling the approach of camels with a ring of bells on each front leg and round the neck. As they advanced slowly along the road with enormous loads, there was a look of immense dignity in their faces which was amusing to see. Bullocks pulling carts often had rings of bells round their necks. If I camped close to a village, I would hear music throughout the evening, the special strains of the Indian music reminding me where I was.

I did not delay in the cities of Allahabad or Kanpur, as another city just beyond beckoned me. Turning south-west off the Grand Trunk Road at Kanpur, I turned north-west again after 40 miles to follow the road running parallel with the Trunk Road. It brought me to Agra, a city which simply had to be fitted into my schedule - as indeed it had to be included in the programme for the majority of visitors to India.

Arriving in Agra in the late afternoon, I cycled out in the evening for a first look at the Taj Mahal by moonlight. Returning in daylight, I gazed in wonder again at one of the most beautiful buildings in the world. The lack of contrast between the white marble of the building and the white sky due to the hot conditions made me concentrate even more on the form of the building. I immersed myself in the story of its construction between 1631 and 1653 by the Mogul Emperor Shah Jahan as the tomb for his favourite wife Arjumand, better known as Mumtaz Mahal, "Ornament of the Palace". She had married Shah Jahan in 1612 and died in 1631 after the birth of their 14th child. Before she died she made her husband promise that he would raise over her grave a mausoleum worthy of the love she had borne him in their 19 years together.

For someone with no wife, yet alone a favourite one, and wondering what destiny held in store, it was a compelling story to absorb myself in. Close inspection of the Taj Mahal revealed a quality of craftsmanship that was almost unbelievable. It wasn't just the form of the building that made it so attractive, but the exquisite carving throughout, both inside and outside the building. There was an earlier example of this craftsmanship across the east bank of the Jamuna River, in the form of the Itmad-ud-Daulah, which I then went along to see. The building was a forerunner to the Taj Mahal, built between 1622 and 1628 by Nur Jahan as a mausoleum for her parents. She was the second wife of Emperor Jahangir, father of Shah Jahan. To please her he raised her father, Ghias Beg, to the highest ministerial position in the State with the title of Itmad-ud-Daulah - reliance of the State. The building was the first experiment in building in white marble with pietra dura inlay, the incorporation of semi-precious stones of different colours to create patterns and pictures.

My enjoyment of this superlative work was marred by an attack of "Delhi Belly". This was the most appropriate description of this affliction as I was just 125 miles south of the capital. I staggered towards it in short stretches, stopping in the intense heat for newly discovered drinks which I could not resist, involving the crushing of mangoes or pineapples, the juice then whisked with iced water to produce the most delicious drinks I had ever encountered. But were the water and ice pure? Were the machines free of contamination? Should I be confining myself to the water which I sterilized? One problem with this was that the sterilizing agents killed only some of the bugs in the water. Some could even resist boiling, so that even the tea I was drinking was not necessarily safe. I was going to be playing roulette with my stomach for some time to come yet.

I recovered from the latest attack before reaching Delhi, and proceeded direct to the British High Commission. With my passport due to expire in less than three weeks, I wasn't sure how long it was going to take to obtain a new one. After the poverty in the countryside, the affluent surroundings in the diplomatic enclave of Chanakyapuri containing the High Commission proved an agreeable environment in which to spend a short time. No, I advised the consular official, I could not provide any references. Following a discussion of my circumstances, the situation was accepted. Four hours after arriving, I left with a brand-new passport to travel towards the older part of the city, to find a small hotel suited to my budget.

Old Delhi throbbed with life, just like Calcutta, India's capital until 1912. New Delhi provided some remarkable contrasts, particularly in the area of the main Government buildings designed by Sir Herbert Baker and Sir Edwin Lutyens. I was glad to have the bicycle with me to travel down the broad, processional avenue of the Raj Path from the President's Residence, formerly the Viceregal Lodge, to India Gate, a First World War Memorial, at the distant east end. I tried to imagine the annual scene on the Raj Path on 26 January, Republic Day, when a huge procession took place involving the Armed Forces and representatives of groups from all parts of the country. It took some time to see the whole spacious layout of the area, including the Secretariat Buildings flanking the President's Residence and the circular Lok Sabha or Parliament House.

It was impossible to visit this area without being reminded of the Raj, the long period of British rule which came to an end in 1947. I went to the Gandhi Memorial Museum to follow the story of the great man who led India on the long road to independence more than any other man. I looked forward equally to visiting the Nehru Memorial Museum, at the former home of India's first Prime Minister. Here was another towering figure on the country's political scene, indeed the world scene, familiar to me through numerous newsreels. Mr. Nehru simply represented India to me throughout all my early years. He was the embodiment of India, dying in May 1964, less than two years before I started my travels.

His home was close to the diplomatic enclave, which I had to return to a number of times. I had confirmed earlier that, as a result of the fighting between India and Pakistan in 1965, the north-west border was open at only one place, Ferozepore. A road permit was required by travellers from the Pakistan High Commission. While waiting for it after the usual form filling, I crossed the road to the elegant surroundings of the British High Commission to read the newspapers in the library.

After collecting the permit, I set off for the Afghan Embassy to obtain a visa for my visit there. I rode along with an unexpected passenger, after being stopped by an English girl with the same mission: it made a change to the normal load on the rear carrier. We arrived to find business closed for the day, necessitating a return the following two days to make application and then collect the visa. I could have delayed this visa until I reached Islamabad, but I was not intending to stay there long. It seemed sensible to arrange all this paperwork in Delhi, where I wanted to spend a number of days.

I fitted in visits to the Jama Masjid mosque and the Red Fort, both built by Emperor Shah Jahan 300 years earlier. A ride out to the south of the city took me to the Qutb Minar, to acquaint me with an earlier period of history. The Qutb Minar, which was either a victory tower or a tower to call the faithful to prayer, rose impressively to 234 ft, the first storey built in 1199. Further stories up to the 4th were added in 1230, and a 5th storey during the next century. It was one of the finest monuments of the period, and an architectural feat. There were sweeping views over the surrounding terrain from the first floor gallery, the area covered by tombs and ruins and reminding me of India's long history.

I was almost ready to leave Delhi. There had been futile attempts to obtain maps of central Asia to assist me on the journey ahead. I had to hope that maps became available as each country was reached. Delhi was a pivotal point on the journey. On the long ride to the capital, I felt I was simply travelling across the country: now, as I departed from Delhi, I felt I was on the way out towards the next country. I left Delhi via Ridge Road, travelling beside the Mutiny Memorial, the Ashoka Pillar and Delhi University. Turning west along the Mall, I was soon out in open country again as the road joined the Grand Trunk Road to Amritsar.

As I reached the urban boundary a sign read "Welcome to Haryana", and marking the start of small industrial units close to the highway. The State of Haryana had been created only in 1967 by taking part of Punjab State. The remaining part became a separate Sikh State, the result of much clamouring by the Sikhs for their own separate State.

A student who rode beside me for several miles confirmed my impression that I was now travelling through a much more prosperous area than so much to the south-east of Delhi. Haze covered the sky for the moment, preventing the sun from producing the normal heat, and allowing me to travel slowly throughout the day against a strong wind.

On the third day away from the capital, I stopped for morning tea at Ambala as the sky cleared to augur intense heat again. If I had turned north, the road would have taken me to the hill station at Simla, built by the British to escape from the intense heat on the plain during the hottest period. The Grand Trunk Road continued north-west to take me to Ludhiana. Sizable towns were now spread out along the highway at regular intervals, allowing the purchase of food, particularly bread, to be much easier for me. Eight miles from Ambala I stopped by a sign reading "Punjab Welcomes You". As the heat came on, I turned off the road to shelter under a bridge for several hours. It was not the best location as the area was covered with thorn-laden bushes. A puncture had to be mended during the stoppage.

Just through Rajpura, a middle-aged history teacher on a motorcycle stopped by me to talk. A few miles further, at a village where I had intended to stop for a break, there he was again, waiting for me to come along. He insisted on buying me soft drinks while we talked further. Contacts like this were helping to leave me with a most favourable impression of this prosperous part of India. The handsome Sikhs in their turbans made a strong impression, as they did wherever encountered.

I stocked up with bread and groceries in Ludhiana before leaving the Grand Trunk Road to turn west to Ferozepore. The main road would have taken me through Jullundur to the Sikh holy city of Amritsar, and directly west to Lahore in Pakistan. But the border was still closed on this route following the fighting in 1965; how much territory was in dispute I could not ascertain. The southern loop to Lahore via Ferozepore was a similar distance, but travellers were being denied the opportunity to see the famous city of Amritsar unless a long detour was accepted. I continued directly west, conscious of the need to keep moving. With the monsoon period approaching from the east, it appeared that I had about two weeks to get off the plain. Stopping east of Ferozepore for my last cups of tea at a roadside stand in India, the operator refused all payment. I had covered over 1,700 miles during 45 days in India. As I prepared to leave an immense, baffling country after merely scratching the surface in an attempt to understand it, this simple act of kindness conveyed a universal message understood by human beings everywhere.

Chapter 24

Over the Khyber Pass

Sunday, 15 June 1969 Pakistan

For my last evening in India, I camped four miles east of Ferozepore, poised to cross the border early the following morning. Ferozepore proved to be a large, spaciously laid out Army town. I passed numerous accommodation blocks on the 10 miles to the border at Husainiwala, reaching it at 8.00am; it was half an hour earlier in Pakistan. It took an hour to get through Customs and Immigration on each side, an anxious time as I looked round at a large number of cars, and a couple of motorcycles, which seemed to have been abandoned. Had their documentation been incomplete? I celebrated entry with a couple of cups of tea before setting off for Lahore 40 miles to the north.

The military environment was a powerful reminder of the uneasy relationship between the two countries, fostered by the continuing feud over ownership of Kashmir since independence and partition, and a fundamental disliking of each other. There was the appalling legacy of the carnage following independence, as millions of Muslims found themselves stranded a long way from the new country created for them, and millions of Hindus and Sikhs equally found themselves in a country where they were no longer wanted. While the visitor to the Asian sub-continent became aware very quickly of the power of religion throughout the region, a power for good in so many respects with its inseparable links with promotion of a life philosophy, the events following independence were a sad commentary on the destructive power of religion. The visitor from the West, with its general scepticism towards religion in the face of the attractions of materialism, was given a lot of ammunition to support this stance. How else was one to come to terms with all these complexities? In the end, of course, every individual had to make their own choice regarding what they believed in. For the moment, I had the opportunity to observe another nation, where religion was such a dominant, underlying force, as I travelled through.

The temperature was rising rapidly as I left the border, necessitating a long rest later in the morning beneath a bridge. It provided the best shade for miles around, as I was in a desert area. About one o'clock I was joined by a large group of local people, including several children, and a herd of cows. A young man with a transistor radio tuned it to an English language station in Lahore, enabling me to hear the news and a record request programme. An elderly man puffed away on a long pipe, the picture of relaxation. I left the shady spot, and company still remaining, at 3.15pm as the sun started to descend, determined to reach Lahore before dark.

Extensive irrigation schemes in the area resulted in scenes of green fields of wheat and maize, with increasing industrial developments as I approached the large city. There were a number of small English cars on the road, in various colours, a contrast with India where virtually all the cars were black, locally made Ambassadors modelled on the Morris Oxford of the 1950's. As I cycled up Ferozepur Road looking around, two men gestured to me as I reached a bridge, guessing correctly that I was looking for the youth hostel nearby. The warden was a charming, elderly man, a former schoolteacher. The welcoming atmosphere he projected reminded me how much I missed the hostels: the last one stayed in had been in George Town, Penang, three months before.

The hostels always had the potential for bringing young travellers together. I had no further company on the first evening, but the following evening a young German from Würzburg arrived on a motorcycle. He had travelled through Europe and Asia, taking the northern route through Afghanistan via Mazar-i-Sharif. Contrary to my previous impression, there was no restriction on travel on this route close to the Soviet Union. However, there was no paved road between Herat at the western end and Mazar-i-Sharif, requiring the fording of a number of rivers. The young German described to me how he waded thigh deep across some of the rivers, with the exhaust on his motorcycle plugged. A paved road took over from Mazar-i-Sharif to Kabul, with bridges across the rivers; he had completed a challenging journey across Afghanistan, during which he met a Japanese cyclist in Kabul.

On the third evening I met again two young Canadians from British Columbia, first met at the Government Tourist Bungalow at Varanasi. I wondered if they had upstaged my journey to Nepal as they gave me the most glowing report of two weeks in Kashmir. A second German motorcyclist arrived, this one on a world tour, and a young Japanese. The German couldn't stand the heat during the middle of the day any better than myself, travelling from 4 to 9am, then from 4pm until darkness.

The German and the Japanese did not venture from the hostel the following day, suffering from the heat. Thankfully, I was managing to cope, as there was so much I wanted to see during three days in Lahore, the cultural and educational centre of the country. The huge Badshahi Mosque was the dominant, historical building, built in 1674 by Emperor Aurangzeb. He succeeded Shah Jahan, the builder of the Taj Mahal. I was frequently looking at my notes to remind me of how all these leading players in the Mogul Empire related to each other. From one of the high minarets of the Badshahi Mosque, there were expansive views over the city and surrounding area, including the Fort. Close by was the tomb of Allama Muhammad Iqbal, the poet-philosopher who first conceived in 1930 the idea of a separate State for the Muslims of the Indian sub-continent. (Whenever I walk through Portugal Place on the north side of Cambridge, my eyes are invariably drawn to a plaque on one of the houses, inscribed: "Allama Muhammad Iqbal - Born 1877 Died 1938 - Poet-Philosopher of Pakistan - Lived here 1905-6 while at Trinity College".)

The Muslim disapproval of bare knees required me to cover up while visiting the Mosque. It made me hotter than ever, I had forgotten when I last wore long trousers. The immense Shalimar Gardens, dating from the reign of Shah Jahan, provided a peaceful, shady location in which to rest during the heat of the day. The Museum provided another retreat. Nearby, in front of Panjab University, was a huge cannon, "Kim's Gun", immortalised by Rudyard Kipling in his novel *Kim*; Kipling lived in Lahore for many years. A sign on the Mall caught my eye, giving directions to the office of the Martial Law Administrator for the area. It was a reminder that Pakistan was currently under military government following disturbances in the then East Pakistan, to become Bangladesh in 1971.

I was pleased to obtain a road map of West Pakistan before leaving Lahore for the next major location of Rawalpindi. I was needing to take extra care on the road, as the bus and truck drivers drove at formidable speed; it would be an interesting contest to pit a Pakistani bus driver against one from Cambodia. Not everyone was moving at such speed, though; a schoolteacher cycled beside me for several miles, buying two melons for me when we stopped, one of which we shared while together. When I stopped for tea later, an English-speaking Pakistani insisted on paying for my three cups of tea after we had been talking. These kind gestures helped to make the heat more tolerable.

South-east of Jhelum the flat plain suddenly ended, giving way to some unusually rugged, undulating terrain. A hazy sky one morning allowed me to reach Rawalpindi earlier than expected, without the normal stoppage for several hours. The neatly kept hedges, flower beds and borders along the Mall reminded me that I was in a military city, dating from the days of the Raj. It was now the headquarters of the Pakistan Armed Forces. I took a room for two nights in a hotel off Raja Bazar in the old part of the city, while I saw some of the sights; but it was insufferably hot in a confined room, and I appreciated the advantages of camping. I spent some time at the Army Museum, one building containing guns, radio sets and other trophies captured during the most recent conflict with India in 1965.

Rawalpindi was serving as an interim capital while construction proceeded apace seven miles north, at the foot of the Margala Hills, of the permanent capital of Islamabad. I went to have a look at it before continuing west. Building commenced only in 1965, but already there were some impressive Embassy and office buildings, houses, schools and shopping centres. I stocked up with food at one of the stores catering for the diplomatic community, enabling me to buy a number of items which I would not find elsewhere.

The undulating terrain continued as I rejoined the main highway. As I rode over a small pass just before Taxila, I stopped by a large column, a memorial to a Lt. Gen. Nicholson, a dashing officer who fought in four Indian Wars to die in the attack on Delhi during the Indian Mutiny. The youth hostel at Taxila enabled me to meet a Japanese motorcyclist on his way to Europe. A journalist, he had sailed to Bombay and spent the whole time during our evening together writing feverishly in his notebook. I didn't know if he was writing about the archaeological ruins nearby, but I visited the largest of them at Sirkap the following morning. They dated from the

2nd Century B.C. when the region was under Graeco-Bactrian rule, a kingdom founded in the north of Afghanistan by one of Alexander the Great's generals.

The hilly terrain gave way to a flat plain, which was unusually green as a result of extensive irrigation schemes in the area. I was close to the mighty Indus River which flowed through the country to the Arabian Sea, joined by tributaries all along its route. Crossing the Indus at Attock, the road followed the south bank of the Kabul River, which started its long course in the mountains west of the Afghan capital before flowing into the Indus. Irrigation had resulted in a major tobacco growing area. It was a very pleasant run close to the river along a tree-lined road, marred by just one factor, the continuing heat. But virtually every time I stopped for tea in Pakistan to refresh myself, someone insisted on treating me. These gestures of hospitality all along the route helped me to forget the conditions.

Twenty miles from Peshawar, a line of hills loomed up to the west. I would soon be in the cooler air of the mountains for a few days at least. On arrival in the city I went to the youth hostel on the University campus, the last hostel I would be able to stay in until I reached Western Europe. I spent a day in the ancient city, soaking up the atmosphere in the bazaar area. Bearded, rifle-carrying Pathans were seen frequently. I sheltered in Shahi Bagh Park during the heat of the day before returning to the youth hostel with two large loaves of bread in preparation for the journey ahead.

The Khyber Pass began 11 miles west of Peshawar, extending for 23 miles to the Pakistan-Afghanistan border at Torkham. The road rose gradually from 1,100 ft at Peshawar to 3,500 ft at Landi Kotal 29 miles away, a swift descent following to the border in a valley. I set off from Peshawar full of excitement, the very words "Khyber Pass" evocative of a history for a mountain passage which must be unrivalled. The initial terrain was quite open, the unsettled nature of the region with a long history of conflict driven home by the sight of fortified villages to the sides of the road. As younger boys ran beside me several times, I was glad to have had the foresight to secure all my baggage straps with small locks. At Jamrud, an unofficial border had to be crossed, the sight of a number of Pathan tribesmen with their chests covered with bandoliers of cartridges reminding everyone in the most forceful way that passage through the frontier area was at the gift of these proud, fighting tribesmen. A large fort looked over the town from an elevated position.

The road wound its way gently as it climbed up into bare hills of black, grey and brown rock. Welcome cloud early in the morning meant that I had gained some elevation by the time it broke up. The heat was then tolerable. After passing a fort of the Khyber Rifles, the road climbed up a wide valley containing many fortified villages. This was the Pass over which had funnelled many of the great invasions of centuries past, including those of Hannibal, Alexander the Great and Genghis Khan. On the hillsides were stone plaques of British regiments which had served in the frontier region in more recent times to try to maintain some sort of order. As I inspected these plaques, I was aware that my tour of just part of the former British Empire was about to come to an end. I had seen something of Canada, Australia, New Zealand, Singapore, Malaysia, Burma, India and Pakistan, the latter, of course, simply part of a larger India during the days of Empire.

*****

Saturday, 28 June 1969 Afghanistan

The market town of Landi Kotal was at the top of the Pass. I stopped for a couple of cups of tea, which would be my last in Pakistan, before sweeping down to Torkham. Within half an hour I was through, relieved, as I had been at the border with India, as I once more surveyed a large number of vehicles which appeared to have been abandoned. I looked down at the cyclometer as I set off: it recorded 450 miles travelled in Pakistan. I also looked down at the road surface, as something felt unusual: it was extremely smooth. The stretch from the border to Kabul had apparently been paved by America in an attempt to secure the allegiance of the Afghan Government. One further positive action was required as I moved away: I needed to cross the road to the right-hand side.

After a first night's camping in Afghanistan, I was up at 4am as the light broke, having set my watch back half an hour at the border. As the days now started to shorten, I didn't expect to be rising any earlier in the future. I was soon riding past new plantations of orange trees. The area had abundant water, with streams running down from snow-capped peaks to the south every few miles. However, preparation of the land prior to planting required a tremendous amount of work as the land surface was covered with stones. I passed an area being cleared of stones by a large team of soldiers. As the streams finished, I crossed a virtual desert until a few miles from Jalalabad, the first town on the route.

I walked round the bazaar area to see what was available. There was no bread, but there was cake. There were biscuits, tea, sugar, jam from Peshawar, apples from Russia, oranges, plums, grapes, tomatoes and eggs. I was not going to starve here. It was astonishing how much food and other items were imported, presumably paid for with loans from America and Russia as they competed for the allegiance of this mountain country, seen as a buffer state for a very long time. The Afghan men in the town were friendly in disposition, although they looked rather fierce. A student enabled me to get a few words of Pushto in my notebook. Here was a proud people who had never been subjugated in war by any foreign country, and could look at any visitor without seeing the word "colonialist" written across his face. The reaction contrasted with the blank stares or looks of hatred encountered a few times in India and Pakistan. It was as if, when they saw me in my pith helmet, I was seen as the embodiment of everything that was wrong with the Raj.

I set off from Jalalabad after stocking up with food for the 90 miles to Kabul, unsure whether there were any sizable communities along the route. I would not be able to obtain a road map until reaching the capital. The valley narrowed after I had approached the Kabul River, and started to follow it upstream through the Kabul Gorge. The road climbed steadily for mile after mile. After a stretch of rapids I came to a dam and hydro-electric power station, built by Germany.

At intervals, perched in a prominent position overlooking the river, was a fort. What events had they been witness to? In 1840 Britain had sent forces into Afghanistan to protect its interests in India. Following failure to take control of the country, did the forts observe the retreat of the British forces and supporters from Kabul in 1842 when they defiled down the gorge? After a number of days, one man staggered towards the garrison at Jalalabad, believing he was the sole survivor of 16,000 men, women and children who started out from the capital. It wasn't sensible to dwell on such matters. Afghanistan was changing rapidly, as the opposing blocs competed for influence with financial aid, and money and personnel flooded in to build roads, factories and power stations.

A large lake opened out above the dam, with ranges of hills stretching away into the distance. I stopped for a pot of tea at the town of Sarobi nearby. The reaction was similar to that in Jalalabad. The people were friendly, but looked only briefly at me or the bicycle. They seemed almost indifferent, as if their daily lives and their faith gave them everything they wanted. I wondered if they really welcomed the foreign aid. The road left the lake to climb over more hills. After entering another gorge, it suddenly narrowed after a number of miles. The road started climbing steeply, the prelude to an even steeper climb as the road doubled back on itself and snaked up the hillside. The Kabul Gorge was far more exciting than the Khyber Pass. I couldn't imagine what the journey through the gorge must have been like before the building of the new road, which included some short tunnels.

As I emerged from the gorge, the snow-edged rim of the Koh-i-Baba Mountains was visible to the west. Kabul lay at the foot of the mountains, reached over a broad valley after passing a number of new factories on the outskirts, including one producing bicycles. I looked forward to spending a few days in the mountain capital at an elevation of 6,000 ft, taking a room in a small hotel near the modern Khyber Restaurant. The number of overland vehicles parked outside what was probably the most popular meeting place in the city, was astonishing. Volkswagen minibuses made up the majority, followed by Landrovers; but there were one or two Citroen 2CVs, proving the resilience of this doughty vehicle.

There was business to attend to after breakfast on the first morning in the capital. As a result of all the earlier problems with tyres, I had written to Michelin to arrange that they send some tyres and tubes to the British Embassy for me. I was conscious that a particular tyre used at home was far superior to anything I had been able to obtain for some time; and I was going to need some heavy duty tyres in Iran and Turkey. The Embassy did not have my tyres, but I came away with a beautifully typed news-sheet for the day, Wednesday, 2 July 1969, informing me of the investiture of Prince Charles as Prince of Wales at Caernarvon Castle. The Malaysian Government was setting up a special department to attempt to solve the country's racial problems, which I had read about in Patna six weeks earlier. On the sports scene, the second cricket Test Match between England and the West Indies at Lords had been drawn, and Rod Laver had reached the semi-finals in the Men's Singles at Wimbledon.

I was directed to the BOAC office, where I learned that my tyres were being held at the Customs building at the airport. As I returned to my bicycle outside the BOAC office, a man came up to me with a startling question: "Do you know Dervla Murphy?" I replied that I didn't know her, but knew exactly who she was. "Have you read her book, *Full Tilt*?" I most certainly had. The book described Dervla's epic cycle journey through Europe and Asia to Delhi in 1963. The man went on to tell me that Dervla stayed with his brother, who was on the British Embassy staff, while she was in Kabul. The man himself was retired and on holiday.

Memories and thoughts flooded my mind as a result of that conversation. While I was preparing for my journey during the year before I left England, Dervla's book suddenly appeared in the bookshops early in 1965 to overwhelmingly favourable reviews in the press. The book was like manna from heaven, providing me with first-hand information on the overland journey as I gathered together all the information I could to assist me with my own planning. I had not been able to obtain much on this stage. Dervla's journey must have been one of the first by bicycle by anyone following the period of recovery and reconstruction after the Second World War. There were no comprehensive records on such journeys, and *Full Tilt* stood out as a landmark in the history of cycle touring. My mind would return to it many times during the next five months - as it had already from Delhi, the destination of Dervla's journey.

By the time I had obtained a waybill for my tyres at the Ariana Afghan Airlines office, it was too late to go out to the airport, but there was time to attend to one pressing matter. As a result of suffering with toothache for a number of days, I had made an appointment to see a dentist. Like many professional people in Kabul, the Afghan dentist had been trained in Germany or by German staff. I recalled my limited German to indicate that I wanted the offending tooth removed, and to tell him a little about what had brought me to his country. I didn't need to be able to say much, a situation well understood by anyone who has ever sat in a dentist's chair. He did a competent job.

I collected my tyres the following morning, before proceeding to the Iranian Embassy for a visa; it was issued without delay. After renewing cholera and typhoid vaccinations as six months approached since the first jabs in New Zealand, I could now concentrate on seeing the city. There were fine views over the city with its mountain backdrop from beside the Nadir Shah Tomb at the summit of a hillside to the east. A soldier on duty along the road indicated firmly that my camera should not be pointed at anything of a military nature. Back down in the central area, there was so much to see in the older bazaar areas and in Western-style stores fronting broad boulevards almost empty of traffic. Besides visitors, there were many foreigners working in the city in connection with the Aid Programmes who would provide some business for these new stores. There were many Russians, the women characteristically stocky, the men indistinguishable from many other Westerners. Twice when I sought information I was on the receiving end of a stream of Russian.

The Afghan people presented a mixture of ancient and modern. Western dress vied with the loose-fitting dress characteristic to this part of the world, contrasts provided by both men and women. Girls and women in skirts and dresses contrasted sharply with others covered by the burqa, the all-encompassing Muslim covering with the wearer viewing the world through a rectangle of embroidered cloth. Where the embroidery was not too close, a pair of eyes could be made out: the sense of mystery was all-pervading. The burqa was worn not only by older women, but by many teenage girls as well. On the older women it was usually ankle length, but commonly stopped just below the knee on teenage girls. Beneath it were contrasting Western clothes of skirt or dress. Did the younger ones retain the burqa to retain privacy, due to shyness, from personal choice, or to obey the wishes of conservative or deeply religious parents? There was no one answer to questions like this, which Westerners found intriguing as Afghanistan was thrust into the second half of the Twentieth Century. Did they want it? Could an ancient country absorb so much change in such a short space of time? Again there could be no simple answers. One sensed a nation at the crossroads.

It was time to return to the countryside. The main road across Afghanistan would take me on an enormous southward loop round to Herat near the border with Iran. While the road from the Pakistan border to Kabul had been built by the Americans, I apparently needed to be grateful to both America and Russia for the paved road from Kabul to the Iranian border. A leaflet collected at the Tourist Bureau advised me that the road was scheduled for completion in 1966. I had the timing right, while Dervla Murphy had to contend with long stretches of gravel in 1963.

I rose early, keen to make a start on the 650 miles to Herat. An early start wasn't needed to compensate for time lost during the middle of the day, since I was high in the mountains. The road climbed gradually for many miles to leave the valley in which Kabul was located. A quicker descent was followed by further long climbs and descents, so that I stayed on a high plateau. There were few trees once I had left the city; areas were covered by golden corn for a time, but more frequent sights were small flocks of sheep, and donkeys and camels being used as beasts of burden. The massive financial aid pouring into the country seemed to be having little effect on the countryside.

The ancient city of Ghazni some 90 miles south of Kabul was the first major place along the route, located a short distance away from the main road. The oldest part of the city stood on a hill, and was built up like a fort. Detouring towards it to replenish food supplies, the contrast with Kabul could not have been greater. Not a single street that I saw was paved, and there did not appear to be any piped water. As I entered the city, I met a young American serving with the Peace Corps, started by President Kennedy in 1961. He told me about the city's most famous resident, Mahmud of Ghazni, who ruled a vast area several centuries ago, every summer going down the Khyber Pass to a plundering campaign in India. The city showed nothing of the wealth which he brought back, as was pointed out by James A. Michener in his stirring novel *Caravans* on Afghanistan, which I had recently finished reading. The young American, who had been teaching in Ghazni for a year, had also read it. He described the procedure he followed, to make safe for eating, fruit like peaches, plums and grapes, where the skins are eaten and cannot easily be separated from the fruit. He would soak the fruit in a bucket of permanganate solution for a number of days: the process did nothing for the taste of the fruit, but at least you obtained your vitamin C. The procedure seemed to me a gross over-reaction to the potential problem of contamination. Clearly, if you could obtain fruit like oranges or bananas, where the skin is easily removed, the problem is eliminated.

The following day, a French motorcyclist on his way to Nepal told me that one of his compatriots was heading my way on a bicycle, followed by an English cyclist several days behind. There was little traffic on the road apart from a few trucks, which were driven in a civilized manner compared with the practice further east. On the surrounding, almost bare terrain I was seeing large herds of camels.

With few trees, I camped with the bicycle chained to a telegraph pole, of which there was one every 50 yards.

It was a long time coming, but about 190 miles from Kabul the terrain made a definite tilt downwards. The land became absolutely bare, posing a problem whenever I wanted to stop for a break, whether long or short. A solution was provided by cylinders below the banked road, which allowed water from the melting of the winter snows to pass through to lower ground. The cylinders were made of corrugated galvanized sheeting; some were oval, though they were generally circular, and at least three feet in diameter. It was usually easy to find a route down the bank to one of the cylinders, taking care to avoid any prickly plants which might result in a puncture. It was remarkably cool inside, perhaps 20 or 30 degrees cooler than in the furnace outside during the middle of the day. I had not anticipated this solution, one which meant that I would not need to find something special each day while in the desert region.

After stopping in one of these cylinders for several hours, I proceeded to Kandahar late one afternoon. I stayed for a day in this second largest city in Afghanistan, an ancient city called Arochosia by the Greeks, and where Alexander built a garrison city, Alexandria of Arochosia. In the main mosque, revered by the Moslem population as a result of holding the Sacred Mantle of the Prophet Mohammed, there was some beautiful pietra dura inlay work similar to what I had seen in Agra. Recent restoration presented some brilliant colours. A slow walk round the extensive bazaar took me past small workshops with fronts open to the road, where men and boys of all ages were industriously turning out different-shaped knives, containers and other hardware. A student who could speak a little English invited me to his home a short distance away, where I sat in a small courtyard along with friends of his. I was glad of this opportunity to get closer to meeting an Afghan family, but the problem of language and the even bigger problem of the purdah in which their women were kept made it impossible for a man to be invited into a family home.

An avenue of pine trees provided shade as I left Kandahar, but I was soon on the open desert. The great mountain range that dominated the centre of Afghanistan was many miles to the north. Herat lay 350 miles to the north-west, a distance which was going to take me either seven or eight days. The daily routine for travel through the hot, desert terrain was well established - rise at daybreak to complete two periods of travel by 10.30am, a long stoppage for lunch and rest in the shade until 3.30pm, followed by two more periods of travel until after sunset. Within this framework, there were subtle variations which made each day's journey unique. I attempted to have the shorter breaks at teahouses along the road, the locations identified by trucks parked outside. If a teahouse appeared as the time arrived for the main stoppage, it was convenient to have a meal there with further glasses of tea, before continuing on to some shade for the rest of the stoppage. The procedure helped to conserve food and water supplies. The problem was knowing where the teahouses were located. There were countless times when I would cover an extra two miles on a stage in the hope of finding a teahouse, eventually stopping in a shady spot, only to come to a teahouse shortly after setting off again. But it was refreshing to rest at a proper stopping place, and to sit at a table in the cooler temperature behind thick walls. I always felt welcome whenever I stopped, although the problem of language limited conversation.

At the end of the day, safety considerations made it desirable to continue to travel until just after sunset. In the failing light, I would scan the ground for a suitable camping area, about a hundred yards off the road so that vehicles would not illuminate my position with their headlights. The bicycle would be supported upright at the front of the tent, using string and extra tent pegs, with a chain leading from the bicycle frame to the tent pole. Nobody was going to be able to walk off with the bicycle without me being alerted. Thankfully, my security precautions were never put to the test.

I knew precisely when sunset occurred. The air was extremely clear in the desert, and, as I headed directly west from Kandahar, the sun would descend directly in front of me like a giant fireball, continuing to emit heat until the very last moment. A bright orange glow followed the sunset, or rather two glows about 15 minutes apart. As the light faded, stars would start to appear. A short time later I would look up at an enormous canopy of stars, seeing thousands that cannot be seen when there is haze or cloud in the sky. A vehicle might pass along the distant road at half hour intervals, but otherwise it was a most peaceful setting. The following morning, after rising as the light broke, I would be outside attending to my ablutions or having breakfast when the sun would suddenly pop above the horizon to start its inexorable daily passage, preceded by two orange glows as at sunset. The heat would be noticeable before I had the tent packed, giving a sense of urgency to getting under way again and able to benefit from the cooling effect of moving through the air. As I experienced one sunrise and sunset after another, I puzzled over the phenomenon presented by the apparent rapid movement of the sun when close to the horizon compared with its speed of movement during the main part of the day, particularly during the middle when it seemed to hover overhead without any apparent movement for such a long time.

As I journeyed westwards, I wondered if I had missed the French cyclist I had been told about east of Kandahar. There was always the possibility that we would pass each other when one of us was at a teahouse or sheltering in the shade of a bridge or a tunnel under the road. About six overland vehicles raced past me each day, not stopping to give me an opportunity to check with them. Then little Citroen 2CVs started to appear in increasing numbers, from two one day to six on each of the next two days. I presumed they belonged to a club. They were surely an indication that the overland journey was no longer quite the ordeal that it had been a few years before. The terrain was harsh but, with a paved road right through Afghanistan, driving conditions were so much easier. The road between Kabul and Herat was a mixture of concrete and asphalt. The stretches of concrete road were apparently due to the Russians, while the smoother asphalt sections had been laid by the Americans.

At Delaram I was able to buy some bread and a jar of jam at a hotel, uncertain when I would next encounter supplies. The hotel manager and a Belgian couple told me of a large hotel further along the road. The road climbed over hills to descend to more desert. Just across the Farah Rod River the most enormous hotel with hundreds of rooms loomed up, built by the Russians. Whether it formed part of some 10 year plan, or 50 year plan, nobody knew, but it was an incongruous sight. The only traffic on the road was a few trucks, overland vehicles and one or two cyclists. There was no one looking for the kind of luxury accommodation which the hotel was built to provide. I had a pot of tea and an omelette in the restaurant while talking to other overlanders, but even that simple request taxed the hotel's resources. A request for two eggs could not be satisfied as the omelette used their only egg.

The road climbed after several miles into rugged hills; black, brown and red rocks predominated, twisted in all directions and suggesting a violent upheaval a very long time ago. I spent the night in a tunnel below the road as the wind declined to ease down. Shortly after setting off, I encountered three Afghanis beside their truck near the top of a rise. As I approached the vehicle, I half expected to see them kneeling on mats and praying towards Mecca, but they were sitting round a primus stove drinking tea and eating nan, the Afghan unleavened bread. They invited me to join them. The tea refreshed me for a continuing battle with a strong wind from the west.

Food supplies were running low as I approached within 50 miles of Herat. With my tin of jam finished, and no eggs, tomatoes or fruit available, I was reduced to meals of sugar sandwiches. I was able to buy eggs at Adraskan, but had to stop there on another account. A cholera checkpoint had been set up as a result of an outbreak of the disease somewhere in the country. I took the opportunity to tell the doctor that I had a sore tongue. He recognised straight away that it was due to vitamin deficiency, not surprising in view of my restricted diet. I came away with a prescription to take to Herat.

The road climbed for many miles to reach a summit of 5,648 ft about 18 miles north of Adraskan. As I set off one morning for the final 31 miles to Herat, the wind of recent days finally disappeared. After a descent for two miles and a final climb, I looked down towards Herat in the distance on a broad plain with mountains behind it. As the road swept downwards I stopped at a teahouse at Guzra a few miles from the city, slowly consuming two pots of tea and a full round of nan.

As I relaxed before entering Herat on Monday, 21 July 1969, I would have had no particular reason to look up into the sky. However, in the world outside, and particularly the world with television, the eyes of hundreds of millions of people were focused on events in the distant sky as they followed the progress of Apollo 11 on its mission to achieve the first moon landing. I knew nothing about this historic flight at the time. Neil Armstrong stepped onto the moon at 10.56pm Eastern Standard Time in America on 20 July, as I drank my tea at what was breakfast time the following morning in Afghanistan.

An avenue of pine trees provided shade as I proceeded into Herat, accompanied by a young Afghani who had just left the airport nearby where he worked in the control room. I found Herat a much more interesting city than Kandahar. Like Kandahar, it had a long history. Prior to the invasion of Alexander the Great, another city, Artakana, existed where Herat was built by Alexander as one of his

Alexandrias. Herat became the capital of Khorasan under the Islamic kings, to be destroyed by Genghis Khan and Tamerlane. During the reign of the Timourid kings during the 15th and 16th centuries, Herat regained a period of splendour. The city was dominated by a huge fort, which overlooked the bazaar. Set into the walls of the fort were open-fronted workshops as in Kandahar. The craftsmanship on old truck tyres and tubes to produce containers, shoes and ropes was amazing to see. Huge piles of melons were built up on the unpaved ground around the fort. Large loaves of the unleavened bread were also on display on sacking on the ground: Westerners bought the bread from this source at their peril. The most outstanding building in Herat was the Great Mosque, the walls covered in inlaid porcelain to produce the most beautiful geometric designs in addition to inscriptions from the Koran. The building was in an amazing state of repair.

I left Herat for the border with Iran with some uncertainty. Due to cholera in part of Afghanistan, the border had been closed a few days before to westbound traffic. However, the situation seemed to be changing from day to day. At the enormous Russian-built hotel beside the Hari Rod River, a French family told me that the border could be crossed, but travellers were held at the border for three days in some kind of quarantine. At the Tourist Office in Herat, a young American with the Peace Corps told me that only about 50 travellers a day, or possibly every other day, were being allowed to cross the border due to the limited quarantine accommodation on the Iranian side of the border. There was no alternative but to proceed to the border 78 miles to the west, and deal with the current situation.

After a final night camping in Afghanistan, I reached the Afghan frontier post at Eslam-Qala the following morning, having lunch at the hotel there after passing through Customs and Immigration. It was six miles further to the border, where I came to a full stop. The quarantine camp was apparently 13 miles further on, but no one could go further without instructions from Teheran. I joined a number of other travellers already waiting to cross, the numbers growing as the afternoon advanced. There we all were, on the open desert, with no food, water, shelter or any facilities whatsoever except what we had with us. A number of hitch-hikers arrived, their entire food supply consisting of two melons. Nobody was being advised of the actual situation at the border, either at Eslam-Qala or at the Tourist Office in Herat. How Iran dealt with the health problem in Afghanistan was clearly seen as an Iranian problem. It was a time for optimism as everyone awaited favourable instructions from the Iranian capital.

Chapter 25

In the Land of the Shah

Thursday, 24 July 1969 Iran

There was plenty of time to think about the journey ahead as an increasing number of travellers joined me at the border with Afghanistan, waiting to be able to cross. During the afternoon of arrival, I spent most of the time in a minibus in the company of an American woman and her daughter, and a young New Zealander on his way to England. A doctor was apparently expected at 5pm, but he arrived without any instructions. 200 travellers apparently crossed the border yesterday; they needed to pass through the quarantine station before there were further admissions.

As we settled down for a night on the open desert, I set my tent up as the sun went down and the wind eased off. The following morning it was soon blowing at full strength as I had a leisurely breakfast and wrote my diary for the unusual day just passed. My attention was distracted by the antics of a number of motorists as tempers became frayed. An attempt was made to block the road to eastbound traffic, with the objective of causing them to turn back and protest to the authorities, hopefully leading to something being done about our plight. But the traffic arriving to enter Afghanistan found a way round the road block. A group then tried to force their way across the border, but were quickly stopped by the soldiers on duty.

In the middle of the afternoon, bread and eggs were distributed, with more at sundown, and blankets for those with no shelter. I passed some time reading two newspapers a few days old, the *Kabul Times* of 21 July and the *Tehran Kayhan* of the following day. Both papers carried a full report on the moon landing. In the Tehran paper I found myself reading a number of times a small news item from Hong Kong, entitled: “11 Killed”. The item read: “Eleven people were yesterday feared dead aboard the blazing British freighter *Eastern Star*, listing critically at anchor in Hong Kong harbour." This was the ship on which I had sailed from Japan to Australia a year before. I wondered about the cause of the fire, and whether any of the officers I had got to know were among the eleven lost.

The following day, the second at the border, was a day of tragedy for another reason. It didn't start off well, with the wind dying down only slightly during the night. The wind apparently came from the steppes of Central Asia where it was much cooler, rushing south to replace the rising warmer air here. It covered a broad front, so that conditions were unlikely to ease for some time. On reflection, the wind was preferable to still conditions, as the heat would have been very difficult on the open desert without air movement. At 7am bread, eggs and a cup of milk were distributed to each waiting traveller. Two hours later a doctor arrived to take specimens for the checking of cholera.

Yesterday evening we were promised a decision by 11am on whether or not we could proceed to the quarantine camp. When 11am passed without anyone arriving with a decision, a group of motorists proceeded to advance inch by inch against a line of eight soldiers across the road. Passengers walked in front of the cars, taunting the soldiers at intervals. After an advance by one car, the corporal in charge punctured one of the front tyres with a penknife. The car reversed to change the tyre.

The incident inflamed tensions, and shortly afterwards a soldier had the magazine of his rifle snatched from him as he attempted to load it with cartridges. A few minutes later someone attempted to wrestle the corporal's rifle from him; the rifle went off, but luckily for everyone the bullet went astray. Then tragedy occurred. The corporal ordered his soldiers to shoot the person who had attempted to wrestle his rifle from him. A shot was fired, but the person for whom it was meant had dodged aside. A young German, seeing himself in the line of fire, raised his hands in the air. Seconds later he fell to the ground, killed instantly by a shot through the head. The soldiers retreated up the road, while the travellers waited for the aftermath.

The commander of the soldiers controlling the border region arrived with reinforcements. A demonstration of strength occurred as the soldiers were ordered to form a line on either side of the road at ten yard intervals, with their rifles in front of them and bayonets glinting in the afternoon sun. An ambulance had also arrived, and the commander sought witnesses to inform him of what had happened. A young American, whose father was a missionary in Iran, acted as interpreter, speaking Farsi fluently. The commander advised us that he had no authority to allow us to cross the border. He had been unable to contact Tehran during the day due to a breakdown along the telephone line. Another officer spoke to the missionary and was asked what would happen to the officer who fired the fatal shot. "He will be executed" was the blunt reply. "And the corporal?" "He will be disciplined". It meant he would lose his stripes and receive other undefined forms of discipline. This was the way things had to be in what was unquestionably a police state. A health official confided, after being harassed for the last two days to obtain permission for us all to go to the quarantine camp, that he was working to escape from the system. He told some of us of the shooting of several thousand students a few years before following a demonstration. The outside world never heard about it.

We wondered if the outside world would hear about the current events at the remote border. Yesterday morning - the day before the tragic incident - an English jeep left for Kabul with a report and films, for posting to the BBC. The report and films highlighted conditions awaiting travellers at the border. It was hoped that publicizing the situation would prompt the Iranian Government to provide proper facilities at the border, and to inform their own and foreign embassies in neighbouring countries in advance of issuing any order to close the border so that prospective travellers could halt at a place with amenities. Apart from the report and films on the way to London, various people were writing to their embassies in Iran. One wondered if previous groups of travellers stranded at the border did anything to inform the authorities of the unsatisfactory conditions. Last year the border was apparently closed for two months; at one stage 500 people were waiting to cross. It seemed to me that we were small fry as far as world events were concerned; it would be doubtful if our situation created headlines in any major newspapers. What was beyond doubt was the stupidity of the behaviour of a few hotheads, who would not accept that one group needed to leave the quarantine camp before the next group could proceed. The notion of provoking ordinary soldiers, yet alone wrestling with them, does not bear thinking about. When the soldiers are conscripts from villages, as were probably most of those at the border, with limited education, they could not be expected to show reserves of self-discipline in the difficult circumstances in which they found themselves.

We were advised to get ready to proceed. While everyone got ready and I took my tent down, the order was overruled by the health department. It was now late in the afternoon. Half an hour before sunset a truck arrived with food and water for the evening. After eating, I unpacked my tent again for a second night at the border.

Just after sunrise we were awoken to be informed that all Europeans were to proceed to the quarantine camp 13 miles away at Taiabad. By the time I had packed my tent away, most of the cars had gone. The camp had 18 large 5-person tents for accommodation, with labels advertising Sears, Roebuck and Simpsons, and a large service building for meals with showers, washing and toilet facilities, plus the essential medical rooms. The meals were excellent. The authorities had set up a perfectly satisfactory quarantine camp. A corresponding effort needed to be made at the border, supported by communication links with embassies and tourist offices. More travellers arrived at the camp throughout the day, including an overland lorry carrying 12 passengers; it was held at the border for just a few hours.

At 10.30 the following morning we were told that we could go. Ironically, we were leaving without the results of yesterday's cholera tests being known, but nobody was going to protest. I was soon through Customs and Immigration just up the road from the camp, and on my way to Mashhad almost 150 miles to the north-west. The events of the last three days faded in my mind as I battled with the gravel road. The entire 900 miles across Afghanistan had been on a paved surface, but my map for Iran showed a very long stretch of gravel road in the eastern half of the country. With a new road under construction parallel to the existing road, I experimented with riding on the sub-bed of the new road, stopping at intervals to lift the bicycle over a raised section corresponding with ducts under the road. It was easier than riding on gravel, and there was the advantage that there was no traffic to shower me with dust as it hurtled past.

Back on the main road, children greeted me with "Hello mister" as I approached Torbat-e-Jam, the first sizable town. The children displayed a vitality which had been absent from the scene for some time. The brighter colours in the clothes of almost everyone were noticeable. Most of the women wore a chador, thus having the head covered, though not the face. I didn't expect to see the burqa as in Afghanistan. The desert terrain became more interesting once I was away from the border region. With irrigation channels crossing the area, large areas of the plain were under cultivation, so that I passed numerous fields of corn and vegetables. Many of the cornfields were being harvested with sickles. I noticed a slightly lower temperature, which was most welcome.

Leaving Torbat-e-Jam, I left the gravel road once more for the new road under construction, eventually coming to a halt at the position of a bridge. The engineer in charge of building the new road from the border to Mashhad was there, and invited me to have tea with him. He realised straight away why I was trying out the new road.

A paved road brought me to the holy city of Mashhad. There was an extraordinary religious fervour in the city as the population was swelled by a huge influx of pilgrims, here to worship at the Shrine of Emam Reza, one of the most revered saints in the Shiite branch of Islam. Emam Reza was murdered and buried in Mashhad in the 8th Century, when the city was just a village. The Shrine was surrounded by the enormous Gowharshad Mosque, all the surfaces covered with the most beautiful inlaid porcelain like the Great Mosque in Herat. Only the faithful were allowed anywhere near the Shrine building. After jostling among so many visitors, I noticed my sunglasses were missing from my shirt pocket as I left the Gowharshad Mosque. I couldn't help thinking that theft sat uneasily beside such deep religious belief.

With the huge number of visitors in Herat, there were surprisingly few restaurants. I settled for one offering kebab. There were far more teashops, where I consumed numerous glasses of tea, and shops selling ice-cream and soft drinks. Cheese, butter and milk were available in the grocery shops; these dairy products had been absent from my diet for some time, but there was no point in buying butter yet as it would turn to liquid until the temperature dropped further. The shops were full of food, hardware and clothing, with market areas having large displays of all kinds of fruit and vegetables. It was all very encouraging, but I needed to be wary of what I bought, particularly of fruit displayed in the open air. I was hoping to put on a bit of weight as a better diet and more plentiful food started to become available. I topped the scales at 8 st 4 lb or 52.5 kg when I checked my weight earlier in the day. The attacks of "Delhi belly" and, more recently, the "Kabul trots", had taken their toll. I wasn't sure of my weight when I left Singapore, but I had certainly lost quite a few pounds.

In my concern over health matters, I noted a report in the Tehran Journal that health organisations in Khorassan Province, the local region, "already engaged in a battle against the entry and spread of cholera in Iran, are now faced with the prospect of a small pox epidemic. Health units have been instructed to watch for and arrest the spread of the disease which has already reached epidemic proportions in some of the neighbouring eastern countries." The existence of an epidemic took some believing, as did another report referring to the Shah ordering the medical profession to organise an insurance scheme for the entire population. He wished them success in attaining this goal.

I was interested to see a variety of bicycles in the larger bicycle shops in Herat, mostly Polish without gears, but both Polish and English machines with hub gears, and some English Raleigh racing bicycles with derailleur gears. It was a reflection of Mashhad's position as a large, modern city, by far the largest city in the east of Iran. I wouldn't be seeing anything further like this until I reached the capital 600 miles to the west.

There were alternative routes for me to take. The main one seemed to be the route skirting the north of the Dasht-e-Kavir, the Great Salt Desert, but I had been told about an alternative to the north via Quchan. One of the German motorcyclists I had met in Lahore first told me about it. Following this up at other opportunities, the view was unanimous that the northern route was scenically much more attractive, and with less gravel road than the desert route. However, the northern route did involve a mountain crossing and was slightly longer. The decision was simple.

I headed north-west for Quchan along a superb road, with the strong wind of a few days before abated. The one disadvantage was that all the communities with amenities were on the older road a mile or so to the side; it would take time for services to become established along the new road. Dervla Murphy had followed the desert road in 1963, taking her through Nishapur about 90 miles to the west of Mashhad. A young Iranian told me in Mashhad that Nishapur held the tomb of one of Iran's most famous poets, Omar Khayyám. My ears pricked up as I recalled an association with my former school in Bury St. Edmunds, the King Edward VI Grammar School. A former student, Edward FitzGerald, translated some of his verses in 1857. In 1956 I was presented with a copy of the resulting work, *The Rubáiyát of Omar Khayyám*, "For Good Work". It was impossible to forget such events: it always fascinated me when seemingly disparate threads came together.

Three miles north of Quchan my swift progress came to a rapid halt as the asphalt ended. As I continued to Shirvan and Bodjnurd, alternating between the older gravel road and a new road under construction nearby, I spent sufficiently long on the gravel surface so that I, and all my baggage and clothing, became covered with a yellowish, brown dust. My khaki shorts were the most appropriate colour, but I couldn't describe my original cycle bags as black any longer. I needed to stop at regular intervals to put fresh oil on the bicycle chain and derailleur gear as the gear clogged up with dust. Climbs over the barren hills afforded wide views over the irrigated green valleys. Villages on hillsides away from the road made interesting pictures at the ends of the day in particular, when longer shadows accentuated the shapes of the simple, rectangular, flat-roofed houses, all the mud-finished surfaces the same colour as the surrounding soil. The flat roofs clearly did not have to deal with much rainfall. Further colour was provided at intervals by flocks of multi-coloured sheep. After lunch in Bodjnurd, I stocked up with food for the next three days for the 150 miles to Shah Pasand, where the paved road would start again. I wasn't certain of food availability between the two towns, and probably would not be in a large enough town or village at lunch times to have a meal in a restaurant. I was trying to do this as much as possible to reduce the amount of food I needed to carry, and to bring me into contact with a few more people. I accepted whatever was on offer, which in Iran meant some kind of pilaff, a combination of rice, meat and vegetables.

There was a consistent reaction in all the towns and villages along the route by the Iranian children. I was asked time and again if I had any English stamps for them, or money or presents. I came to the conclusion that I was meant to be on a gift distribution run, but, even if my bags had been full of small gifts, I could not have satisfied the demand. Some decided to help themselves, taking clips off baggage straps when I was away from the bicycle in a tea-house or store. At one small community I came back to the bicycle to find the Union

Jack on my saddlebag ripped off. I had not encountered minor theft like this in any previous country.

But these incidents did not compare with an earlier one after I had stopped for lunch in the shade of a tunnel below the road. I was suddenly joined by a big, surly-looking man, who squatted near the entrance to the tunnel while I had my lunch. He made no attempt to speak to me, but it was clear that he hadn't come there just to shelter from the sun. As I packed things away later prior to departing, the man indicated he wanted something of mine before allowing me to pass. He gestured to my jumper, a small part of which projected from the saddlebag. Knowing I would need it later, I deflected his attention to my watch. It looked valuable, though it wasn't, and had stopped working a few days before. I explained by gestures that, with a little attention to it, he could soon have a valuable possession. The bluff worked, and I was soon on my way up the road as fast as I could pedal, not looking back for some time. When I did, the surly-looking man was shaking the watch, trying to get it to work. The incident was a reminder of the need for continuous caution, and the importance of trying to ensure that my position was not observed whenever I stopped in an isolated place.

My food supply was stretched to the limit as the road became rougher, and I had to stop and fit one of the Michelin tyres collected in Kabul. The daily milage dropped below 30 miles for three days. As I started going downwards after one climb, it quickly became apparent that I was on an important descent. Small bushes gave way to larger bushes, then small trees appeared; in a space of two or three miles I was riding through forest, with thick cloud overhead.

The desert was left behind as I entered the cooler and wetter terrain close to the Caspian Sea. The hills I had just crossed acted as a barrier to rainfall further east. I followed a river down the valley, the river getting bigger and bigger as tributaries joined it from the thickly forested hills. Rain started to fall after I had stopped to camp beside the river. When I set off the following morning, the road surface was one of sticky mud until the sun could dry it out. After descending for several more miles the hills parted, the valley growing wider and wider until I was on an apparently limitless plain. It was a fertile plain covered with fields of wheat, cotton and watermelons. As I passed field after field of watermelons, I reached the paved road to end a run of 226 miles on gravel from north of Quchan. With 132 miles from the border to near Mashhad, it made 358 miles of gravel in eastern Iran. Within a year or two this should all be paved.

I stocked up with food before starting a leisurely ride westwards, with more time now to look round at the fields instead of needing to focus on the road surface. I stopped early to give the bicycle a good clean and to oil it. A few miles west of Gorgan I had a first sighting of the Caspian Sea. I looked forward the following day to riding beside it on the 23 miles between Babolsar and Mahmudabad, but the road ran between half a mile and a mile from the sea with a ridge of sand cutting off the view except at a few points.

Disappointed, I turned away southwards towards Tehran. The next stage was a complete contrast as the road climbed over the Elburz Mountains. The land sloped upwards very gently at first as the road followed the Haraz River upstream. The thickly forested slopes of the foothills quickly gave way to sparser vegetation. Soon the mountain slopes were bare, with just oases of greenery close to the river. As the road climbed to give a succession of memorable views, the first of several unlit tunnels was encountered, making for a tense journey as my dynamo attempted to show the position of the tunnel walls. A steady stream of cars and buses came to my aid, each vehicle lighting up the tunnel for some distance ahead as it came up behind me. Out in the open to the west was the conical peak of Mt. Damavand, rising to 18,963 ft with patches of snow on the upper slopes. As the road started to zigzag upwards, I guessed the top of the pass was near. The road climbed to 2,100 m, or 6,888 ft, when I put my jacket on before starting a long descent. After a few miles the road looked down on the major winter ski resort of Abali. It was difficult to imagine snow on the surrounding bare slopes as the road descended and the temperature rose once more.

An important event occurred on the descent involving a small piece of bicycle equipment: the cyclometer, which recorded my milage, passed through 10,000 miles. It was the first one to achieve this distinction, the previous two seizing up some time after 9,000 miles. (The latest unit was still in use at the end of the journey, after measuring a further 3,600 miles.)

As I arrived in Tehran and looked back on the journey of the last two weeks from Mashhad, a journey of great variety, it was difficult to conceive that the desert route to the south could be as interesting. Tehran was a landmark on the overland journey, but I found the capital a big, noisy, characterless city. However, it was a city I wanted to spend a few days in to get to know it. I bought a newspaper to catch up with the news, reading about riots in Northern Ireland. At the Post Office I was disappointed to find no mail waiting for me. Either letters home from Kabul were not received, or replies did not get through to Tehran. It made two successive letter failures, as an earlier one from Kathmandu produced no reply to Kabul. I would have to write again while in Tehran to attempt to assure my family that I wasn't lost somewhere in Central Asia. A letter would have been welcome to boost flagging spirits, as I suffered an attack of the local variation of "Delhi belly". My weight was down to 112 lb, the lowest for a long time. But I couldn't recommend the associated diet as one to follow to lose weight; the side effects were altogether too disagreeable.

I walked and cycled along the broad avenues of the city, and round numerous squares, as I attempted to get my normal energy back, stopping to visit the Golestan Palace and the Crown Jewels, symbols of a grandeur of which the Shah saw himself such an integral part. All attempts to ask anyone what they personally felt about the rule of the Shah met with a frozen stare; a climate of fear gripped the city, no one being certain about the extent of the ears of the secret police.

A pass obtained at the Tourist Office to allow me to visit the National Assembly building produced some interesting reactions when I went along there. I didn't know if many people visited the Parliament building, but my pass was regarded by one official after another as a document of considerable importance. Discussions occurred as to who was going to escort the visitor, while an assessment was being made of my actual importance: I was eventually assigned to one of the junior staff. As he took me to the main chamber and various meeting rooms, he could not enlarge on what the eye beheld, as he spoke not a word of English, French or German. I was left with a favourable impression by the offer of a small glass of tea at the end of the tour.

There was a more relaxed atmosphere at the Traditional Gymnasium, where seven men performed exercises in an octagonal enclosure to the accompaniment of music and chants. Some looked extremely fit, the exercises apparently having a high standing in Iran. I recalled seeing a photograph in *Time* magazine a few weeks earlier of the American Secretary of State, William Rogers, hoisted on the shoulders of a group of the athletes during a stopover in the city.

I was still regaining my fitness when I left the capital, eventually reaching open country after travelling through a sprawling industrial district. As I crossed a vast, bare plain in continuing heat, my butter supply soon turned to liquid. I would have to postpone buying any more for the time being. The Elburz Mountains were just to the north of the road, while to the south stretched the open plain. A short turn south-westwards was made at Qazvin, but otherwise the road ran north-west to the Turkish border.

The map suggested a straight, uneventful journey, but it could not convey a number of unexpected features which arose as the journey progressed. After turning north-west at Takestan, the road followed a river for many miles, the river's path defined by a broad band of green in contrast to the brown hills to either side. Initially I was on a new road some distance from the valley, but interest improved as the road approached the fertile valley. It was a prime fruit growing area, with many fields of grapes.

The temperature was no longer oppressive, so that I didn't need to stop for a long period during the middle of each day. With a paved road, the daily milage improved again. In the circumstances I could have stopped earlier each day, but I considered it wiser to continue until sunset so as not to advertise my camping spots to every Ali Baba in the district. The day was still long, with sunrise at 5.45am and sunset at 6.45pm. I could afford to spend a little more time at the tea-houses for the shorter breaks and at eating places in the towns for lunch. Food was more plentiful at the shops in the towns, which allowed me to build myself up again after the recent setbacks.

South of Mianeh the road and river entered a scenic gorge, with granite hills looming on either side. Groves of poplar trees were all along the valley, and small orchards on flat pieces of ground. The road climbed to give sweeping views over rolling hills, much of the land under cultivation. A familiar sight in the villages was the threshing of corn, with cattle circling round and round on a layer of corn on the ground, dragging a sled with spiked wheels to chop up the corn. This was then tossed into the air to separate the grain from the chaff. It had been some time since I had seen similar scenes in the east of the country.

After reaching a summit, the road descended to Boston Abad, only to begin another long climb. The road ran beside a deep blue lake, all the more attractive since it was unexpected. The descent from the next summit brought me to Tabriz, the capital of Azarbaijan province and by far the largest city in the region. I approached the centre along a broad tree-lined avenue divided in the middle. Late in the evening a small coach party arrived at the hotel where I was staying, on the way to Tehran. At breakfast I found myself in conversation with an American black girl and a retired Canadian couple. They wanted to see something of the city during the morning before the coach departed in the afternoon, but the girl in particular was looking for some company, judging it was unwise to go out walking unescorted. I spent the morning in an unexpected role, as the four of us went out together to see some of the sights, including the Citadel, the Blue Mosque and the bazaar. Following an earthquake which struck Tabriz early in the Nineteenth Century, the Citadel and Blue Mosque were still partly in ruins, but the Citadel had been made safe to allow ascent to the top, from where there were fine views over the city.

It was an interesting situation as our group explored the city. The local men could see that the Canadian couple were together, but just what was my relationship with the attractive, black girl? As the Tabriz men contemplated my apparent good fortune, I judged that the looks of disapproval were outweighed by others of envy. Our time together was over all too quickly. Returning to the hotel, I spoke for some time to Piers, a Cambridge University student who had been in Iran for five weeks, principally to study folk music.

The visits to the damaged Citadel and Blue Mosque reminded me of major earthquakes in Iran in recent years. A newspaper reported the visit of the Shah to Gonabad and Ferdowsi south-west of Mashhad, on the first anniversary of the earthquake which caused the loss of 40,000 lives. The same paper reported bad weather in parts of the country, with rain in Tehran and snow in other locations. Here in the north-west, fine weather continued.

I left Tabriz for the border almost 170 miles away feeling happy after discharging a new role as male escort. Shortly afterwards, I was amused to meet a young Frenchman on a mobylette, one of those very French motorized bicycles driven by a tiny engine on top of the front wheel. It was something I never expected to see; but, if I could do the journey by bicycle, it could surely be accomplished with engine assistance. Jean François seemed to be having little trouble with his machine, which was clearly being tested to its limits.

Around Marand I passed field after field of melons reminding me of the fields of watermelons seen earlier east of the Caspian Sea. The border region had an air of remoteness as communities became scarcer, and the road ran within a few miles of Armenia. In the undulating terrain, the road was continually going down into one valley before climbing gradually to the top of the next rise. In one valley were fields of sunflowers, the seeds being harvested by beating the heads with sticks.

The terrain became more arid, much of the land unusable as a result of being covered with lava from volcanic mountains to the west. The road suddenly left the wide, lava-strewn valley to enter a gorge, climbing to Maku. This last town in Iran for travellers going west had the most unlikely setting, vertical walls of rock towering all round. After stocking up with food, I relaxed to enjoy my last glasses of tea in Iran. Four miles on, as the road emerged from the gorge onto a broader valley once more, I headed into trees by the river bank to camp in a secluded position prior to crossing the border the following day.

I could only look forward to an easier crossing than the previous one from Afghanistan. It seemed a long time ago now: it was, in fact, just under six weeks, during which another 1,350 miles had been covered, and through quite varying terrain. In particular, I had avoided a long desert stretch in the east. The journey had not been without its unsavoury incidents, but it had exceeded expectations.

NORWAY
Oslo
SWEDEN
Stockholm
FINLAND
Helsinki
Leningrad
RUSSIAN FEDERATION
Moscow
ESTONIA
LATVIA
LITHUANIA
SCOTLAND
N.I.
EIRE
WALES
ENGLAND
DENMARK
Copenhagen
0
200
400
Miles
Bury St. Edmunds
London
Dover
Ostend
NETHDS
Hamburg
Berlin
POLAND
Warsaw
BELARUS
Kiev
Stalingrad
UKRAINE
BELGIUM
Brussels
GERMANY
Koblenz
Rudesheim
CZECH REP.
Paris
LUXG
Rothenburg
Augsburg
Munich
Salzburg
SLOVAKIA
FRANCE
Berne
SWITZD
AUSTRIA
Graz
Maribor
HUNGARY
ROMANIA
ITALY
Novisad
Belgrade
YUGOSLAVIA
Nis
BULGARIA
Sofia
Plovdiv
Black Sea
GEORGIA
ARMENIA
Madrid
SPAIN
CORSICA
Rome
ALBANIA
Edirne
Istanbul
Bolu
Ankara
Yozgat
Sivas
Erzincan
Erzurum
BALEARIC Is.
SARDINIA
SICILY
GREECE
Athens
TURKEY

Chapter 26

Farewell to Asia

Wednesday, 3 September 1969 Turkey

Cloud covered the sky as I woke up, but dispersed while I had breakfast and packed my bags for the 11 mile ride to the border. I looked north over rising ground to Mt. Ararat, my eyes continually drawn towards it as the road continued up the valley to the frontier at the top of a small pass. There was surely no more scenic frontier in the world. I had to take my turn in a long queue behind motorists with complicated carnets to be examined and stamped. It took one and a quarter hours, but it simply gave me more time to admire the famous mountain ahead. Focusing intently on the slopes, yes, I thought I could see ruins of Noah's ark.

Turkey, like Iran, had just one time for the whole of the large country, requiring me to now set my watch back 1½ hours. I would now be getting up at 4.15am instead of 5.45, and stopping at 5.30pm instead of 7.00 if I wanted the same full day. I needed to do this as the days started to shorten. The plan for crossing Turkey was a simple one of taking the direct route from Erzurum to Ankara via Erzincan, Sivas and Yozgat, then sweeping north-west via Bolu to Istanbul. The mountain route appealed to me in preference to branching north-west near Erzurum towards the Black Sea, and following the shore for 300 miles before turning towards Ankara. The place names would become ingrained in my memory as arrival in each location during the next five weeks signalled onward progress. I was going to be on a high plateau in mountainous terrain for most of the journey. All being well, I would be out of the mountains before the onset of winter weather. It seemed extraordinary thinking like this, when only a few weeks earlier I had been sheltering from the heat during the middle of the day; but it was now September, and the fine weather could not last forever.

On both sides of the frontier were groups of nomads, the women dressed in brilliant colours of oranges and reds. There were camels everywhere and the unusual sight of cattle saddled with sacks of corn like donkeys. Shortly after leaving, cloud rolled over the sky, obscuring the 16,940 ft peak of Mt. Ararat and allowing me to concentrate on the journey ahead. The road was paved but bumpy, winding its way over undulating, grass-covered terrain on which grazed many flocks of sheep and herds of cattle.

The small town of Dogubayazit was my first one in Turkey. I stopped for afternoon tea and to explore the bazaar. The prospect was promising for foodstuffs, with a range of groceries available and large loaves of white bread compared to the thin, unleavened bread in eastern Iran. If I could obtain this white bread throughout the country, I should continue to restore lost weight, having already recovered 8 lb since leaving Tehran. The teahouses were now separate from the restaurants, and a number of distinctive additional buildings appeared on the scene, full of tables occupied by men playing cards and board games. Tables spilled out onto the pavements, creating a characteristic scene which would be repeated in every town where I stopped. I picked up my first words of Turkish from two young boys, for entry in my notebook. The procedure was now a little easier as one of the reforms introduced by Kemal Atatürk, the founder of modern Turkey, was to change from Arabic to the Roman alphabet, or at least something very close to it. Accents or other symbols appeared above or below various letters to indicate a particular pronunciation. Pictures of Atatürk were to be seen frequently, contrasting with images of the Shah in Iran.

Dogubayazit was dominated by a castle built in 1380 high on the hillside to the south. After my first night's camping in Turkey a few miles west of the town, I emerged from the tent at 4.30am, about 15 minutes after the light broke. With the temperature dropping considerably during the night in this high region, I waited patiently for the sun to rise to warm the air. The frontier region was apparently the coldest part of Turkey. As the journey continued over grass-covered plains and hills, Mt. Ararat slowly disappeared from view as I looked back. At Agri, the first large town on my route, I spent some time walking round the bazaar before continuing west. The road started to climb before Eleskirt, changing to gravel as I left the town. The gradient increased, taking me to the highest elevation on the entire journey across the country as far as a contour map indicated. From about 8,000 ft, I admired the wide mountain views before descending to a broad, cultivated valley.

The first stretch of gravel lasted for 63 miles, to a few miles before Pasinler. I stopped for lunch in the town before climbing out of the valley to descend to Erzurum, easily the largest city in the east of Turkey. I decided to spend a day in the ancient city, a city with a complicated history going back at least 1,500 years. Control of the whole region changed many times during this long period due to its strategic location. It was interesting just walking slowly round the central part of the city, seeing the main buildings including the mosques built in different eras, and absorbing the atmosphere.

There was no question about Erzurum's strategic location, with its closeness to the Soviet Union, Iran, Iraq and Syria. There was a large barracks in the city, just as there was in almost every town I had so far passed through. As I approached Erzurum, a convoy of some 200 vehicles passed me heading east, the equipment all looking in good condition. I could only wonder about the amount of money being spent on the army, money which could surely be better spent in raising the general standard of living.

Walking round the city, I found an excellent tea-room at a hotel near the one I was staying at, where I was served with a pot of tea accompanied with a second pot of hot water. The restaurants served a wide variety of meals, the principal one in this area being döner kebab. It was a familiar sight at the restaurants, the combination of small pieces of meat, tomatoes and onions mounted on a skewer held vertically in a stand; a charcoal fire running vertically beside the rotating skewers grilled the meat to produce a very tasty meal. I was already enjoying the food in Turkey. At an ice-cream parlour, bringing Erzurum into the modern world, I had a long talk with a courageous American family from Illinois, travelling with two young children. They were the only Westerners I met in the city apart from two hitch-hikers.

I was pleased to obtain a large road map of the country before leaving Erzurum to continue west, having caught up with washing and having a haircut so as to be able to cope better with all the dust I expected to be thrown at me from further stretches of gravel road. It was a paved road, however, as far as Askale, where the road divided; one fork went north-west towards the Black Sea, while I took the south-west fork to Erzincan. I was immediately back on gravel, which lasted this time for most of the next 200 miles. After a climb for seven miles, a long, gradual descent began. I realised I would be going down all the way to Erzincan as a small river appeared on my left, the map showing it continuing beyond the city.

The coldest day I had experienced in Asia was immediately followed by an even colder day as the sun showed itself for only a few seconds as it went down. Conditions were changing. I was having to wear long trousers again, also a sweater and jacket. The road and river entered a rocky gorge, the valley widening near Tercan only to narrow again after a few miles. Several doubtful-looking suspension bridges were passed, built for man to cross but not vehicles. The cloud dispersed after a couple of days to herald a return to hot, sunny weather.

The road ran high up the hillside as the valley widened again, giving a bird's eye view of a large, cultivated area as I approached Erzincan. The city didn't warrant a long stay; lying in an earthquake zone, it had been destroyed and rebuilt many times, the most recent earthquake prior to my visit occurring in 1939. Most of the buildings were therefore new, with several large, well-kept cemeteries a testament to the destruction. After a ride round the new city, stocking up with food and having a cup of tea, I started off for the next major city of Sivas. (Update: Erzincan was destroyed again in 1983.)

As the road climbed, I looked for evidence of earthquakes on the hillsides in the form of landslides, but everywhere appeared normal. The road turned north-west for a few miles, leaving the Firat River behind as it turned south-west; it would soon turn south, become the Euphrates and flow on its long journey into Syria and on across Iraq to the Persian Gulf. The road climbed to the top of a pass at 2,100m (6,888 ft), before beginning another long descent. Five miles west of Refahiye, I had to decide whether to take the direct route to Zara or a curving route to the north via Susehri. By all accounts the direct route involved a very bad road, though construction work was taking place to improve it. I decided on the longer route. Long climbs were followed by long descents, all done slowly on the gravel surface. Numerous tractors passed me, pulling trailers piled high with wood, as the local people built up stocks of firewood for the long winter ahead. I stopped often at the teahouses to get the dust out of my throat, including at the town of Susehri which was built in a most improbable position on a steep hillside. As in most of the small towns, the road surface was cobble stones, a difficult surface to climb on.

In the desolate terrain which I was travelling through, special attention was needed at the end of each day with selection of a camping spot. My location was revealed one night, not by the lights of a passing vehicle, but through unexpected circumstances. Writing my diary during the evening while camped on the open plain, I became aware of sounds in the distance, which quickly increased in volume. I opened the tent doors to see, in the faint moonlight, that the tent was in the path of a flock of sheep being moved to new pasture. One sheep after another tripped over the tent's guy ropes as they moved past. The shepherd coming up behind was as surprised to see me as I was to see him. After exchanging words of greeting, I thought about lighting my primus stove and offering him a cup of tea; but the idea quickly became redundant since the shepherd needed to keep moving to attempt to keep his flock in sight in the very poor light. Quiet returned as fast as it had disappeared. I tried to take in what had happened, wondering if I should pack everything up and move to another location. As I attempted to count how many sheep were in the flock, I fell asleep. Thankfully, the night passed without further incident, but it served to put me on my guard. The next morning I looked over the surrounding terrain for my unexpected visitors, but they were nowhere to be seen.

Reaching Zara at lunch time, I reflected on a procedure which was becoming quite common at the restaurants of being ushered into the kitchen to make my choice of meal. Few people, including waiters, could speak any English, while I was frequently asked if I was German. Several men spoke a little German, and some had possibly worked in West Germany. German seemed to be the first foreign language for most students. Unexpectedly therefore, I found myself recalling my limited German in the restaurants, teahouses, shops and on the streets.

I looked forward to an easier run from Zara, as the road followed the Kizil Armak River west, but the road ran about two miles north, going up and down over the hills. Sivas proved to be a large, modern town with many Western style buildings in the centre. Erzurum, Erzincan, Sivas, Yozgat, Ankara - there was now just one more significant town on the route before reaching the capital. Thirty miles west of Sivas the gravel road came to an end. There had been a total of 287 miles of gravel road in eastern Turkey, compared with

358 miles in eastern Iran. However, while Iran's figure was coming down rapidly, I wasn't aware of any programme for the road through the middle of Turkey. The country did not have the oil wealth of Iran to fund what would be very expensive construction through mountainous terrain.

The route I was following had taken me north of one of the world's most troubled areas, the Middle East. While my route involved challenging terrain, a route through the Middle East would have presented difficulties on a different scale altogether. The combination of desert and political difficulties made such a route practically impossible. On a paved road, I could relax now in one sense, but not in another, as I was still in the mountains. At first glance most of the undulating terrain looked untouched, the parched grass on the higher slopes of the hills blending with the stubble in the harvested cornfields. Trucks passed me every day laden with sacks of corn being taken to the mills.

After a long steady climb, I looked down from near the summit of the road on Yozgat, built on the slopes of the hillsides below. I replenished food supplies and had tea in the attractive town centre before following a small river, or rather its present dry bed, down a winding valley where it met the Delice Irmak River. A further winding run beside this river allowed me to complete more than 50 miles in a day for the first time in Turkey. Seeing the terrain dropping away to the west, it looked as if I had made a permanent drop from the higher plateau behind me.

A build up of traffic occurred near Delice as the road reached the junction of the road to Coram, Samsun and the Black Sea. I didn't know if I had missed any spectacular scenery by not following the Black Sea route, but I sensed that my route across the middle was the quieter one. A heavy stream of buses and trucks now roared past in both directions. Amenities along the road increased, so that I was disappointed to reach Baliseyh for lunch to see no sign of a restaurant, and Kirrikale later for tea to see no teahouses. Grapes grew in abundance in the area, and many watermelons. The following morning I had some watermelon with glasses of tea before climbing to about 1,250 m (4,100 ft).

Ankara lay 400 m lower and 23 miles away, approached via the most gradual of descents along a valley which was a vast market garden supplying the capital. Arriving at Kayas for lunch, the steep hillsides lining the valley were covered with little white houses with red tiled roofs. As the houses continued down the valley, I realised that I had already reached the outskirts of the capital. I looked forward to a few days in the city as, apart from one day in Erzurum and two in Tabriz, I had been on the move continuously for a month since leaving Tehran.

Ankara was another landmark on the overland journey. I was delighted to collect mail at the Post Office, thus re-establishing contact with my family in England after a gap of three months during which letters were not getting through in one direction or the other. After taking a room in a small hotel, I spent some time having a shower to rid myself of the dust of the previous two weeks before going out to acquaint myself with the city.

I was impressed by Ankara in every way. I didn't have to move far from my hotel in the northern part of the city to see historical features of the old Ankara; there were the remains of the Temple of Augustus, dating from just before the birth of Christ, and of the Roman Baths built in the 3rd Century A.D.; there were the Byzantine Citadel and the 15th Century Haci Bayram Mosque. But it was the modern Ankara which now dominated the scene. Ankara was just a small, provincial city in 1923 when it was decided to make it the capital of the new Turkish Republic, following the defeat of occupying armies by Turkish forces led by Kemal Atatürk. The wish was that the new Ankara would be worthy of a modern, Westernized state. I enjoyed walking along the broad, main boulevards, seeing the public monuments, squares and gardens. On Atatürk Bulvari, the main boulevard, were many restaurants and cake shops, several with outside tables. In the commercial area to the south, there were several bookshops with English books and maps, and I was able to buy recent issues of *The Daily Telegraph* and *Time* magazine to catch up with the news. The walk south took me to the huge Atatürk Mausoleum on top of a hill, the location giving fine views over the city. Down in the central area, I spent many hours in Gençlik Park, sitting at a table overlooking the large central lake, drinking tea and watching life go by. A bonus was provided one evening as I sat in this most attractive park, looking at the city lights with a full moon, and listening to the sound of Cliff Richard's *The Young Ones* and other records wafting over from an adjacent fairground. In its scenic setting, the lights from houses on the hillsides all around reminded me of Wellington, New Zealand.

I was trying to eat as generously as my budget would allow while in locations like Ankara. With milk now available, and butter and cheese, I decided that I could discontinue the vitamin tablets which I had been taking since Herat in Afghanistan. Checking my weight, I had put on a pound since Tabriz, with stomach upsets now behind me. Since I was eating well, I concluded that my present weight of 121 lb wasn't going to change much while I was burning up so much energy.

After three days in Ankara, it was time to burn up some more. Fine weather continued, but I now had my sweater on most of the time as it was distinctly cooler. Although I was still in the hills, gradients were easier as the busy, paved road took cuttings through some of the hills, and embankments lessened the drops. On the first day out, as I looked like ending the day very close to the town of Kizilcahamam, the Army suddenly ensured that I would finish several miles before the town. Along with an ever-growing queue of cars, trucks and buses, I was stopped along the road at midday for about an hour. With all the military vehicles on the road, it was made clear that no photographs should be taken. The Army was conducting manoeuvres further down the road, resulting in the boom of a large gun or cannon at intervals. While waiting to proceed in the shade of some trees, I spoke to a number of English and American travellers who had crossed from Afghanistan into Iran just a week before; no one was being held at the frontier any more. Everyone seemed to have heard of the tragic incident two months earlier when I was there, but they were hearing highly imaginative stories concerning what happened.

I reached Kizilcahamam the following day for morning tea after climbing to a summit at 1,140 m (3,740 ft) just before the town and sweeping down to it in a long valley with many apple orchards and vineyards almost the whole length of the valley. The terrain was surprising me, or maybe it was wishful thinking on my part about the ending of mountainous terrain west of Ankara, since another very long climb followed. The scent from the pine trees on the higher slopes was very pleasant. A road marker recorded the summit this time at 1,560 m (5,100 ft). Long descents and climbs followed, one descent taking me down into a broad valley where I could see the town of Bolu in the distance. West of Bolu the road passed through several small communities which specialised in basket making. The roadside was lined for two or three miles with women and girls trying to sell the fruits of their labours.

After a steep climb I stopped for tea at a restaurant at the summit at 900 m (2,950 ft) to savour the view. It was clearly the final climb. The road went down and down from the pine-clad slopes to a fertile valley. Houses were spread all along the valley. At a position where the river flowing down the valley came close to the road, I decided, with the sun setting, that it would be a suitable place to camp. There were no houses nearby, but a group of teenagers arrived shortly after I had erected the tent. They did not stop long, being unable to see much in the fading light. The experience drove home to me that I was once more in a populated region. The desert with its wide open spaces was now left behind. Looking back, my last, long descent would present a challenge to any cyclist travelling in the opposite direction, signalling in the most dramatic way the movement up to the high plateau which characterised most of Turkey.

A warmer night followed now that I was down to a low elevation, at no more than a few hundred feet above sea level. A road from the Black Sea joined the main road at Düzce, resulting in a bigger roar of traffic. As the road passed over a line of hills, there were splashes of red from the maple trees on the slopes, as the leaves changed colour with the approach of autumn. The main road now by-passed most of the towns on the route, making it desirable to detour off it to find quieter, smaller restaurants than those beside the main road. A bigger detour through Sapanca allowed me to follow the shore of a large lake to the north, the quieter road also making it easier to find a camping spot for one evening.

Progress was slowed as I hit a stone on the road while admiring the deep blue colour of the lake. The front tyre went flat in an instant. As I examined the front wheel, the decision was made to replace the tyre and tube. The tyre had served me well, covering a record distance of 7,472 miles since fitting in Sydney, but the casing was ruptured in a number of places. I fitted my second spare tyre collected in Kabul, and a new inner tube; they should get me back to England without any further attention. The road did not run as close to the lake as I hoped, but it kept me off the main road for a few miles.

The area became increasingly industrialised as I returned to the main road near Izmit, shortly afterwards having my first view of the Sea of Marmara. When the road turned inland slightly to cross rolling hills, the slopes of which were covered with grape vines and apple orchards, I decided I had reached a suitable area for my last night's camping in Asia. An undulating run followed the next morning to Üsküdar on the eastern side of the Bosphorus. I had been able to cycle every yard of the 5,800 miles from Calcutta, but a change was now required. 7,500 miles had also been completed since leaving Singapore seven months earlier. I felt good as I enjoyed my last meal in Asia close to the ferry terminal, poised to return to Europe.

Chapter 27

Through Eastern Europe

Wednesday, 1 October 1969 Turkey

The ferry ride across the Bosphorus to Istanbul was so short, involving a distance of a mile crossed in five minutes, that I hardly had time to contemplate its full significance. After seven intensely interesting and varied months in Asia, I was returning to Europe. The date, 1 October, seemed significant: it was a reminder that winter would soon be approaching. Having arrived in Europe, time must not be lost in completing the overland journey. There could be no certainty, however, about how quickly conditions might change. A spirit of optimism prevailed as I looked back on a September of fine, warm weather, with rain on just one day, while I had been crossing the high plateau of eastern Turkey. It was difficult to tell myself that these conditions would not go on indefinitely, at least for the next two months, the time it would take to get back to England.

I wasn't dashing off anywhere for a few days, though, as I had arrived in one of the most historical cities in Europe. Surveying the scene, I could imagine the opposition to the decision in 1923 to make Ankara the capital of the new Turkish Republic instead of Istanbul. The ferry crossed to the northern part of the city, an area with some very modern buildings dominated by the multi-storey Hilton Hotel. I made for the Tourist Information Office nearby, the steep roads in the very hilly region being a test for the low gears on the bicycle. I gained a few looks as I appeared to climb effortlessly towards the heavens. Western faces were everywhere in the vicinity of the Tourist Office. After collecting information on the famous city, I headed south across the Golden Horn via the Galata Bridge to the older part of the city to find a suitable hotel.

The first morning was taken up by visits to the nearby Aya Sofya, or Church of St. Sophia, completed in 537, and to the more recent

Sultanahmet Camii, or Blue Mosque, built early in the 17th Century. A superb flower garden occupied the square adjacent to Aya Sofya, allowing fine views of the building, which was far more attractive outside than in. It was dull inside, possibly the result of the removal of a number of high level windows following rebuilding after earthquakes. The opposite was the case for the Blue Mosque, the entire vast interior being richly decorated in one predominant colour. A number of stained glass windows allowed light to enter the building, resulting in a great, dignified edifice. I moved south towards the waterfront to view the building with its six minarets from some distance, stopping on the return journey to visit the impressive Mosaic Museum.

At the Topkapi Palace in the afternoon, I felt I already knew something about the treasures there as a result of the film *Topkapi* starring Peter Ustinov. Moving through the huge complex of buildings within the Palace walls, I came close to the buildings of the harem. This area was divided off to necessitate a separate visit. As I came the closest I had ever been to such a fascinating institution, I mused on how well I would have fulfilled the role if different circumstances had caused me to occupy the throne of the sultan during the centuries of the Ottoman Empire.

With its long history, Istanbul had a large number of mosques and museums imposing on the time of the visitor. The city was noticeably dirtier than the smaller Ankara, but thronged with Western visitors, including many young ones. Mini-skirted girls were everywhere, a sight which the Turkish men seemed to have difficulty getting used to, unless constant staring was simply a permanent attitude. As I sat outside at the restaurants and cafés, I contemplated how to spend my time. I wanted to take a cruise up the Bosphorus, but found my plans thwarted by the weather, which had turned cloudy. It was an unusual situation in which to find myself, but I wanted some sunshine in which to view the sights from the boat.

A day was spent seeing the northern part of the city, which I had seen briefly on my arrival. I crossed the Galata Bridge after walking down the steep, winding, cobbled Raviali Caddesi to the Golden Horn. A large Russian liner was berthed at the terminal just across the Galata Bridge, requiring a walk close to the waterfront to have a closer look. The liner apparently cruised the Mediterranean and was on its way back to a Black Sea Port. I went up through the shopping district and past the Hilton Hotel as far as the Military Museum. After absorbing myself in the country's military history, I returned to my hotel via the Atatürk Bridge, west of the Galata Bridge, and up a maze of steep, winding streets, getting well off the regular tourist routes.

After a further cloudy day, I simply had to set off up the Bosphorus. The days, the weeks and months of unbroken sunshine were over. There were patches of blue sky as I walked down to the quay beside the Galata Bridge, but they quickly disappeared. A cool journey followed as the boat headed into a breeze, travelling about 20 miles to the most northerly point at the small town of Rumeli Kavagi. With the Black Sea clearly visible 5 miles further to the north, the boat stopped for an hour to allow the passengers to disembark for lunch. A transformation occurred in the light as the cloud cleared, making for an enjoyable return journey; the succession of small towns on both banks, along with all the mosques and fortresses, now stood out clearly in the sunlight. The journey had been worthwhile after all.

I departed from Istanbul feeling that I had had a reasonable introduction to the city, but aware that I had only scratched the surface. There were still so many places to see, but there was a reasonable chance of being able to return to locations like this in the future. After all, Istanbul was in Europe, not in some remote spot. I bought a new tyre before leaving, so that the reassurance resulting from carrying a spare tyre could continue. I had views of the Sea of Marmara for most of the first day, often from an elevated position as the road travelled inland over treeless terrain, which rose and fell in great swells.

Meeting a Canadian hitch-hiker also travelling west, I was interested to learn that it was now possible to visit Burma for a longer period. Compared with the 24 hour maximum in April, 3-day visas became available in August, allowing some travel outside Rangoon, including to Mandalay: it was a definite improvement. Later, I was even more interested to meet two young Londoners, a young man and his girlfriend, on their way by cycle across Asia. After exchanging information for an hour or so, I wished them well, but was very apprehensive about the weather they might encounter as they entered the mountains in eastern Turkey, yet alone further east. They had read the story of Dervla Murphy's ride through Asia to India, but I couldn't help thinking that Dervla was the exception to the rule as far as being able to accomplish the journey during winter.

The encounter meant that I was still close to the Sea of Marmara at the end of the day, a situation I would not forget as it provided me with an idyllic camping spot overlooking the deep blue water. The following morning my road turned north-west away from the sea at a junction, while the road west went towards Greece. The traffic diminished, along with housing and amenities. I passed fields of wheat on the rolling, treeless terrain, plus tomatoes, sunflowers, cabbages and other vegetables. All that remained of the sunflowers were the stalks, which were being cut down and carried away in wagons, possibly to be used for fuel.

I spent my last evening in Turkey camping a few miles east of the city of Edirne, and just 18 miles from the border with Bulgaria. Edirne made a positive last impression for anyone about to leave Turkey: likewise, it must make an impact on anyone entering Turkey at this position. Approaching the city, the view was dominated by the Üç Serefeli Mosque straight ahead along the main road, with its unique feature of four differently shaped minarets. Another mosque soon commanded the attention, though, the Selim Mosque by Sinan, built in 1569-75. It was considered to be one of the most beautiful works of Islamic architecture, and the crowning-piece of his life work during which he was responsible for several hundred buildings, both religious and civil. After visiting the Selim Mosque, and admiring it from various positions, I stopped at a teahouse on the main street for my last cups of tea in Turkey. With the sun shining from a bright, blue sky, I could only feel good about my five weeks there, bringing me 1,200 miles closer to England. The remaining stages, as measured by the time spent in each country and the distance covered, would all be much shorter.

*****

Thursday, 9 October 1969   Bulgaria

It was an easy run from Edirne to the border 12 miles away, a following wind blowing me along a valley which was noticeably green compared with much of the earlier terrain, past fields of sugar-beet, maize and other crops. I looked left across the Meriç River into Greece, three countries coming very close together near the crossing into Bulgaria. The frontier formalities took just a short time, with the Turkish and Bulgarian officials declining to inspect my baggage at all. I couldn't recall if my baggage had ever been inspected, a sign perhaps that a touring cyclist would not be expected to be carrying anything controversial; however, I could not be sure of the situation as I entered a Communist country for the first time.

As I filled in an identification card for Bulgaria, I was confronted with the Cyrillic alphabet for the first time, used throughout the Communist world. I was aware that I knew virtually nothing about the country, except to recall reading at some time in the past that it had one of the strictest and most conservative regimes, with strong adherence to the Moscow line. I had not been able to collect any literature on the country prior to arrival, so that it was unfortunate that the Balkan Tourist Organisation office at the Customs building was closed for lunch. The woman normally there could not have known of my pending arrival!

I had not proceeded very far before the appearance of the first of many signs indicating that horses and bicycles were prohibited from using the main road. The sign was at every track and road joining the main road. Not a word had been said to me at the border, so the officials must take the view that foreign cyclists have been briefed on the situation prior to arrival. I was puzzled about the supposed mechanism for this, since it was a very unusual situation, one I had never encountered before. I was therefore grateful for having met the cycling couple as I left Istanbul. They told me that the barring of cyclists from the main road was waived for foreign tourists. If I hadn't met the couple, I would have seen the first prohibition signs with some bewilderment.

I felt in a privileged position. On the other hand, could I not expect to encounter resentment from local cyclists? The answer to this was surely in the negative: if the concession for visitors was decreed by the authorities, then in a Communist country it had to be accepted. Moreover, the local cyclists might feel pleased that foreign cyclists were interested in seeing their country by a means they understood, were putting in a clear effort in doing so, and not flaunting a luxury Western vehicle to which they couldn't hope to aspire. I was getting carried away with my rationalizations.

Progress was slow for two reasons as I passed through a village or small town every few miles, on a journey through gently undulating terrain; there was so much to see both in the countryside and in the towns and villages with being in a new country, and the road through every village and town was cobbled. The roadsides were lined with trees, and I quickly became aware of a rich and varied agriculture. I passed apple orchards and fields of grape vines, maize, cotton and other crops. Long buildings on the farms were a reminder that the farms were worked collectively; huge signs carried exhortations to satisfy various goals for the State.

I stopped in the first town, Svilograd, to get a feel for what was in the shops. At a pastry shop I encountered for the first time a feature of the Eastern European world - the Communist queue. I joined a long line of women who were queuing very patiently. The grocery stores tended to be very large buildings, but the size seemed to accentuate the relative lack of food for sale. Perhaps I needed more time to form a broader picture. Food was also available in the towns at kiosks along the road.

While Svilograd was the first town passed through, Harmanli became the first large town the following morning on my first full day in Bulgaria. The main shops selling clothing, footwear and hardware were in huge buildings. There were radios, televisions, record players and tape recorders, washing machines, refrigerators and electric cookers, in short all the hardware the Western world took for granted. But there were large areas of empty floor space in the stores. I had need for very little, but for the first time I had difficulty in obtaining batteries for the torch I used while camping. As soon as I found some, extra ones were purchased in order to have some in reserve.

During the afternoon it looked as if I would be ending the day close to an organised campground west of Haskovo. I was therefore disappointed to find it closed for the season, and looking very forlorn and deserted. I felt I had complied with regulations as far as possible, a leaflet collected at the border emphasizing that "CAMPING in areas not specially designed for this purpose is FORBIDDEN". The leaflet was written for motorists, but I couldn't expect a separate leaflet to be prepared for cyclists. If I was stopped, I felt I had a reasonable explanation for not camping at an authorised place, and would thus avoid transportation to Bulgaria's equivalent of Siberia.

Camping a mile further down the road west of Haskovo, the temperature dropped noticeably as the sun went down in a clear sky. It was another reminder of the approach of winter. The following evening I camped on the edge of an apple orchard, resulting in a visit the following morning by two men on patrol. Through gestures

I was asked many questions about my travels, before being offered four apples. Having a picnic lunch beside the roadside later after passing through Plovdiv, I was offered a bunch of grapes by a man patrolling large vinefields nearby. I was pleased to accept them, but with undoubted reservations. I hadn't touched a grape since Kandahar for fear of the "Kabul trots" and related afflictions. The grapes were delicious: all I awaited now were the consequences.

The fruit was ripe everywhere and ready for picking. It was an interesting commentary on the Communist regime to find the orchards and vinefields being patrolled to deter theft. Nevertheless, I couldn't help feeling, even in my insignificant circumstances, that the system was on trial when it came to relations between the Communist and Western worlds. It was a matter of honour for each side not to present itself to the other in a bad light. Thus I felt inherently safe in this new world, and sensed it was an insult to the character of the local people to lock the bicycle up to the extent I had become used to whenever I stopped at a shop or café. I dispensed with the locks on every baggage strap and on the gear controls. The bicycle attracted the normal interest, but there was no interference.

I was making contact with a number of people along the road as well as in the towns and villages whenever I stopped, with younger ones enabling me to get a few words and phrases in my notebook. After passing through many towns and villages, I noted with regret the coming to an end of the teahouse, that great institution which I had become increasingly fond of since India. I encountered cafés selling soft drinks and cakes, but tea and coffee were less frequent. I had my first cup of coffee in Plovdiv: it was awful! I stayed only briefly in Bulgaria's second city, deciding in preference that I would have a day in the capital, Sofia, 100 miles further on.

The exit from Plovdiv was one of the most memorable ever, with the leaves of the poplar trees lining both sides of the road a brilliant yellow. An easy run followed for many miles up the broad Maritsa valley before the road entered hills and pastoral country. With cotton grown in the area, an attractive sight occurred several times of a woman spinning a ball of cotton while tending sheep or cattle. I had been enchanted the day before by the sight of an elderly woman spinning cotton on an ancient spinning wheel as she sat outside her house by the road.

I arrived in Sofia mid-morning after an easy run over a broad plain, and relieved that there was no reaction to the grapes of two days earlier. Finding a hotel proved a formidable task. After trying a number without success, I returned to the Tourist Office for assistance: the hotels I approached clearly did not want a Western visitor. A stay in a private house was quickly arranged, or rather a room in a fifth floor flat, with use of the amenities there. I could speak little to the middle-aged couple in the flat, but they were content to take my receipt from the Tourist Office and give me a key; they had clearly done this before.

The most attractive building for me in Sofia was the Alexander Nevsky Cathedral. Named after a Russian prince and military leader of the 13th Century, it was now a museum, but in a fine state of preservation. The walls and ceilings were covered with paintings of biblical scenes and of saints. The basement contained further paintings, which I understood were salvaged from other churches throughout the country when the Communist mantle fell over Bulgaria. It was a sad sight in other towns travelled through to see birds' nests on the top of church towers, indicating a falling into decay. It was difficult to work out the attitude of the authorities to the Cathedral, since they could not judge whether anyone in the building was not engaged in silent worship. The authorities had invested considerable money on it, to the extent of floodlighting it at night.

To further my education, I made a visit to the Museum of Bulgaro-Soviet Friendship. It contained many photographs involving the Russian leaders, as did numerous notice boards throughout the central part of the city. There were almost always people looking at them, but there was a constant crowd outside the American Embassy looking at photographs from the flight to the moon.

Stopping for coffee on the way back to my room after admiring the floodlighting of the Cathedral, I found myself in conversation with a foreign trade student conversant with seven languages. He gave me an insight into the way in which the food stores operated, telling me that the people working in them cared little how long it took to serve you since the stores were owned by the State. While buying food earlier, I had encountered the iniquitous system of paying in advance for items required. Thus I queued first at the cashier's kiosk where, after payment for everything required, I was given a slip of paper with a list of the items and the individual prices. I then moved to another queue at the appropriate counter, to hand over the slip of paper and be issued with the items. It was a cumbersome, time-consuming procedure. The system must have been instituted to deal with problems of theft, or of customers simply forgetting to stop at the cash desk after collecting goods at the food counter, but the difficulties can be imagined when you cannot define in words at the cash desk what you require or what quantities. Needless to say, if you had omitted an item or ended up with something not wanted or in insufficient quantity, the whole, laborious procedure had to be repeated. Many cafés also operated on the pay-first system.

The frustrations of food shopping in Bulgaria would soon be behind me, as only one more day remained in the country as I left the capital for the border with Yugoslavia 35 miles away. A slow ride out of Sofia on the cobbled surface speeded up on reaching the outskirts, and a wide, smooth road traversed a broad plain. The terrain started to undulate just before I stopped for lunch. After a long, gradual climb, the road descended a narrow valley, which became a gorge after passing through Dragoman. Since it was now late in the afternoon, I resolved to stay in Bulgaria for the evening. The terrain opened out to present a broad valley ahead. As I looked towards trees wondering where I might camp, I rounded a bend to see the Bulgarian Customs Building just ahead. Looking at the trees so much, I had misjudged the distance travelled, thinking the border was still a mile or two away. I was going to have to cross the border now, rather than the next morning. But one more stage was complete, a short stage of 233 miles during eight days full of interest.

*****

Wednesday, 15 October 1969   Yugoslavia

The sun was setting as I went through the border formalities, which thankfully were the shortest ever, with no identification card to fill in for the new country. I sped away and into the trees once out of sight of the border, to get my tent erected during the fading light. I entered Yugoslavia better prepared than for Bulgaria as a result of finding, in a bookshop in Istanbul, the *Gateway Guide to Yugoslavia* published by Methuen. It was one in a series of booklets on European countries which I had found invaluable from my first cycling days on the continent; they were a mine of information and very compact, ideal characteristics for the cyclist's bag.

The booklets were written with motoring tours in mind, however, so that they contained no specific information relating to cycling. Following the experience in Bulgaria, the key questions to be resolved referred to the subject of cycling restrictions. Problems loomed ahead, as a number of motorways had been built in recent years. I had no wish to travel on any motorway, but part of my route north-west was going to take me towards a motorway, with no realistic alternative anywhere near it; the old road was no longer available as a continuous entity, the motorway having been built by upgrading parts of it. It was a problem which had arisen before, in America: it seemed a long time ago. I wasn't sure what roads had been followed by the couple I met west of Istanbul. They told me that cycling was not permitted in the larger cities in Yugoslavia: you could either ride on the pavement or walk. There were going to be some interesting situations.

These problems were all in the future as I set off towards Nis on my first full day in Yugoslavia. It was a warm, cloudless day, allowing the varying terrain to be seen to good advantage. The road travelled first over a broad valley, past scenes of maize stalks, now brown, dried up and brittle, being cut, stacked in shocks, and loaded onto wagons to be hauled away either by oxen or horses. A change occurred west of Pirot as the road climbed through hills ablaze with autumn colour. As the valley narrowed, I entered a steep-walled gorge through which ran the Nisava River. The railway linking Belgrade with Sofia also ran through the gorge, both road and railway making use of tunnels to find a passage at times.

At a position where the hills receded slightly, I camped before continuing along the gorge the following morning. As the hills dropped away after a few more miles, Nis was approached over a broad plain. It had been a spectacular introduction to Yugoslavia. On the eastern outskirts of Nis I stopped at Cele-Kula to have a look at the macabre skull tower incorporating the heads of 952 Serbs, built by the Turkish Pasha of Nis after an unsuccessful Serbian rebellion in 1809. I looked in vain in the attractive town centre for somewhere to have a cup of coffee before proceeding to the Tourist Office to discuss my onward route.

I was relieved to be told that I could cycle on the motorway, a position confirmed by a young Yugoslav who spoke to me as I prepared to set off. It wasn't long before I encountered restriction signs. The following day a policeman stopped me to advise that bicycles were forbidden on the motorway! I could only tell him about the advice received in Nis, and showed him on my map how I intended to leave the motorway later in the day at Svetozarevo, where an alternative route presented itself. He was quite happy about it. After a run through undulating farming country along the Morava valley, I left the motorway to take an alternative route through Kragujevac to Belgrade. I would not again be involved with this kind of conflict, as along every remaining part of my journey there was an alternative to the motorway.

Before turning off, I had an excellent cup of coffee at a motel at the turn-off to Krusevac, a particularly memorable location as the motel lounge contained a very modern juke-box with a TV-type screen above it. As the music played, the artists featured were seen in performance; I had never seen anything like it before. The odd thing was that the motel was almost in the middle of nowhere. Someone had the vision to build a modern motel at the location, perhaps anticipating growing future demand, and reminding me of the giant hotel on the desert in western Afghanistan.

Poring over my map while enjoying the coffee and the music, I saw that I could leave the motorway a few miles on at Paracin, and 11 miles before Svetozarevo. The road was continuous but very bumpy, passing through Cuprija. Now that I had left the motorway, I started to encounter an incredible number of horse-drawn carts on the road, the main form of transport for the country people in the absence of cars. The route via Kragujevac involved very undulating terrain through good farming country. As I approached the town early one afternoon, I came towards a car stranded beside the road. "Do you have any petrol?" the driver asked. "Of course," I replied without batting an eyelid, as if it was the kind of question asked regularly. The two pint container serving my primus stove was almost full, so that I was happy to oblige a fellow traveller, giving him sufficient to get to a petrol station. As I replenished my supply a short time later in Kragujevac, I wondered if the stranded motorist had thought I was on a motorcycle when he first saw me. It was the only time I had ever been approached for petrol.

As the days shortened and the nights became cool, especially after a cloudless day, my primus stove was all-important during the evenings and early mornings. Throughout most of Asia, I closed only the inner mesh doors of the tent in order to dissipate heat. The main doors started to be closed before reaching Istanbul. Now, a few weeks later, I would have just one cup of tea with my evening meal. The second cup would be postponed until I was ready to retreat into my sleeping bag for the night. My watch was currently recording sunrise at 6.50am and sunset at 6.40pm, so that I was getting up at 6.15am and stopping at 5.45pm. However, I had noticed that the time on the clock tower in Nis was an hour behind that shown on my watch. I decided to leave my watch as it was until Belgrade: it was more acceptable getting up at 6.15am rather than 5.15.

There seemed to be a more relaxed atmosphere in Yugoslavia compared with Bulgaria. There were no billboards with pictures of idealized workers exhorting everyone to greater efforts, no slogans, no outdoor broadcasting systems, no display of output figures and no pictures of Lenin. Yugoslavia was following its own Communist path under the powerful personality of President Tito, perhaps the only leader in the Eastern Bloc strong enough to stand up to criticism from Moscow.

Fruit in abundance was being gathered as I travelled towards Belgrade, especially grapes. On one section, where the roadsides were lined with apple trees, piles of fruit lay on the ground, much of it unspoiled; as I picked up just a few apples, I told myself it seemed a pity to let it all go to waste. About 15 miles from the capital, Mt. Avala came into view. A detour from the main road took me up through forest to the large Memorial to the Unknown Soldier by Ivan Mestrovic. The elevation allowed a wide view over the surrounding terrain in all directions, but there was little to see, particularly in the direction of Belgrade, due to haze. A photographer told me that rain was needed to clear the air: I had almost forgotten what that was.

I descended towards the capital, walking the last half mile in the centre as the first of a plethora of signs restricting cyclists, motorcyclists and horse-drawn carts was encountered. They were meant to be obeyed. After my experience in Sofia, I lost no time in the search for accommodation, and took a room in a private house after finding that Yugoslavia operated a similar scheme. I decided to spend two full days in Belgrade, as it would be my last stopping place for about two weeks. The city resembled closely any Western European city, and was very modern as a result of almost complete rebuilding after destruction during the Second World War. The shops were stocked with all kinds of goods; there was none of the cumbersome paying in advance as in Bulgaria, and none of the queues. Almost the entire range of English newspapers and magazines was available, with no apparent censorship, at countless kiosks throughout the city. Pin-up magazines were on sale, but what was particularly startling in Belgrade was the widespread display of the centrefold in the kiosk windows. At every kiosk there were usually several pictures like this from different magazines, showing a freedom of expression not permitted even in most Western countries. I was curious as to the Communist philosophy on the subject. *Playboy* was available here, as it was also in Istanbul, Ankara and Tehran - a symbol of a modern city.

A reading room on the main street was full of American newspapers and magazines. Large photographs of the Apollo 11 astronauts occupied the windows, and were being looked at constantly. Interest was high as the astronauts proceeded on a triumphal world tour, visiting Belgrade on 20 October, two days before my arrival. I walked to Kalamegdan, the large park north of the central area containing the ruins of an ancient fortress. I stopped on the way to visit a fine church, the Saborna Cathedral. Although there was freedom of worship in Yugoslavia, the absence of pews or seats seemed to indicate less than total support by the State. From the park I looked down on the confluence of the Sava and Danube Rivers; my first view of the great river showed it far from blue.

I left Belgrade feeling refreshed and ready for a long ride north-west. The main route through Zagreb and Ljubljana was a motorway, but my map showed an alternative route running parallel about 40 miles to the north through Osijek and Maribor. My guidebook ignored the route completely: I was therefore quite intrigued by the prospect of what I might find. The first stage to Novisad took me over a flat plain covered with fields of maize being harvested, before crossing hills to descend to a large cultivated area beside the Danube. Finding a camping spot looked difficult until a sheltered area appeared overlooking the bridge spanning the river to Novisad on the north bank.

After a warm evening I crossed the bridge the next morning to follow the north bank of the Danube as far as Backa Palanka. A ferry took me across to the south bank to a minor road going west, joining up with a main road east of Yukovar. It was now a straightforward run along this route for the next 200 miles to Maribor, through farming country with a village or small town along the road every few miles. I left the Danube behind after passing through Yukovar, as its path turned towards Budapest to the north. Shortly afterwards my road started to run close to a tributary, the Drava, which formed the boundary with Hungary west of Osijek. I looked north across the Drava valley into Hungary, at one point the road and river being only four miles apart. To the south the road skirted an almost unbroken line of hills from Nasice onwards.

There was virtually no traffic on the road for mile after mile apart from the occasional cart being pulled by bullocks or horses, and a number of bicycles ridden by men and women of all ages; teenage girls in mini-skirts tugged at their skirts as we passed! It was an idyllic scene moving through this pastoral landscape in the warm autumn sunshine, the leaves on the trees all shades of yellow, orange and brown. In village after village, I became familiar with a characteristic scene of single storey farmhouses at right angles to the road.

Camping about 30 miles south-east of Maribor, I awoke with some discomfort to a severe frost; it took some time to warm my shoes in readiness for the last full day in Yugoslavia. A crisp, clear day followed. The single storey farmhouses gave way to houses of two storeys with balconies and paintings on the external walls. Suddenly everything started to look Austrian. Morning tea in the old town of Ptuj was followed by afternoon coffee in a hotel in the large town of Maribor, as I celebrated virtual completion of 540 miles across Yugoslavia, and completion of another wonderful month. Setting off on a winding run, I stopped well short of the frontier 11 miles away, determined to remain in Yugoslavia for one more night as the light started to fade, and not wishing to rush across as I found myself doing two weeks earlier when entering the country.

Chapter 28

Nostalgic Return

Saturday, 1 November 1969 Austria

I felt I was almost home as I crossed the border after just four miles from my overnight camping spot. I was now in a country which I had been in before, having travelled in a small part of Austria during the summer of 1965 while on my third two week holiday on the continent in consecutive years. It was a holiday which had started and finished in Munich, involving a tour of Eastern Bavaria which brought me into Austria near Salzburg and out again at Passau. I would always look back fondly on that tour, as for the first time I had the wide range of gears on the bicycle which seemed to open up the world before me. I no longer had to walk up any hill: if the low gears could deal with the gradients in southern Bavaria, they could deal with the gradients anywhere in the world.

The plan, now that I was in Western Europe, was to continue north-west through Austria, Germany and Belgium on a route which would take me on parts of the earlier tours. Of all the possible routes to follow through Europe, this would also be a fairly direct route, an important consideration with the onset of winter. A glorious day followed for my first day in Austria, and the first day of another month. The sun rose in a clear sky so that, as the road followed the River Mur upstream towards Graz, a succession of colourful autumn scenes occurred. As in Yugoslavia there was a community every few miles, with one community virtually merging with the next. Almost all the houses were large, neat and brightly painted; I was constantly passing signs reading "gasthof" and "gasthaus", and houses with rooms for travellers, but I was looking out for anyone who might possibly know the location of any youth hostels along my route. I was starting to get wary about camping, as a penalty for a bright, blue sky during the day was a plunging temperature as the sun went down.

There was a note of prosperity everywhere, and almost everyone was smartly dressed. It was the weekend, a time when all the shops shut, work stopped and the Austrian people concentrated on recreation. I was glad to already have some food in my bags so that I was going to be able to camp. A constant stream of cars passed me in both directions, many of those going south doing so apparently to allow the occupants to drink inexpensive Yugoslav wine. 1 November was All Saints' Day, a remembrance day, so the roads were unusually busy. With everywhere shut, I did not stop in Graz, but proceeded a few miles further north before stopping to camp for my first night in Austria.

There was just a touch of frost, similar to the last night in Yugoslavia, and a second glorious day followed as the road continued to follow the River Mur, turning west at Bruck an der Mur. A turn north-west after 15 miles put me on the road to Bad Ischl and Salzburg. I followed a tributary of the Mur as the road climbed towards the Schober Pass at 849 m, or 2,784 ft. The snow-covered Erzberg peak dominated the immediate view. The climbing helped to keep me warm, but I needed every bit of extra clothing on as I descended to the next valley.

I was very pleased with the performance of a recent additional item of clothing, a waistcoat fashioned from the many pages of a *Daily Telegraph* bought in Belgrade. It was somewhat stiff but, once in position between my sweater and jacket, served as a complete windbreak and eliminated the wind chill factor. All gentlemen of the road knew of the merits of newspaper for keeping warm! I could wear my rain cape to achieve the same effect, but was reluctant to do so in the absence of either rain or snow. I received enough odd looks wearing a Balaclava helmet to keep my face and ears warm. The cape was the next, and final, line of defence if needed; I had last resorted to it for this purpose in the Snowy Mountains in Australia. It not only dealt with the wind chill factor on the body, but also the arms and, in particular, the hands. Then, by conserving heat in the body, the blood flowing to the feet, the other vulnerable extremities, would be warmer than otherwise. The much-derided cape had many advantages.

A sprinkling of snow was visible on the tops of the surrounding hills as I descended from the Schober Pass. A severe frost occurred the following night as I camped near Liezen in the valley of the River Enns; I awoke to ice on the water left in my container after making tea the night before, and there was even ice in my main gallon reservoir. That was it: if the temperature dropped later in the day, I would seek shelter under a solid roof. I set off with maximum clothing on - plus my rain cape. The road turned away from the Enns to climb steeply before descending to another broad valley of rolling meadows and pine-clad hills, with large houses dotting the countryside. It was very much the characteristic view of Austria. As the valley narrowed, I followed a river downstream through thick forest to the town of Bad Aussee. From the Pötschen Pass beyond I looked down on the five mile long Hallstätter See to the south.

The falling winter sun had already put in shadow most of the valley to which the road descended. As the temperature fell I looked for a gasthof, to spend the evening in unaccustomed luxury. The air was noticeably warmer than the day before as I set off on the final stage to Salzburg, due to rain which fell throughout the morning, followed by snow for an hour. The unfavourable weather could not conceal further attractive country beside another large lake, Wolfgang See.

The first waves of nostalgia came over me as I reacquainted myself with Salzburg, wandering slowly round the central area, visiting again the Cathedral and Mozart's birthplace on Getreidegasse: it was like going back to a shrine. But, hadn't I been back to Salzburg since that cycle tour in 1965? I had, of course, in my mind, like millions of others who had seen the film *The Sound of Music*. It was fascinating to walk again through the Mirabell Gardens; wasn't there a faint echo of Julie Andrews and the von Trapp children singing choruses from "Doh - Ray - Me - Fah - Soh"? I climbed once more to the Fortress Hohensalzburg for the spectacular views over the city.

A large, modern youth hostel welcomed me, replacing the small hostel stayed in four years earlier. Having expected to freeze, I luxuriated once more in a centrally heated building. The hostel was almost full, including Americans, Canadians and Japanese on extended holidays, and other hostellers from all over Europe. I was pleased to have such company again, the first since the hostel at Peshawar in Pakistan in June, meeting in particular a young Swedish cyclist heading south to Greece; he had travelled through Poland and Czechoslovakia to reach Austria. We discussed ideas for keeping warm.

With the increasingly cooler weather, a change in plan became desirable. The intention had been to head directly west through the

Bavarian Alps to Garmisch-Partenkirchen, retracing in reverse the route followed in 1965. However, travelling through the mountains in November would be very different to conditions in mid-summer. After 200 miles in Austria, a more northerly route was therefore selected for the first stage in the next country.

*****

Saturday, 8 November 1969   Germany

I crossed the border without formality a few miles north-west of Salzburg: the procedure no longer warranted even a stamp in my passport. At Freilassing, almost immediately after crossing the border, a secondary road passing south of Waginger See allowed me to get off the main road as I travelled over a gently undulating plain. In addition to the main road, an autobahn took the majority of traffic between Salzburg and Munich, but it was more relaxing on an even quieter road. To the south the Alps rose abruptly from the plain, defined by a line of jagged peaks.

After a warm, sunny day I camped in pine forest near Obing. The following morning near a gasthof outside Wasserburg, I noticed several people looking north from the rim of a precipice. Joining them to see what the attraction was, the most astonishing sight was revealed of the town of Wasserburg far below, built on a small neck of land formed by the River Inn as it made an almost complete loop. I found myself in conversation with an Austrian doctor from north of Salzburg, who invited me to join him and his companions for refreshments in Wasserburg. I followed his car on the swift descent into the town, joining him and two young women; one was a daughter, the other an American girl from South Carolina staying with them and fluent in German. After refreshments, I accompanied them on a walk round the historic town. I would remember this hospitality on a Sunday morning, enjoyed in exceptional surroundings.

Proceeding towards Munich, I found myself on the outskirts earlier than expected, taking a room in a hotel as camping became impracticable. It was ironic that, in an area with a large number of youth hostels, and in the country which started the marvellous organisation in 1910, I couldn't stay in them. A few years earlier an age limit of 25 in Bavaria had caused me to maximize the situation with successive summers there. The age limit had since been increased to 27, but it wasn't quite enough; older hostellers at Salzburg told me the limit was being strictly enforced.

When I received my hotel bill, I needed no further persuasion to return to camping until I had left Bavaria. Funds were running low, as the return journey was taking significantly longer than expected, requiring some careful budgeting during the remaining weeks. I did not delay in Munich, continuing north-west to Augsburg. Stopping at a cycle shop on the way into the city, I met by chance an interesting man there. He spoke English quite well, having been a PoW in England for two years, spent in several places, including Bury in Lancashire. Seeing the Sturmey-Archer hub gear in my gear system, he gave me a leaflet on the German equivalent, the Torpedo gear by Fichtel and Sachs. It was much appreciated, as my experience had led me to develop an interest in all hub gears.

At Augsburg I met *Die Romantische Strasse,* the Romantic Road. There was nothing romantic about much of the southern section of this creation of the travel industry, particularly the route from Augsburg to Donauwörth up the flat valley of the River Lech. Then a major change occurred, as the road travelled north-west through a succession of picturesque towns to Würzburg. I had travelled up this road in 1964 on my second tour on the continent, which started and finished in Rüdesheim on the Rhine; it had taken me south to the Black Forest, along the border to Garmisch-Partenkirchen with a short period in Switzerland, before turning north. Reaching Donauwörth to cross the Danube, I looked forward to the miles ahead, to seeing again Nördlingen, Dinkelsbühl, Feuchtwangen, Rothenburg ob der Tauber and Bad Mergentheim.

As I began a nostalgic return along the route, I found myself reliving that early love affair with Germany and its beautiful countryside, thinking once again about the many interconnecting factors which had put me on a very special course during the last few years. From the beginning, cycle touring gave me immense pleasure, enabling me to travel the countryside at an optimum speed to enable the ever-changing views to be observed. A cyclist had freedom to choose the speed of travel, being able to stop or slow down at will for any view that caught the eye. Travelling in the open, the cyclist could smell the scents of the countryside, and cyclists moved silently, an advantage to be enjoyed on the open road everywhere when away from other traffic.

I referred in an earlier chapter to my identification with a phrase which the Youth Hostels Association used in its early publicity, the belief in the virtues of exploring the countryside "under one's own steam". With gear equipment allowing the physical effort involved in cycling to be reduced to a level manageable by any moderately fit person, the health benefits accruing from regular cycling become substantial. I would never forget the feeling of elation two days into my first tour, in North Wales in 1960, when my stamina improved to an extent I never thought possible. It was not a fluke: it resulted from the steady exercise. Far from the physical effort being a drain on the system, the exercise was entirely beneficial to health. The same improvement in stamina occurred on succeeding tours in Europe, a situation then reinforced a thousandfold on the current longer tour.

It was necessary to recognise one's individual capacity, the distance that could be cycled on an average day, and then repeated day after day, without running the system down. That capacity had to be determined by experiment. If you then stayed within that limit, you could go on indefinitely. I had been practising this on every stage during the last four years, whether it extended for six months or nine.

A bonus from this background was that there was no need for any undue concern about health matters while travelling for an extended period, with problems at times of harsh terrain, extremes of weather and doubtful diets. The continuous health-promoting exercise meant that one not only felt in superb condition generally, but the invigorated condition of the body inspired confidence concerning the ability to deal with any illness in minimum time.

If only this level of fitness and health could be maintained permanently, the ability to enjoy every aspect of life would become enhanced correspondingly. Real life isn't like that, of course: other pressures impose demands on time. Nevertheless, the benefits of regular cycling - involving a slight increase in load on the cardio-vascular system compared with the normal demand - make cycling one of the exercises most beneficial to health that is available with so little effort. The activity of cycling helps to keep the leg muscles supple, so important a factor in personal mobility.

The medical profession should be shouting from the rooftops about all these beneficial effects: but it does not. Isn't there a major problem of cardio-vascular disease in the country? A number of factors motivate against positive promotion. We live in the age of the car, which attracts massive advertising to promote its advantages for many purposes. In an age of uncertainty about status, the bicycle can be conceived as sending out the wrong signals to society in general. In this overall background, promotion of cycling by the medical profession in the interests of general health comes across as weak. The public could be forgiven for believing that there was any promotion at all. It was one of the paradoxes of modern life that cyclists understood the enormous health benefits of their chosen activity, while the medical profession ignored the phenomenon for all practical purposes.

When I started cycle touring, promotion of the activity in America was given weight by eminent surgeons lending their names to publicity campaigns. Perhaps ordinary cyclists, writing about their experiences, had a part to play in promoting an activity which could be so beneficial and the source of so much pleasure. The general reader might be prompted to think: "There may possibly be something in this for me." If there was an outstanding lesson to communicate from my experience, it was the extent of the benefits to be derived from this chosen method of travel. It went far beyond the immense enjoyment obtained on a personal level. I mused often on such thoughts as the miles rolled by.

I stopped for tea at Donauwörth, before leaving the flat plain and climbing into hills. On the winding run, the memories came back of the towns along the route with their lovely, medieval-looking centres, Rothenburg being the gem of them all. Following the River Tauber from Rothenburg, I remembered reading about an outstanding carved altar, in a church off the main road near Creglingen, by Tilman Riemenschneider. Why could I always recall names like that, when I couldn't remember what was said to me five minutes before? There were many vineyards on the hillsides on the long, winding run down the Tauber valley to the spa town of Bad Mergentheim. I was the sole guest at the youth hostel, where there was no heating, no hot water and no meals provided. I had come prepared; at least I had a solid roof over my head, now being outside Bavaria as defined by the hostel organisation. The Bad Mergentheim hostel had been so much busier when I stayed there during the summer five years earlier; a boisterous school party sang German folk-songs in the dormitory until their teacher decided I might like some sleep.

I continued down the Tauber Valley to Wertheim, the river winding its way through the hills in great loops from north of Tauberischofsheim, where I left *Die Romantische Strasse*. At Wertheim the Tauber flowed into the River Main which I followed west in another series of great loops to Miltenberg. The Main was about 200 yards wide and deep enough to support commercial traffic, so there was the sight of great barges chugging up and down the river. It was very relaxing following the rivers for so many miles. Five years earlier I continued to follow the Main through Aschaffenburg and Frankfurt to its confluence with the Rhine at Mainz, but decided this time to avoid such large centres of population in favour of a quieter run over the hills to Darmstadt.

At Miltenburg, with its fine setting south of a big bend in the river, I turned north to follow the Main a few more miles, turning away westwards at Obernberg. I had interesting company at the youth hostel at Darmstadt in the form of two young men from my home county of Suffolk, one from Troston and the other from Long Melford. They were on their way to work as cooks at an American Forces base nearby. I was able to catch up with a lot of news on events at home. After a ride over a broad, flat plain to the Rhine near Mainz, I followed the north bank to the delightful, little town of Rüdesheim.

Rüdesheim would always have a place in my affections. It represented the most distant location on my first cycle tour on the continent in 1963, which had brought me across Belgium and Germany to the Rhine at Koblenz. A cruise up the great river to Rüdesheim preceded the return journey by a more southern course involving the Moselle River, Luxembourg and Belgium. It seemed only fitting the following summer to take the train as far as Rüdesheim before exploring further a country which had captured my imagination. On these first two tours I had to walk part of the way up the steep hill to the youth hostel in its commanding position overlooking the town. It seemed so easy now with the additional low gears on the bicycle.

In a wave of nostalgia, I now followed in reverse the outward part of the 1963 tour, but this time cycling down the Rhine valley to Koblenz along the quieter east bank. The valley had looked so much better in the warm sun of mid-summer, lighting up the vine-clad slopes of the high hills bordering each bank. Perched at the top were a number of castles, while down on the river huge barges reminded me of the commercial importance of the great river. From the elevated position of the Fortress Ehrenbreitstein on the east bank opposite Koblenz, I looked down on the confluence of the Moselle and Rhine, and west to the Eifel Hills.

After sweeping down to the river from the Fortress, where the youth hostel was located, I was delighted after crossing the long bridge to Koblenz to collect three letters at the Post Office. While buying postcards as a result, two older Germans spoke to me. One told me he was in England during the Second World War for 2½ years, showing me with pleasure his PoW identification slip, which he carried in his wallet. This unexpected encounter reminded me that it was now 24 years since the end of that conflict. I had been astonished when I first came to Germany six years earlier to see the extent of economic recovery, and the air of prosperity. I wasn't the first to feel that Germany had recovered rather more quickly than Britain, considering the scale of devastation in Germany. There was a positive mood as we now worked together to build a different kind of world.

A long climb followed as I moved away from the Rhine. I seemed to be climbing for most of the day, any descents being short and rapid, while the ascents were long and gradual. I was keeping my fingers crossed concerning the weather as the road advanced across the Eifel Hills; there had been just a few showers to contend with during the previous 12 days since entering Germany, but a fair amount of cloud ensured warmer nights than in Austria. This was appreciated as one more night was spent camping in Germany, after failing to reach a planned youth hostel due to the climbing, and fighting a keen wind.

On my last full day in Germany I remembered vividly one particular section of the route followed six years earlier, as the road took me for two miles beside part of the Nürburg Ring. Several motorists were on the motor racing circuit, moving at such a speed that I decided it was unwise to even consider taking the bicycle on it, even if allowed. A long descent took me to a lower elevation, and away from low cloud. Rain fell as I left Blankenheim after afternoon tea, but left off before I reached the youth hostel at Kronenburg. As expected on this quiet route, and at this time of the year, I was the only guest in the hostel. I didn't mind, as I looked back with pleasure on a nostalgic journey of almost 500 miles through Germany.

*****

Thursday, 20 November 1969 Belgium

It was just nine miles to the border, where I sought out an official in the Customs and Immigration building. He looked at my passport with disinterest for a few seconds. That was it: I was in my final country with the same lack of formality as at the previous frontier. With a leaden sky and the wind blowing strongly against me for a third consecutive day, I took things steadily as there was still a fair amount of climbing to do while now in the Ardennes. A curving ride north-west brought me to Malmedy, scene of a major offensive by Germany during the final stages of the Second World War. A long climb out of the town brought me to Belgium's motor racing circuit at Francorchamps. Unlike the Nürburg Ring, it used public roads for much of the circuit. High fenders on the bends indicated that I was no longer on an ordinary road. I waved at thousands of invisible spectators as I passed one of the stands, acknowledging the imagined roar of applause before leaving the circuit shortly afterwards to continue to the health resort of Spa.

After much difficulty I located the youth hostel in rapidly failing light, only to be told by the warden that it was closed for a few weeks. With funds low I resolved to camp, heading out of Spa down a river valley as fast as I could. Fortunately the sky was clear, and a full moon was just two days away; it wasn't difficult in the bright moonlight to find a camping spot, so that I was able to erect the tent without needing to switch on my torch. The next morning, on a bright autumn day, I continued north down the valley to Pepinster; here the river ran into the Vesdre, which I followed on its winding course through the hills to Liege, where the Vesdre itself ran into the Meuse. I remembered this attractive journey from six years earlier; travelling then in the opposite direction, it had been such a welcome contrast after the journey over the relatively flat plain of northern Belgium.

I left the hills behind me as I climbed slowly up cobbled streets in Liege towards the road to Tongeren and St. Truiden. In 1963 I had taken a direct route between St. Truiden and Liege, but I now opted for the longer route. It proved to be quiet as I had hoped; after the climb out of Liege, the road stayed high on an undulating plain as it took me through a succession of communities in a densely populated, cultivated countryside. I passed many fine houses, with characteristic tinted glass in the windows, behind which were masses of plants. At the cafés there was little but drinks; I missed the delicious cakes which were so prevalent in Germany.

At St. Truiden I met the main road west and increased traffic, confirming that I had been on a quieter road. A secondary road from Leuven allowed me to approach the Belgian capital on a delightful run through the Forest of Soignes, then passing through the great Victory Arch. My memory allowed me to find the youth hostel without difficulty, where there was interesting company as expected in a major city.

After very undulating terrain east of Brussels, the undulations became gentler the further west I progressed, on another warm, cloudy day. I was being blessed concerning the weather, a situation I was grateful for as I had to camp outside the historic city of Ghent, learning in Brussels that the youth hostel was closed. It would be my last night of camping. A keen wind blew from the north-east as I set off for Bruges, where I sat in the central square for a picnic lunch, soaking up the atmosphere in a city which I remembered with such affection from the first visit in 1963. Regrettably I wasn't there at a suitable time to hear again the carillon of 47 bells at the top of the 13th Century Belfry.

I had to dive for cover as a storm moved overhead, and rode most of the way to Ostend with waterproof clothing on as a succession of storms passed over. I hadn't travelled every mile along the same road as six years earlier, unable to forget how I departed from Ostend for Bruges on my first cycling miles on the continent with features all around me corresponding with the autoroute. Several miles had to be covered before the first turn-off was reached. It was not an auspicious start to international travel, but would get better.

*****

Tuesday, 25 November 1969 England

I checked the ferry times before going to the youth hostel in Ostend for my last evening on the continent. Arrival completed 200 miles across Belgium and the final stage of the overland journey which had started nine months earlier in Singapore. The cyclometer recorded the distance cycled as 9,350 miles. There were still a few miles to go to get home. I felt in buoyant mood as I reported to the ferry terminal for departure at 10.30am. A fairly calm crossing of the

Channel followed, but the waves were high enough for me to spend much of the journey in a horizontal position below deck.

After almost four years away and a mass of badges on my saddlebag recording travels in 21 countries, I wondered how quickly I would get through Customs: it took 10 seconds. I emerged from the Customs building in Dover to a heavy shower of sleet and a bitterly cold wind. There was a strange feeling of anti-climax. I needed to tell myself that on journeys such as I had undertaken, the destination was not the important matter: it was the journey itself. Only I knew, in my mind, just what that journey had involved. There would hopefully be opportunities in the future to share with others some of the experiences of that journey. My mind was bursting with memories of a richness which I could only dream about four years earlier. I uttered a silent prayer in gratitude for having been able to translate that dream into reality.

I reached the centre of Dover just in time to be able to withdraw funds from a dwindling bank account to cover expenses for a few more days. At the youth hostel it was an irony to be told about an Indian cyclist on a world tour who had stayed there two nights earlier: how I would have loved to meet him. As I set off for London the following morning, a light covering of snow covered the roadsides and adjacent fields. I opted for the quieter route via Folkestone, stopping overnight in Maidstone. Although I had probably judged correctly, there was no getting away from a deafening roar of traffic as I reached the outskirts of London.

Before going to the King George VI Memorial youth hostel in Holland Park, I could not resist a nostalgic ride along the Albert Embankment, gazing across the Thames to the Houses of Parliament. Crossing the river at Westminster Bridge, a short ride brought me to Trafalgar Square before turning up the Mall to Buckingham Palace. Plans to watch the Changing of the Guard the next day had to be abandoned when snow started to fall. I had lunch with contacts at the Michelin Tyre Company, whose products had been invaluable on the arduous terrain in parts of Asia. As we left a restaurant, one of the employees, a young Australian, came up to me and asked: "Didn't I see you in Nepal?" The company I was with were amazed: so was I.

I left the capital the next morning under an ominous sky. Snow was soon falling heavily until the middle of the afternoon when I passed through Chelmsford. A severe frost was forecast for the night, which was spent in Braintree. As I strapped my bags on the bicycle for the final time, the air felt comfortable. Thankfully, there had been only a touch of frost, so that the road was not slippery, though often covered with packed snow. After lunch in Long Melford, there was more nostalgia as I reached the villages to the north which I knew so well, including my home village of Hartest where I lived for the first nine years.

The distances seemed so much shorter now, as I found myself approaching Bury St. Edmunds during the middle of the afternoon on Sunday, 30 November 1969. My family were awaiting my arrival. It was difficult to know what to talk about first; so many things needed to be discussed. After some time the question was asked: "Have you heard about Amy?" I looked up. Amy? Amy who? I didn't know anyone called Amy. It soon became apparent that the focus of attention was a character in a soap opera currently gripping the country's attention. It was understandable how the fictional characters in this daily drama would mean more than real life stories about the Rocky Mountains or the Khyber Pass. If I was going to relate more closely to those around me, I was going to have to immerse myself in the events which impinged more closely on their daily lives. For a start I was going to have to watch *Crossroads*. It was going to be a long struggle.

Appendix 1

Inventory

There is no agreed list of items which the long distance cyclist should carry, but a list of the items carried by an individual cyclist serves as a useful reference point. The list answers a host of queries concerning what can be, and sometimes is, carried on a bicycle.

Saddlebag:
(Made by the author to enclose all the items listed below)

- Tent: Black's "Good Companions Standard". Wt. 7lb 6oz.
- Sleeping bag: Black's "Icelandic Standard" with full zip. Wt. 3lb.
- Airbed: Black's "Good Companions" Lightweight. Wt. 2lb.
- Bag of clothing:

  1 shirt | 1 vest
  1 pair of pants | 2 pairs of socks
  3 handkerchiefs | 1 pair of pyjamas
  1 round neck sweater | 1 polo neck piece
  1 balaclava helmet | 1 pair swimming trunks
  1 pair of long trousers (assume shorts being worn)
  1 windproof jacket | 1 pair of gloves
  1 towel | 1 YHA sheet sleeping bag

- Waterproof clothing:

  Cape | Leggings
  Sou'wester | Overshoes

- Miscellaneous:

  Camera: Yashica J 35mm with delayed and long exposure settings
  1 spare 3-speed trigger control
  1 waterbottle cleaning brush
  Teatowel | Tripod
  String | Wire

Close-up lenses	Sheets of foam rubber
2 bicycle locks	2 spare wheel spokes
1 spare pump connection	Plastic bags

Handlebar Bag:

(Size 12″ x 10″ x 6″ - adapted by the author from a Karrimor 12″ x 12″ x 6″ pannier bag)

- Maps, guidebooks, travel literature
- Novel
- *Cycling Book of Maintenance* by Temple Press
- Films
- Stationery
- Prints of bicycle
- Small bag containing:

Passport	Notebook
Diaries	Health Certificate
Biro	Suntan lotion
Wallet	Penknife
Mosquito spray	Travellers Cheques
Keys	Fly spray
YHA Card	12 small locks

- Drugs, pills, slimming tablets, tranquillizers etc:
    4 Aspros
- Supplement in desert states of U.S.A.:
    Salt tablets
- Supplements in Asia:
    Salt tablets
    Enterovioform tablets (to cure bacillary dysentery)
    Anti-malarial tablets
    Hexaform tablets (to cure amoebic dysentery)
    Water purification tablets
    Vitamin B tablets
    Eyedrops

Handlebar Bag Mapcase:

(Size 10¼″ wide x 10¾″ long with 8¼″ wide x 9″ long window, and including stiffening wire inside long edges due to overhang of handlebar bag - made by the author from a Karrimor pannier bag, heavy duty plastic and steel wire.)

Pannier Bags:
(Size 12″ x 12″ x 6″ by Karrimor)

- Righthand Bag:
  Optimus 8R petrol stove. Packed size 5″ x 5″ x 3″. Wt. 1lb 9oz.

Cup, eggcup, sponge	Toilet bag and mirror
2 Pint tin of petrol	Shoe polish, brush and rag
Funnel	Torch and 2 spare batteries
2 boxes of matches	Travelling clock
2 billy cans	Spare cyclometer

- Plastic bag containing spare keys, rubber bands, string, shoelaces, bag straps, 6 pegs, biro, pencil, sellotape, plastic bags and sewing kit - reels of black and white cotton, button thread, thimble and scissors.
- First Aid kit:
  Packet of Elastoplast Snake Bite kit
- End Pocket of Righthand Bag:
  2 inner tubes, rim tape, 3-speed control wire, 1 lock, cycle clips, insulating and plastic tape, string, wire and rags.
  Tin of spares: 3-speed indicator chain, chain links, rear axle nuts, 2 cotter pins, 2 brake blocks, derailleur gear control lever screws, hub gear pawls and springs, dynamo and torch bulbs, valves and caps, cyclometer striker, ball bearings, wire, miscellaneous nuts and bolts.

- Lefthand Bag:
  Half gallon plastic water container
  Plastic containers for tea, sugar, butter, eggs, salt and pepper
  Plastic plate
  Knife, fork, dessert spoon, teaspoon, tin opener, bottle opener, tea strainer, billy can holder
  Food

- End Pocket of Lefthand Bag:
  1 inner tube
  Toolkit: Adjustable spanner, dumbell spanner, wheel axle cone spanner, 1 large and 2 small screwdrivers, pliers, chain rivet extractor, spoke nipple key, file, 2 tyre levers, pump connection.

Puncture repair kit including 2 tubes of rubber solution and a large number of patches.

Tin of oil, tin of grease, rags, pieces of bag cloth for repairs.

- Spare tyre - laid on top of pannier bags.
- Sun-hat.

Total weight of baggage - approximately 70lb when including 1½ gallons of water and 2 days supply of food.

Weight of bicycle - 45lb.

Notes:
Complete inventory not carried all the time. Major items not carried initially, but considered desirable to be carried in retrospect:

1. Camping equipment - to minimize costs.
2. Half gallon plastic water container - to give more flexibility in choice of campsites, and to provide a reservoir of drinking water in any hot weather.
3. Spare tyre - to save concern about replacement.
4. Camera tripod.

Other major items not carried initially:

1. Sun-hat and gallon plastic water container - both required only in extreme heat.
2. Salt tablets.
3. Tablets for water purification, dysentery and malaria.
4. Insect repellents.

Appendix 2

The Bicycle

Raleigh semi-sports bicycle with 26″ x 1 3/8″ wheels and North Road raised handlebar. In the author's view, this handlebar is the most comfortable handlebar ever invented - an important consideration on a long tour.

Original bicycle with Sturmey-Archer 3-speed AW wide ratio hub gear. Gear system increased, to obtain lower gears, by adding an additional rear sprocket, replacing single chainwheel with a double ring unit, and adding a derailleur mechanism and chainwheel changer.

- 48 tooth chainring and 21 tooth sprocket give the three original gears of 79.2″, 59.4″ and 44.6″, suitable for general use.
- 48 tooth chainring used with new 28 tooth sprocket gives the first lower gear of 33.4″ with the hub gear in "Low".
- New 32 tooth chainring used with 28 tooth sprocket give two lower gears of 29.7″ and 22.3″ with the hub gear in "Normal" and "Low".

Thus gear range of bicycle = 79.2″ - 22.3″.

This is not the place to discuss details of the technical equipment involved in the gear system which served me so well. However, a few salient points need to be mentioned about this hub-derailleur combination, known as a hybrid system. A suitable gear range, in particular the provision of low gears, is central to successful cycle touring. The range above was, at the time, exceptional. It was not available on any standard bicycle, but had to be specially fitted, whether the bicycle started with a hub gear or a derailleur system.

The situation changed with the advent of the mountain bike, and the corresponding need for low gears in order to climb steep hillsides. Suddenly the gears above became available as standard on any mountain bike.

Again, it is not appropriate here to discuss the merits of one system against another, the steps needed between gears, or availability of equipment in changing market conditions. The overwhelming consideration, in the author's view, is to have some low gears on an extended tour.

Appendix 3

Statistics

Countries visited:

America	Singapore	India	Turkey
Canada	Malaysia	Nepal	Bulgaria
Japan	Thailand	Pakistan	Yugoslavia
Australia	Cambodia	Afghanistan	Austria
New Zealand	Burma	Iran	Germany
			Belgium

Tour Summary:

Time:	Journey:	Distance cycled (miles):
April 1966 - September 1966	Across North America	6,100
October 1966 - March 1967	(Work)	0
April 1967 - October 1967	West of America	8,600
November 1967 - March 1968	(Work)	0
April 1968 - June 1968	Japan	2,400
July 1968 - November 1968	Eastern Australia	5,700
December 1968 - January 1969	New Zealand	2,700
February 1969 - November 1969	Singapore - England	9,500
		Total:
		35,000

Costs

Region	Cost/day
North America	£2
Japan and Australasia	£1.50
Asia and Europe	£1

Item	Cost
Cycle journeys	£1,380
Sea and non-cycling land journeys	£ 700
Films	£ 200
Total cost	£2,300

Overnights

Accommodation	No. of Nights	Percentage
Camping	470	50.3
Youth hostels	107	11.4
Hotels	164	17.5
YMCA's	83	8.9
Relatives, private homes and other	111	11.9
	935	

Thus overall average cost/day while cycling

$$= \frac{£1380}{935} = £1.50 \text{ approx.}$$

The table above is included to highlight the importance on the tour of camping, which provided so much flexibility in the choice of overnight stopping positions, and helped significantly to control costs. Considering that the first stage of the tour, across North America, involved no camping at all, an overall percentage of 50.3 % shows its growing importance on the succeeding stages.